FEEDING FASCISM

Feeding Fascism explores how women negotiated the politics of Italy's Fascist regime in their daily lives and how they fed their families through agricultural and industrial labour. The book looks at women's experiences of Fascism by examining the material world in which they lived in relation to their thoughts, feelings, and actions.

Over the past decade, Diana Garvin has conducted extensive research in Italian museums, libraries, and archives. *Feeding Fascism* includes illustrations of rare cookbooks, kitchen utensils, cafeteria plans, and culinary propaganda to connect women's political beliefs with the places that they lived and worked and the objects that they owned and borrowed. Garvin draws on first-hand accounts, such as diaries, work songs, and drawings, that demonstrate how women and the Fascist state vied for control over national diet across many manifestations – cooking, feeding, and eating – to assert and negotiate their authority. Revealing the national stakes of daily choices, and the fine line between resistance and consent, *Feeding Fascism* attests to the power of food.

DIANA GARVIN is an assistant professor of Italian at the University of Oregon.

FEEDING FASCISM

THE POLITICS OF WOMEN'S FOOD WORK

Diana Garvin

UNIVERSITY OF TORONTO PRESS
Toronto Buffalo London

Reprinted in paperback 2023

ISBN 978-1-4875-5157-5 (paper)
ISBN 978-1-4875-2818-8 (cloth)
ISBN 978-1-4875-2820-1 (EPUB)
ISBN 978-1-4875-2819-5 (PDF)

Publication cataloguing information is available from Library and Archives Canada.

Cover design: Sandra Friesen
Cover image: Jonathan Horn

We wish to acknowledge the land on which the University of Toronto Press operates.
This land is the traditional territory of the Wendat, the Anishnaabeg, the Haudenosaunee,
the Métis, and the Mississaugas of the Credit First Nation.

University of Toronto Press acknowledges the financial assistance to its publishing program of
the Canada Council for the Arts and the Ontario Arts Council, an agency of the Government of
Ontario.

For Dad, Professor Garvin Sr.
All my love,
Diana, Professor Garvin Jr.

CONTENTS

ILLUSTRATIONS

ACKNOWLEDGMENTS

I am very grateful to the following institutions for their support of this project: the American Academy in Rome, the Wolfsonian-FIU Museum, the Council of Library and Information Resources, the Mellon Foundation, the Julia Child Foundation, and Oxford University. At the University of Oregon, I am thankful for the support of the Oregon Humanities Center, the Department of Romance Languages (special thanks are due to David Wacks, for his thoughtful leadership, and Nathalie Hester, steadfast champion of the Italian sector), the Food Studies Program (Stephen Wooten, for forging UO's food community), and the Center for the Study of Women in Society (Michelle McKinley, for creating camaraderie among emerging scholars). A special thank you to Karen Ford, for her warmth and mentorship. I am also grateful for the support of the Office of the Vice President for Research and Innovation, especially Kate Petcosky, my fellowship yenta and friend, for brilliance, foster kittens, and rosé. A Faculty Club pinot noir toast to my awesome cohort, Devin Grammon, Linni Mazurek, Carolyn Fish, Noah Eber-Schmidt, and Abigail Fine. Nothing beats laughing with you guys at the end of a tough week.

At Cornell University, I owe thanks to the Mario Einaudi Center for International Studies (Sydney Van Morgan and Cindy DeLorme at the Institute for European Studies deserve special thanks for kindness and supreme organization), the Institute for Comparative Modernities, the Society for the Humanities, and the Department of Romance Studies (Rebecca Davidson, alias "The Godmother," and the formidably elegant Kora Battig von Wittelsbach, protector of TAs). I am grateful to the Feminist, Gender, and Sexuality Studies Program (and to Kate McCullough and Jane Juffer especially) for their intellectual rigour, their fire, and their fun. The Center for Teaching Excellence (under David Way's expertise at the helm) provided a pedagogical counterpoint to this research. And finally, many thanks to my dissertation committee, Medina Lasansky, Kate McCullough, and Tim Campbell, for inspired questions, for illuminating ideas, and for being wonderful teachers across the board.

Over a decade of research in Italy and the United States, this project was helped by the Musei delle Aziende, as well as the Archivio Centrale dello Stato and the Ministero state archive system. It has been a pleasure to work with Giancarlo Gonizzi, whose leadership of the Biblioteca Gastronomica di Academia Barilla exemplifies broad vision coupled with attention to detail. Much admiration is due to Antonietta Pensiero for her pioneering design and ongoing management of the Health Ministry library catalogue and for insightful recommendations. Nadia Lodi at the Museo della Figurina provided critical historical context as well as sneak peeks of risqué ephemera. The Wolfsonian Museum feels like home away from home. Thank you all so much for your warmth and knowledge, particularly Frank Luca for superb library leadership, Niki Harsanyi for modernist marvels, Amy Silverman for interwar tea parties, Lyton Gardiner for photography lessons, Silvia Barisione for curatorial innovation from Miami to Genova, Jon Mogul for post-conference pep talks and excellent advice, and Micky Wolfson for his love of gyros and dystopian fantasies and for the vision and fun behind this museum. You make the research sing.

Deep gratitude is due to Stephen Shapiro at the University of Toronto Press for his intellectual dedication to this project, and to this book's careful readers. Jaimee Garbacik, Footnote Editorial developmental editor and my friend, forged order out of chaos. She vowed to make "the recipes gleam like the very finest *beurre blanc* sauce," and she has done so, with anti-Fascist passion and editorial genius. *Grazie tanto* to illustrator Jon W. Horn for detailed discussions of interwar aesthetics – from Boccasile bodies to interwar typography – for the book cover. You captured the complexity and the punch of this period in your art. It is dynamite.

My writing group, Jennie Row, Julie Elsky, and Topher Davis, patiently pruned many chapters. I am grateful for their interdisciplinary insights, rambunctious meetings at the Boston Public Library, and delicious dinner parties in Cambridge. Many thanks to the Romance Studies cohort, Mozelle Foreman for *Doctor Who* marathons with Hero, Eddie Curran for coffee at Stella's, and an extra hug to Sylvia Hakopian-LeBouteiller, for Italian sector solidarity, friendship, and teaching me how to make dolmas. The Cornell Dames, Ophélie Chavaroche, Mariam Wassif, Julie Désangles, and Jennie Row, provided sparkle and oysters at Maxie's. A prosecco toast to the AAR crew, especially Jess Peritz, Lauren Donovan Ginsburg, Anna Majeski, Liana Brent, and Cate Bonesho. *Un abbraccione* for Rita Di Muro, for morning market visits and so many wonderful conversations. Home Sweet Rome will always be your house.

Warm thanks to Kate Ferris, leader of the European Food History Early Career Workshop at St. Andrews. Your mentorship lifted the emerging scholars in our group and made us feel like Real Academics. *Grazie infinite* to my academic brother Brian Griffith for solidarity across Rome, Edinburgh, and New York City. I can't wait to watch your research on wine under Fascism change the field. To Emily Contois, my fellow Gastropeep, for many years of Food Studies friendship. Hugs to Carly Anderson, for joy during the hardest year. Since college, the Estrogen Mafia has provided the soul, and an airtight alibi if needed. Kay Schwader, Kate Condon, Joy Jauer, Claire LeGoues, Eva Xia-Privitera, Camille Johnson, and Théa Morton: I would take a bullet for you.

An additional toast to Medina, who taught me to research fearlessly. You believed in this project from day one, and your extraordinary mentorship changed my life. If this research is good, it is because of you.

To my best friend Mackenzie Cooley and *carissimo* Brian Brege, the Renaissance and her scholar, my beloved co-founders of the Alpine Italianists Workshop: thank you so much for your excellent edits and friendship over five-hour lunches in Mantova and annual downhill swooshing in the Dolomites. Looking towards the brightness of the future, I am overjoyed to be Artemis's godmother. *Fiamma e fama!* To Sean, my love, and to Joan, Mel, Bridget, Phil, Anna, Ella, and the epic Griffith clan, I am so lucky to have you. You have taught me to live with greater thoughtfulness and connection, that is, in a warmer, kinder way. Mageet, I miss cooking with you. You are the cup of tea and the shot of whisky. To Cindy, the dynamite, and to Mom, the star: I love you more than anything. You make me laugh. You make me think. You keep me sane. I have never had so much fun in the world as when we were just chatting at dinner together. Here's to many more years of road-tripping, toasting, and diagnosing with the Doctors Garvin! Dad, I love you and miss you and hope that you are having a wonderful time in the Sedona hiking trails in the "wilderness area" adventure in the sky.

FEEDING FASCISM

TABLETOP POLITICS

The Italian table provides an intimate stage for national politics. Whether in a public trattoria or in a private kitchen, the table resonates deeply with Italian culture and society; it is the centre of everyday life in Italy. In the pre-Fascist period, the table had been the site of ancient Roman excess amongst the elite and intense privation for the poor; during the Fascist period, it was the site of initiatives to nationalize and Italianize. From the economic boom to the contemporary period, the Italian table has remained a vital component of public policy debates that ask what it means to be Italian today. The concept itself is a convivial one, building connections between the national and the regional, the government and the individual, the abstract and the concrete, the public and the private. Food provides the means to invite these disparate concepts into a cohesive conversation. Put another way, the Italian table encompasses not only the polenta and couscous served on it, but also the political debate that occurs above it.

Food matters: how food is produced, purchased, cooked, eaten, and represented illustrates social norms as well as personal choices. Further, food constitutes the point at which politics physically touch the individual through the material reality of everyday life. It can connect women's political lives with the places where they lived and worked and the objects they owned and borrowed. It also points to new archives and materials for historical analysis. Culinary ephemera can provide concrete evidence to investigate abstract ideas, a method that food studies scholars refer to as using "food as a lens." This approach suggests that that plate of polenta provides rich cultural information which traditional historical materials cannot capture. Analysing dinner plates and café menus in conversation with work songs and love letters allows the historian to critically examine state narratives using a broad body of evidence but also draws upon the cultural history of women and the masses, not just the male elite. Food complicates the idea of an all-powerful government monolith by revealing the local variations of manufacturing, construction, and financing for state enterprises. These regional histories demonstrate the unexpectedly significant extent of women's involvement in shaping the Italian industry and agriculture, even under a regime that aimed to exclude women from public life.

This book analyses various women's experiences of Fascism by examining the material world in which they lived in relation to the historical archive of their feelings, thoughts, and actions. To maintain the bright sound of these voices, I focus on site-based case studies to demonstrate that women's feeding work certainly involved the kitchen but also transcended it: working-class women worked in middle- and upper-class women's kitchens as well as in urban factories and rural fields. Moreover, they breastfed the next generation of Italian citizens inside public obstetric clinics that housed the most intimate form of feeding. These interlinked sites fuse the public and the private spheres of life, casting paradox in stone.

Feeding Fascism contributes to the growing body of scholarship that attempts to posit a more complex portrayal of women's daily lives under the dictatorship. It aims not only to explore women's quotidian interactions with Fascist policy by opening the kitchen cupboard, but also, more broadly, to explain how women experience the material dimensions of politics in their daily lives. For this reason, I follow women's food work. Food work includes cooking. It also encompasses agricultural labour and industrial food production. In this book, I use the term "women's food work" to make visible the broad range of gendered activities that all had to work on together in order to produce the ingredients for meals. Collectively, these chapters contribute a new perspective to recent debates in the lived experience of autocracy and dictatorship.

This is not a story of an uprising or a tragedy but rather a story of everyday toil and strategies for endurance. It focuses on the objects and messaging that informed women's decisions about whether to breastfeed in private or in public, how to organize the kitchen, and how to manage female bodily needs while working in the factories and fields. Feminist theory informs my historical focus on the tabletop politics of Fascism: whenever possible, I use women's own conceptions of gender, class, and region to describe social categories. In terms of style, these historical subjects express complex thoughts and emotions in clear speech. Their words remind me that educated sources will sometimes use convoluted phrasing as a power play, framing opacity as expertise. Predictably, these two styles shape debates in different ways. Clear speech starts conversations, and opaque speech ends them. To apply this lesson, I try to use direct, vibrant language to describe these histories.

Most past discussions have suggested either that using food, cooking, and feeding to decipher women's daily political lives recreates patriarchal power structures and reduces women to domestic roles or that the culinary does not constitute a sufficiently serious topic for inclusion in the history of gender. This book responds to this earlier scholarship by providing for a food-based material culture studies reading. Women's food work enlarges our notions of political action because women actively engaged with the regime through their farming, home design, office work, and writing. Indeed, the study of food and foodways is important precisely because women spent much of their daily lives engaged in these activities. Further, focusing on this aspect of women's history could potentially help to deflect the historic denigration of practices, work, and spaces associated with women. To contribute to these scholarly debates, this book situates new examples of cultural history within the broader context of power negotiations between women and the state, ultimately adding an adaptive and resourceful approach to the scholarship of the modern history of gender and culture.

Tabletop politics blend domestic affairs and domestic life, an amalgam informed by feminist historians' long-standing effort to eschew characterizations that impose the categories they claim only to describe. The everyday serves theoretical and methodological ends if we recognize it as such. To this end, this book is in conversation with a theoretical disciplinary question regarding the role of food studies in reconstructing women's history and a methodological question concerning the relationship between the local and the national, as well as between individual bodies and the body politic. To reconstruct the history of women's daily lives under Fascism through tabletop politics, this book proceeds iteratively, place by place, object by object, so as to document and make sense of the assemblage, rather than stand back and explain the whole. I look at the material culture that surrounded these women to understand their capacities, gestures, movements, location, and behaviours. If one were to believe the family stories told about the Fascist period today, Italy would appear to have been populated almost exclusively by resistors. Those who lived under Fascism typically do not want to talk about it or remember it in detail. My guiding assumption is that historical objectivity cannot exist: we cannot represent the everyday world holding it at arm's length. As a researcher, I am always enacting my knowledge of archival ephemera, objects, and built environments. More broadly, my understanding of social constructs like gender, race, class, and region also reflects my own cultural milieu. My hope is that acknowledging this potential for bias will disarm it to a certain degree.

Women produce culture through everyday habits and rituals. They are not pure consumers who unquestioningly receive cultural messages from above. They are actors, interpreters, and critics: they accept, modify, and reject. Buildings, texts, and objects do not exist in a vacuum: they are processes of signification materialized by women's use of them. The consumer is a producer of culture. Everyday decisions have enormous power not just because they add up to the national, but also because they construct people's sense of themselves as citizens. In the home, individuals and the state come into contact with each other through industrial design. Pushed further, this line of reasoning suggests that power lives in things as potential energy, which individuals can either use as directed or make use of in novel ways. With creativity, consumers can unlock additional meanings and uses for any household object. But in either case, interacting with state-produced goods means making political choices. Power in the private sphere is in a constant state of flux and negotiation. The power of an individual may not be equal to that of the state, but even small choices can create moments of independence. Even the smallest assertion of will constitutes a form of power.

Methodology: Fascism as Magnifying Glass

The question of Fascism's essential nature often rests in the uneasy place of identification without explanation. Despite a century of debate, little consensus has emerged regarding the relative importance of the conditions of Fascism, the total number to be met, or the conditions themselves.[1] Is Fascism a generic concept or a national variation of historically specific political instances? Can we draw a sharp distinction between political thought (Fascism as ideology) and political institution (Fascism as state)? What models can we use to study Fascism without replicating destructive power structures? Notable historical models include Benedetto Croce's Fascist parenthesis, Roger Griffin's Fascist minimum, and Robert Paxton's Five Stages of Fascism.[2] Hannah Arendt's seminal study built terror into the definition of totalitarianism.[3] But while violence as analytic frame captures the horrors of the Holocaust and Stalinist Russia, systematic terror did not define the everyday experience of Italian Fascism. Rather, haphazard brutality was an omnipresent threat. The regime exerted violence on the body through beatings and incarceration and in the body by weaponizing common laxatives. One regular tactic for punishing suspected partisans involved the forced consumption of castor oil (*ricino*) to induce diarrhoea. Fascism militarizes people and land. Food and feeding connect the two, a link that dictatorial regimes exploit through Fascist foodways: the politicized seizure of local culinary culture for the promotion of national demographic goals.[4]

This historical period (1922–45) provides a particularly clear lens for studying women's food work. It is not representative of Italian culture – rather, it is hyperrepresentative in that the bombast of dictatorial politics ballooned concepts that predated the March on Rome. Women did not suddenly feed their families in completely different ways under Fascism, although as this book will show, the smaller changes they did make held political significance. Rather, the great utility of using the Fascist period to study women's feeding work lies in its ability to amplify general tendencies in women's work that are often too subtle to see during the Giolitti period or the post-war years bookending the *ventennio*, the twenty-odd years of Fascist rule. The Fascist period thus provides a key to unlocking other historical periods. Philosopher and historian Benedetto Croce was wrong: Fascism is not a parenthesis. It is a magnifying glass.

Frugal Italian dietary models predate Fascism and helped set the stage for the nation's culinary consent to regime dictates. Peasant foodways celebrating breaking bread as conviviality, intertwined with the Catholic Church's veneration of *il nostro pane quotidiano* (our daily bread), created continuities, as Nuto Revelli's oral histories of Piedmontese countrywomen born between 1884 and 1958 have shown.[5] These continuities meant the Battle for Grain, a ten-year propaganda campaign to boost Italian wheat production, was not a stark innovation but an appropriation that repurposed the long-standing Italian celebration of the sacredness of bread.

Furthermore, Fascist Italy was not alone in drawing on earlier cultural models of peasant eating for new political purposes. Writing on Nazi Germany, Corinna Treitel has convincingly argued for the emergence of the "natural diet" in the decades prior to German unification and World War I. With the involvement of racial scientists, the earlier health claims cast völkisch diets in political terms.[6] In Italy, World War I further conditioned Fascist foodways. Whereas World War II would bring terrible and enduring food shortages to Italy, World War I did not. Because of Allied, and especially British, loans and supplies, many Italians ate better from 1915 to 1918 than prior to the war. Soldiers ate particularly well, enjoying 375 grams of meat per day. Memories of full bellies in wartime, a legacy of World War I Allied food policy, likely conditioned Italian responses to the Fascist preparations for food shortages during World War II. National food policies also conditioned later imperial projects by enhancing or limiting the viability of aggressive military expansion.[7] What's more, the United States emerged as a major producer and exporter of cheap wheat after World War I – it was hardly in short supply. Because Fascism built autarky in part out of women's work, it is significant to note that isolated production was in some ways a choice on the part of the regime rather than a necessity.

Three core arguments emerge from my analysis of women's everyday lives under Italian Fascism. First, I posit a broad theoretical position about the role of interdisciplinary enquiry in illuminating women's history, focusing on how thematic approaches, such as gender studies, food studies, and material culture studies, might be combined with the pre-existing methodologies of established historical fields to produce new insights that neither open studies nor closed disciplines can achieve in isolation. Women, like food, have historically been treated as objects, that is, as pieces of material culture. I argue that focusing on the relationship between the female body and the actual material world reveals how knowledge is produced through the body and embodied ways of being in the world. Lynda Birke's assertion that "bodies may consistently undergo interior change, but within apparent sameness" applies not only to the interior cycles of the female body but also to the ways in which food physically reforms the body through the digestion and incorporation of proteins, fats, and nutrients.[8] Eating leads to the "unravelling of all bodily essentialisms," as Kyla Wazana Tompkins has put it.[9] Moreover, eating reveals how the self is enmeshed in the material world. Breastfeeding provides an excellent example of this idea, in that the producer of food, the mother, physically links to the consumer, the infant. At a very basic level, these trajectories explore how subjects and objects emerge.

Second, I suggest that these everyday practices of food production and consumption (eating, feeding, and cooking) coalesce at both regional and national levels because the individual body figures the body politic. These interlinked methodological questions address current debates about the relationship between local food choices and global foodways and challenge the assumption that personal choices must have a noble goal in order to have a positive impact. Choices need not be conscious to be meaningful. Feeding Fascism is the governing metaphor of the bottom-up process by which individual women across the peninsula participated in and rebelled against Fascist political projects. Whether women agreed or disagreed with the regime's dictates, the fact that they engaged with them daily proves Fascist ideology and policy to be omnipresent, even in apparently apolitical moments of daily life. In line with Ian Hodder, I argue that food, and more broadly, material culture, transforms, rather than reflects, social organization.[10] To connect the local to the national, I avoid the practice of analysing spaces and objects as static text and instead focus on bodies and objects as they travel. Following Arjun Appadurai's focus on "things-in-motion," I study the ways in which people and objects move between social contexts, gaining new meanings through successive recontextualizations.[11] Agricultural sections of the Fasci Femminili viewed Gino Boccasile's propagandistic pamphlet, *Mangiate Riso*, as a teaching document to instruct countrywomen in new domestic technologies at Fascist festivals and rallies. But when the pamphlet switched hands at these events, its meaning changed as well: working-class women saw the pamphlets as an incursion on their right to cook the dishes they pleased. The pamphlet's cheap paper kindled their cooking fires. Following such trajectories allows me to examine people, places, and things at distinct moments in their lifespan, at the points of manufacturing, circulation, use, and disposal. Perhaps even more importantly, this methodological approach reveals places and things as indicators of individual actions and recurring practices whose meaning derives from the broader historical context of Italy's Fascist period.

A third, historical argument unifies my theoretical and methodological propositions. In this text, I question the nature of political interactions between women and the regime, focusing on quotidian situations so as to characterize these negotiations in realistic terms, grounded in actions rather than analysis. Essentially, I ask how politics and women's subjectivity related on a daily basis – what types of interactions cannot be characterized by polarities? What happened *between* rebellion and consent? In this task, I pay close attention to the prescribed and actual use of culture. In line with social historian Michel De Certeau's theory that consumers do not passively use culture but actively make use of it, I predicate my analysis on the assumption that trends move from the bottom up and from side to side as well as from the top down. When women modified Fascist messages to suit their own ends, they also inscribed their own value systems into the current political paradigm. Women did not simply absorb Fascist dictates but rather reconfigured its commands for personal use. What characterized these food-centred strategies for survival was not patriotism but practicality.

Whenever possible, I avoid extensive histories of the great and powerful and instead focus on reconstructing working-class women's history through popular materials. This body of evidence not only leads to new conclusions regarding the nature and extent of women's involvement in national political projects, but it also reframes current historiographical debates by integrating traditional approaches to women's history with a new emphasis on material culture. Against the dominant characterization of women's response to Fascist regime dictates as one of passive consent, I contend that female citizens and the state actively negotiated for sovereignty over women's labour in both the public and the private sphere through food, ultimately revealing how political power worked from the bottom up as well as from the top down.

Many scholars of Italian history, and particularly those focused on Italian Fascism, such as Ruth Ben-Ghiat, Mia Fuller, and Medina Lasansky, have shifted away from the study of literature and film in isolation and towards the integration of their analysis with the social contexts and built environments that surrounded the works in question. This book is part of this larger cultural history vein of Italian studies. By combining close readings of culinary ephemera with histories from private food industry and women's first-hand accounts, *Feeding Fascism* contributes to this current body of work, most notably Carol Helstosky's *Garlic and Oil* and Emanuela Scarpellini's *Material Nation*. It is also part of the general move in Italian studies away from high society. *Feeding Fascism* employs Medina Lasansky's comprehensive approach to the lived spaces of Fascism as explored in *The Renaissance Perfected*, in terms of both its materials and its archives. Moreover, this project contributes a deep study of women's professional lives to the general histories accounted for in Victoria De Grazia's *How Fascism Ruled Women*. In its attention to the clinic, the home, the factory, and the field, *Feeding Fascism* also builds on works focusing on similar sites, such as Elizabeth Whitaker's *Measuring Mamma's Milk* and Perry Willson's *Peasant Women and Politics in Fascist Italy* and *The Clockwork Factory*. Similarly, this book aims to build on the work of scholars like Natasha Chang, Karen Pinkus, Stephen Gundle, Marcia Landy, Millicent Marcus, and Robin Pickering-Iazzi, who have written about Fascist iconography of women in print advertising and in film with great sensitivity and skill.[12]

Mapping the Political Landscape

Human geography informs my selection of these case studies, which focus primarily on Northern and Central Italy. I emphasize Lombardy, Piedmont, and Emilia-Romagna, with a secondary consideration of Umbria and Lazio due to the intense relationship that these regions had with the Fascist regime. These were, at once, the zones of the greatest adherence to and the strongest resistance against the regime. Moreover, the regime engaged with Northern and Central Italy more frequently and directly than they did with Southern Italian regions due to the accessibility, productivity, and thus the perceived modernity of the north vis-à-vis the government capital in Rome. Milan, Turin, and Genoa created an industrial triangle, a powerhouse of factory work and the pulsing centre of modern urban life, all easily accessible by the recently nationalized train system.[13] Along with Bologna La Rossa (Bologna the Red), these cities crackled with Communism. Their long labour history was pockmarked by associated strikes. And yet, the opposite political pole stood in the same location: Mussolini was born in the small town of Predappio in Emilia-Romagna, and Fascism spread across Northern Italy before marching south across Umbria to reach Rome in 1922.

The Po River valley's vast floodplain held the majority of the Northern Italian population during this period. Agriculturally as well as industrially, Northern Italy was very productive: rice and wheat grew in abundance, and migrant workers were needed to weed the paddies in the spring and to thresh the grain in the fall. A profusion of regional dialects including Piedmontese, Lombard, Emilian, and Romagnol rang through the work songs of the fields. Urban dialects, such as the Bolognese of Emilia-Romagna, rarely appear in field work songs, as these women would stay local to work in factories. But whereas you will not hear Bolognese in field songs, you will sometimes hear Emilian or Romagnol songs sung in the workshops of urban Bologna. Women often moved from the country to the city for work. Because of this migration, rural women's political beliefs also entered urban factories.

Thick fog, a regional peculiarity, cloaked the Po valley from October to February, an atmospheric condition that mirrors this period's rising pollution due to high levels of urban industrialization and winds blocked by the Alps to the north and the Apennines to the south. In short, Northern Italy was enticingly productive in both fields and factories, making it an ideal laboratory to test new incarnations of Fascist modernity, like rationalized agriculture and Taylorist factory work; yet these same working groups leaned left, meaning it was also a hotbed of Communist dissent. Making the north visible as a geographic category guards against projecting these case studies as universalisms that apply to the Mezzogiorno, that is, to Abruzzo, Apulia, Basilicata, Campania, Calabria, and Molise, to say nothing of Sicily and Sardinia. More broadly still, discussion of Italy's imperial projects in Ethiopia, Eritrea, and Somalia merits books, not chapters.[14] Here again, I aim for a complete analysis of a few significant arenas of everyday life rather than for exhaustive coverage of all possible places.

At the height of Mussolini's popularity, Antonio Gramsci broached the idea of the Southern Question, the idea that the Italian south exists in a permanently marginalized position with respect to the north.[15] The Southern Question framed Italy as being composed of two parts: a desirable European north and a south that deviates from that model.[16] Fascism pledged to forge a cohesive national whole, in theory providing an answer to the Southern Question. In their line of reasoning, southern agriculture shaped culture, which in turn informed politics. Poverty and Catholic devotion, underpinned by lean ingredients and simple preparations, marked Mezzogiorno cuisine to a relatively greater extent than they did Northern Italian cookery. The craggy, semi-arid climate of the Mezzogiorno favoured citrus, olives, and grapes. These crops required a long waiting period before harvest. Although the regime promoted these products through tourism by inaugurating regional festivals, economic outlay went to quick-harvest crops like grain, which could be profitably grown only by sizeable estates. Agriculture then shaped class structure: the majority of the peasantry worked on the large-scale farms run by the rich landowning few. With no middle class to speak of, urban poverty and mafia violence ruled Catania and Palermo. Meanwhile, the Fascist regime claimed that the Mediterranean climate degenerated culture; thus the south could not rule itself and needed a strong central government to impose order from above. Italian Fascism and Benito Mussolini hailed from Northern Italy. Through the Ministero delle Corporazioni, five key Partito Nazionale Fascista groups oriented around cereals, sugar, oil, wine grapes, and fruits and vegetables, moved to create a new form of culinary nationalism by imposing northern foods and recipes on the southern populous by intensifying the regime's promotion of autarky. But despite these highly visible attempts to nationalize the Italian diet, it makes sense to view things regionally because region played a central role in determining the menu. In many ways, the cuisine of the north – meat tortellini, balsamic vinegar, parmesan cheese – came to stand for the whole of Italy.

Narrative Trajectory

Women fed their families most obviously by cooking but also by weeding the rice paddies, working the factory line, and breastfeeding. By following a trajectory that mimics historical events, I present the paradoxes of Fascist interventions, revealing the intimacy of food factories and crop fields and the publicness of domestic kitchens. To emphasize the fusion of women's food production and reproduction that took place under Fascism, my book focuses on three topics: (1) working-class women's lived experience of feeding their families under Fascism, not only by cooking but also through gardening, foraging, and agricultural labour; (2) the blending of Fascist autarkic food policies and state surveillance of the female body through the biopolitics of breastfeeding in the Perugina chocolate factory; (3) the surprising financial connections and professional overlaps between female cookbook authors, male kitchen architects, and the Fascist regime. To conclude, I bring the reader full circle, exploring the translation of abstract government policies into tangible cooking methods and recipes in the ideal Fascist kitchens, an architectural legacy that endures today.

I do not claim to discuss every space relevant to life's events, particularly with regard to the public sphere. Schools and summer camps would provide fascinating sites for analysis, as would canonical locations such as the church and the piazza.[17]

Instead, I focus on the domestic realm with regard to national geography as well as interior spaces. This strategy also emphasizes the secondary argument that the Fascist regime intertwined women's feeding work with their reproductive labour, connecting them under the aegis of autarky.

To present a clear strategy for the reader to think about feeding as it relates to women's food work, these chapters unfold along an axis of increasing state intrusion into women's daily lives. This narrative trajectory carries the reader from the field to the factory to underscore how people, places, and objects became politicized under the dictatorship. At the same time, this succession traces the widening cracks between Fascist ideology, what the regime hoped to achieve, and the historical reality of what eventually transpired. These caveats serve to contextualize the changes introduced by the regime in a realistic way. Signalling the difference between Fascist ideology and practice provides a trace on the regime's hesitations and second thoughts, as well as its failure to implement coherent food policy. Pointing to the other cultural models that were at work, be they the power of the religious tradition in the countryside or the new models conveyed by the popular American culture in the cities, situates the historical continuity of the Fascist period within the broader arc of Italian history and culture and Italian women's lives.

Book Overview

Chapter 1 establishes the economic stakes for tabletop politics. Today, Italian cuisine without spaghetti sounds inconceivable. But under Fascism, the abolition of pasta centred dictatorial food policy. The Battle for Grain prompted artist-provocateur Filippo Tommaso Marinetti to call for the end of pasta. Culinary propaganda carried this message to the dinner table through decorative bread plates, topped by Benito Mussolini's command to "Love Bread." Producing and consuming only Italian food products promised economic immunity to international markets as well as to League of Nations sanctions against Fascist military aggression abroad. Fascist women's groups like the Massaie Rurali worked alongside private food companies to put alimentary autarky into action. In place of doughy bellies of spaghetti, muscular arms formed by autarkic rice and rabbit stew promised to realize Mussolini's dreams for hyperproductive fields and factories.

In chapter 2, I move to rural rice paddies and grain fields, contrasting propaganda for the Battle for Grain and the Battle for Rice with first-hand accounts of women's agricultural labour. Country almanacs financed by the regime followed seasonal cycles, naturalizing new Fascist holidays and legislation of rural labour to frame both as timeless traditions. This temporal propaganda relied heavily on photocollages to eliminate unacceptable images, like a rice worker staring stone-faced at a jubilant Mussolini, and to emphasize acceptable ones, such as a side profile of a thresher as she helps Il Duce with the harvest. By casting political edits as artistic ones, the regime could cut and paste consent. Women's work songs of the period suggest widespread antipathy for the regime for paying them in compliments rather than cash. Rice weeders sang of their disgust for rice and beans. Rumbling bellies led to what many women refer to as their first political acts: food theft of frogs and wild bird eggs from landowners' marshes. In time, culinary revulsion curdled into political revolt: the *mondine* (female rice weeders) lay across the railroad tracks from Vercellese to

Molinella to assert their right not just to the calories required to live but also to the delicious tastes necessary to thrive.

Chapter 3 opens the doors of the Perugina chocolate factory to investigate the surprising ways that women's industrial food production foreshadowed the regime's approach to reproductive healthcare. Founder Luisa Spagnoli seized Fascism's autarkic moment by creating new candies like Bacio chocolates and marketing new fabrics like angora fur. As an entrepreneur, Spagnoli provides a case study for the political ambiguities involved in reaching the heights of business success in the early years of Fascism. Spagnoli's paternalistic approach to her female factory workers blended social welfare with social control. By installing the first industrial breastfeeding rooms and nurseries at the Fontivegge plant, she made the labour force more efficient by optimizing every bodily movement in the workday, ideas that the regime later deployed towards social control of female factory workers in parallel industries like paper and textiles. With the creation of ONMI (Opera Nazionale per la Protezione della Maternità e Infanzia, or the National Bureau for the Protection of Maternity and Infancy), the regime moved to rationalize reproductive healthcare: newsreels like *Per la Protezione della Stirpe* and *Alle Madri d'Italia* promoted new clinics that Taylorized breastfeeding, turning it into a prescriptive public practice. By controlling the quantity and quality of breastmilk, the regime hoped to shape the future body politic from the inside out.

In chapter 4, I examine how cookbook authors Amalia Moretti Foggia (pen name Petronilla), Lidia Morelli, and Ada Boni debated Fascist food policies of autarky and rationing. What is particularly interesting about this story is that it shows how a group of professional women built their writing careers under a regime that considered a women's place to be in the home. Book dedications speak to the layers of formal and informal associations between writers and publishing houses. Asides to other writers in the cookbook texts show how women maintained collegial connections through brainstorming sessions and letter exchanges. Their recipes reveal that women collaborated with one another by integrating new ingredients into pre-existing dishes, prompting the question of political collaboration with the regime. Financial records and advertising within these books push this question further, illuminating the complex calculations involved in the construction of political identity through women's writing on food.

Chapter 5 looks inside model Fascist kitchens to illustrate how apparently apolitical spaces enacted policy through design. Specifically, Lidia Morelli's popular home encyclopedia *Dalla Cucina al Salotto* provides a template for understanding how politics shaped kitchen design and use during the 1930s. Just as the regime refurbished factories to increase speed and hygiene, so too did kitchen designers. Glide and gleam, the speed and cleanliness of kitchen work, fused the management of domestic spaces with government goals for economic productivity. I also examine how architecture journals such as *Domus* and *Casabella*'s *Costruzioni* advocated rationalist kitchen design in the new *case popolari* (public housing) to increase the productivity of women's domestic labour. At this nexus of architectural and political history, the changing 1930s kitchen reveals Fascism's modernizing impulses as they apply to food, as well as to the state's increasing surveillance of the female body at work.

In the conclusion, I examine the legacy of Fascism in contemporary Italian kitchens and foods. Culinary innovations and deprivations dating from the Fascist period dissolved in the post-war years only to crystallize during Italy's economic boom of the 1950s and 1960s. In the kitchen, as well as in the field and the clinic, relics like autarkic cooking, gendered agricultural labour, and Taylorist breastfeeding not only persisted but actually gained cultural traction and even wider popularity under new names that obscured their origins in Fascist political policy. I also consider avenues of future research, including a consideration of underutilized archival materials.

I have organized the book's structure in this way primarily to focus on women's subjectivity and secondarily to underscore the importance of location and material conditions in shaping habits and identity. The women discussed in each chapter are different from one another. They lived in rural and urban settings. They worked in different occupations. They belonged to different socio-economic classes. They related to their families in different ways. But they all addressed the task of feeding their families, a challenge filtered through their gendered experience of the Fascist state. Because women thought deeply about the daily decision of what to cook and eat, the same woman might support Fascist food policy in one situation but resist it in another. By tracing these paths across the private and the public sphere, I demonstrate how women transformed the body politic through daily practices of food and feeding. They fed their families by cooking but also by labouring in fields and factories and by breastfeeding. Ultimately, this trajectory aims to broaden the way that we think about how women provided for their families during the Fascist period.

CHAPTER ONE

TOWARDS AN AUTARKIC ITALY

Tabletop politics are particularly useful as a means to understand women's lives during Italy's Fascist period (1922–45). During this time, the Italian state attempted to control food in its many manifestations – cooking, feeding, and eating – to assert and negotiate power. As such, the Fascist *ventennio* is not so much representative of Italian cultural history as it is hyper-representative.[1] It blows up violent tendencies that are present in other time periods in inactive or ineffective forms. That darkness is always there, but Fascism hands it a doctor's stethoscope, a professorial chair, or a judge's gavel. Amplification and hyperbole in governmental rhetoric and policy provide a magnifying glass to observe the quotidian interactions between female citizens and the state that less bombastic regimes often obscure. Further, many of the Fascist state's key projects used food as a means to accomplish political goals. Autarky stood at the centre of these policies. This mandate for economic self-sufficiency dictated that Italian citizens eat only domestically produced and locally sourced foods. Yet this was already common practice, particularly among the rural poor. In other words, autarky did not create new food practices but rather redefined pre-existing ones by framing economic necessity as a patriotic gesture.

Dictatorial regimes in Italy, Germany, and Spain nationalized different elements of their regional cuisines, transforming their local ecology into a new, national biology. Two historically specific conditions come together to produce this phenomenon. First, in the totalitarian contexts of the European interwar period, women's worries become national interests. Controlling the contents of each family's cupboard through a combination of new food policies and propaganda evoked successful supervision of the entire country's food supply. As Alice Weinreb observed of Nazi Germany, "While previously it had been housewives who worried about the contents of the soup pot, such issues suddenly consumed the entire population."[2] Second, dictatorial regimes exploited the fact that bodies are constructed through the digestion of food, using local ecology to define citizens' biology at the national level.[3] The Fascist state operated not just on the bodies of the most vulnerable members of society but also inside of them. Manipulating culinary culture could fortify the future body politic. Ultimately, Fascist regimes mobilized recipes for eugenic cookery: to prepare people as well as food.

The Fascist regime began to push for pronatalism, the bearing of numerous, healthy children, largely because of a perceived problem of low population levels. One could make the case that they had reason to worry: heavy loss of life due to World War I, the Spanish flu in 1918, and extensive emigration took their toll on the Italian population. This was particularly true in Southern Italy, which was historically prone to emigration, both internally (to Northern Italian cities) and externally (to foreign countries such as Argentina and Brazil, Canada, and the United States). Mussolini's preoccupation with Italian demography coloured his Ascension Day speech. Delivered in 1927, the discourse addressed the national decline in fertility.[4] The intensity of his fear, and the fact that it seems to have resonated with the population at large, helps to explain the period's obsession with demographic statistics. After Mussolini's speech, the regime sought to marshal the nation through numerical analysis. In an era that equated a large population with military and economic might, pronatalism thus emerged as a key issue for the regime.[5]

Birth More Infants, Farm More Food: Women's (Re)productivity under Fascism

Pronatalism emerged as a guiding principle of Fascist domestic policy due both to the regime's intense preoccupation with Italy's declining birth rate and its potential implications for political and economic dominance abroad and to conservative social politics seeking to keep women in the domestic sphere.[6] But the success of pronatalist policies depended on the participation of Italian women, particularly those who were pregnant, nursing, raising small children, or engaged in several of these activities at once.

To combat infant mortality, the Senate established the National Bureau for the Protection of Maternity and Infancy, known by the Italian acronym ONMI. Originally titled Opera Nazionale Fascista per la Protezione della Maternità e dell'Infanzia, a subsection of law #2277 created this group on 10 December 1925.[7] On 15 April 1926, additional regulatory procedures for ONMI were published.[8] Collections of the 1927 Bachelor Tax, which assigned an increased tax to able-bodied, adult men for every year spent single, went straight into ONMI coffers. The Fascist Party provided the primary push in ONMI's initial legislative creation and continuing financial sustainment. Prevention, rather than treatment, of disease was the focus of ONMI's activities. Breastfeeding, formerly an intimate connection between mother and child, became a primary target for government intervention.

Breastfeeding bonds mother to infant through the fleshy connection of nipple and mouth. No time, space, or additional actors stand between the food producer and the food consumer. The mother feeds as the infant eats – because these actions are simultaneous, breastfeeding simplifies and essentializes all other foodways. Although we rarely think of them in such broad terms, breastmilk is a food and breastfeeding is a food chain.[9] Investigating breastfeeding distils the complexity of local, regional, and national foodways down to the most elemental form: a one-to-one exchange of nutrients, fats, and proteins. Just as breastfeeding provides a key to unlock the meaning of foodways, foodways can also be used to denaturalize breastfeeding as a cosy, caring act insulated from political meaning. Put another way, breastfeeding connotes the maternal, the domestic, and the private, terms often scorned for their supposed lack of political significance and limited national importance. But breastfeeding holds the power to shape the demography of future generations. By reimagining breastfeeding as a foodway, we can strip away the patronizing tone of contemporary debates that minimize its biopolitical implications.[10] Economic, social, and political concerns do not stop at the transom of the home but rather intensify as they are enacted through cooking, feeding, and eating. This is where words become actions. Abstracting breastfeeding as a foodway demonstrates how the public and the private spheres of life merge at the level of the everyday.

During the interwar period, democratic and dictatorial governments alike demonstrated a profound concern for how food powered and shaped the body, from infancy to adulthood.[11] But the Italian Fascist regime went further in its attempt to harness the biopolitical power of food in preparation for military dominance. First, alimentary autarky promised economic self-sufficiency, the first step to diplomatic impunity. More infants born today meant more Fascists to support state ambitions tomorrow. Second, the regime promoted its own ideas of what healthy bodies looked like and what kinds of foods could create those bodies. Nutritional science promised to build ideal mothers and soldiers, the two demographic roles that the regime considered to be the most critical for success in war.[12]

Consider the regime's *ricettari*, the mass-produced recipe pamphlets that used these new nutritional studies to push state-approved foods and foodways. Giving lie to their name, the recipe text in *ricettari* typically amounted to less than half of the total page count. Graphics, graphs, and testimonials composed the majority of the pamphlets' pages. The artistic illustrations and scientific graphs produced by Fascist boards (Ente Nazionale Risi, or the National Rice Board) and the food industry (Dahò, Maizena, Centauro) merge scientific expertise with biopolitical governance. They emblematize Fascism's attempted control of the insides of homes and people, a bid for control evidenced by domestic literature and didactic newsreels that aimed to teach regime-approved cooking methods and child-rearing practices.[13]

Society was imagined by Fascists as a body to be defended against threats both external and internal. Examining the body politics of *ricettari* demonstrates how these documents cast infancy and age as forms of sickness to be cured through food.[14] In the words of David Horn, these are "bodies at risk" which can in turn "pose risks to a more encompassing collectivity."[15] By pathologizing what had been normal stages of life, these documents elevate mild physical vulnerability to complete biological breakdown. Propaganda framed food as an edible panacea. By fortifying vulnerable age groups, it suggested that women could use their cooking skills to remove the stumbling blocks to the regime's ascendant demographic power.

Meanwhile, on 14 June 1925, Benito Mussolini launched the Battle for Grain to liberate Fascist Italy from the "slavery" of foreign bread. This ten-year campaign focused on increasing consumption of grains other than wheat, and to a lesser extent on decreasing consumption of bread and pasta, with the goal of promoting economic self-sufficiency. But because bread and pasta were so important to Italian foodways, the regime had to offer a substitute. In place of these wheat-based staples, the regime advocated rice and rice-based products. To push rice as a replacement for pasta in propaganda, the regime established the Ente Nazionale Risi in January 1928 and the National Day for Rice Propaganda one month later. The board hawked rice to home-makers by pointing out its versatility and thrift. Rice could be flavoured with nearly anything, and the resulting scraps could be moulded into inventive forms to trick family members into eating leftovers. Here, private and semi-private food companies enacted governmental food policy.

These tips attempted to meaningfully address a specific legacy of wartime cook-ery: the struggle between citizen and state over the right to flavour and the need for calories. Many Italians, particularly Southern Italians, resisted the official line that rice offered superior nutrition and flavour due to lingering associations between this product and the privations of World War I, when the government distributed rice as a bread substitute. Moreover, incorporating rice into the Southern Italian diet ran directly counter to traditions of regional foodways: pasta ruled the Mezzogiorno menu. The ensuing tug of war between the regime's emphasis on culinary economy and citizens' dual concerns exemplifies a broad phenomenon – under Fascism, power struggles that linked public politics to private practices materially manifested in food.

Mussolini was not above creating his own propaganda. Stripping bare to the waist, Mussolini cast himself as a virile farm worker to join in Sabaudia's first wheat threshing, a bit of political theatre memorialized on the July 1935 cover of *La Cucina Italiana* (Fig. 1.1). The co-founder and editor of *La Cucina Italiana*, Delia Notari, en-thusiastically supported Fascism and used the magazine to promote autarkic cooking. In fact, the magazine regularly covered Fascist events that were completely devoid of culinary associations.[16] Politics, not cooking, was the centre. With similarly absurd posturing, Mussolini strutted across the literary arts front. His famous poem "Amate il Pane" ("Love Bread") encouraged Italians not to waste this precious product. The poem reads, "Amate il pane, cuore della casa, profumo della mensa, gioia del focolare" (Love bread, heart of the home, perfume of the table, joy of the hearth). While the phrasing and title ("Amate il Pane") suggests that bread is the "cuore della casa," the heart of the home more typically refers to the kitchen or fireside. Positive emotive

1.1. "Il nostro pane quotidiano" (Our Daily Bread), *La Cucina Italiana* magazine cover. Published 1 July 1935. (Academia Barilla Gastronomic Library, Parma, Italy)

terms such as "amate," "cuore," and "gioia" elevate bread eating from a rote act of filling the belly to a pious ritual of quasi-religious significance, as with the consumption of the host. Only the state had the authority to oversee the holy rite of bread consumption, precious as it was.

As banal as it was ubiquitous, this poem appeared everywhere from women's almanacs to decorative dinner plates (Fig. 1.2). Sienna wheat stalks and midnight-blue cornflowers at the wide lip of the plate wreathe the injunction to "love bread." The centre of the plate shows the open fireplace of a country kitchen, flanked by stylized wheat spikes drawn in a relatively larger scale than the kitchen. By using the open hearth as a backdrop for Mussolini's verse, ceramics maker Virgilio Retrosi casts the country kitchen as the symbolic space for daily autarkic practices such as conserving bread.[17]

1.2. Virgilio Retrosi, "Amate il Pane" (Love Bread), Rome, 1927. Bread plate, manufactured for Fabbrica Ceramiche d'Arte (Ceramic Arts Factory), ceramic, 35.5 centimetres diameter. (Wolfsonian Institute, Miami, 84.7.30)

Dubious stunts and bad poetry by Mussolini seem to invite smiles and ridicule. But the core of their message – consume rice, conserve bread – evoked a more serious concern, the fortification of Italian bodies for war. Popular injunctions like "Non togliete il pane ai figli dei nostri lavoratori, acquistate prodotti italiani" (Don't take bread from the children of our workers, buy Italian products) and "Assicurate il pane dei nostri figli" (Protect your children's bread) (Fig. 1.3) focused on the power of bread to nourish children specifically, the future of the nation and the ultimate targets of the Fascist body project.

Fatness in particular conveyed ideal health. Carol Helstosky has examined how this association pervaded Italian language during the early twentieth century: "Gustatory metaphors applied to happiness and success. A *uomo di panza*, or 'man with a belly' was a successful man; a *uomo grasso* or 'fat man' was not obese but a man of importance. To 'swim in lasagna' or 'invite someone over for pasta and meat' also carried connotations of generosity and success."[18] Mussolini, stout and muscular, himself embodied this quality: propaganda celebrated his square, neckless profile as a symbol of fortitude.[19] Gino Boccasile's cover (Fig. 1.4) for the Ente Nazionale Risi *ricettario* exemplifies this association and sought to connect fatness with the abstract concept of plenty and with the concrete foodstuff of rice. A robust blond baby flops atop a

1.3. "Assicurate il pane ai vostri figli" (Protect your children's bread), poster. (Centro Studi e Archivio della Comunicazione, Parma, Italy)

bulging burlap sack, spooning rice into its mouth from an oversized white plate. The baby's gender is unclear, as the face is cast in shadow. In effect, this is not a specific baby but an iconic one. Subjectivity of taste gives way to the apparent objectivity of nutrition's salubrious effects. Vitamins and minerals act internally to recreate the external appearance of the baby, plumping its cheeks and adding a rosy tint. Rice's nutrition appeared as a medical fact.

This image evokes the interlinked associations of fatness, plenty, and rice in two ways: first, the infant's disproportionate size in relation to the women in the background and, second, the rice's exceeding of the sack and plate's boundaries. The plate suggests that there is plenty of rice to eat today, and the sack assures us that there will be plenty to eat tomorrow. Alongside this image, the text connects these three ideas: next to the baby's face, we see the words "Rice is Health," written in white. Even the font reinforces this theme. The *ricettario*'s titular command, "Eat Rice," swells to absorb the bottom half of the page. Like the baby shown in the centre, the thick orange and black letters seem to have fed on the rice and grown fat as a result of this autarkic nosh.

1.4. Gino Boccasile, *Mangiate Riso* (*Eat Rice*) *ricettario* cover, 1935, published by Ente Nazionale Risi (National Rice Board), 19 by 16.5 centimetres. (Wolfsonian Institute, Miami, ITAL 2XB1992.1798)

Because the *ricettari* draw attention to the importance of nourishing weak bodies, especially those of young Italians, they also point to importance of the *massaie* (country housewives), not only in the production of food but also in the reproduction of children for the nation. Decreasing infant mortality constituted the centrepiece of reform and led to the founding of ONMI, with its explicit goals of raising domestic birth rates and decreasing infant mortality so as to increase the total number of Italians living in Italy.

Fascist demographic policy dovetailed with its autarkic policies in that it conflated the productivity of farmers with their farms. In particular, the beauty of rural Italian women – their florid cheeks and robust figures – denoted their fertility and implied a capacity for doubled production of babies and wheat. By birthing future soldiers and mothers while farming the food to fuel the new nation, hyperfertile rural women promised a solution to the autarkic problem.

The symbolic figures of the good girl from the country and the bad girl from the city figured heavily in newspapers and cartoons, as their juxtaposition provided an exemplar of the Fascist rules for living as a woman. This dichotomy proved so important to director Alessandro Blasetti that he devoted an entire film, *Terra Madre* (*Motherland*, 1931), to exploring it. In brief, this film concerns the urban protagonist Marco's personal transition from henpecked urbanite to powerful master of his family's rural estate. Ruth Ben-Ghiat argues, "The estate thus appears as a synecdoche for Italy before the event of Fascism – a sterile, disoriented country that suffers from an absence of leadership and collective purpose."[20] Marco comes to know and love his native countryside through a *paesana* (country woman) by the name of Emilia. Symbolic of the countryside even in her name, Emilia specifically evokes the *terra madre* of Benito Mussolini, who was born in Predappio, in the province of Forlì-Cesena in Emilia-Romagna. *Paessaggio* (landscape) is mediated through the human figure of the *paesana*. Blasetti seems to be testing the limits of the idea that the specificities of one region can be used to evoke the national whole. The final scene of the film *Terra Madre* makes the idea explicit: Marco, the protagonist, has just rejected his fiancée Daisy, an archetypal *donna-crisi* ("crisis woman") emblematic of the city's sterile pleasures. He turns to Emilia, his new love, joyfully pitching a mound of hay. He asks, "Didn't we say that when the machines arrived the women were supposed to stop working? Don't you want a child someday?" The two run off across the fields together, and in the final shot, an unseen hand playfully throws a handful of grain at the camera lens. This conclusion suggests that just as the countryside bears grain, so will Emilia soon bear children. Both *paesaggio* and *paesana* are idealized as fertile, productive bodies, producing an autarkic product for the good of the Italian nation.

Ideas for ways to reshape the national body came from unlikely venues. In 1909, Filippo Tommaso Marinetti published "Manifeste du Futurisme" ("The Manifesto of Futurism") in the French newspaper *Le Figaro*, launching the Futurist movement. Becoming a Futurist meant being forward-thinking and disruptive. For this reason, Marinetti and his followers exalted urban evidence of modernity: the industrial city, speeding machines, and flight. Professors and politicians, the Futurists claimed, wrongly looked to the past for Italian identity. Nostalgia had turned the nation into a museum, static and impotent. To remake Italy, the Futurists would start by revitalizing the arts. Futurist manifestos proliferated, advocating bold new approaches to literature, sculpture, architecture – and cuisine.

In three key ways, Futurist cuisine heralded the modernizing impulses that drove Fascist food policy in the late 1930s and early 1940s. First, this artistic movement celebrated cooking as chemistry. Fascism would later echo this optimistic characterization of lab-born foods to justify the proliferation of cheap food substitutes in the years of the sanctions. The Futurists also anticipated the Fascist dream of mobilizing the curative properties of food to re-engineer the national body in anticipation of global war. These methods are best demonstrated by the fusions and elisions of modernity

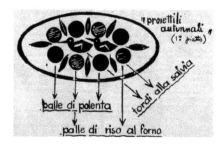

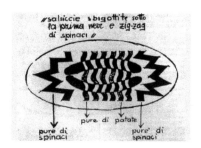

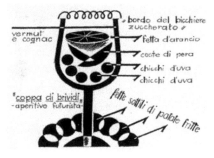

1.5. Illustrated "formulas" (recipes) for *La cucina futurista* (*The Futurist Cookbook*). Recipes by F.T. Marinetti. Art by Fortunato Depero, 1931. Archivio per il Catalogo Generale delle opere di Fortunato Depero, Rovereto, FD-3431-DIS, Rovereto, Italy.

in Marinetti's *La cucina futurista*, first published in 1932.[21] *The Futurist Cookbook* and the Santo Palato tavern in Milan served as Futurist cuisine's Bible and church. Suites of recipes (Fig. 1.5), composed for an "Extremist Banquet" and a "Dynamic Dinner," added a eugenic twist to the old idea of food used as medicine. In Italian, *ricetta* means both culinary recipe and medical prescription. "We invite chemistry immediately to take on the task of providing the body with its necessary calories through the equivalent nutrients provided for free by the State, in powders or pills, albumoid compounds, synthetic fats and vitamins." With this idea, the Futurists took the doubled meaning of *ricetta* to the logical extreme. Wolfing down heaping plates of spaghetti made the populous heavy, brutish, slow, and pessimistic. Popping pharmaceuticals instead promised to revolutionize Italian dinners, the first step towards evolving Italian diners. Or rather, it would beatify them: Futurist cuisine proposed that new eating habits could force an evolutionary process that would raise man from animal to demigod: "Until now, men have fed themselves like ants, rats, cats, or oxen. Now with the Futurists the first human way of eating is born."[22]

Eating dinner in the form of chemical foams, powders, and pills runs counter to the logic of day-to-day dining. Thus, Futurist cuisine was never broadly consumed. That said, it was still highly influential, as Futurist cuisine and Fascist politics held one another in high esteem. Common aesthetics bound both groups: speed, modernity, science, and war. Futurist cookbook authors Marinetti and Fillìa (Luigi Colombo), as well as the ever-shifting Santo Palato tavern cast of chefs and poets, waiters and painters, were enthusiastic Fascists of the first hour. Ultimately, Futurist practitioners provided a laboratory for new ways of thinking about food as an edible agent for

1.6. "Prodotti Autarkici Liebig: Vegedor e Italdado" (Liebig Autarkic Products: Vegedor [vegetable extract with yeast] and Italdado [vegetable extract]), advertisement in *Il nuovo casadoro: Piccolo consigliere della signora moderna*, 2nd ed. Printed by Liebig in Milan, Italy, c. mid-1930s. (Museo della Figurina, Modena, Italy)

bodily reform. Over the arc of the *ventennio*, the wild fantasies of Futurist cuisine were diluted and morphed, but then eventually stamped and signed into formal food policy by the regime.

Additionally, the mere existence of and chatter surrounding Futurist food may have prepared the populace to accept food products created in laboratories rather than kitchens. Private food industry seized the culinary moment. In the 1940s, companies like Liebig and Dahò increased production of extracts and gelatins, the very powders and gels so beloved by Marinetti and his fellow Futurists, providing food-like substances to bridge the gaps left by sanctions and rationing.[23] Private food companies brought Futurist food to the broader population in the later years of Fascism, albeit under the household names of Italdado and Vegetine (Fig. 1.6). Hyperproductivity from the laboratory powers the advertising visuals: a cornucopia of edible rationalist squares tumbles from the cylindrical can as the double-vision arrows shoot quality, fragrance, and economy through the sky.

Futurist food prefigured the regime's enthusiasm not only for lab-based preparations but also for colonial ingredients, like coffee, and even for particular substances found in these foods, like caffeine. After all, both Futurists and the regime abhorred lethargy, sterility, and generalized lack of vigour. Marinetti famously blamed what he viewed as Italy's essential backwardness on its citizens' excessive pasta consumption, "an absurd Italian gastronomic religion." In an even more obvious vote of support for Fascist food policies of autarky, Marinetti's diatribe against pasta proposed introducing rice as a patriotic substitute for spaghetti.[24] Although wilfully provocative, this controversial stance both introduced and began to normalize the edict to eat less pasta. Marinetti's avant-garde stunt later allowed Mussolini to appear relatively moderate when he attempted to curtail pasta consumption in Italy through the Battle for Grain. In place of these lulling carbohydrates, stimulating drug foods like coffee, chocolate, and sugar would energize Italian bodies, the first step towards militarizing them.

The regime was so enamoured of the concept of drug foods as national panacea that it nudged private banks to subsidize their promotion in mass media. For example, the regime regularly funded the sugar advertisements in the racialist periodical *Difesa della Razza*.[25] In a typical example, we see a child, mouth open in a scream of delight as he rides a sugar cube like a hobby horse; the text confirms, "Sugar fortifies and restores" (Fig. 1.7). Advertisements for drug foods and other exciting new products are often rendered in *pugno nell'occhio* or "punch in the eye" style, a design that conveys an idea with a single punch of a graphic – the food product to be sold, in vivid colour against a black or white background, as in artist Federico Seneca's chocolate advertisement for Perugina (Fig. 1.8). The aggressive visual burns the brand into the shopper's memory, ready to resurface when they face the grocer's shelf. Here a golden wasp consumes a candy bar, sweet as honey. Artist Fortunato Depero's coffee advertisement for Cirio (Fig. 1.9) emphasized the speeding buzz of Brazilian coffee beans, perfected by the power of Italian manufacturing. Caffeine jolted workers. It could push them to accomplish twice the work in half the time. "Noi fermiamo il tempo!" (We stop time!) the ad copy promises. It is illustrated by a mechanical human figure who pulls back the clock's minute hand to halt its noonday chime. But it was Cirio's technology – its swift steamship lines and patented can closures – that made its coffee attractive to consumers by ensuring freshness and aroma. Brazilian coffee, perfected by Italian technology, promised to improve bodily efficiency.

As these examples show, Futurist food prefigured many of the methods and goals of the Fascist body project. To incarnate the fertile mothers and muscular soldiers needed for war, F.T. Marinetti and Fillìa seized on the advent of the nutritional sciences, modifying their methods and goals through the Futurist principles of acceleration and unbounded limits. Military planners had already relied on the quantification of nutrients to marshal scarce resources during World War I, a move that

1.7. Sugar advertisement, "Lo zucchero fortifica e ristora" (Sugar fortifies and restores). In *La difesa della razza* (*The Defence of Race*), 20 September 1938, 45. (ACS, MCP, f. "La difesa della razza," Rome, Italy)

disseminated the nutritional sciences along with relief supplies to stricken areas of Europe.[26] Dietics aimed to use new knowledge of nutrition to fortify and preserve bodies, and demography meant might. Futurist cuisine sent these principles into hyperdrive. Futurists believed harnessing the science of food would break the biological speed limit, hastening the next step in human evolution: the birth of a new species, the ideal Fascist man. Adding nutrients would strengthen male bodies to heroic dimensions and would allow female bodies to multiply the population by undreamt of factors. Subtracting germs through kitchen hygiene would decrease tuberculosis infections, slowing or eliminating infant mortality.[27]

Although statistical measures evoke objective rationality, the nutritional sciences were far from politically neutral. Dietary interventions divided the population by prescribing different foods for different bodies, factualizing cultural assumptions about what is good to eat. As Nick Cullather has argued, calories render food, and the

1.8. Poster advertisement for Perugina chocolates, designed by Federico Seneca, "Cioccolato Perugina," Perugia, Italy, 1925. Permission by concession of the Ministero per i beni e le attività culturali e per il Turismo. (Museo Nazionale Collezione Salce, Direzione regionale Musei Veneto, Venice, Italy)

eating habits of populations, politically legible.[28] In interwar Europe, nations wielded the nutritional sciences as an instrument of power to authorize and guide a succession of different schemes of imperial and autarkic food management.

Industrial cookbooks for mess hall chefs framed cooking as an ever-shifting trinity of taste, economy, and nutrition. Dario Fornari's *Il cuciniere militare* exemplifies this genre.[29] The cover to the second edition, published in 1932, the same year as *La cucina futurista*, points to the new addition of "il valore nutritivo degli alimenti: Le analisi semplici per conoscerne il grado di purezza e le norme per convervarli, L'igiene dell'alimentazione, ecc" (the nutritional value of foods: the simple analyses to determine the degree of purity and the norms for conserving them). Patriotic recipe titles show that the military cooks fed troops with dishes named for the Italian Army's specialized divisions. Sauces move from the general "salsa militare" (military sauce) to the specific "salsa alla bersagliera" (sharpshooter sauce). Appetizer plates reference both the mountain and field infantry, with "manicaretto all'alpina" (alpinist dainties) and "manicaretto

1.9. Cirio coffee advertisement, "Noi fermiamo il tempo!" (We stop time!). Designed by Fortunato Depero, Turin, Italy, c. 1930s. (Ministero per i beni e le attività culturali [MiBAC], Milan, Italy)

all'artigliera" (artillery dainties). Dishes ranging from gnocchi to flans are prepared in the colours of the *tricolore*, with stripes of green spinach, red beets, and white potatoes arranged in tribute to the Italian flag. Moreover, the cookbook honours Mussolini by highlighting the cuisine of his region and hometown with recipes like "risotto alla Predappio," featuring sanction-friendly rice flavoured with fried onions and sausage, topped with a sprinkle of parsley. Fornari frames the cookbook as a how-to manual, one that will "interessa tutti perchè insegna a mangiar bene con poca spesa" (interest everyone because it teaches how to eat well at little cost).[30]

The rhetoric of battle conquered domestic territory as well, as evoked by titles like *La cucina italiana della resistenza*.[31] This cookbook, published by Emilia Zamarra in 1936, did not present partisan cuisine. Instead, her rallying cry from the cover called for culinary resistance to the sanctions – "Difendiamoci contro l'iniquo assedio economico!" (Let us defend ourselves against the unjust economic siege!) – through chapters devoted to dishes designed to substitute eggs and vegetables for meat, such as a "frittata economica."

Promoting nutritious food provided an apparently virtuous justification for facilitating a widening of the state's supervision of the welfare and conduct of whole populations via the dinner plate. While this authoritarian impulse and the desire for total control evoke Fascism and Nazism, the eugenic element of the nutritional sciences and their pedagogic partner, home economics, was broadly popular during the interwar period. These trends spanned the Atlantic, with key practitioners hailing from democratic and dictatorial nations alike.[32] Futurist cuisine, however, was born under Italian Fascism. It thus provides a lab to test how these broader transatlantic trends moved through Italian interwar food culture. Futurist cuisine seized on math as well as science, quantifying food and its effects on the body with the ultimate goal of fleshing out ideal Fascist physiques.

Food Production for the National Body

For the regime, the battles for grain and rice would defend the alimentary front of a larger economic war: the struggle for autarky. Autarky signified economic self-sufficiency at the national level. For the Fascist regime, financial sovereignty also translated into political autonomy. In a loop of tautological reasoning, autarky served as both the end and the means for unilateral action and conquest in the greater Mediterranean. That is, to increase domestic production and reduce the need for goods from elsewhere, Italy first needed to augment its domestic territory. Thus, Mussolini invaded Ethiopia in September 1935, establishing the Italian Empire in East Africa. In October, the League of Nations countered with a raft of economic sanctions against Italy, curtailing trade with key partners such as Turkey, from whom Italy received the majority of its wheat imports.[33] To stay afloat, the regime shifted its focus from expanding the boundaries of the domestic to increasing the capacity of production, formulating policies to rationalize and modernize Italian industry. By reducing imports and increasing production, the regime hoped to attain economic self-sufficiency and imperviousness to war.

The Fascist regime clearly recognized the outsize impact that food had on the local and national budget: groceries accounted for nearly 70 per cent of family income during this period. Government memos and communiqués repeatedly suggest that food provided a key means to push for the larger autarkic project because the majority of family budgets, regardless of region or class status, went towards food. Emanuela Scarpellini cites pricing data suggesting that within these food budgets, extras like butter, coffee, and beef stood in stark contrast to basics like starches and grains. She includes the average annual consumer prices for one kilogram of the following products in lire: bread: 2.06, pasta: 2.96, rice: 2.30, potatoes: 0.65, butter: 14.16, coffee: 32.27, sugar: 6.50, and beef: 10.99.[34] The regime also realized that the regularity of food purchases meant more opportunities for government invention in citizens'

1.10. Photo of a girl with her prize-winning cauliflower. (ACS, MRF, 1934–6, b. 90, f. 151 sf 6–12, 907–34)

choices. Urban women who went to the market for food had to make daily or weekly choices regarding what to buy for their families, whereas other purchases, like clothes and housing, occurred far less frequently.

Mobilizing regional Italy to produce more and better food promised to fill the empty bellies that had been constricted first by general poverty and later by the specific privations of wartime. To this end, the Partito Nazionale Fascista's women's groups, under the umbrella of the Fasci Femminili, emphasized the rural sector by founding the Massaie Rurali.[35] Pedagogy was at the centre of the Massaie Rurali model. Teachers travelled to the gates of Rome to learn new methods for raising rabbits and poultry at the Sant'Alessio Training College. Upon graduation, they dispersed across the countryside to lead evening classes and weekend workshops, instructing rural women in party-approved methods for cooking, gardening, and farmyard animal raising. Modernization marked both the means and the goal of these didactic interventions: spraying chemical fertilizers and building rationalized rabbit hutches meant that women would put less toil into the earth but reap more and bigger fruits. Competitions for the biggest squash, pumpkin, or cauliflower (see Fig. 1.10) took root in rural townships from Piedmont to Umbria.[36]

1.11. Photo of a woman in a white rabbit fur coat and rabbit fur hat with her white Angora rabbit. (ACS, MRF, 1934–1936, b. 90, f. 151 sf 6–12, 407–34)

The productive drive meant not only producing bigger varieties of the same vegetables but also promoting foods that were naturally abundant or prolific. This is one reason why the regime pushed *conigliatura* (rabbit raising): famous for their reproductivity, rabbits made an excellent substitute for scarce and expensive pork products. It is hard to overstate the ubiquity of rabbits (and the aforementioned rice) in Fascist-period mass media: they hopped all the way from the recipe columns to the fashion pages, where hats and coats fashioned from angora fur emblematized the new autarkic style (Fig. 1.11). Many popular women's magazines, such as *Bellezza*, *Cordelia*, *Grazia*, and *La donna italiana*, included regime-friendly articles featuring autarkic fashion spreads composed with photos like the one in figure 1.11.

To provide a more extreme example, *La Cucina Italiana* constitutes a unique case of a hobby magazine's direct adherence to state dictates. Founders and editors Delia and Umberto Notari enthusiastically supported the Fascist regime by promoting Mussolini's autarkic campaigns with reader contests and letters to the editor. Umberto Notari's adherence to Fascist political doctrine appears to have developed in his early twenties, during his collaboration with Filippo Tommaso Marinetti on the magazine *Poesia*. His enthusiasm for social conservatism in general and Fascist racial policy in particular manifested in many of his publications, from *La donna "Tipo Tre"* to his signature on *Manifesto della razza* and *Panegirico della razza italiana*. But it was Delia Notari, not Umberto, who pushed for the creation of *La Cucina Italiana*; furthermore, she controlled the editorial slant of the magazine as director. A widow of engineer Joseph Magnaghi and the owner of the Salsomaggiore thermal baths, Delia Pavoni later married Umberto and appears to have shared his pro-Fascist politics.

Delia Notari encouraged contributors to incorporate recipes for autarkic eating to support the regime, even before government sanctions began to pressure Italians to change their eating habits. During her tenure from the first Milan-produced issue of 15 December 1929 to her final Rome-produced issue of December 1934, she encouraged contributors to incorporate recipes for autarkic eating to support the regime. Proponents of Fascism from the literary arts world such as Giovanni Pascoli, Ada Negri, and Margherita Sarfatti contributed articles as well.[37] Futurists Massimo Bontempelli and Filippo Tommaso Marinetti served on the tasting committee, whose enviable duties extended to sampling the magazine's recipes before publication.[38]

As *La Cucina Italiana*'s sudden enthusiasm for rabbit and their inclusion of Fascism-friendly columnists suggests, not all women's narratives of autarkic cooking contested the regime dictates. Rabbits and poultry emerged as primary autarkic meats because housewives could raise them themselves quickly and cheaply in their yards. Whereas beef and pork required time and specialized skill to butcher, these smaller animals provided protein to families on a budget. *La Cucina Italiana* recipes' content underlines the intensity of this shift. Prior to the sanctions, the 1934 index of *La Cucina Italiana* provides only three rabbit recipes in the twelve-issue total. In December 1935, just after the November call for autarky, twenty-two recipes for rabbit appeared in a single issue. Other proteins rose in prominence as well. In 1936, *La Cucina Italiana* began to emphasize fish dishes to such a degree that editors provided a new column heading in that year's index to collect them. *La Cucina Italiana* further attempted to cast autarkic cooking as a means to demonstrate one's modernity to other women. Illustrations showing fashionable women holding autarkic fare such as plucked pigeons and elaborate French recipes featuring the poorer meats tried to cast autarkic cooking as stylish, as in the line drawing of an elegant wife that accompanied an article on hunting and its related sanctions-inspired recipe competition (Fig. 1.12).

But even housekeeping manuals that wrote admiringly of the regime continued to treat autarkic meats as less prestigious than pork, or less commonly beef. Variously, they note that these meats provide less protein or flavour than those desirable alternatives. In framing rabbit and poultry comparatively against other meats, they establish pork and beef as the ideal standard against which all other meats' nutrition and taste should be judged. Even when obvious comparisons to pork and beef are absent, rabbit, fish, and chicken recipe narratives evoke their primacy. For example, *La Cucina Italiana* regularly heralded autarkic meats for their lightness and digestibility. Such statements simply cast the housekeeping manual's contention of low nutritional value in a positive light. They also suggest that pork and beef, being heavier, offer more

1.12. Bruno, magazine article illustration, line drawing accompanying the article "Mogli di cacciatore, vittime ignorate" (Wives of hunters, ignored victims). (*La Cucina Italiana*, September 1935, p. 15)

nourishment pound for pound than lean meats. Still, taste went unmentioned, a conspicuous exclusion for a magazine ostensibly concerned with good eating. As such, autarkic meats, while good for the nation, emerged as almost definitionally not good for the palate. And since few families possessed the funds to consume pork or beef on a weekly basis, even less prestigious meats such as chicken, rabbit, or fish would have been a rare treat after a week of grain-based dishes. Thus, these texts document not so much a nationwide change in diet as a redefinition of how the social value of these foods were purposefully recharacterized because of political events such as the sanctions. As Carol Helstosky puts it, "What was miserable and inadequate in the nineteenth century became healthful and patriotic under Fascism."[39]

Fascist food policy had little effect on Italian foodways.[40] What we see in these magazines does not represent a large shift in what Italians ate – and gardened and raised and wore. Many women were already tending courtyard plots and keeping henhouses. Rather, pushing autarkic food constituted a bid by the Fascist Party to shift perceptions about the relative prestige of different domestic products, both within categories (pork versus rabbit, wheat versus rice) and between them (meat versus vegetables).

1.13. Photo of a woman with her prize-winning squash under electric wires. (ACS, MRF, 1934–6, b. 90, f. 151 sf 6–12, 907–34)

The lasting effects of Fascist food policy were subtle but irrevocable. Autarky required hyperproductivity from factories, laboratories, and farms alike – in the pursuit of bigger and better vegetable harvests and grain yields to feed the nation, the seasonal cycles of the countryside were held to quantifiable urban standards of ever-increasing speed. Despite their best efforts, the biological impossibility of increasing autarkic output to fully compensate for trade deficits was aptly, though perhaps accidentally, evoked by the name of the Massaie Rurali training program, "Women with a Hundred Arms." Instead, technology began to accomplish what people could not: electric wires and telephone lines buzzed, emitting bright noise down country lanes. Even the Massaie Rurali made use of modernity to make their message heard, capitalizing on the popularity of radio by broadcasting the *Ente Rurale*. Advice from this popular "how-to" radio hour may have even helped women such as the one pictured in figure 1.13 learn about the right fertilizer to grow enormous squash (Fig. 1.13). Yet contrary to the fulsome images of regime propaganda, neither farmwomen nor the farm could be kept in socially conservative bubbles, floating outside of time and

Belle donne italiane: salute e garanzia della razza

1.14. "Belle donne italiane: Salute e garanzia della razza" (Beautiful Italian women: Health and promise of the race) in "La Battaglia vittoriosa e il premio delle donne italiane," *La cucina italiana*, July 1936, p. 3.

change. To boost domestic production through women's food work, the regime forged propaganda from paradoxes. Hyperproductivity brought speed and technology, traits more often associated with Futurism and with cities, into the countryside.

Speeding up the farm's seasonal cycles of growth and fertility to increase production was not the only way that autarkic policies melded dichotomies like modernity with tradition. The Fascist regime also invented new culinary "traditions" like the Festa dell'Uva along with a host of other regional *sagre* (food festivals). *Sagre* functioned like country fairs, with cooking and gardening competitions and product displays used to promote local products such as grapes, oranges, chestnuts, and snails, as well as such recipes as crescentine and ravioli. Newborn traditions like the *sagre* lay at the heart of Fascism's key mythos: the resurrection of an idealized national past.[41] The regime framed these events – which were recent, urban inventions – as regional conventions. Costumes, parades, contests, and costumes were planned as though they were theatrical productions to showcase a picturesque version of rural life. The *sagre* mapped social conservatism onto geographic space. Consider two photos published in *La Cucina Italiana* in July 1937: "Belle donne italiane: Salute e

Un gruppo di donne nei pittoreschi costumi della Sardegna forte e gentile

1.15. "Un gruppo di donne nei pittoreschi costumi della Sardegna forte e gentile" (A group of women, strong and kind, in the picturesque costumes of Sardinia) in "La Battaglia vittoriosa e il premio delle donne italiane," *La cucina italiana,* July 1936, p. 3.

garanzia della razza" (Beautiful Italian women: Health and promise of the race) (Fig. 1.14) and "Un gruppo di donne nei pittoreschi costumi della Sardegna forte e gentile" (A group of women, strong and kind, in the picturesque costumes of Sardinia) (Fig. 1.15).

These photos accompany articles that describe regional *sagre,* as well as other Fascist food events aimed at women. While there are general thematic correlations between the text and the photos, no textual evidence supports the notion that these photos were actually taken at said events. So while these stock images may be loosely affiliated with the regime, it appears that their primary purpose within the context of *La Cucina Italiana* is to provide visual variety to the magazine page. In "Belle donne italiane," we see a line of four women holding up a piece of fabric, each with their right arm artfully crossed over their neighbour's left. Not only are the women posed, but they also appear to be situated in an area specifically designed for such staging: in the background, we see a wall of leaves and a striped paper lantern. The "forte e gentile" women of Sardinia are shown against a nearly identical wall of leaves. This background evokes nature but is in fact artificially constructed.

1.16. Advertisement for Ornamental Littorio Stamped Saint-Gobain Glass by Ventrunione Cristalli, Milan. Printed in *Domus*, June 1938, p. 45.

Domestic Industry, Architecture, and Design

Autarky, unlike the Battle for Grain, was not strictly a food-based policy – rather, it promoted the production and consumption of Italian goods, both material (linoleum, marble) and abstract (Italian labour, Italian language). Both of these ideas changed kitchen design during the Fascist period. Aluminium, along with glass and concrete, could be produced in Italy at low cost.[42] Modernist aesthetics in the kitchen derive partially from the hygienic shine of these materials, which proliferated from the concrete ceilings to the ceramic-tiled walls and down to the linoleum floors. Even the dishware – the Moka coffee pot on the stove and the maiolica bread plates on display by the cupboard – were made of domestically sourced materials.

Key regime architects like Gio Ponti used the pages of *Domus* to celebrate these materials as exemplars of Fascist materials for their literal support of the regime. Glass, already an autarkic material, could be stamped with images of the *fascio*, as in this advertisement by Saint-Gobain's Milanese glassworks, a private company advertising specialized windowpanes for the exclusive use of state- and parastate-authorized groups (Fig. 1.16). Materials mattered to the economics of autarky but also to its physical aesthetics and written and image-based content.

Ceramics boomed under Fascism. Industrial designers like Lino Berzoini, along with private companies like Calderoni and Motta, translated autarky into decorative plates and serving dishes that brought Fascist messages into private kitchens. Berzoini had found early success in ceramics as a painter of doll faces for Lenci manufacturing. This work provided financial stability and name recognition for the artist to launch his own ceramic work and paintings to acclaim, participating in the Venice Biennial in 1938. In the same year, he signed Marinetti's *Manifesto della ceramica futurista*. Here, the ceramicist and the Futurist first invented and then romanticized the Italian national past – a Brigadoon that served the regime's call for autarky by celebrating pastoral bounty through social conservatism. Ceramic plates and bowls bore illustrations of pristine country kitchens and hearty farm work. Along with Virgilio Retrosi's "Amate il Pane" (Love Bread) ceramic plate and Eugenio Colmo's "Autarchia" ceramic bowl, these pieces prescribed autarky as a means to food conservation.

Although mass-produced, these objects were not in wide circulation: because Berzoini, Retrosi, and Colmo designed these plates as limited-edition pieces for the Fascist state and sold them directly to the government, their total production numbered in the hundreds.[43] But despite their low numbers, these pieces had high cultural visibility. On Fascist holidays and at the *sagre*, plates like these were given out to women as prizes for productivity. Plates went to women who raised the largest cauliflower, spun the most angora fur, and, most importantly, raised prolific families.[44] Set high on the wall, such pieces mapped these new traditions onto heavy ceramic and tin. They reminded diners to save bread by framing food conservation as the practice of moral value, a celebration of hearth and homeland.[45] But upon a closer look, scratches and cracks suggest that women served and scraped from these plates. Economic need pushed the purpose of these objects from decoration to service. This move from prescribed to actual dishware use speaks to the distance between the idyllic country kitchen scenes shown on these plates and the harsh realities of the kitchens in which they served endless dinners of beans, rice, and the other economical legumes and grains that formed most families' daily diets.

Decorative bread plates offered the ample, flat surface area necessary for detailed pictorial odes to autarky. Because of widespread grain scarcity and a national push for conservation, bread consumption (how much, how often, by whom) sent charged political messages, whether the consumer intended it or not. Placed in the kitchen or dining room and thus highly visible around mealtimes, these objects were meant to display and communicate the importance of bread conservation when such messages could have the greatest effect on rationing behaviours.[46] Despite their intended purpose as dining room decoration, many women ignored their artistic qualities and focused on their functional ones, serving minestra on these plates at family mealtimes.

While we cannot say with certainty where individual plates fall on a continuum from decorative to functional usage, their physical characteristics provide hints. Lino

1.17. Eugenio Colmo, Autarchia Bowl, 1938, ceramic, 30.5 centimetres diameter. (Wolfsonian Institute, Miami, xx1990.627)

Berzoini's bread plate for Calderoni appears functional, as it includes an undecorated eight-inch-diameter space at the centre where one might place the bread. By contrast, his plate for Casa Giuseppe Mazzotti provides a ridged design in the centre and lip of the plate that would make it difficult for bread to stay in place during service, suggesting that it may have served a decorative function. Creamy risotto or spicy amatriciana would have covered the plate's Fascist imagery and neutralized the political meaning of this object when in use. How do the aesthetics of these objects evoke simplicity and rurality? And how do these traditions promote alimentary autarky? As the following example demonstrates, these dishes overtly trumpet political messages with text and graphics but also evoke the political climate with their material composition and their elements of design.

A 1938 Turinese glazed ceramic bowl (Fig. 1.17) designed by Eugenio Colmo stridently conveys the fusion of urban and rural food industries to support a common autarkic goal.[47] The bowl features six black figures engaged in various activities of labour and production against a bottle-green background. At the centre of the bowl, near the lofted pickaxe of a miner and the vegetable basket of a countrywoman, a soldier brandishes the wind-blown banner encompassing them all, "Autarchia." Each figure incarnates one of four key activities – colonization, mining, nourishment, and textiles – in support of this central theme, all named at the lip of the plate under the figures' feet. Based on the fact that he carries the encompassing message of autarky, the soldier, under the title of "Difesa" (Defence) appears to hold central importance. In reality, the Fascist troops invaded Ethiopia. They acted as aggressors in others' territory, not defenders of domestic turf. By inverting these roles, this image casts Italian colonizers in Africa as the wronged party, allowing them to seize the moral high ground. Depicting autarky as a form of domestic protection, the plate raises the stakes for women's participation in food production and conservation in the context of the kitchen and dining room, where this plate would have been visible. By linking the home and the home front through public and private forms of labour, the bowl feeds Fascism by celebrating women's labour as belonging to the regime's autarkic project. The design frames food work as a key plank in the autarkic platform.

A similar plate made of patinated tin (Fig. 1.18) goes even further in enmeshing modern and traditional forms of labour under the aegis of autarky. Aesthetics as well as context conflate the two: stamped scenes rounding the rim depict a seamless succession of agricultural and industrial activities involved in wheat growth and harvest. This treatment inscribes manufacturing within the cyclical rhythms of agricultural production. Both the technique (metal stamping) and style (use of successive, static images to suggest the passage of time) date back to medieval artistic traditions. The artistic treatment of this plate flattens aesthetic distinctions between fields and smokestacks by depicting all associated activities as temporarily frozen moments of a harmonious cycle. Metal kitchen objects often, but not always, evoke the streamlined speed and power of an imminent machine age. But this plate shows that the cultural meaning of metal was not fixed. Here, the copper hue provides a muted palette of earth tones on a rough, non-reflective surface to evoke tradition, a parallel plank in the autarkic platform. A material generally associated with speed, urbanity, and modernity now communicates slowness, rurality, and convention. This newborn national history lies at the heart of the Fascist autarkic project for increasing domestic food production. By blending farms and factories, this plate naturalizes the Fascist push for increased industrial production to support the autarkic cause.

But design alone could not change how women cooked, served, and ate. Dishware's form also provided a powerful way to modify these behaviours so as to promote alimentary autarky. First among these qualities is these bowls' large size. Mounted on a pedestal base and extending just over thirty-five centimetres in diameter, the hefty dimensions of the Autarchia bowl could hold vegetable soup for fifteen or risotto for ten. In use then, this bowl would have prompted multiple generations or, better still for the pronatalist cause, many children to gather at the table to eat together. Here

1.18. Lino Berzoini, Bread Plate, Milan, c. mid-1930s, designed for Calderoni and manufactured by Motta, patinated tin, 25.5 centimetres diameter. (Wolfsonian Institute, Miami, 84.9.12)

again, multiple forms of gendered labour – including women's reproductive work of birthing children and their productive work of cooking – converge in a single object of Fascist propaganda. Indeed, this interpretation reflects how a cook would have acquired this autarkic dishware in the first place. The regime often awarded bowls such as this to hyperproductive *massaie* as prizes for their cooking, gardening, and rabbit- and chicken-rearing skills. Productivity and reproductivity blend here as well.[48] The regime also bestowed these bowls on prolific mothers.[49]

By examining physical details like a bowl's size and shape, we see how a mass-produced object would have supported the autarkic cooking and eating practices promoted by the Fascist government. This bowl's concave cup dips wide and deep. A pork *bracciola* would look absurd placed in the centre of this giant bowl. It would be nearly impossible to bear down with a knife to cut a meat fillet in this deep recess. Such a form suggests that liquids, not solids, should be served. Perhaps a minestrone filled with homegrown vegetables or a porridge made of domestically produced grains like polenta, oatmeal, or rice? Ultimately, this bowl unites decoration and form while forcing function: the shape and size of the Autarchia bowl would make bread service impossible and meat service challenging.

As this bowl demonstrates, Fascist Italy provides a particularly fruitful time and place for the analysis of gender and material culture for two reasons: first, because the self-mythologizing tendency of dictatorships boosts the production of politically inflected design and offers a wealth of materials to study; and second, because the period presents a hyperbolic cultural moment that makes subtle phenomena more readily observable to the historian. The scope and intensity of these state interventions into private life are not unique to Fascism: indeed, their legacy persists today in farms and factories, kitchens and clinics. But the Fascist period offers a useful point of departure for the study of women's tabletop politics because of the regime's own intense interest in the private lives of its female citizens.

Autarky Elsewhere: Nazi Germany and Stalinist Russia

Militarized nations run on their stomachs. The Italian Fascist government was not alone in embracing autarky as a means to unilateral martial action. German Nazism and Russian Stalinism pursued autarky for analogous motives, but the geopolitics of their national foodways created divergent culinary effects.[50] These three dictatorial states shared a common framework in their initial approach: each relied on regime-affiliated women's groups to promote autarky to working-class mothers as a classed and gendered culinary project.

In Nazi Germany, organizations like the National Mothers' Service (the Reichsmutterdienst, part of the Deutsches Frauenwerk) and the National Economy and Home Economy Boards (Volkwirtschaft and Hauswirtschaft) counselled women on patriotic practices for the market and the kitchen by suggesting specific food choices and preparations for national shortages. The Home Economy Board recommended vegetables over meat and heavily promoted the *Eintopf* (the "one-pot dish") as the meal of sacrifice for the nation. It advised German civilians to develop a "political stomach" to face wartime cookery. As in Italy, patriotism offered one justification for augmenting foodways, but advocating self-denial to promote national interests failed to convince women to change their recipes. Recognizing this, Home Economy propaganda increasingly supplemented the call for culinary sacrifice with practical tips to point out the personal benefits that autarky provided for housewives. For example, later *Eintopf* preparations emphasized the health benefits of eating vegetables and the time saved by preparing one-pot dinners.

German Nazism attempted to promote alimentary autarky as a cultural and nationalistic issue, but for Italian Fascism, such practices originally arose from economic necessity. Wartime food shortages created larger culinary shockwaves in Germany than they did in Italy, where autarky simply provided a new name for the way that families had eaten for centuries. Many Italian women had extensive experience with *la cucina povera* (the "cooking of the poor"), but *Hamsterfahrten* ("hamstering trips" into the countryside to forage for food) and black markets constituted new social phenomena for the German women who came of age during Nazism.[51]

On the other hand, certain elements of Italy's history of culinary austerity found a corollary in the traditions of the Russian kitchen. The *obshchestvennitsa*, or "civic-minded woman," movement drew tens of thousands of women into the Stalinist reconstruction of daily life through their volunteer work and influence in the domestic sphere. This group constituted one element of the broader movement to modernize Russian motherhood by applying principles of science and design to the home in general and to the kitchen specifically. Like their Italian counterparts in the Fasci Femminili, these modern mothers sought to prepare meals for their families using the latest nutritional information provided by state science boards.

But the communal nature of Stalinism meant that alimentary autarky also applied heavily in public dining settings: members of the *obshchestvennitsa* supervised meal preparation in factory cafeterias as well as in family homes. By contrast, the Italian Fascist women's groups rarely cooked for public groups, instead supervising food preparation at communal kitchens in nurseries and soup kitchens as part of their volunteer efforts. Supervision of cooking even extended into the private homes. The Board for the Protection of Motherhood and Childhood (ONMI) used volunteer social workers (*visitatrici* – typically the wives of middle- and upper-class Fascist officials) to inspect the cooking and cleaning habits of the working-class mothers who relied on state cafeterias to supplement their family food budgets. As such, social class control shaped the Italian Fascist promotion of domestic cookery in a way that it did not in its Stalinist counterpart.

The promotion of alimentary autarky in Russia was also less rooted in the cult of domesticity than it was in either Germany or Italy. This was due in part to the collectivization of daily life and in part to women's greater participation in the workforce. Although similar rhetoric connected home and homeland – the *obshchestvennitsa* was to be the "housewife to the nation" – these inventions were primarily aimed at the public sphere and benefited women workers as well as men.[52]

Moreover, the Italian Fascists was not alone in their manipulation of food and foodways to shape the future body politic by fortifying individual bodies. Other Fascisms approached this equation as a dual movement – they attempted to strengthen certain populations by weakening or eliminating others. Under Spanish Fascism, Francisco Franco pursued a policy of autarky from 1939 to 1959 to disastrous results. Poor harvests and excessive food exportation to Germany led to nearly 200,000 deaths during the 1940s, a decade known as the "years of hunger."[53] Michael Richards has convincingly argued that the Francoist regime deliberately deployed autarkic food policy on political opponents and their families, part of the post–civil war punishing and redeeming of the defeated republicans – a process achieved through death by starvation.[54]

Similarly, German Nazi Party leader Herberte Backe created a plan to manipulate food-supply routes in the occupied Soviet territories with the dual goals of feeding and strengthening German soldiers while weakening the local populous through systematic starvation. Known as the Hunger Plan (der Hungerplan or der Backe-Plan), this economic management scheme called for an immediate and full exploitation of the occupied regions in favour of the war economy of Germany, particularly in the areas of food and oil.[55] As Lizzie Collingham has argued, the Nazi Hunger Plan amounted to no less than an engineered famine – it aimed not only to shape the German military population but also to eliminate specific Soviet populations.[56] In an era that equated a large domestic population with international political might, consumption patterns appeared to presage military victory or defeat. This belief had biopolitical implications: a new focus on nutrients over flavour aimed to fortify individual bodies, with the ultimate goal of readying the national body for war.[57]

Private food companies like Cirio and La Rocca seized on this charged moral rhetoric of feeding the nation through liquids flowing from heart to breast. La Rocca created advertising ephemera like tax stamps and *chiudilettere* (stamps to seal envelopes) featuring images like a noble tomato (Fig. 1.19), who bravely cuts into his own red flesh with a cooking knife to feed the nation with his bloody red juice. Through anthropomorphization in this La Rocca ad, the tomato incarnates the transformation of Italian foods into Italian bodies that cookbooks only mildly evoke: "Il suo succo purissimo e il generoso sole di Puglia nel concentrato di pomodoro La Rocca" (His very pure juice and the generous sun of Puglia in La Rocca tomato concentrate).

Broad questions of how foodways formed the national body under Fascism are compressed into this tiny one-inch stamp. *Ius sanguinis* (right of blood) defines Italian citizenship. Blood – figured here as tomato juice – is never far from racialized discourses of nationality. What is inside us defines where we belong. Put another way, fruits from Italian soil build the Italian body. In the case of this *chiudilettere*, Pugliese sun and soil define Italianità, whether we are talking about a person or a tomato. Instead of food forming a person, this advertisement visually inverts the terms, showing a vegetable that evolves to a man through his patriotic self-sacrifice. It does not matter whether blood or juice flows through the veins: what matters is that that liquid is Italian and pure. Through digestion, an Italian citizen who ate those Italian tomatoes increased the total volume of Italianità coursing through their veins. In Nazi Germany, the idea gained even greater popularity as "Blut und boden" (blood and soil). In Italy, *sangue* and *suolo* provide the material terms for determining one's nationalism. This was true of both people and tomatoes.

Totalitarian regimes curate reality, elevating the times and places of perceived national unity and international dominance to stand for, and above, the entirety of the nation's past. Periods marked by liberal politics and foreign influence fade into shadow.[58] This paradox – a newborn history – is always socially conservative,

IL SUO SUCCO ·PURISSIMO
E IL GENEROSO SOLE DI PUGLIA
NEL CONCENTRATO DI POMODORO
LA ROCCA

Navarra S.A. - Milano   Ediz. Uff. Propag. LaRocca   Creaz. SCARANO

LORENZO LA ROCCA - BARI (ITALIA)

1.19. *Chiudilettere* of La Rocca tomato concentrate. Designed by Scarano of S.A. Navarra in Milan for La Rocca. Financed by La Rocca of Bari, Italy, c. 1937. (Museo della Figurina, Modena, Italy)

normalizing the new Fascist regime as an apparently natural rebirth of the nation's original state.[59]

Under Fascism, some parts of the nation's past were considered to be more Italian than others. This line of reasoning applies not only to eras but also to regions and citizens. Nationalizing the regional does not mean equal representation; rather, it means selecting those geographic areas that best symbolize the goals of extreme conservatism and amplifying them to stand for the whole of the country. Marginalized people, such as working-class women, and marginalized places, like the isolated farms and villages hidden deep in the countryside, are held as exemplars of the new Fascist ways of thinking due to their role as repositories of the cultural memory. Unfortunately, they also bear some of the regime's worst exploitation.[60] Fascism slurs ecology into biology to accomplish eugenic goals. In Italy, it leveraged women's cooking work, changing what people eat so as to reform the body, ultimately creating new definitions of nationality that operated at the level of the cell.

CHAPTER TWO

AGRICULTURAL LABOUR AND THE FIGHT FOR TASTE

"Bisogna ruralizzare l'Italia" (Italy must be ruralized). The regime held rural Italy in high esteem. It was seen as a repository for tradition thanks to its conservative gender roles and robust birth rates. In Fascist Italy, progress did not mean just the skyscrapers that surged upwards over Milan or the military planes buzzing over Rome's Ciampino Airport. The regime seized the Italian countryside as a living laboratory and a centrepiece of their vision for the future. Far from the sterile cities, roaring machines and chemical wizardry promised to send Italian fertility into hyperdrive. It was a rigorous demonstration of Fascist modernity that vowed to secure the nation's food supply. A less overt part of the broader eugenic program, tractors and fertilizers aimed to increase autarkic production, that is, to enhance the vigour and reproductive capacity of plants, animals, and even people. Farming bodies were believed to be healthy bodies. Fascist slogans framed agricultural work as a means to cultivate the national body as well as raw products like fruits and vegetables. The regime approached the task of strengthening the Italian population through campaigns for food production that depended almost entirely on rural women's agricultural work. Under Fascism, food brought rural Italy into focus.

In contrast to the nineteenth-century labour shifts of the United States and Great Britain that held a woman's place to be in the home, Italy maintained its time-honoured tradition of female agricultural work well into the twentieth century. Women weeded rice paddies in the spring and threshed grain in the fall. Rice and wheat stood at the centre of Fascist alimentary policy along with the labour that produced them. Named for their springtime work, the *mondine* (female rice weeders) worked the region's rice paddies, their arms and legs deep in the mud, backs bent for eight hours each day during the forty-day *monda*, the summer rice-weeding season. This particular form of agricultural labour took on heightened political significance under Benito Mussolini's dictatorial rule, when the Fascist state demanded that domestic products – and those who produced them – fuel the nation's economy. Under the Fascist regime, bread conservation and rice consumption intertwined in the dovetailed goals of the Battle for Grain and the establishment of the National Rice Board (Ente Nazionale Risi), which pushed Italians to balance the national budget by growing more grain while eating more rice.

In 1927, the Fascist ruralization campaign began in earnest with the founding of the Istituto Nazionale di Economia Agraria the following year. The institute conducted a photographic survey of Italian agricultural work in 1929, as well as a census in 1930 to assess the state of Italian agriculture and identify arenas for financial savings. Minister of Agriculture Arrigo Serpieri spotted an opportunity: women worked the fields, and they could be paid less than men. In 1934, he introduced a new labour law: women's agriculture work was valued at 60 per cent of a man's, regardless of her output. Thereafter, this notorious calculation bore its maker's name: the *coefficiente Serpieri*.[1]

By recognizing rural Italy as an industrial sector with productive capacity akin to that of urban manufacturing, the regime could apply policies of economy to paddies and fields as well as to plants and factories. In the case of the typical *mondina*, precarious finances meant that staying at home was not an option. The necessities of the working class eclipsed gender dictates that placed women in the private sphere. Although rural working-class Italian women had historically taken on agricultural work outside the home, they generally did so on a piecemeal basis to augment household income. Rice-weeding traditions departed from these general working norms in that women planned to participate in the year's *monda* (forty-day weeding season) in advance to generate what was often the only liquid capital their families possessed. Thus, in the context of Italian agricultural labour, the economic necessity of the female presence in the rice fields contradicted socially conservative state narratives of prosperity.

Popular literary culture, including novels and magazine articles, also pointed to this previously untapped resource of women's migratory agricultural labour. Yet this insight did not solely celebrate women's agricultural work; it also opened the rice paddies to intervention from the regime. The state's call for increased domestic production of consumers and consumables alike played out both on and in the female body. But as women's first-hand accounts and work songs demonstrate, Fascism's vision of hyperproductive female bodies collectively working to support autarky disintegrated when women demanded the right to consume a diet that was not only nutritious but also flavourful.

This chapter investigates the history of those women who did not live in the urban milieu and who attended only elementary school or less. What did countrywomen farm and eat during the Fascist period? How did they feel about the demands for increased food production placed on them by the regime? How did their agricultural labour fit in – or not – with the rest of their lives? By examining regime propaganda of rural life in tandem with the work songs and testimonies of female farmworkers, we can understand the degree to which daily life was marked by Fascist aesthetics and appreciate the full spectrum of opposition that women employed to resist the regime's ruralization policies in daily life.

As James Scott has observed, open revolt is a luxury for subordinate classes. For agricultural workers, "political activity was risky at best, reckless at worst." By contrast, ambiguous actions like "foot dragging, dissimulation, desertion, false compliance, pilfering, feigned ignorance, slander, arson, [and] sabotage" did not carry the risks of outright collective defiance.[2] Scott notes that these actions share certain features: they "require little or no coordination or planning; they make use of implicit understandings and informal networks; they often represent a form of individual self-help; they typically avoid any direct, symbolic confrontation with authority."[3] These low-profile resistance techniques provided ordinary weapons to relatively powerless groups. This investigation draws on Scott's characterization of everyday forms of peasant resistance, here namely food theft and illegal foraging, as "weapons of the weak." As this chapter will highlight, rural women's resistance took many forms in the face of insidious propaganda and massive attempts by the state to control their work, food, and bodies.

Speed and Productivity in Rural Propaganda

With the regime having identified the countryside as the solution to the nation's financial and demographic problems, cultivation speed rose as a primary social goal on the Fascist horizon. By accelerating natural cycles through the application of new scientific methods and rationalist work methods, wheat fields and their female threshers would provide the nation with more food and more people. To showcase this particular group, the regime deployed a cyclical form of propaganda specifically geared to disseminate imagery of rural life: the country almanac.

Country almanacs had been part of rural Italian culture since the seventeenth century, when they were often read aloud to groups of farmers. Almanacs typically advised rural, working-class men in farmwork and animal care through a calendar that emphasized monthly work cycles and the Catholic feast days. The 1903 and 1918 editions of Bemporad's *Almanacco Italiano* are representative examples. Ads for this and other almanacs could also be found in periodicals aimed at male workers, such as *Le Industrie dei Cereali*. By the late 1800s, farmers had their choice of publications, including *Almanacco Agricolo*, *Amico Contadino*, *Annuario Agricolo*, *Campagnolo Agricolo*, and *Coltivatore*. In the early twentieth century, famous titles such as *Il Barbanera di Foligno* and *Lo Schieson Trevisan*, or the more religiously oriented *Frate Indovino*, spread into private households as literacy rose. Come the 1930s, publishing companies Domus, Bemporad, and Marzocco began to produce almanacs aimed at women instead of men, with a new focus on articles espousing home economics, calendars that blended Fascist and Catholic holidays, and photocollages celebrating agricultural contributions to the regime, as suggested by the paragraph below, which opened Domus's popular almanac of 1938. These new additions replaced the agricultural tips, weather patterns, and horoscopes of yore. Specifically, festival dates often combined Christian holidays with newly created Fascist celebrations. In *Almanacco della donna italiana 1936*, the catalogue included Epiphany, the Assumption, and All Saints' Day alongside the Anniversary of the March on Rome, the Anniversary of the Foundation of Fascism, and the Anniversary of the Declaration of War. In this way, the regime took a pre-existing form of popular culture and reconfigured it to serve as a particularly intrusive form of propaganda: They used old seasonal farming calendars to inscribe new Fascist events, holidays, so-called traditions, and activities into women's lives.

The Fascist state seized on almanacs' long-standing associations. Almanacs are, by definition, tied to the rhythmic cycles and punctuating events of one specific year. Their presentist focus made them ideal bridges between domestic politics and the domestic sphere. For improving agriculture, instructing in religion, and addressing semi-literate audiences, almanacs were well suited for reconfiguration. In contrast to the housekeeping manuals, which families purchased once, almanacs required cyclical acquisitions. They are ephemeral documents, used intensely for one year only. So while annual purchases would eventually equate to or surpass the cost of a housekeeping manual, almanac readers would never have to spend a significant lump sum. Almanacs also provided an ideal, pre-existing vehicle for the state-sponsored promotion of rural speed.

The introduction to Domus's almanac *Libro di Casa 1938* places woman at the kitchen window looking outwards. And what does she see, from this "tiny opening on the immense life of the new Italy"? To judge from the propagandistic bent of the book, the view is decidedly Fascist.

> L'Almanacco è un libro-di-figure-per-i-grandi. E' indispensabile come un lunario ma non pretende di essere meraviglioso come un libro di strenna di mezzo secolo fa. E' utile, rassenerante, augurale. E' una finestra ancora aperta sull'annata appena chiusa: spiraglio minimo sulla vita immensa della nuova Italia.

> The Almanac is a picture book for adults. It is indispensable like traditional almanacs but doesn't pretend to be marvellous like the Christmas publications of half a century ago. It's useful, calming, auspicious. It's an open window on the barely closed year: a tiny opening on the immense life of the new Italy.

Almanac writers managed Fascist politics at two key stages: first at the level of the publishing company through financial management, and then at the level of the text through almanac content. In terms of the first issue, Bemporad's dealings with the Fascist Party provide a useful case study. Bemporad, a Florence-based publishing company, in connection with *La Donna*, a Rome-based women's magazine, released a total of twenty-four almanacs from 1920 to 1944. Silvia Bemporad, wife of founding publisher Enrico Bemporad, served as the editor from 1920 to 1936. During this time, her husband regularly sent sample books to the regime, including Italian almanacs.[4] He also sought commercial relations with the Fascist government: in a 13 January 1932 letter, Bemporad offers to supply textbooks to elementary schools in the colonies. Three years hence, Enrico sought protection from the regime as well. A 9 April 1935 State Publishing Institute (Istituto Poligrafo dello Stato) memo from the Undersecretariat of the Press (Sottosegretariato Stampa) to Mussolini summarizes his letter, noting that Bemporad's partners (*soci*) "lo hanno cacciato dall'Azienda" (chased him out of the business) and that he "invoca un posto di lavoro nel suo campo d'azione dove possa ancora rendersi utile" (requests a work position in his field where he might still make himself useful). These behind-the-scenes mechanizations suggest Enrico Bemporad's growing dependence on state intervention regarding commercial concerns.

Almanac content reflects publishers' increasing reliance on the Fascist Party for financial assistance. Cultural contributions from female writers and artists abound during the 1920s editions, while the almanacs take a decidedly more political and socially conservative turn in the mid-1930s, especially with the arrival of a new director, Gabriella Aruch Scaravaglio, who made many changes to almanac content and graphics. Elisa Turrini credits Scaravaglio with "fascistizzando" (Fascistizing) the almanac from 1936 to 1938.[5] A third editor, Margherita Cattaneo, served from 1939 to 1943, during which time Bemporad's extreme financial difficulties led the group to sell the almanac production to rival publishing house Marzocco. These personnel changes, business moves, and government communications evoke the complex blend of personal and political interests inherent to the domestic publishing business. This is not to say that the Fascist government is directly responsible for co-opting almanacs so that working-class women would support autarkic policies. Rather, it reflects a more general social phenomenon: domestic literature fused the public and private sphere through women's food work.

Interactions at the level of the firm and the government, such as that between more stridently Fascist Bemporad editors like Scaravaglio and Cattaneo, ought to be viewed within the larger framework of how individual writers managed the modern period's politicization of the kitchen, previously characterized as timeless space. Whereas *Domus* featured ideal kitchens requiring an architect for construction and housekeeping manuals offered a mix of ideal kitchens and practical tips, almanacs focused on kitchen solutions with an economic bent. These documents also offer a particularly rich picture of how major companies, which often advertised in their pages or even served as financial backers, seized upon the national importance of autarkic kitchen practices and patriotic rhetoric in order to promote their own products. Consider Bemporad's *Almanacco della Donna Italiana 1936*. From the cover design, featuring disembodied female hands with a wedding ring and thimble darning a girl's baby bonnet, one might expect an interior filled with household tips for cooking, sewing, cleaning, and child-rearing. Instead, we see explicitly political tracts.

Almanacs were meant to provide a sort of propagandistic rural news summary for urban audiences. Illustrated articles predominated: titles including "L'Italia cambia viso: Effetti delle sanzioni" (Italy changes its face: Effects of the sanctions), "Massaie rurali" (Rural housewives), and "La donna e le sanzioni" (Woman and the sanctions) cast the political machinations leading to the sanctions in hyperbolic terms to trivialize world events. For example, in "L'Italia cambia viso," the Geneva Convention's protocols are described as "sciocca, sciocca e superba, com'è tutta intera la Società delle Nazioni" (silly, silly and arrogant, as is the League of Nations as a whole).[6] Simple, descriptive language glossed the Fascist territorial seizure of Ethiopia. This approach had the potential to spark the reader's emotional arousal and participation in sanctions resistance while obfuscating the role of Italian imperial aggression as the sanctions' cause. Although the tone and vocabulary of the texts appear more accessible than those found in newspapers, common content (international and domestic politics) and format (articles, political cartoons) united the two. In turn, that political content was meant to motivate women to follow the autarkic cooking preparations contained in these prescriptive guides. Across Domus, Bemporad, and Marzocco almanacs, food preparation in the kitchen became a political act demonstrating either patriotism or selfishness. And that patriotism or selfishness was directly determined by the cook's degree of dedication to autarkic cooking.

But almanac writers also seemed to have realized that Fascism alone might not convince women to support the autarkic cause: for this reason, they couched autarky as helpful to Italy and Italians, citing its utility to Italian industry, to Italian workers, to workers from specific towns such as the farmers of Monte S. Guiliano e Castellammare near Trapani (*Almanacco della donna italiana 1936*), and even, in the mid-1940s, to the Italian resistance of Nazi occupation (*Almanacco della donna italiana 1943*).

Almanac authors like Ada Felici Ottaviani, Nina Milla, and Guidalestro consistently connected imperialism with daily frugality, the sanctions with careful shopping, and Ethiopia with Italy.[7] Here we see how international policy abroad affects domestic kitchens: seizing the lands and crops of Italian East Africa resulted in economic sanctions, which led the Italian government to institute similar policies of labour optimization and conservation of goods at home with autarkic practices. Ottaviani points to the Battle for Grain and electrification of the Italian countryside as projects worthy of the reader's support. Collapsing distinctions between national industry and the individual countrywoman's industriousness under the common heading of "nostra vita materiale" (our material life), Guidalestro advocates the twinned functions of autarky and rationalism to conserve and optimize effort and goods. Put another way, one might say that these authors domesticize the sanctions, rendering the significance of international events as on the scale of everyday life.

Recipes and household management tips present the Fascist constraints on rural life as a political rainy day: unpleasant in the short term, but necessary and natural. By separating the cause of the sanctions (imperial invasion) from their unpleasant effects on daily life (less meat, dairy, sugar, and coffee), almanac articles minimized the importance of bare cupboards, turning politically driven food scarcity into just another problem for women to solve. The natural cycle of the almanacs was in some ways a means to impose a veneer of normalcy on an atypical period, famously referred to as "tempi eccezionali" (exceptional times) in Amalia Moretti Foggia's cookbook of the same name. Lack of wheat is framed as normal and inevitable, akin to other common annoyances like moulding grout or painful teething.

Neutralization of the negative daily effects of Fascism on women's lives appears in the *Almanacco*'s article "La Donna e le sanzioni." Here, author Nina Milla takes up the question of assigning specific actions in the home to address the sanctions. Making an explicit connection between avoiding spending that would benefit the "paesi sanzionisti" (the sanctioning countries) and not wasting national products, she argues that one can still prepare family meals in new and tasty ways through small savings, such as using a bit less electric light and gas, or simple substitutions like planting potatoes, beans, tomatoes, and onions in place of Dutch tulips. Similarly, almanac recipes exulted cheap meats such as poultry, rabbit, and fish. Working-class women could raise these animals at home, unlike pork and beef.

In "La Donna e le sanzioni," Milla uses economy to mean the rational spending of goods through use. This goal emerges in terms that suggest an implicit trade-off, wherein increased ingenuity on the part of the homemaker must compensate for decreased availability of material goods.

> Instaurare il regno della più rigida e illuminata economia: studiare tutti i mezzi, tutti gli accorgimenti, perchè nulla si disperda, in casa e soprattutto in cucina: perchè tutto sia utilizzato e sfruttato al massimo: perchè ogni spesa sia ridotta, ogni consumo diminuito.

> Install a reign of the most rigid and enlightened economy: study all the means, all the tricks, so that nothing is wasted, in the home and above all in the kitchen: so that everything is used and exploited to the maximum: so that every expense is reduced, every consumption diminished.[8]

In defining rationalism as "uno sfruttamento sempre maggiore delle materie prime" (an ever-increasing utilization of primary materials) and then arguing for its wide adoption by housewives, Milla's article raises questions of countrywomen's agency in the deployment of almanac prescriptions for the home. Because Milla opens this argument with the inclusive *noi* form, this regime could refer to every homemaker in

2.1. Almanac cartoon, republished by Bemporad in *Almanacco della donna italiana 1936*, originally published in the Florentine newspaper *Il Brivido*, 20 by 15 centimetres, p. 97. (Wolfsoniana Collection, Genoa, Italy)

the country or just to the reader of this specific manual. Similar articles generally address readers as agents capable of making choices about kitchen practices who should adopt autarkic and rational practices for patriotism and personal benefits.[9]

Accompanying illustrations conflated food with politics, with visual puns underscoring the material effects of trade disputes. An almanac cartoon contextualizing these recipes with the sanctions, "Pol...litica estera" (foreign politics) (Fig. 2.1), turns on the common sound of *pol-*, using this as a homonym syllable to connect poultry to politics. This promotion accounts for the cartoon's chortling bovine: autarkic cooking saves her from imminent slaughter. Moreover, this image would have suggested all the milk and cheese to be gained from eating less beef: Italians could have their own Laughing Cow, a reference to La Vache qui Rit, a spreadable, single-serve Comté. This French cheese dominated Italian grocery shelves during the 1920s, even as Galbani and other domestic concerns were attempting to gain a foothold in the European market. But with the onset of the sanctions, Galbani's Bel Paese, an individually wrapped Alpine style cheese much like La Vache qui Rit, surged in popularity. Moving from milk to meat, we return to the cartoon. Anxious roosters consult panicked pigeons as to the culinary politics produced by the sanctions: "La nostra posizione è un po' ingratella!" "Io mi sento già sullo … spiedo della guerra!" ("Our position is a bit racked!" "I already feel as though I am on the skewer of war!") Here, both *ingratella* and *spiedo* refer to kitchen tools: metal grills and roasting spits. Their conversation continues in text below the image: "Che ne dici della situazione?" "Uhm! … La pentola bolle!" ("What do you think of the situation?" "Hmm! The pot is boiling!") A second culinary pun obliquely links the national and the domestic here, tying the problem of economic sanctions to the solution of a dietary shift away from beef and towards poultry. As the political realm heats up metaphorically, so do the hearth fires.

Rationalist kitchen practices promised to increase not only working-class women's productivity but also their reproductivity. In "Massaie Rurali," an article in *Almanacco della Donna Italiana 1936*, Ada Felici Ottaviani argues that countrywomen ought to standardize food preparation in rural kitchens "con metodi igienici e moderni e evitando loro fatiche esagerate che invecchiano precocemente e danneggiano il fisico e la maternità" (with hygienic and modern methods and avoiding their excessive efforts which age [them] prematurely and damage the body and maternity). She states that her article's goal is to "rivelare l'importanza politica e sociale di questa sezione rurale femminile del Partito Nazionale Fascista" (reveal the political and social importance of this rural female section of the Fascist Party). At once seeking to further elevate the reader's perception of the role of the *massaia* (housewife or countrywoman) in public affairs and also evoking their perceived immateriality to the political realm, Ottaviani concludes, "Anche le donne della campagna partecip[ano] ai grandi destini dell'Italia nostra" ("even country women participate in the grand destiny of our Italy"). Yet rural poverty and illiteracy likely precluded many, if not most, peasant women from reading Ottaviani's herald and from realizing the grand Fascist vision for rural women's productivity.

A photocollage (Fig. 2.2) suggests that fusing modernity with tradition could promote blooming, booming growth: flower-filled windows brush against modern train stations, a baby's smiling face sits beside an oversize *fascio*. Traditional figures and symbols, such as children, nuns, and shafts of wheat, take on modern meanings in the political context of Fascism's Battle for Grain and the construction of new maternity centres, clinics, and nurseries. Over successive pages of similar photocollages, modernity overwhelms tradition: images of Futurist post offices and train stations as well as streamlined ocean-liners and airplanes predominate.

Strong visuals make the message impossible to ignore: almanacs spanned home and home front, linking household management to national preparedness for war. In figure 2.3, we see Mussolini threshing grain, jubilant Italian soldiers of the African colonies, and everywhere massive, cheering crowds, pictured from above, from planes aloft with Futurist speed (Fig. 2.3). It suggests the permeability of kitchens to the political rallies congregating just outside the window. These images and others like it

2.2. Almanac inside cover photocollage, published by Bemporad in *Almanacco della donna italiana 1936*, 20 by 15 centimetres. (Wolfsoniana Collection, Genoa, Italy)

2.3. Almanac photocollage, published by Bemporad in *Almanacco della donna italiana 1936*, 20 by 15 centimetres, pp. 5–6. (Wolfsoniana Collection, Genoa, Italy)

in Domus's *Libro di Casa 1938* craft evocative dystopian scenes. Overall, the effect is one of dizzying multiplication: technology promises to speed both territorial invasion and terrestrial productivity. Planes zoom across the page; tractors till beneath the bombardiers. No distinction is made between urban and rural contexts: each piece supports the overall vision of machine-driven hyperproductivity and the masses of willing soldiers ready to advance the Fascist cause. Within the context of the country almanac, such support means adopting the cooking and farming methods suggested in the book's articles and recipes.

Increasingly, the photocollages in women's culinary and agricultural publications, including home economics guides and magazines like *La Cucina Italiana*, portrayed military men in motion.[10] En masse, they charged through fields of all sorts, fields of battle and fields of wheat. Here, the photocollage provides patriotic context for engaging in the autarkic cooking prescribed in the opposite pages, proclaiming, "Noi tireremo diritto ... l'Italia farà da sé" (We'll push ahead ... Italy will do for itself). The phrase came from a popular martial tune composed by E.A. Mario in 1935 and quickly became a rallying cry for culinary defiance of the sanctions.

"Noi tireremo diritto," E.A. Mario (1935)

Noi tireremo diritto,	We'll push ahead,
faremo quel che il Duce ha detto e scritto:	we'll do what the Leader has said and written:
serenamente rimarremo paria,	serenely we will remain the same
figli di questa Italia proletaria,	sons of this proletarian Italy,
serena e forte contro tutte le viltà!	serene and strong against all cowardice!
Giacché la Lega delle Nazioni	Even though the League of Nations
vuol regalarci	wants to gift us
le sanzioni,	the sanctions,
giacché la Lega contro noi s'ostina,	even though the League is obstinate against us,
sopporteremo	we will manage
con disciplina,	with discipline,
cantando allegramente una canzon:	happily singing a song:
Noi tireremo diritto;	We'll push ahead;
l'amor di Patria non fu mai delitto ...	love of the Fatherland was never a crime ...
Se il fante in guerra va senza paura,	If the child goes to war without fear,
chi resta a casa stringa la cintura:	who stays at home tightens the belt:
anche il digiuno, in questo caso, è salutar!	even fasting, in this case, is healthy!
Durissima vigilia pei ghiottoni	Very difficult eve for gluttons
saranno certo	the sanctions

le sanzioni:
le pance tonde più non le vedremo,
ma noi, frugali,
non moriremo
per questa dieta di frugalità…

will certainly be:
round stomachs we will no longer see,
but we, frugal ones,
we won't die
of this diet of frugality …

Noi tireremo diritto,
né mai ci mostrerem col viso afflitto.
La carne manca? Poco ci rincresce!
Abbiam tre mari, abbiamo tanto pesce
che, a chi lo vuole, lo possiamo regalar!

We will push ahead,
we'll never show a troubled face.
There's no meat? We've no regrets!
We have three seas, we have so much fish
that, to whomever wants it, we can give it
    away!

Sono applicate ormai le sanzioni:
stoffe e belletti
non più a vagoni:
ci mostreremo in tutto nazionali,
saremo in tutto
più naturali,
ci mostreremo insomma quel che siam!

By now the sanctions have been applied:
fabric and rouge
no longer fatsos:
we will show all the nations,
we are overall
more natural,
we will, in sum, show them who we are!

Noi tireremo diritto,
faremo quel che il Duce ha detto e scritto:
serenamente rimarremo paria,
figli di questa Italia proletaria,
serena e forte contro tutte le viltà!

We'll push ahead,
we'll do what the Leader has said and written:
serenely we will remain the same,
sons of this proletarian Italy,
serene and strong against all cowardice!

Noi tireremo diritto,
se pur la Lega ci taglieggia il vitto …
Questa è l'Italia: un popolo poeta:
crede e combatte, fisso alla sua meta,
ed obbedisce, se obbedir non è viltà.

We'll push ahead,
even if the League has cut our food …
This is Italy: a poetic people;
believe and fight, fixed on their goal,
and obey, if obeying isn't cowardice.

It was not the only popular song to do so. Although less culinary, the 1934 song "Sanzionami questo" (Sanction Me This) was composed by Rodolfo DeAngelis, a Neapolitan Futurist, and sung to his "former girlfriend," understood here as the League of Nations. The chorus goes, "Sanzionami questo / O amica rapace: / lo so che ti piace / ma non te ne do" (Sanction me this / O rapacious friend: / I know that you like it / but I won't give any of it to you).[11]

Propaganda spoke through sensory language: songs like "Noi tireremo diritto" travelled acoustically through radio waves and visually through almanacs, whose messaging hummed the same tune. Popular music and art both targeted country-women's cooking in hopes of shifting diets. This song obscures the Fascist regime's invasion of East Africa by focusing solely on the League of Nations sanctions, with particular attention to how those who stay at home should show a brave face, tightening their belts as round bellies disappeared. In so doing, they appealed to women by casting them as the heroines of a new machine age of speed and multiplication. Inverting the typical association of countrywomen and historical past played on women's sense of value: praising someone's valour makes them want to take further actions to live up to the compliment. Patriotism took a culinary form in avoiding pork or beef and instead eating fish or chicken and wild game, as the almanac advocates. Lyrics suggested that, despite the moaning of gastronomes, frugal citizens would be just fine. Countrywomen, though often unnamed, stood at the centre of the regime's propagandistic efforts to shift the Italian diet. Photo-collages and songs worked in tandem, targeting semi-literate rural women through images and music with the ultimate goal of convincing them to "tirare diritto." Because, of course, Italy could not "push ahead" without rural women.

Rural women, as a group, possessed the specific skill sets necessary to fix the sanction-based problems caused by the regime's decision to invade Ethiopia. The regime desperately needed countrywomen to support the anti-sanctions narrative in particular and the project of alimentary autarky in general because their low wages provided the most economical way for the regime to produce rice and wheat, the two most important grains in Italy. Not only did they control what their families ate, but they also controlled how much food was available to the nation at large. This section has shown how the regime addressed these women through almanacs, but how did it deal with them directly? When photocollages depicted rural women, what did they show, what did they hide, and why? And second, how did rural women feel about their representations by the regime and about Fascism's alimentary policies at large?

Constructing Consent: From *Ricettari* to Photocollages

Recipes blended public politics and private practices into a heady cocktail, one that worked to cast autarkic cooking as women's personal war front. In culinary propaganda, the regime celebrated countrywomen, and the *mondine* in particular, as an emblem of ideal Italian femininity: robust, florid, rustic, maternal, and working class. Engaged in the twin occupations of producing autarkic staple foods and Italian bodies, the *mondine* constituted a symbol of gendered hyperproductivity based on and in the female body.

Recall Gino Boccasile's recipe pamphlet cover, with its robust blond baby. In the background, *mondine* labour in the fields behind the baby to produce his bowl of

rice, providing a living backdrop. Black-and-white photographs of *mondine* lever-
age a greyscale realism that places these images within the context of newspapers,
newsreels, and documentary photography. Although these media forms suggest
ideological neutrality and the pursuit of truth, their content typically parroted the
party line. Their persistent presence in Ente Nazionale Risi propaganda stems partially from their physicality: the regime connected bounteous hips and reddened
cheeks with fertility, tradition, and social conservatism. They appeared to epitomize
Fascist womanhood.

In reality, most of the *mondine* considered themselves to be Socialist or Communist, and, as evidenced by their persistent strikes, many were overtly hostile to the
Fascist regime's economic policies.[12] The *mondine* memorialized these strikes through
their work songs, including the famous "Se otto ore vi sembran poche" (If Eight
Hours Seem Too Few).[13] Showing the *mondine* on Boccasile's cover suggests their
consent to Fascist policy and links the women's production of rice to the baby's consumption thereof. Because the *ricettari* draw attention to the importance of nourishing weak bodies, in particular those of young Italians, they also point to importance
of the *massaie*, not only in production of food but also in the reproduction of children
for the nation.

This is the point of the *mondine*'s presence: to birth the baby in the foreground
and to grow the rice it eats. Health frames the project and serves as the implicit goal
in promoting autarkic foodstuffs. This *ricettario* was one of many. Like the almanacs, this was a regionally specific form of propaganda but with a distinct purpose.
International commercial groups began to print and circulate colour lithograph recipe pamphlets for food products as early as the 1850s. Along with this early form
of advertising, food companies began to develop distinctive brands and packaging
during the mid- to late-1800s. Political *ricettari* of the Fascist period built on these
earlier commercial models. Illustrating the emergence of branding with a peek into
a bourgeois family's kitchen cupboard, Emanuela Scarpellini lists the major companies of the period as including pasta from Buitoni, Barilla, and De Cecco, biscuits
from Lazzaroni, chocolates from Venchi and Caffarel, preserved fruits and vegetables from Cirio, cheese from Galbani and Soresinesi, and olive oil from Bertolli, as
well as new food products, like meat extract, broth concentrate, and dried milk from
Liebig, Knorr, and Nestlé.[14] Few extant studies analyse *ricettari*, perhaps because they
were the opposite of an heirloom. Flimsy and mass-produced, their physical qualities
begged the trash bin. Because the regime had little funding for public education
efforts, *ricettari* were produced on cheap paper measuring roughly fifteen by ten centimetres and bound with staples. Whereas a cookbook could withstand years of use,
stains and splatters from just a few recipe preparations would destroy the *ricettari*.
Inside, these hybrid documents combined cookbooks, food advertisements, and medical manuals. Neon graphics and watercolour images enlivened scientific graphs and
expert testimony.

Because of their apparent similarity to cookbooks, *ricettari* could advance totalitarian goals that could not be achieved through more traditional forms of propaganda. Most rural working-class Italian women would have had extensive exposure to state propaganda through political posters pasted on city walls. On movie screens, they would have seen newsreels and feature films produced by the Fascist Party's cinema arm, the Istituto Nazionale Luce (L'unione Cinematografica Educativa, or LUCE).[15] But unlike posters, films, and newsreels, *ricettari* were physically small, used in private, and highly interactive. Cooking, the professed subject of *ricettari*, conveyed political neutrality – it falsely marked the documents as feminine and innocuous. So too did design: small and light, these stapled leaflets could be easily rolled up and stuck in an apron pocket. Portability thus insured that these documents could cross the threshold from the public rally to the private kitchen. They could enter private homes to directly address women, and once there, they could modify behaviour in ways that would change the body from the inside out. Each *ricettario* hawked a single, autarkic grain product, typically rice, oatmeal, or cornmeal. These documents exemplify Carol Helstosky's concept of "the cooking of consent," the widespread promotion of food policies favourable to the regime.[16] As such, *ricettari* might be characterized as a closer relative to the original, medical conception of recipes than the modern, primarily culinary variants. Through what Jack Goody called "prescribed actions," recipes attempted to create physical and mental change.[17] This medical conception of the recipe helps to account for the obsession with sickness and hygiene running through these documents.

Improving the health and hygiene of the Italian citizenry buttressed the larger Fascist project for demographic growth. The rice *ricettario*, with its flashy cover outside and nutritional charts and recipes inside, is a domesticated version of ONMI's pronatalist propaganda. In many ways, this medicalized concern for nourishing weak bodies through autarky to promote demographic growth might foreshadow what Scarpellini refers to as *la cucina di guerra*, the cooking of extreme privation that would characterize Italy's culinary climate during World War II. This *ricettario* cover placed an infant front and centre, suggesting a potential connection between the apparently disparate government initiatives for autarky and pronatalism. While it would be an overstatement to claim that *ricettari* constitute an explicit government bid for demographic manipulation, these documents do evoke multiple, concurrent projects of the Fascist regime.

The images featured in *ricettari* went beyond directing consumers towards autarkic goods; they were also overtly manipulative in their representation of rural women. Because the *mondine* incarnated the regime's propagandistic push for agricultural autarky and pronatalism, graphic designers had to reconcile the state's reliance on the *mondina* as a symbol of ideal Fascist womanhood with the far more critical opinion that the *mondine* had of the regime. Figures 2.4–2.7 speak to the successive stages involved in creating a propagandistic photocollage and demonstrate how the regime relied on the artistic process to construct false images of consent. Graphic designers working for

2.4. Photo cutout for propagandistic collages, Crescentino, Italy, 1932, in folder *Milano: Ente Nationale del Riso, Contributi del Duce per l'assistenza alle Mondariso.* (ACS, PCM, 1934–6, b. 509.488, f. 2)

2.5. "A me il riso piace moltissimo" – Il Duce ai risicoltori di Crescentino 25 ott. 1932 ("I really like rice" – the Leader to the Rice Growers of Crescentino Oct. 25, 1932), photocollage piece, in folder *Milano: Ente Nationale del Riso, Contributi del Duce per l'assistenza alle Mondariso.* (ACS, PCM, 1934–6, b. 509.488, f. 2)

the regime used photography to evoke veracity. But they also heavily mediated these images by discarding those parts that did not support their message and by combining images taken in different times and places. In figure 2.5 and figure 2.7, the contrastive scale of the two photographs used for the foreground and background highlights the extensive editing involved in the construction of photocollages (Figs. 2.5, 2.7). This juxtaposition miniaturizes the agricultural workers even as it aggrandizes the shafts of wheat, suggesting that the two are bound together in a relationship of patriotic production to support the regime's goal of autarky. Rather than hiding the cut-and-paste approach, this form of propaganda highlights the extensive editing involved in its construction, casting revision as an artistic move rather than a political one.

This series of images reveals the artistic techniques used by the regime to obscure the *mondine*'s general distaste for the Fascist regime in general, and Il Duce in particular. Figures 2.5–2.7 show a spectrum of obeisance in their finished or near-finished collages. Side profiles and turned heads all served to hide the *mondine*'s

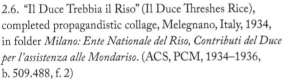

2.6. "Il Duce Trebbia il Riso" (Il Duce Threshes Rice), completed propagandistic collage, Melegnano, Italy, 1934, in folder *Milano: Ente Nazionale del Riso, Contributi del Duce per l'assistenza alle Mondariso*. (ACS, PCM, 1934–1936, b. 509.488, f. 2)

2.7. "Il Duce Trebbia il Riso" (Il Duce Threshes Rice), completed propagandistic collage, Melegnano, Italy, 1937. (Author's photo of completed postcard.)

facial expressions, which often evoked unacceptable emotions ranging from neutrality to incredulity to distaste.[18] By contrast, a single piece destined for a larger collage reveals an almost comical level of contrast between Mussolini's enthusiasm and that of the rice weeders present (Fig. 2.4). As Mussolini poses with his hand on his hip in full military regalia, his mouth open in a grin, the *mondina* stares down the audience, poker-faced, as the *mondino* glances at Il Duce and continues to work. The rice worker's facial expression communicates her distaste for the leader of the regime and his transparent bid for positive publicity as a hero of workers. The regime decided to discard this image, electing to use other, more mediated images for propagandistic purposes instead. Successful photocollages were eventually published in Ente Nazionale Risi propaganda, like the postcard made from the photograph of the rice weeder and Mussolini (Fig. 2.7). Note that the same woman, wearing the same patterned skirt and head-kerchief, appears in three of these pictures (Figs. 2.5, 2.6, 2.7). In a telling move, the regime chose to widely publish the image with her head turned away from the camera, rather than the image that reveals her profile.

Suffice to say, despite the regime's enthusiasm for the *mondine* as emblems of a socially conservative national past projected onto a hyperproductive future, the *mondine* rarely reflected a similar admiration for the regime. They did not see Fascism as responsive to their interests, and indeed, letters and memos between town-level representatives of the Ente Nazionale Risi and the regime reveal a near-constant state of protests catalysed by socio-economic concerns.[19] Investigating this history means reading these almanacs and photocollages against their prescribed audience and artistic subjects. Female agricultural workers were very well informed as to the regime's alimentary policies, and they largely dissented from these protocols. As the next section will show, female agricultural workers viewed the politicized economic context surrounding their fieldwork in class-based terms that they translated into culinary forms of dissent.

Who Were the *Mondine*?

The *mondine*'s physically taxing rice-weeding work, and their affinity for strikes and Socialism, predated Mussolini by nearly fifty years. As Augusta Molinari has observed, the *mondine* had already organized themselves into leftist unions and participated in rural workers' struggles by the late 1800s.[20] Most famously, the *mondine* strike of 1909 gained the eight-hour workday for all Italians. In this historic protest, the *mondine* laid across the railroad tracks, shutting down the Northern Italian railway system from Vercellese to Molinella. The protest was memorably captured by illustrator Achille Beltrame for the cover of the popular newspaper *Domenica del Corriere* (Fig. 2.8). Recurrent references to this early strike in songs and testimonials point to the enduring significance of this protest for the *mondine*.

By the time the blackshirts marched on Rome, 80 to 95 per cent of all weeders were women.[21] As noted by Perry Willson, rice growing was seasonally very labour intensive, employing roughly 160,000 to 170,000 hired hands.[22] Those enrolled with the Confederazione Fascista Lavoratori Agricola composed a mere sliver of this larger workforce: in 1938, the Confederazione counted 62,500 weeders, just 2.64 per cent of all rice weeders.[23] As this chapter will show, the *mondine*'s connections with the political traditions and organizational structures of liberal politics remained strong during the Fascist period. Yet the *mondine* were omnipresent in regime propaganda.

The disproportionally high representation of rice weeders in magazines and newsreels bespeaks the critical economic and symbolic roles that the *mondine* held for the Fascist regime. By 1935, their labour produced 700 million kilograms of rice annually,

2.8. Newspaper illustration of the Rice Weeders' 26 May 1909 protest, drawn by Achille Beltrame. The caption reads, "Dal Vercellese a Molinella" (From Vercellese to Molinella), a reference to the train line running through the heart of Italy's rice belt, successfully blocked by the *mondine* protesting for the eight-hour workday. (*Domenica del Corriere*, 6 June 1909)

the most in Europe.[24] At a time when the regime struggled to conserve wheat, rice appeared to provide an abundant autarkic alternative for domestic consumption and exportation. Rice weeding allowed the regime to export 250 million kilograms of rice annually, worth over 200 million lire. But despite their role as linchpins in the agricultural economy and their celebration in propaganda, the *mondine* who weeded the paddies were ill-treated by the regime.

Under Il Duce, the *mondine*'s working conditions worsened in two ways: their salaries plunged and their private lives were subject to greater state surveillance. First, regressive policies targeting women's wages, like the notorious Serpieri coefficient, pushed their salaries down by 25 per cent between 1925 and 1933, and they stayed at this low level for the remainder of the *ventennio*.[25] Predominant attitudes towards the low relative value of women meant that employers could pay them half or two-thirds as much as they would pay male labourers (*braccianti*) for the same work. The *braccianti* earned 1,038 lire per year in 1938, at a time when 1 kilogram of rice cost nearly 2 lire.[26] For forty days of work during the weeding season, *mondina* Erminia Confortini recalled being paid 220 lire, plus "a few kilograms" of rice.[27] *Mondina* Ermanna Chiozzi recalled being paid 16 lire per day in 1927.[28] National Rice Board publications offered ad hoc biological arguments for employing women to obscure these economic reasons: they argued that only women had the patience for weeding, that their bodies were lighter and more agile, and their fingers were more delicate and thus less likely to damage the tender plants. Francesco Pezza, the public health officer of Mortara, Lombardy, went so far as to note that women's flexible backbones naturally suited them for this arduous labour.[29] Put more broadly, officials like Pezza drew on gendered stereotypes to naturalize occupational gender segregation. Many women bent these arguments to their own purposes, taking pride in their ability to perform work that men could not endure. And yet these same women also seem to recognize the latent justificatory edge of such statements. As Milena Scalabrini recalled, "Nella risaia erano occupate solo le donne perché più brave, svelte, precise, pazienti nel togliere le erbacce e perché venivano pagate meno degli uomini" (In the rice fields there were only women because [they were] better, faster, precise, patient in pulling the weeds and because they were paid less than men).[30]

In its pursuit of alimentary autarky, the Fascist state issued waves of legislation to tighten state control over the rice paddies and the women who worked there. On 7 August 1936, the regime created the Pro-Assistenza Mondariso program, providing rice-paddy nurseries to aid *mondine* with small children. Daily operations of the nurseries were managed by ONMI, who required a trade.[31] To access such services, women were supposed to renounce their work songs. If a *mondina* sang a Socialist work song, she would be ineligible to place her children in the nurseries. The Fascist regime's propaganda of the *mondine* as happy workers clashed with the reality of their liberal political orientation and the protests that came with it. Many former *mondine* recorded their experiences of agricultural work under Mussolini to attest to this schism.

> Io, Ermanna Chiozzi, ho dipinto sulla bianco tela della mia dote la mia vita di braccianti e mondina. / Le mie vicende sono come quella della nostra gente. / Con i miei colori di vita e d'amore, di sacrificio e di tanto sudore, miseria e sfruttamento, i bei campi dorati e immense risaie fangose e grigie. / Questo per non dimenticare e ricordare alle future generazioni il mondo di una mondina pittrice, ormai scomparso, come quello della civiltà contadina.

> I, Ermanna Chiozzi, painted on the white cloth of my dowry my life as a hired hand and a rice weeder. My life's events are like those of our people. With my colours of life

and love, of sacrifice and much sweat, misery, and exploitation, the beautiful golden fields and the immense rice paddies, muddy and grey. This, so as not to forget, and to remind the future generations [of] a rice-weeder-painter's world, by now gone, like that of country culture.

Ermanna Chiozzi (Fig. 2.9) was born in Copparo, a village in the province of Ferrara, in 1920. Her diary begins at age thirteen, when she, having gone to elementary school but no further, travelled north to weed rice fields in the spring and to thresh wheat fields in the fall. Because of the Italian economic boom in the 1950s and 1960s, many former *mondine* learned to write later in life. As a retiree, Ermanna provided twenty-seven pages of art and testimony to the Archivio Diaristico Nazionale with a specific goal in mind: "To remind the future generations of a rice-weeder-painter's world." This historic quirk – a social-class jump within a single generation – means that we

2.9. Self-portrait of Ermanna Chiozzi. Charcoal on cloth, photographed inset in testimony of Ermanna Chiozzi, "Io ricordo: Ermanna nella storia fra arte e racconti," 1933–46. Transcript of manuscript MP/Adn2 4626, Archivio Diaristico Nazionale, Pieve Santo Stefano, Italy.

have a kaleidoscopic view of early twentieth-century field work, as voiced, and in some cases painted, by the women themselves. With charcoal and paintbrush, Ermanna depicted herself, always in a polka-dotted dress (Fig. 2.10): sending winged love letters writ in flowery language, with ivy symbolizing devotion and sacrifice ("dove m'attacco, muoio" [where I attach, I die]) (Fig. 2.11) to her young husband at the Eastern Front in the 1930s. He died soon after returning, and Ermanna changed her medium, from paper drawings decorating his letters to paintings on the cloth meant for her dowry. Although her mother was at first furious at this artistic rather than practical use of such valuable cloth, having a house filled with Ermanna's art soon won her over. She even gave Ermanna the sheets off her own bed to paint.

Fortunately, this account of a *mondina*'s daily life does not stand alone: Ermanna's testimony is part of a chorus of sensory details found in *mondine* testimonials of agricultural life under Fascism. Another diarist, Antonietta Chierici, recorded her early memories of their rural *bracciante* household in the town of Correggio, in the

2.10. Self-portrait of Ermanna Chiozzi (in polka dots) with fellow *mondine*, "1935: Risaia – Tramonto" (1935: Rice Paddy – Sunset). Charcoal on cloth, photographed inset in testimony of Ermanna Chiozzi, "Io ricordo: Ermanna nella storia fra arte e racconti," 1933–46. Transcript of manuscript MP/Adn2 4626, Archivio Diaristico Nazionale, Pieve Santo Stefano, Italy.

2.11. Self-portrait of Ermanna Chiozzi with ivy, "Dove m'attacco, muoio" (Where I attach, I die). Charcoal on cloth, photographed inset in testimony of Ermanna Chiozzi, "Io ricordo: Ermanna nella storia fra arte e racconti," 1933–46. Transcript of manuscript MP/Adn2 4626, Archivio Diaristico Nazionale, Pieve Santo Stefano, Italy.

inland Emilia region of Emilia-Romagna, North Central Italy. The heart of her story, written in 2006, beats with the sayings, habits, and movements of her mother, who remains paradoxically nameless in Antonietta's writing. Copies of *Grand Hotel* lay hidden under her mother's straw-filled mattress. Photos of Togliatti, Gramsci, and Lenin sat next to images of Jesus, Mary, and Joseph on her parents' dressers. We smell the woodsmoke from the hearth and winter mould in the walls. We hear her father's evident and oft-stated pride in her mother's "corpo da lavoratrice robusto e svelto" (robust and agile worker's body) and in her work as a *mondina*. "Sei il mio uomo di casa" (You're my man of the house), he cooed when she returned from the fields.

In testimonials donated to the Archivio Diaristico Nazionale, former *mondine* provide a range of responses to their politicization writ in the sensory details of everyday life. Like Ermanna Chiozzi, Angela Baldi, Ivana Cipolli, Laura Scalabrini, and Maria Verzani lived in Emilia-Romagna and worked as *mondine* during the Fascist period. Their five testimonies refer to the same arc of time and were recorded between 1960 and 2010.[32] These women share Chiozzi's central positioning of female family members in their narrative construction, as well as their emphasis on the early sensory impressions of everyday life and its lasting effect on the women's conception of themselves as gendered and classed subjects. Selections from Marco Minardi and Franco Castelli's transcribed interviews from 108 *mondine* from across Northern Italy and related ephemera (personal photographs, work contracts, rice tax stamps) further help to contextualize the detailed recollections in these testimonies. These additional testimonies offer alternate catalogues of specifics of the *monda* (forty-day weeding period), along with a broad body of evidence to guard against essentializing the accounts.

The interviews speak to the specialness of these female relationships. Their bonds are noteworthy both for their duration (many women stayed friends into their nineties) and for their warm intensity. Women recalled keeping secrets, making promises, staying loyal to one another. They were proud of having been rice weeders. Secondarily, the former *mondine* all remember the work as very physically taxing and testify to this at length. Third, they often use their songs (sometimes bursting into melody mid-interview) to provide examples of what their lives were like. As a group, the *mondine* are frank and very funny. Listening to them, one does not have the sense that they had anything to prove. They are happy to tell their stories, but they are not desperate for a listener. A chorus of voices resound from the centre of this story: the work songs, diaries, and art created by Northern Italian rice weeders. Ultimately, this leader-ensemble format evokes the range of women's voices, in both their diversity and their harmony.

Although the *mondine* did not write cookbooks, they did record what they cooked and ate, as well as how they felt about their daily diet in relation to Fascist politics. Reading these testimonials in isolation, one might be tempted to frame them within the regime's narrative trope of the rural, socially conservative national past. After all, the women characterize their deep friendships as a direct result of the material conditions of their labour, including the distance from home, the absence of family, and the difficulty of the work. One might be tempted to insert these women into propaganda's picaresque spectacles as the merry labourers, happily going about their work with frequent bursts of song. Indeed, Fascist ideology often involved the creation of an idealized national past, coupled with the related myth that only dictatorship can deliver its rebirth. As applied in the geographic context of the Po valley, this meant that women should embody physical characteristics that historically demarcated female beauty, specifically nineteenth-century ideals of robust fecundity, and they were expected to gestate the future generation of Italians as well.

But this Fascist fairy tale shatters at the first word from the *mondine*. In her testimony, Antonietta Chierici provides a telling account: as a young girl, she was horrified by the physical toll that the rice fields had taken on her mother's body by the end of the *monda*. Seeing her daughter's stricken face, Chierici's mother responded, "Eh si, guarda bene com'è la campagna, non come la leggi sui libri, ma com'è per chi la lavora" (Uh huh, take a good look at the country, not how you read it in books, but how it is for those who work it).[33] This chapter takes Chierici's mother up on her challenge by considering *mondine* testimonials and grounding its analysis of the rice workers' often romanticized songs within the material context of rice-weeding labour. By placing rural Italian women's voices in conversation with the rustic dishes and illustrated almanacs that they used every day, we can understand the degree to which daily life was marked by Fascist aesthetics and appreciate the full spectrum of quotidian opposition that women mobilized to resist the regime's ruralization policies in daily life. More broadly, this story underscores the historiographic importance of considering non-textual source materials and reading government narratives of who ate what and why in the years leading up to World War II.

Moreover, the *mondine* left another body of historical evidence: their work songs.[34] And what can the narrative themes and musical techniques of the *mondine* tell us about female collectivity under Fascism? Choral testimony reveals that physical conditions of labour in the rice fields directly shaped the music that the *mondine* sang through constricted diaphragms, backs bent to plunge hands deep into the bog. Corporeal strain – sore muscles and empty stomachs – catalysed the musical corps. According to their own testimonies, the *mondine* sang to make their labour feel easier and to make the workday pass faster. To weed the rice paddies, women worked in teams of four to twenty. Walking through knee-deep mud, they spent eight hours at a time with their backs bent, picking weeds from among the rice shoots. Hot from the work, damp from the standing water, and blinded by the glare of the sun on the paddies, women managed the physical toll of rice weeding by singing work songs together. In short, they sang to change their own perception of the labour, to alleviate its physical effects with an activity that required light mental concentration and moderate physical participation. Women sang as a direct response to the physical demands of rice weeding. Reciprocally, their songs then influenced their weeding, regulating its speed and intensity.

Although I use the following culinary-themed songs as case studies, these specific songs do not represent the full song corps of the *mondine*. Rather, they provide widely shared sentiments on a very specific topic: what the *mondine* ate and how they felt about it. As women's work songs relate, their dismal diet and dining conditions sparked vivid food fantasies during the forty-day *monda*. The next section uses music to explore the yawning gap between *mondine*'s culinary desires and realities to demonstrate that the right to taste as well as to nutrition emerged as a key point of contention between *mondine* and landowners, a gap that later produced uniquely culinary forms of rebellion.

Culinary Protest Songs

Culinary-themed work songs describe meals through absence as much as presence. In the Emilian song "Alla mattina il latte c'è" (In the Morning There Is Milk), the dietary necessity of milk is there but the palate-enticing sugar for sweetening the beverage is not. Like many Northern Italian agricultural workers, the *mondine* had historically faced culinary privation and acquired foraging knowledge to cope well before the wartime sanctions.[35] Moreover, the *mondine* regularly ate meals cooked with stale ingredients while away from home at the northern weeding sites. Descriptive stanzas list the repetitive meals, largely comprising low-quality carbohydrates.

Monotonous meals and poor-quality ingredients stemmed from the economics of migrant field work: agricultural contracts were arranged by middlemen who profited from constricted food budgets. Daily fare for *mondine* consisted of nothing more than a loaf of bread made from mixed wheat and corn, a dish of rice soup, and a dish of beans with a bit of salt, pepper, and lard. The resulting diet was at once heavy in volume and low in nutrients. Moreover, the ingredients were prepared in haste: a designated cook boiled rice leftovers from previous harvesting seasons on the banks of the rice paddies during the day and in the converted horse and cow stalls that served as dormitories at night. Even rice-paddy cooking conditions appear in work songs: "O cusinéra mèt via la caldera / che dumà de sera / che dumà de sera / O cusinéra mèt via la caldera / che dumà de sera / la minestra la vören pö." (Oh cook put away the boiler / because tomorrow night / because tomorrow night / Oh cook put away the boiler / because tomorrow night / we don't want any more soup.)[36]

Endless rice filled the menu: *minestre* of rice, rice and beans, stale rice-flour bread, and germinated rice, interrupted only by the occasional gluey pasta. In their obsessive repetitions, culinary songs like "Alla mattina il latte c'è" and "Trenta giorni di polenta" (Thirty Days of Polenta) differed from the emotive crescendos and minutely conceived atmospheric details that characterize the majority of music in the *mondine* song corps. Choruses switch from general description of the meals to personal accounts of the effects of such a diet: it beats and wrecks the *mondina*. Lamentations like "com'è lenta" (how slow it is) and "com'è lesta" (how poorly done) blend similar sounds, an acoustic melding that evokes the culinary repetition that "Trenta giorni" decries.

Similarly, triplicate echoes sound within the chorus of "In the Morning There Is Milk," both across the section with the repeated opening of "si diventa" (one becomes) and within each separate phrase, as in "gnec gnec gnec" (beat beat beat). Repeating these words acoustically captures the monotony of the meals, perhaps the most common and intensely felt complaint among the *mondine* regarding their diet. Here, the song recites the meals of one day, with food in the morning, midday, and evening. Others rely on a weekly format, as in the song "Non più riso e fagioli" (No More Rice and Beans), and more still speak to the monthly cycles of meals, as in "Thirty Days of Polenta" and "Or son passati quaranta giorni" (It Has Been Forty Days). Adjectives in "Alla mattina il latte c'è" clip the full word down to a single identifying syllable – "fiac," "strac," and "gnec" – just as the abstemious diet pares down the body's contours.

Alla mattina il latte c'è

Alla mattina il latte c'è
ma senza zucchero, ma senza zucchero
Alla mattina il latte c'è
ma senza zucchero, perchè non c'è
Coro:
A manger poc poc poc
Si diventa fiac fiac fiac
si diventa strac strac strac
si diventa gnec gnec gnec
A mezzogiorno la pasta c'è
ma sembra colla, ma sembra colla
a mezzogiorno la pasta c'è
ma sembra colla da cartolèr
(Coro)
Alla sera il brodo c'è
ma è acqua calda, ma è acqua calda
e alla sera il brodo c'è
ma è acqua calda per lavari i pè
(Coro)
A la matèina da clasiòun

In the Morning There Is Milk

In the morning there is milk
but without sugar, but without sugar
In the morning there is milk
but without sugar, because there is none
Chorus:
Eating little little little
One becomes weak weak weak
One becomes wrecked wrecked wrecked
One becomes beat beat beat
At midday there is pasta
but it seems like paste, but it seems like paste
at midday there is pasta
but it seems like paste to glue
(Chorus)
In the evening there is broth
but it is hot water, but it is hot water
and in the evening there is broth
but it is hot water to wash your feet.
(Chorus)
In the morning at breakfast

acqua fresca e pan tiròun

amor amor amor, e la rosa l'è un bel fior

E da mesdè e da disnêr

is dan dal ris cl'è da mundèr

amor amor amor, al magna i pòver e brisa i signòr.

fresh water and stale bread

love love love, and the rose is a beautiful flower

And from midday to dinner

they give us rice that's to be weeded

love love love, the poor eat it and not the rich.

Trenta giorni di polenta

Trenta giorni di polenta

come l'è lenta

come l'è lenta

Trenta giorni di salame

o che fame

o che fame

in mezzo al mar.

Trenta giorni di minesta

come l'è lesta

come l'è lesta

e via che andùmma a ca.

La brutta vita le brutte notte

ris e pagnòtte mi g'ó mangià

ris e pagnòtte pan de risína

sö Lumelina mi ga ö pö

solo una volta per contentarmi

mi ànno dato fasoi e ris.

Thirty Days of Polenta

Thirty days of polenta

how slow it is

how slow it is

Thirty days of salami

oh what hunger

oh what hunger

in the middle of the sea.

Thirty days of soup

how poorly done

how poorly done

and away we will go home.

The ugly life the ugly nights

rice and bread I am going to eat

rice and bread made from rice flour

I am Lomellina I am going to the Po

only once to make me happy

they gave me beans and rice.

In a conclusion that is as comical as it is heartbreaking, the singers of "Alla mattina il latte c'è" face a bowl of rice so old that it has already germinated. They do not know whether to eat or to weed it. The only fresh "food" consumed is water, which the women contrast against their breakfast of stale bread and their lunches and dinners of germinated rice. In other words, first-hand participation in the Battle for Grain was often a miserable affair. The women weeded rice in knee-deep water all day, hence the reference in "Trenta giorni di polenta" to the *mondine* singing out like wasted sirens from the middle of a land-bound ocean ("in mezzo al mar").[37] They then consumed rice and water for the majority of their meals. Doubled emphasis on water and rice across work and meals beats at the heart of almost every *mondina* song about food, as with "Da ber ci dan dell'acqua": "Da ber ci dan dell'acqua / da mangiar ci dan del ris / se la continua ancora / ci tocca da morir" (To drink they give us water / to eat they give us rice / if that continues further / we are going to die).[38] Through digestion, this diet merged women's bodies with the seasonal rhythms and watery green contents of the paddies themselves.

By contrast, desired foods resided at the front lines of the Battle for Grain: the *mondine* dreamed of wheat-based pastas. Consider the lyrics of "Or son passati quaranta giorni": "Or son passati quaranta giorni / siamo stanche di riso e fagioli / le tagliatelle vogliamo mangiar" (Now forty days have passed / we're tired of rice and beans / tagliatelle we want to eat).[39]

In "No More Rice and Beans," we hear a similar wish for noodles: "Non più riso e fagioli tutta la settimana / al mercole e al giove / pasta napoletana / alla domenica carne / e un bicchier di buon vin / evviva il nostro Duce / che è Benito Mussolin" (No more rice and beans / all week long / on Wednesday and Thursday / pasta napoletana / on Sunday meat / and a glass of good wine / and long live our Duce / who is Benito Mussolini).[40] Here, we see culinary commonalities (the common wish for more pasta and less rice), yet political divergence marks this song. As previously noted, the vast majority of *mondine* aligned with the political Left and disliked Mussolini and the Fascist regime.[41] They grieved their alliance with the landowning classes and their economic exploitation. "No More Rice and Beans" is rare. This song has been found in one tiny township, recalled by one singer, a certain Pina Pedini of Pieve di Cento. Nevertheless, I include it here because it demonstrates the power of culinary propaganda. As Castelli observes of this song, "non si sbaglia a considerarla come strofa propagandistica nel quadro della campagna di cattura del consenso delle masse rurali" (it would not be wrong to consider it a propagandistic verse within the campaign to capture the consent of the rural masses).[42] This is a point especially well taken given that this group stood at the forefront of the Battle for Grain and the rice sector. The effectiveness of this offer of pasta, meat, and wine resides in its awareness of the symbolic value that the *mondine* accorded to food: rice was the fare in soup kitchens and in prisons and a staple of war rations.[43] As a food, it signalled bare nutrition, as well as disdain for the social values of eating, like pleasure and love. Promising tasty foods indicated that the regime cared about the *mondine*. But here a paradox emerges: Mussolini appears to have attained popularity, at least with this small Cento-based township, by making culinary promises that directly contradict the goals of the rice campaign. To get support for the regime, which wanted people to eat less grain and more rice, he has to promise the rice weeders that they can eat more grain and less rice.

In sum, although these songs demonstrate that the *mondine* objected to both the ingredients and the repetition of this diet, it was truly this latter quality, the monotony, that they hated. Whereas the regime attempted to address the *mondine* through cyclical propaganda in almanacs, the *mondine* explicitly rejected weekly repetition of food through their songs. This differentiation comes through most stridently when comparing and contrasting songs based on the foods wished for and the foods eaten. After all, not every song objected to rice: when served polenta and salami for forty days straight, women came to crave the rice and beans ("solo una volta per contentarmi mi ànno dato fasoi e ris"). But rice and beans were broadly rejected, as in the Cremonese refrain of "Or son passati quaranta giorni" ("siamo stanche di riso e fagioli") and the Cento tune, "Non più riso e fagioli." Again, these songs emphasize the distaste for repetition in their very style and structure. By the end, even the listener is sick of rice. Luckily, these songs were not the *mondine*'s only way to resist the fare: the *mondine* began to supplement their menus, and these choices took on political resonances. Ultimately, anti-Fascist beliefs translated into culinary rebellion.

Foraging and Food Theft

Small actions can combine over time and number to massively resist oppressive state structures. For the *mondine*, political revolt began with a bird egg. Purple herons, black-winged stilts, pygmy cormorants, and whiskered terns laid their eggs in the low-lying marshlands from Lombardy to Piedmont – or, as in the famous song "Son la mondina," along the boggy belt that stretched "from Vercellese to Molinella."[44] Nimble hands snatched the eggs from nests, and hungry mouths swallowed their liquid contents. They took frogs and fresh birds' eggs from the rice fields and, less commonly, potatoes from the storerooms. Milena Lavagnini recalled "drinking the eggs fresh in the fields."[45] The *mondine* used food theft as one of Scott's "weapons of the weak" to regularly enact class-based principles of ownership and labour.

Women were slightly more likely to take food from the field than the pantry, a preference based on the dual considerations of proximity and opportunity, as well as their complex concept of ownership. In their testimonials, many former *mondine* suggest that the process of working the land confers ownership of its fruits. This line of reasoning helps to explain why women did not take garden vegetables as often as they did wild-growing foods – they did not personally work in the potato fields or in the pantry. As such, the *mondine* would eagerly share their field-found foods with friends while covering evidence of their activities from the *padrone*. Meanwhile, they were more likely to tattle on their compatriots when kitchen- and storeroom-based foods were stolen. So while potatoes had to be stolen, eggs could simply be drunk. But the larger message remained constant across the majority of *mondine* testimonials: women consistently highlighted the circumstances and rationale behind their first theft of food from landowners, an act that nearly all recalled as being personally and politically significant. Their songs indicate awareness that the regime controlled and regulated the market from the top down. As the lyrics to "La Lega" admonished both landowners and Il Duce, "E voi altri signoroni che ci avete tant'orgoglio, abbassate la superbia e aprite il portafoglio" (And you other big shots who are so proud of us, lower the arrogance and open the wallet).[46]

Fascist policies consistently favoured rural landowners over migrant workers, and the land itself over those who laboured on it. Political and economic motives meshed: the Fascist Party was indebted to the landlords and rich farmers who provided the money and the arms that had cleared their way for victory over left-wing movements in the Italian countryside. As a result of this history, the *mondine* would have felt the heavy hand of the Fascist economy through the regime's suppression of peasant landholding and land use (*usi civici*), as well as through loan-fixing schemes and the higher taxes that they paid proportional to their take-home income. New policies of market standardization and hygiene also favoured large estates over small farms, as only wealthy landowners could afford to meet the new regime policies for spraying, sorting, and packing agricultural goods.

Further, these policies targeted the products themselves on a classed basis: the purchasing power of commodities produced by northern commercial farms and the great southern estates (rice, wheat, tobacco, sugar beets) increased or remained stable during the 1930s thanks to Fascist tariff protection, direct subsidies, organization of markets, and wage cutting. By contrast, the purchasing power of products that provided the livelihood for peasants (vineyard, orchard, and garden crops) enjoyed no such government protections. Their financial value plummeted. The commercial stakes of these food policies were soon evident: Istituto Centrale di Statistica del Regno d'Italia (ISTAT) data shows a major reduction in peasant ownership of small farms and homesteads and a rise in tenant farming. Between 1921 and 1931, the number of operating owners declined by nearly half a million, while the number of cash-tenants rose by nearly 400,000. The *mondine* were not working in a free labour market, and they knew it.

But while they lacked economic buying power, the *mondine* were not without agency. Enduring such a limited diet pushed their limits. One might even say that rice launched the *mondine*'s battle for taste. Colourless, textureless, and above all tasteless, rice provided the *mondine* with the calories required to function but not the flavour required to thrive. Chierici's testimony underscores the message of the *mondine*'s food songs: "Il vitto era sempre e solo riso" (the food was always and only rice).[47] For many women, the monotony of their forty-day diet affected food preferences for years to come. Chierici's mother, for instance, refused to eat rice even into her old age. Scalabrini experienced a similar reaction to her mother's rice dishes after having worked as a *mondina*: "Il riso cotto, anche se fatto con tanto amore sempre riso è, l'aspetto orrendo nel piatto mi sembrava di vedere dei vermi cotti, per quanta fame avessi non riuscivo mangiarli certe volte." (Cooked rice, even if made with love, is still rice, the horrible appearance of the dish seemed to me like cooked worms, as hungry as I was sometimes I couldn't eat it.)[48] This points to a class-based reaction wherein former *mondine* asserted their contested right to variety as well as basic nourishment.

Pushing this line of reasoning further, some *mondine* asserted that they were entitled to sneak the eggs and frogs because they could not afford to pay for them. They note their goodwill towards traditional notions of ownership but also argue for flexibility in the face of economic hardship. They explain that if they could have paid for these foods, they certainly would have. But because they could not, they argue, they should not be faulted for taking them, because every person has the right to enjoy a varied diet. In most accounts, women characterized their actions as "taking" (*prendere*) rather than "stealing" (*rubare*). They characterize the latter action as immoral and something that they themselves would never do. As the relative frequency of taking eggs and frogs versus potatoes suggests, the *mondine* characterized ownership not as a strict dichotomy of "mine" and "his" but as semi-collective, relative, variable, and existing along a spectrum of relative possession punctuated by situational exceptions.

Terminology provides a window into the range of relative fault the *mondine* associated with partaking of various foods. Milena Lavagnini recalled how she "shook with fear" at the thought of being caught "stealing" tomatoes and chicken eggs from the *padrone*'s vegetable garden. Not only did she fear "qualche grosso guaio" (some big trouble) for herself, but she was also greatly concerned by how her actions would reflect on her weeding squad, which was "molto rispettata perché eravamo brave e svelte" (very respected because we were good and quick).[49] Lavagnini's designation of the activity as "stealing" due to its location in the *padrone*'s vegetable garden underscores the idea that many *mondine* defined the morality of food theft as a relative function of location rather than inherent in the action of appropriation itself. Further, her concern for how her actions would reflect on the reputation of her squad, respected for its workswomanship, illuminates the boundaries within which she constructed her definition of an ethical action.

For the *mondine*, identity could be demarcated by degrees of hunger and categories of agricultural work. These two tendencies suggest that they treated social class as a relational system: its composition and qualities shifted in relation to where one stood within it. To wit, they tended to name their social class by their own profession. They did not say, "I am working class." More specifically, they stated, "I am a *mondina*, and I generally have enough to eat." In contrast to middle- and upper-class women who used patriarchal profession or inheritance to understand their own social class, the *mondine* described their standing in terms of subsistence and the forms of labour they engaged in.[50] References to the profession of male spouses are notably absent from women's descriptions.

The *mondine* also typically characterized their standing in terms of whether or not they were hungry and how often. As former *mondina* Laura Scalabrini notes, "Lavorarli faceva svuotare la pancia ma il raccolto non riempiva lo stomaco" (Working [the fields] emptied the belly but the harvest didn't fill the stomach).[51] Maria Verziani similarly recalled, "Lo stipendio che percivamo era poco perciò mi sono messa di buona volontà e nelle ore libere andavo a vendemmiare, a mietere il frumento, a castrare i galletti per arrotondare il bilancio famigliare" (The wages we earned were low [and] that is why in the free hours I voluntarily went to harvest the grapes, to thresh the grain, to castrate the roosters to round out the family budget).[52] Tellingly, Verziani's definition of free time does not indicate leisure but rather suggests an opening to assume supplementary agricultural labour. With regard to work, many noted that although rice weeding paid well, its physical toll meant that women only took on this work when their families began to skip meals.

The *mondine* understood class not only in terms of their own work but also in terms of the way they were treated in comparison to women of other classes. This is illustrated by the character of the trip *mondine* took to reach the fields in weeding season. Starting in early May, the *mondine* travelled to the Vercellese, Novarese, and Lomellina fields composing Italy's rice belt. Some came from nearby, arriving by bike. Others came from up to one hundred miles away. Scalabrini recalled the sensation of vast distance between her hometown in Casteld'Ario in Mantua to Vercellese as feeling "come oggi andare a CUBA" (like going to CUBA would be today).[53]

For many *mondine*, the train station served as a moment of dawning class consciousness. The low social value accorded to their status as migrant agricultural workers was underscored by the fact that they travelled in the *carri bestiame*, train cars meant for animals, to arrive at the fields. The Parmentese *mondine* frequently lodged complaints with the prefecture and police headquarters, asking for "carrozze normali, riservati … Un modo di viaggiare un po' più umano" (normal cars, reserved ones … A more humane mode of travel).[54] These trains would stop "for hours" at each station, to allow for the paying passenger trains to pass. Forced pauses to defer to wealthier travellers suggest the perception that the rice workers' time held relatively lower value. Once the *mondine* arrived at the fields, their dormitories consisted of converted barns and stalls, underscoring their role as the human workhorses in the fields. Despite local cultural divergences, numerous former *mondine* pointed to the space of the train depot and the moment of departure for the rice paddies as an emotionally resonant threshold. Many women recount this event with a great level of sensory detail, recalling the vendors who gathered to sell the *mondine* their characteristic straw hats, used to protect their eyes from the afternoon glare of the sun on water.

Given the little baggage space available to these women, their near-unanimous decision to privilege flavour in their food and beverage choices is significant. They carried sacks and cardboard suitcases filled with salami, cheese, and other preserved foods to add variety to the daily board of "rice rice and more rice" provided by the *padrone* as part of their contract. Chierici recalls that her father slipped a small bottle of Marsala into her mother's bag, saying "una piccola cosa per tenerti su" (a little something to perk you up).[55] As Chierici's father clearly realized, small luxuries raise the human spirit, particularly when under conditions of sensorial privation and physical strain. These carefully selected luxury foods served a powerful psychological purpose for the *mondine* by reaffirming their self-worth under working conditions that cast them as purely physical beings. A bit of salami in a sea of rice not only excited the palate but quietly reminded the *mondina* that she deserved delicious taste as well as basic nourishment.

From Culinary to Political Resistance

The song creation process was communal and social. Consider the text transcribed from an interview with former *mondine*, which appears in choral form.[56]

> J.: Quindi, insegnavate alle giovani …
> B.: Quelle giovani …
> F.: Canzoni sovversive …
> B.: … a cantare. E le insegnavamo …
> J.: Questo in pieno periodo fascista …

> J.: So, you would teach the young …
> B.: Those young ones …
> F.: Subversive songs …
> B.: … to sing. And we would teach them …
> J.: This in the middle of the Fascist period …

Between two and three speakers contribute to each sentence, suggesting not only a deep social ease through fluid turn-taking but also political concord in the characterization of the women's collective history. The women break their turns along clause lines, evoking the ascendant importance of the idea over formal sentence structure. Central themes discussed concern the intersection of youth, politics, and song. Teaching unites the three, as the women note that they used to instruct the younger *mondine* in the history of the working class by teaching them Socialist and Communist songs in the field. In their use of repetition through refrain, the songs provided a sound pedagogic tool to aid in the retention of lyrics and the ideas therein. Intense use of this technique also meant that the new *mondine* could quickly acquire a sense of class-based identity through the collective history that the song corps teaches. In a sense, the songs can best be understood as both a transfer of experience and knowledge to the young and an expedient manner of politically indoctrinating new workers.

As with a new quilt sewn from old cloth, these songs must be understood as a form of culture that consumes (other songs' melodies and lyrics) as it produces ("new" songs), constantly acquiring new meanings with each original configuration and context. Such stitching took place both at the level of song and at the level of each workday's singing. The *capa*, using suggestions from the *squadra*, would knit together the day's songs in the field, selecting the following song in the moment on the basis of artistic and practical needs. She might select the next song because it built on a theme or mood in the previous song or because the team needed to change their weeding pace.[57] The *mondine* sometimes paused in their singing, discussing amongst themselves the best way to continue a song or the day's singing.

Just as the *mondine* fit the music to their work based on practicality, they also assigned musical parts on the basis of ability rather than hierarchies of age or experience. Counterpoint as well as dissonance could be used to build the melodic daisy chain:

> Ad esempio ad una canzonetta quale "Vola colomba vola" poteva far seguito "Montenero" secondo il prinicipio del contrasto, a cui poteva aggiungersi "Cara biondina capricciosa garibaldina" e poi "Crumiri schifosi" seguendo un filo riflessivo, ma anche "La strada di Cento" incatenando le "stellette" dei soldati con "la stella vicino al cuor."

> For example, to a popular song like "Fly Dove Fly" one could have followed with "Black Mountain" according to the principle of contrast, to which one could have added "Dear Capricious Little Garibaldian Blond" and then "Disgusting Scabs" following a reflective thread, but also "The Road of Cento" linking the "little stars" of the soldiers with "the star close to the heart."[58]

The concatenation that Staro describes here points to the idea that no song existed in isolation. Similarly, Castelli diagrams Angiolina Balocco's account of song linking guidelines.[59] This pictorial presentation suggests that concatenation depends largely on lyrical echoing in the opening lines of the songs. In sum, each individual song served as a subsection of one meta-song, communally created over the course of a day's work. The songs were never truly begun or finished; and in fact, competition between different *squadre* resulted in successions of interrupted songs, as many women enjoyed "stealing" (*rubare*) songs from nearby groups, an act that consisted of taking a lyric fragment and using it to begin a new song.[60]

One could seize the spotlight between songs as well: rival groups often took the opportunity provided by a brief silence or conversation to launch into a new song.[61] This tendency highlights the primary purpose of the work songs, which was to alleviate and ameliorate the physical pain and mental boredom that accompanied the repetitive work of rice weeding. These songs are, at their most basic, a vocal extension of manual labour. Not only do cries and yells provide emotional emphasis to the song; they also offer a physical vent for working bodies under duress. Nowhere is this more apparent than "Se otto ore," a song memorializing the 1909 *mondine* rail strike, which gained the eight-hour workday for all Italian workers.

Se otto ore vi sembran poche	**If Eight Hours Seem Too Few**
Se otto ore vi sembran poche	If eight hours seem too few
provate voi a lavorare	try to work them yourselves
e troverete la differenza	and you will discover the difference
di lavorar e di comandar.	between working and commanding.
E noi faremo come la Russia	And we will do like Russia
noi squilleremo il campanel	we will ring the bell
falce e martel	sickle and hammer
e squilleremo il campanello	and we will ring the bell
falce e martello trionferà.	sickle and hammer will triumph.
E noi faremo come la Russia	And we will do like Russia
chi non lavora non mangerà	He who does not work will not eat
e quei vigliacchi di quei signori	and those cowards of those gentlemen
andranno loro a lavorar.	will go to work for themselves.

Women used "Se otto ore" to pass the workday in the fields and to coordinate the pulling of weeds with the rest of their *squadra*. The music emphasizes the regularity of these events in its highly repetitive form, suited to the repeated action of pulling rice weeds. In a musical instance of form following function, women would have marked time in the fields by singing this song about the cycles of rebellion. This move suggests that women also used the temporal content of "Se otto ore" to maintain hope in a more egalitarian future, one in which all classes would work the fields. Such a transition, of course, would not be easy: the inherent irony of the title, that eight hours seem too few, frames this song as one half of the contentious debate between the rice workers and landowners over the length of the workday. By opening with this rebuttal, the song uses the history of failed diplomacy to declare the imminent necessity of resorting to riotous revolution, with its rising flags and clanging bells. In the meantime, passing the workday by singing this song allowed the *mondine* to symbolically link their present condition to the time clock of Russia's revolt.

Historical time governs this song, in that the lyrics reference Russia's revolutionary past as prologue to the song's vision of a Socialist workers' utopia in Italy. The *mondine*'s verses invoke both past and present and frame Italy as being the next logical wave of an international sea change. Using the future tense rather than the conditional, the lyrics treat the hypothetical Italian revolution as the inevitable result of poor working conditions. This emphasis on work affects the song's treatment of history in two ways: First, it collapses geographical distinctions between Italy and Russia even as it emphasizes striations between the social classes of those who work and those who command. Second, the lyrics treat this global workers' history as a smooth flow of events, which proceed towards a brighter future through the fits and starts of local struggles. This contextualization lends international significance to the women's daily work by connecting the daily to the historical. But perhaps more importantly, rewriting history in terms of revolutionary cycles would have provided women with a sense of solidarity with the global working class.

If rice weeding benefited the Fascist economy, then how could the *mondine* reconcile their liberal politics with their food work on behalf of the regime? The content and use of song, as characterized by "Se otto ore," shows how the *mondine* redefined the meaning of their labour. To accomplish this mental feat, the *mondine* emphasized the local over the national, as demonstrated in their interviews and testimonials. This tactic allowed them not only to sustain dissent to the regime's landowner policy and disparaging treatment of peasant and tenant farmers, but also to maintain personal identity in the face of state attempts to appropriate the *mondine* as a figure of jovial rurality and political consent in Fascist propaganda. In a limited sense, the *mondine* did work on behalf of the regime in that they produced the rice, bodies, and rural culture crucial to the state's autarkic, pronatalist, and nationalist goals. But in a more powerful way, the content and use of their songs demonstrate that the *mondine* constantly and carefully negotiated dangerous political stances, sublimated unspoken emotional desires, and endured the physically exhausting effects of state policy, all while bent over, knee-deep in the mud.

Songs led to strikes. From 1932 to 1939, almost every Fascist campaign for rice was followed by agitation by the *mondine*. More than twenty strikes rippled across the sixteen miles between Novara and Vercelli in June 1931 alone.[62] Agitation intensified the following year: the *mondine* interrupted weeding and organized picket lines. They protested in front of the mayor's office, then burst into the municipal offices to make their demands to Fascist officials in person. On these occasions, the *mondine* not only objected to the regime's pay policies, but they also openly manifested their loyalty to Socialism and Communism. When the Ravennese *mondine* united for the workers' protest in Conselice in June 1932, they sang leftist hymns like "L'Internazionale" and "Bandiera rossa." In 1937, the Fascist Confederation for Rural Workers was forced to reconfirm the legitimacy of the eight-hour workday established by the *mondine* protests roughly twenty years prior. Item one set base pay at 11.20–13.00 lire for one day of weeding and 11.60–13.45 for rice planting. Overtime hours were to be compensated at the base pay rate plus 25 per cent, and 50 per cent on holidays.[63] For the *mondine*, fighting for fair wages was part of a larger battle for human dignity. The salary and work hours were key concessions from the regime.

In a culinary victory, the *mondine* also fought for and won the right to better food. Food quality and variety was so important to them that "miglioramento vitto" (improved rations) appeared as item two in the lengthy list of the Fascist Confederation's 1938 concessions to the *mondine*. Each weeder was now entitled to a daily ration of 0.6 kilograms of bread, 0.3 kilograms of rice, 100 grams of beans, 50 grams of lard, 15 grams of tomato paste, and a quarter litre of milk. Once per week, they were to receive 150 grams of meat and a quarter litre of wine.[64] No more rice and beans? Not quite. But thanks to the *mondine*'s demonstrations, they won the right to Sunday dinner.

Speeding Seasons, Rationalized Rurality, and the Flower of Revolt

The difference between how the Fascist regime addressed and represented rural women and how those women saw themselves was the difference between a full belly and an empty one. Reading propaganda against the grain reveals the obsession with plump bodies to be a foil for the *mondine*'s growling guts. Almanacs provided a distinctly rural form of propaganda that advocated seasonality and productivity as a solution to the wheat crisis. Obscuring the Fascist invasion of East Africa as the cause of the League of Nations sanctions, the almanac articles instead focus on promoting women's participation in the Battle for Grain and the push for rice production and consumption. Countrywomen were to solve the problem caused by the regime through rationalized rurality. Women weeded rice for half the pay that men received; meanwhile, they were expected to cook and eat more of this unpopular foodstuff and to birth more children than ever before. Because many rural women were semi-literate, photocollages visually conveyed these ideas next to the almanac articles. The steps involved in photocollage construction of the *mondine* demonstrate that graphic designers manipulated angles, scales, and viewpoints to suggest that rural women supported the regime, a process that I term "cut-and-paste consent." Tractors and tanks collapse the distinction between farming and warfare. Through these pictorial representations, the regime evoked the acceleration of biological cycles of fertility across country fields and rural female bodies as a key means to increase autarkic food production and the Italian population. For the regime, countrywomen, and the *mondine* in particular, stood as the symbolic saviours of the Fascist nation. Their big bellies – full of autarkic rice and pregnant with the next generation of Italians – marked the finish line, the goal of the Italian race.

But this admiration was far from mutual. And as the subjects of a regime hostile to working women, the *mondine* proved themselves to be anything but willing soldiers. The *mondine* despised the regime and the doubled economic burden they were expected to cheerfully endure. Their work songs spoke to the monotony of rice and beans and to the longed-for pasta dishes of home. This gap between culinary wishes and realities exemplifies the Battle for Grain. If anything, this propagandistic project whet women's appetites for tagliatelle and pasta napoletana. Rice became even more strongly associated with deprivation under Fascism, in terms of both its flavour and the work involved in its production.

We know all of this because the *mondine*'s diaries, artwork, and field songs conjure the flavours and smells of everyday life, revealing how rural working-class women contextualized their migrant agricultural labour in the rice paddies of Lombardy and Piedmont within the larger political context of Fascist food policy and economics. They defined themselves by their seasonal fieldwork. Former *mondina* Ermanna Chiozzi painted the daily travails of rice weeding and the arrival of the war – the long bicycle rides at 4:00 a.m. to get to the paddies, the bonfires they lit in November to

2.12. Self-portrait of Ermanna Chiozzi in rice paddy, "Son la mondina … son la licenziata"
(I am the rice weeder … I am the fired one). Charcoal on cloth, photographed inset in testimony
of Ermanna Chiozzi, "Io ricordo: Ermanna nella storia fra arte e racconti," 1933–46. Transcript of
manuscript MP/Adn2 4626, Archivio Diaristico Nazionale, Pieve Santo Stefano, Italy.

stay warm. Other paintings show the Fascist army trucks that brought the *mondine*
to the rice fields when rubber became so scarce that the bikes had no tires. In a combination of the two, one painting pictorially recounts how she was fired one season
because a gust of wind blew her straw hat from her head and she splashed across the
paddy to chase it. She concludes the episode with the joke "Son la mondina, son la
licenziata" (I am the rice weeder, I am the fired one), a pun and trenchant commentary
on the popular song "Son la mondina son la sfruttata" (I am the rice weeder, I am the
exploited).

This chapter has investigated the quiet, personal moments wherein lie the origins
of political revolt. In doing so, I am also underscoring the historiographic importance
of considering non-textual source materials and contrasting them against government narratives of who ate what and why in the years leading up to World War II.

The *mondine*'s words, in testimony and in song, demonstrate that rebellion should be understood as an ongoing process composed of daily questions rather than as a singular, heroic moment of conversion. By grounding this study of social identity in the specifics of what rural women said and did, I hope to avoid implying an essential group personality. And yet, two common characterizations of the *mondine*'s labour unites this population: although these women only worked in the rice fields for forty days out of the year, they point to this experience as a rite of passage to adulthood and class consciousness and also describe it as a powerful developmental arena for forging their voices and opinions. As such, the *mondine* viewed political revolt not as an isolated event but as a gathering force. They relied on a wide spectrum of politicized forms of resistance to negotiate for control over the conditions of rice production and consumption, and by extension over the political meaning of women's agricultural work in the rice fields in Fascist Italy.

Clear revolts are born of ambiguous nativity scenes, each one as delicate as a dandelion puff. Individual acts of foraging, borrowing, and stealing food from the landowner's stores prompted the *mondine* to question property ownership and workers' rights. Collective work-song authorship based on borrowing and stealing lyrics forged a female working-class identity powerfully inflected by anti-Fascist sentiment. Full-blown political resistance includes rallies and strikes, but the rice workers' chorus catalogues the early series of quiet, electric moments when the resistance first took root in their minds. Revolt flowered from these bursting seeds.

CHAPTER THREE

RAISING CHILDREN ON THE FACTORY LINE

Waged labour figured prominently in the lives of many Italian women. In the mid-1920s, women represented 15 per cent of the total workforce. But as Fascism took hold, greater numbers of women sought employment outside of the home. Indeed, the Fascist state monopolies employed many of these women directly: in 1926, female state workers numbered 16,037, of whom 13,478 were employed in monopolies, 603 in the arts industries, and a further 1,839 in theatre alone.[1] Contradictory edicts from the regime celebrated specific groups of female workers for their contributions even as they maintained that a woman's place was in the home.

By the 1930s, women made up 25 per cent of the total workforce.[2] The majority of these labourers remained in the countryside, weeding rice and threshing grain.[3] But not all workers toiled outside of the city limits: one in four worked in factories, primarily in textiles, paper, and food production.[4] Additionally, hospitality employment for café waitresses and hotel maids shifted traditionally feminine domestic duties like serving food and changing bedsheets into the public sphere.[5] With the internal variety of this workforce in mind, this chapter turns from the country to the city to explore Northern Italian women's food production in relation to Fascist politics towards female employment in the urban sector. Specifically, the regime attempted to rationalize factory workers' bodies to increase the production of food and the reproduction of children. Their intent was to remove blockages (fatigue, ill health) to make them run faster and more productively (birthing more children), like a machine.

It was not the first time that the regime aimed for women's stomachs. The Fascist romanticizing of female sacrifices embodied by the *mondine*, along with other living archetypes like prolific mothers and war widows, took on added complexity when women entered traditionally male spaces like industrial plants. Government bodies like the Centri di Cultura paired with private industry like the Propaganda Corporativa to produce the Diritto del Lavoro booklet series, which included practical guidelines for new gender-based legislation. In *La donna operaia e lo stato fascista*, they outlined the mutual constitution of Fascist ideology and gender roles in the urban workplace:

> Il Fascismo non è femminista, se nel femminismo si identifica la lotta di un sesso contro un altro; ma nella practica ha dimostrato di seguire un serio e sano feminismo, quando nei contratti stipulati attraverso i sindacati non ha fatto distinzione di sesso, ma si è esclusivamente occupato dal lavoratore in quanto era un lavoratore, anche quando si trattava di una lavoratrice.

> Fascism is not feminist, if in feminism one identifies the struggle of one sex against another; but in practice it has proved to follow a serious and healthy feminism, when in the contracts stipulated through the syndicates it has not made distinctions of sex, but it has only dealt with the worker as a worker, even when it dealt with a female worker.

Such an assertion may have been true, but only within the context of this legislative summary. In practice, women workers were subject to gender-specific work restrictions and state surveillance of their fertility. The booklet provides a brief overview of labour law, article by article. For instance, Article 5 establishes the workweek (*orario di lavoro*) at forty-eight hours. Article 7 (*lavoro straordinario*) covers overtime payment, set at base pay plus an additional 15 per cent thereafter for daytime hours and 30 per cent for nights or holidays. The rules seem reasonable: workers could not smoke, bring food into the factory, or refuse surveillance visits. Absences had to be accounted for to avoid a series of fines. The first subtracted three days' salary, the second incurred one week with no work. The third absence terminated employment. Employers could also fire workers for engaging in acts associated with competition and poaching. Inviting non-employees to the factory, sketching the machines, and using the machines for one's own independent production was considered comparable to inciting riots, performing criminal acts, and extreme negligence and had correspondingly severe consequences.[6] Because these rules focused on the employer-employee interaction, judgment, and value, they also implied new approaches to gender roles.

Fertility in the factory centred these debates. In 1934, writing in *Il popolo d'Italia*, Mussolini declared that, for women, working outside of the home was physically dangerous. It could even cause infertility. By contrast, the same labour when performed by men was described as a source of "great physical and moral virility." Mussolini also blamed women's entry into the urban workforce for the lack of jobs available to men.[7] But the low wage historically accorded to female workers was simply too profitable for the regime to risk excluding them entirely. Recall that the Serpieri coefficient dictated that female agricultural workers could only earn half of men's pay. For this reason, the state used a scalpel rather than a hammer to intervene in the world of work.

Taylorist Breastfeeding and the Industrialization of Motherhood

During the Fascist period, Benito Mussolini's regime exhorted Italian mothers to breastfeed. No previous Italian government had ever deemed breastfeeding to be a matter of national importance or made nursing the subject of propaganda and legislation. Recognizing breastfeeding as a tight, and thus powerful, foodway helps to explain why governments, especially dictatorial ones like the Italian Fascist regime, paid so much attention to breastfeeding and food preparation for toddlers and young children in this era. Amongst all foodways, breastfeeding connects human bodies most intimately. With one link, breastfeeding physically connects the producer (mother) and consumer (infant) in a simultaneous act of feeding (mother to infant) and eating (infant from mother).

The Fascist regime made two foundational assumptions regarding the nutritive capacity of breastmilk: first, that good nutrition led to strong character, and second, that mother-child bonding led to strong bodies. Underlying both ideas is a biopolitical belief that food could create or change physical and mental traits in the inchoate infant body. Although anachronism bars any possibility that the regime could have described breastfeeding as a national foodway, their treatment of this act evokes and foreshadows this characterization. Regime officials and their media mouthpieces celebrated breastfeeding as a nutritive as well as an emotional bond between mother and child. Through posters, films, and even architecture, Fascist propaganda abstracted breastfeeding as the individual practice of a national norm. And inside government clinics and mother's refectories, dietary directives and nutritional tables demonstrate that the regime conceived of breastfeeding as a body-to-body exchange of nutrients that could be manipulated to favour demographic increase; the logic went that better breastmilk would result in lower infant mortality. By manipulating how working-class women and their children ate, the regime attempted to control the formation of their bodies. Ultimately, these interventions sought to strengthen the national body as a whole.

Over the span of the Fascist *ventennio*, ONMI normalized a new reproductive practice: collective breastfeeding in factory-like clinics. Rationalist ONMI centres were built as an architectural solution to a seemingly vast demographic problem: low birth rates coupled with high infant mortality. Facing rampant poverty, women utilized ONMI complexes en masse, as the centres included cafeterias and milk dispensaries along with breastfeeding rooms and obstetric clinics. The regime obsessively tracked the number of bodies processed by these healthcare offices. In the year 1935 alone, 255,605 pregnant mothers came to an ONMI-run obstetric clinic for their first visit, and 485,958 infants were taken to their first visit to an ONMI-run paediatric clinic, according to ISTAT, the Fascist government's official arm of statistical analysis. Further ISTAT data details visitor totals for ONMI's refectories, milk dispensaries, and nurseries, listing increasingly specific and numerous public institutional settings for the years 1936–46.

State interference in the mother/child relationship was not unique to Fascism. In Nazi Germany, compulsory membership in the Nazi League of German Girls (Bund Deutscher Mädel, or BDM) taught girls ages ten and up to embrace motherhood as their social role. Indeed, motherhood centred Adolf Hitler's racialized goal of *Volksgemeinschaft*, the ideal Aryan community. The Nazi movement valued women for their biological power as generators of the race in the Third Reich. Military strength and colonial expansion in eastern Europe depended on aggressive population policies, like the 1936 *Lebensborn* (Fount of Life) movement, an extension of the SS Marriage Order of 1932. Soaring birth rates, not familial connection, was the point of this state-run program. It constructed shelters that provided birth documents and financial support for single mothers and aggressively sought adoptive parents for the children. The SS Marriage Order also dictated that every male member of the Nazi Party sire four children, in or out of wedlock; at the same time, the state increased punishments for abortion.[8] In later years, the German Nazi Party shifted closer to Italian Fascist tactics in their policies. They provided marriage loans, dispensed family income supplements for each new child, and publicly honoured prolific families by bestowing the Cross of Honour of the German Mother on women who birthed four or more children.

Italian Fascist social welfare programs did not aim to help mothers; rather, they attempted to use maternal bodies as a means to improve the next generation. This was done primarily through food – not only breastfeeding but also by feeding the mother particular things to pass their nutrients on to the child. In 1933, LUCE and ONMI released a newsreel, *Per la protezione della stirpe* (*For the Protection of the Race*). In it, a day in the life of a Casa della Madre e del Bambino unfolds as a set of variations on the same central theme: large collections of mothers, children, and infants working, eating, and feeding in the clinic complex and the nearby textile factory (Figs. 3.1–3.4). As propaganda, it manipulates these three variables to create an equation: built environment plus food aid equals more working-class mothers surveilled by the regime's nascent healthcare system. Let us examine the gifts proffered, and then follow the strings attached.

At its core, the newsreel concerns interactions between food, bodies, and built environment. The heart of the newsreel seats the viewer in the mother's refectory, a critical space found in nearly every clinic. Prior to the Fascist period, the Catholic Church managed the majority of Italy's charitable soup kitchens and clinics. Funding for these social services came from the local gentry, as well as from the church itself. During the 1930s, many of the priests and nuns continued their work in these aid centres, although their approval and opprobrium of the regime varied widely.[9] A shot lingers over the mother's refectory menu. Offerings range in content but all are cheap and filling – Monday offers minestrone with rice and tripe with potatoes, Friday brings risotto, codfish, and tuna with salad. These proteins, tripe and codfish, evoke economic concerns in that they cost far less than meats like beef or pork, but they also speak to both old religious traditions and new eugenic thinking. The Catholic tradition of meatless Fridays dictated fish for that day's dish.[10] Regime nutritionists heralded tripe for its high quantities of easily digestible proteins, ideal building blocks for strengthening fetal formation.

Looking more closely, we see that the menu privileges two foods: milk and rice. Milk appears every day, in an obvious conclusion at the end of every meal selection. Rice appears nearly every day as well, though masked as rice minestrone (Monday), rice in broth (Wednesday), and risotto (Friday). Pasta (Tuesday, Thursday) and raw and cooked vegetables (daily) round out the menu. The milk and rice evoke broader Fascist policies: the promotion of pronatalism and of autarky through social services. The Fascist regime believed feeding milk to mothers improved their breastmilk. According to the regime's nutritional studies, mothers' diets controlled the quality and quantity of breastmilk available for their infants. This reasoning accords enormous biopolitical potential to flavoursome breastmilk by suggesting that it moulds the next generation. It also demonstrates that ONMI ranked the infant's supposed desires above those of the mother, privileging the formation of the inchoate national body over the personal preferences of the maternal body. ONMI considered anything other than breastmilk to be a nutritional disaster for infants. And good-tasting breastmilk enticed the infant to eat more, resulting in its physical fortification. Hence, refectory menus largely eliminated plants from the Alliaceae family, like garlic, onions, and leeks, as well as some Brassicaceae, like cauliflower and broccoli. These vegetables were believed to diminish the flow of breastmilk and to give it a sour or bitter flavour that infants supposedly did not appreciate. Further, dense, solid foods and loose, liquid porridges were added or subtracted to thicken or thin breastmilk consistency. Put telegraphically, ONMI believed that the dishes on refectory menus could directly impact the physical and spiritual development of breastfeeding infants. This is why, as a *Maternità ed Infanzia* article on the mother's refectories put it, only the pregnant or breastfeeding "woman as mother" and the "child as potential energy" were eligible for ONMI aid.[11] Food served a prophylactic purpose: feeding mothers translated to feeding infants, the future of the race.

Per la protezione della stirpe gives filmic form to this line of thought. This newsreel constitutes an explicitly eugenic forerunner to *Alle Madri d'Italia*, the pedagogical film discussed in the following section. After the still shot of the weekly refectory menu, we see images of women eating and then breastfeeding. By temporally linking these scenes, the activities appear causally connected as well. And that is why every day of the week, the cafeteria provided milk for the mothers to drink, underscoring the regime's hopes of feeding infants through mothers, rather than feeding women as an end in itself.

For the regime, demography and economics went hand in hand. The milk- and rice-forward menu of *La protezione della stirpe*'s model refectory shows how ONMI pushed for pronatalism through thrifty meal plans. But it also speaks to the regime's subtle cross-promotion of another concern: autarky. Economic policies of reducing imports and stimulating domestic production promoted the regime's political goal of

3.1. Publicity photograph of the ONMI mother's refectory for *Per la protezione della stirpe*, 1933. Film code D065901. Footage supplied by Istituto LUCE Cinecittà.

3.2. Publicity photograph of close-up at the ONMI mother's refectory for *Per la protezione della stirpe*, 1933. Film code D065901. Footage supplied by Istituto LUCE Cinecittà.

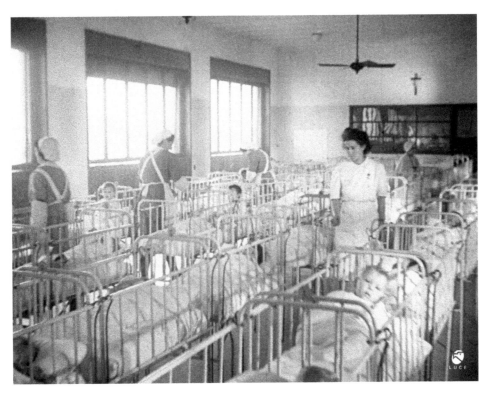

3.3. Publicity photograph of ONMI nursery for *Per la protezione della stirpe*, 1933. Film code D065901. Footage supplied by Istituto LUCE Cinecittà.

3.4. Publicity photograph of milk dispensary for *Per la protezione della stirpe*, 1933. Film code D065901. Footage supplied by Istituto LUCE Cinecittà.

3.5. Magazine cover "Verso la Vita" (Towards Life). The caption reads, "L'Assistenza all'infanzia alla mostra delle colonie estive" (Early childhood assistance at the summer colonies display). (*La Cucina Italiana*, August 1937)

national self-sufficiency. The refectory menu speaks to these objectives directly in its emphasis on autarkic foods. Little wonder then that rice figured prominently on refectory menus: working-class mothers had little choice but to eat what the clinics provided.

Because mothers ate autarkically, their infants did as well. Although regime propaganda does not refer to breastfeeding as an autarkic activity, the factory-like setting of the ONMI clinics and the denigration of baby formula produced abroad suggests that the regime considered the economic implications of breastfeeding and characterized it as a form of domestic manufacturing. Propaganda related to the production of autarkic food and breastmilk make parallel cases for the finer flavour and nutrition of domestic products. Women's magazines such as the cooking magazine *La Cucina Italiana* promoted these activities as forms of culinary patriotism (Fig. 3.5). By contrast, imported foods, including Nestlé infant formula (Fig. 3.6), drew coins from domestic coffers and deposited them in foreign wallets. Thus, Fascist propaganda tried to tip the scales in

3.6. Severo Sepo, artist's study for Nestlé artificial milk advertisement, Paris. (Archivio della Communicazione, Parma, Italy)

favour of breastmilk. A wide variety of periodicals for women supported the regime's push for breastfeeding. These included both hobby and lifestyle publications that assumed a female readership and professional publications aimed at men concerned with maternal and infant care, such as ONMI's publication *Maternità e Infanzia*. Meanwhile, ONMI, in partnership with LUCE, produced a variety of didactic films and newsreels directly related to breastfeeding, such as the aforementioned *La protezione della stirpe*, and short features to publicize award ceremonies for prolific mothers, showcases of new clinic openings, and instructions for hygienic infant feeding practices.

Given this, we might view the promotion of breastfeeding in the context of other regime-advocated activities, such as raising rabbits and chickens or creating a home garden. By recognizing breastfeeding, cooking, cleaning, shopping, and gardening as forms of work like manufacturing and business, the regime could apply policies of economy in the domestic sphere as well as in the industrial sector. Once the regime

placed these forms of gendered labour within the broader frame of autarkic and pronatalist production, they could shift interventions from the public market to the private
and thus control productivity at the level of everyday life. This framing did not valorize
women's labour so much as open their private lives to government interference.

The connection between women's factory work and breastfeeding is front and centre in the regime-sponsored film *Alle madri d'Italia*. This film celebrated the maternal body as a productive apparatus. Produced by the Istituto Nazionale LUCE and
directed by Pietro Francisci, this forty-one-minute silent film was commissioned for
the tenth anniversary of the ONMI organization to instruct women how to hygieni-
cally breastfeed and care for their young children.[12] This film states its pedantic intent
at the very beginning: "Questo film dimostra come l'Opera prepara la donna alla sua
missione di madre e le insegna ad allevare e i propri figli sani e forti" (The film shows
how the Institute prepares the woman for her divine mission of motherhood and
teaches her how to raise her children to be big and strong). Industrial motherhood
emerges from the film's conflation of manufacturing and maternity under the aegis of
gendered bodily labour. Motifs of surveillance and order fuse the textile factory and
the factory nursery, establishing twinned areas of production and control.[13]

In an early sequence that highlights ONMI's role in creating nurseries for factories, we see a group of women working in rigid rows. The camera angle shoots
downward so that the audience viewpoint is merged with that of the factory boss.
Fabric-based debris is utterly absent from this hygienic space of production: no fabrics mound the factory floor, no dust motes dot the air. The rhythmic choreography
of human hands and mechanical gears signals industrious production. As such, the
factory allows female workers to manufacture two autarkic products: Italian textiles
and Italian babies. In both cases, the female labourers are under constant surveillance.
The camera then cuts to a close-up of a clock. "E quando dovranno tornare al lavoro
potranno allattare i loro bambini che sono assistiti nel nido della fabbrica" (And when
they must return to work, they can breastfeed their infants, who are taken care of by
the factory nursery). As one, the sombre workers rise. In a swift shift of emotional
tone, the next shot depicts them blissfully breastfeeding their infants in the nursery, a
petite Victorian building that bespeaks bourgeois femininity. Lacey patterns of sunlight and shadow, cast by the elaborate latticework of the doors, cloak every vertical
and horizontal surface in a single looped pattern. Although the nursery is under the
auspices of the factory, its small scale, light colour, and playful decorations mark its
separateness. In its resemblance to a country cottage, the nursery appears to be a feminized space of production.

The sudden sentimentality suggests that breastfeeding brings these women greater
happiness than their work at the textile factory. It also underscores the regime's contradictory support of certain types of female labour in the public sphere, like textile
work, rice harvesting, and Taylorist breastfeeding, as well as its denigration of female
labour in manufacturing plants and refineries. The cut from the factory to the nursery

further undermines state claims that women belong solely in the home by showcasing how easily these women combined factory work and childcare – ignoring that the state assisted this process. As a puericulture expert looks on with approval, a smiling woman breastfeeds her infant, her face bathed in sunlight. The camera then zooms in, cutting off her head to focusing on the infant's mouth at her breast. Her body becomes pure productive capacity, doubly monitored by the regime's representative and the camera.

Throughout the Fascist *ventennio*, women continued to work at the depressed wages advocated by the regime, with added state interventions to guard their reproductive capacities. In 1934, a new law dictated that any factory with more than fifty female workers ages fifteen and older had to have a breastfeeding room with hygienic conditions. Law 653 restricted the hours women could work as well as the total weight they could carry. Night shifts were eliminated, and fifteen- to twenty-one-year-old women were banned from certain jobs that were thought to diminish fetal health, particularly in mining. Moreover, every female worker was required to have a *Libretto di iscrizione delle operaie alla cassa nazionale di maternità*, a laywoman's copy of the ONMI employment laws.[14]

In reality, however, these regulations had almost no effect on the total number of women employed in the public sector. Perry Willson has noted the ironically progressive unfolding of these paternalist dictations: "Some of this meant changes that could actually make it easier for women to work outside the home, such as improvements in maternity leave and the provision of nurseries and breastfeeding rooms."[15] In other words, Fascism was fundamentally corporatist: principally concerned with output and efficiency over and above even its own purported politics. Whether out of ideological allegiance or economic practicality, most businesses supported Fascist policy. But what would happen if the corporate leader of a major food industry were female? How might she negotiate regime policy?

Perugina: A Woman-Founded Factory under Fascism

Although a mere 893 female workers were employed in the Italian food industry by 1926, nearly a third of that force worked at the chocolate company Perugina alone, rendering it worth studying as one of the leading employers of women in industrial work in the 1920s and a model for other companies to come.[16] Journalist Maria Guidi described the management style of founder Luisa Spagnoli in laudatory terms,

> Questa industria così fiorente, ormai tra le primissime della nostra patria, è stata fondata da una donna, la signora Luisa Spagnoli. Ella affronto coraggiosamente le difficoltà della Guerra, seppe schivare e sorpassare le asprezze e le lotte, uscire vittoriosa da tutte le crisi del dopoguerra. Creatura energetica e volitiva, ha impreso nobilmente nello stabilimento ordine, decoro, signorilità.

> This industry, so blooming, by now among the first in our country, was founded by a
> woman, Madam Luisa Spagnoli. She courageously confronted the difficulty of the War,
> knew how to dodge and overcome the severity and struggles, coming out victorious
> from all the crises of the post-war period. An energetic and wilful creature, she has
> nobly impressed the factory with order, decorum, and elegance.[17]

Spagnoli was rare for achieving such success as a female entrepreneur at the height of
the Fascist period, a feat that she managed by leveraging regime policies to promote
chocolate.[18]

Charting Perugina's development illustrates what it took to grow a business under
Fascism. Started as a drugstore in central Perugia, Perugina became a major industrial
concern in a matter of a few years. Spagnoli made use of Fascist projects like pronatalism, autarky, and rationalism to market Perugina chocolates, while Fascist policies promoting the Italian food industry favoured Perugina's growth in return. Spagnoli read
the political moment and interpreted it through the lens of human needs and desires.
Her entrepreneurial approach looked inward to factory personnel as well as outward to
the customer base: Spagnoli's monitoring innovations to factory-based women's welfare
projects were later enshrined in the regime's doctrine – indeed, it can be argued that
she anticipated and may have even inspired some of their policies around breastfeeding
and women's labour. That said, no records indicate whether Spagnoli self-identified as
Fascist; we only know Perugina expressed Fascist goals when the regime's legislations
supported the company's economic goals. More interesting is the manner in which
Perugina and Spagnoli interacted with Mussolini and the regime's pet projects.

Well before the Fascist regime translated its abstract demographic goals into specific legislation, Spagnoli took an authoritarian approach to female factory workers'
reproductive health. As a founder and employer, she was early and active in her provision of factory-based social welfare for the female employees who composed most of
her workforce. From the moment Perugina opened its doors in 1907, the factory provided workers with an Ufficio di Assistenza Sociale that distributed coupons (*buoni*)
to support employees' physical health outside of factory hours. Specific benefits covered basic food and medical visits (house calls included) and expanded in 1936 to
include visits to ocean, mountain, and heliotherapeutic colonies.[19] Healthy female
factory workers of Perugina could thus feed the nation in two ways: first, through
the industrial production of chocolate, but second and less obviously, through the
production of breastmilk. Even before the Fascist regime and the state's push for pronatalism, Spagnoli built breastfeeding rooms and nurseries at Perugina for her workers; once the regime was established, however, she applied to the regime's pronatalist
ONMI group for additional funding to open those rooms to the Fontivegge community beyond the factory. One might say, what started as an independent breastfeeding
initiative became a Fascist one. Furthermore, female factory workers were required to
sign up for maternal healthcare insurance but were also guaranteed dowries and even

pensions for their husbands if they fell ill.[20] In other words, Perugina engaged in what Barbara Curli described as "feminine paternalism."[21]

In ways both good and bad, Spagnoli herself had extraordinary force of personality. Charismatic and confident, Spagnoli projected authority in a way that drew the Perugina factory workers behind her goals. Both her sociability with her employees and her willingness to regulate their private lives foreshadow later moves by the regime to blend paternalistic care with governmental control. Perhaps Benito Mussolini's visit to the Perugina factory in 1923 provided early inspiration for the regime's later attempts to rationalize maternal healthcare. The visit was certainly useful for Spagnoli's and Perugina's reputations.

Social control of the female factory worker lay within the realm of the family and the gender roles supported by the Fascist regime. Luisa Spagnoli modernized this role by deploying the efficiency of social hygiene to personnel management, with the ultimate goal of increasing factory productivity. This brings us to the larger political context of these industrial innovations. Under Fascism, Italian breastfeeding became corporate policy with a specific political meaning. The regime attempted to intervene in what all Italian citizens ate. Newborns were no exception. And these interventions first appeared in factory settings before later expanding into factory-inspired clinics and refectories. A broad body of evidence attests to the Fascist government's exploitation of the biological capacity of breastmilk towards eugenic ends.[22]

Nowhere is the idea of Taylorized and maternal working women's bodies clearer than in a newsreel hailing the social welfare provided to female factory workers by Perugina chocolates. On 21 April 1937, director Arnaldo Ricotti released a newsreel on the eighteenth Fiera di Milano, a popular event celebrating Italian industry at the height of autarky.[23] Distant pan shots encompass the fair, a temporary city composed of pavilions and posters for key foreign and Italian companies – over thirty-one in total spread across the public and private sectors. The energetic male voiceover announces the addition of two new themed pavilions – one for textiles and the other for mechanics, additions of central importance to economic autarky. What he does not state, but is suggested everywhere in this clip, is the extent to which these two types of urban factory work were gendered, with women being in the textile sector and men in mechanics. In 1936, 25 per cent of the industrial labour force was female (1,377,373 women workers). They worked mainly in a few sectors: textiles (where they made up 75 per cent of the labour force), paper (50.7 per cent), leather (40.8 per cent), chemicals, printing, mechanical industries, and – to be studied here – food production.[24] Underscoring the association of women and textiles, the camera lingers over a chorus line of female mannequin legs, all kicked towards the sky to display the hosiery produced by the young woman working the nearby machines. Achille Starace, party secretary for the Partito Nazionale Fascista, marches through this section of the fairgrounds with a group of uniformed Fascist soldiers. Costumes and uniforms further underscore the gendered divide. Their severe dark uniforms show off shining

3.7. Perugina pavilion with statistics and bassinette. Stabilimento Fotografico Crimella, 1937. (Fondazione Fiera Milano, Archivio Storico, photo code 1937_550, Milan, Italy)

medals, whereas the woman at the hosiery machine wears a flower crown, with her hair in decorative twists. The soldiers bring the warfront to this urban gathering, and the factory woman brings the blooming, fertile countryside.

Machines matter almost as much as people in this newsreel. In addition to the industrial work done by the women on these textile and paper machines, the newsreel also lingers over the display of agricultural machines and motors, showcased alongside airplane propellers. Note that this display echoes the collapsing of farm equipment and war machines seen in the almanac photocollages in the previous chapter. The newsreel also focuses on machines for transportation, including the display train car – complete with a *fascio* on its nose, destined for the new Venice-Milan-Turin line. The voiceover notes Starace's fascination with four machines – "le macchine cartarie, grafiche, la filatura e la tessitura." Starace's attention to the papers, graphic, sewing, and fabric-producing machines mirrors the key industries for female urban employment. To this list, we can add food production, as Perugina represents the sector. The Perugina chocolate booth sells rabbit fur sweaters for women from Luisa Spagnoli's other business, a fashion house. Connecting rabbit raising and chocolate production suggests the omnipresence of women's autarkic textile work and its rural associations even in the urban food industry sector.

3.8. Film still of Perugina sales clerks with baby dolls, "18° Fiera di Milano," dir. Arnaldo Ricotti, 21 April 1937, duration 00:02:15. (Archivio LUCE, Giornale LUCE B/B1079, film code B107908)

In the Fascist context, rurality and rabbits also inevitably evoke the question of reproductivity. The newsreel promotes this fusion by heralding the Perugina chocolate company's support of the regime's demographic campaign. Pairs of doves holding hearts in their beaks fly across the Perugina pavilion façade (Fig. 3.7). "100 000 lire di premi in contanti, 1000 bambini nutriti gratuitamente per un anno" (100,000 lire of prizes in cash, 1,000 children fed for free each year). An enormous baby in a bassinet hovers below the promise. The next shot shows grown women, store clerks to judge by their matching white garments and haircovers, happily bouncing baby dolls in their laps (Fig. 3.8). Because this is a newsreel, Perugina must have intentionally composed this scene by providing their workers with these pronatalist props. In other words, Perugina used the idea of feeding children to advertise their company in an autarkic context. Chocolate was a luxury product in the 1930s; thus, demonstrating their investment in food for the less fortunate was critical to the company's reputation and to securing Fascist support of their industrial concerns. The announcer celebrates Perugina's social engagement through economic subvention of procreation within the nuclear family unit, noting their "premi di nuzialità e di natalità," prizes for marriage and birth.

A busy Perugina store shows saleswomen packing up boxes for the eager crowd: one large box of Buitoni pasta, one smaller box of Perugina chocolates, plus a participation form for their *concorso*, featuring "Il feroce saladino" and the Three Musketeers. The last scene of the film features a well-dressed woman pushing a baby buggy through the crowd, a balloon gifted by the Perugina company trailing merrily behind. All in all, the emphasis on child-rearing in the chocolate factory was truly intense: one might say that chocolate went hand in hand with mother's milk.

The Industrial Biography of Luisa Spagnoli

Luisa Sargenti Spagnoli (1877–1935) was an exceptional entrepreneur (Fig. 3.9). Her ability to think strategically and maintain long-term focus while executing each step of her business plan with determination and precision made her a powerful leader in Italian industry. She started out poor, the daughter of a fishmonger who died early, leaving her mother to take in laundry for neighbours, and young Luisa to help. At thirteen, she began to work as an assistant to a local seamstress in town. For eight years, she cleaned the atelier, took customer orders, and learned to cut and sew, occasionally sneaking scraps of colourful ribbons and fabric home to play with as toys. Luisa Sargenti met Annibale Spagnoli (b. 1872), a young man from Assisi, when he came to play with the town band. After his military service, Luisa and Annibale married in 1899, when she was twenty-two and he

3.9. Portrait of Luisa Spagnoli, Perugia, Italy, c. 1910. Photo accession number GBB-F-005146-0000. (Archivio Alinari, Florence, Italy)

was twenty-seven. It was with the money from the army and Luisa's sewing savings that, in 1901, the couple decided to buy a small drugstore that specialized in *confetti* (candies) production and began to make chocolates by hand.

Luisa Spagnoli gave birth to three sons – Mario, Armando, and Aldo – in almost as many years, and the economic difficulties of feeding so many mouths caused her to ask how to optimize the drugstore's output. In 1904, Luisa introduced semi-mechanized production to the Via Alessi establishment, changing the store's candy production from artisanal to mechanical in short order. By age thirty and thirty-five, respectively, Luisa and Annibale were managing a true industrial establishment: the Società Perugina per la Fabbricazione dei Confetti. To do so, Annibale brought a number of Umbrian industrialists onto the new company board in 1908. The group included mayor of Umbertide Francesco Andreani, Ancona-based businessman Leone Ascoli, and Francesco Buitoni, whose father, Giovanni Battista Buitoni, founded the Buitoni pasta factory in San Sepolcro in 1827–8. With 70,000 lire and fifteen workers, they opened the Perugina factory.

The new division of labour required both Annibale's and Luisa's involvement to manage the operation of the store and the employees. It was difficult work, especially for Luisa, who spent the entire day with the workers inventing new products to enter in the national competitions (*concorsi*) among Northern Italian candy companies. Yet the business kept growing: by 1913, Perugina had fifty workers (thirty-six men and fourteen women) and produced 300 kilograms of chocolate, candies, pastilles, and bonbons per day. Activity took off in part thanks to the marketing talents of Giovanni Buitoni, Francesco Buitoni's son. Giovanni was only eighteen years old when Francesco called him back from his studies in Germany to help with the company, and he quickly assumed primary control of the business at Fontivegge. Perugina was now a substantial factory, boasting almost 200 workers, the majority of whom were women.

When the Great War broke out, Luisa and her oldest son, Mario, then thirteen years old, substituted for the men who left to fight, running the business and managing the remaining 150 female employees. During this period, Luisa invented new roles for the factory workers, although these were largely aimed at the middle-class employees, like the new saleswomen positions that offered more managerial autonomy than before. Running what was temporarily an all-female factory, Luisa turned her attention towards women's welfare, creating the previously discussed in-factory nursery, as well as providing food and clothes. She even started a retreat, a *colonia marina*, where the workers were temporarily entrusted to nuns and would return "più laboriose e buone" (more industrious and good), suggesting that the women returned as harder workers and also as morally elevated ones – for the company's benefit.

Astounding as it may seem that a luxurious product was continually produced in wartime, the decision to leave the Perugina doors open was socially shrewd. In World War I, Antonio Salandra's government ceased all sweet production except for chocolate because it was a useful food for the front. It provided a quick hit of energy as well as a powerful boost to morale. Consider what it must have felt like to be a country soldier presented with a daily piece of chocolate, in a time when this tasty treat denoted social esteem and romantic love.[25] This is why Perugina was able to expand right after the war ended rather than having to take time to get back on its feet. And because all sweets except chocolate were considered unnecessary luxuries and were not permitted for sale, Luisa converted the plant to all things cacao. The idea was a successful one and made Perugina the Italian chocolate industry leader. World renown arrived in 1922, with a kiss.

The Bacio, invented by Luisa Spagnoli 1922, crafted luxury from leftovers. Making truffles and bonbons resulted in excess chocolate and hazelnuts. Realizing the value that lay in castoffs, Luisa rolled a small handful of loose chocolate into a ball, topped it with a single hazelnut, and covered the creation in fondant. She named it the *cazzotto*, or punch, because the resulting form resembled a closed fist, with one nut-knuckle popping out of the top. But offering one's lover a box full of punches was not very romantic. In Federico Seneca's famous advertisement (Fig. 3.10), *cazzotti* turned to kisses.

3.10. Poster advertisement for Bacio chocolates, designed by Federico Seneca, "Baci Cioccolato Perugina," Perugia, Italy, 1923. Permission by concession of the Ministero per i beni e le attività culturali e per il Turismo. (Museo Nazionale Collezione Salce, Direzione regionale Musei Veneto, Venice, Italy)

In the next five years, over 100 million *baci* were distributed. The company (*azienda*) became a corporation (*società*). Perugina had 400 workers (300 women and 100 men) and produced 3,000 kilograms of chocolate per day, ten times its pre-war production. Saving scraps was not only lucrative but also an increasing necessity given the broader political picture. With importation constricted, fewer cacao pods were coming in. Luisa needed to get every last bit out of the pods that did arrive on Italian shores. To stretch the available product, she introduced new chocolates featuring domestic ingredients that were available in abundance, such as preserved citrus fruit. The *tavolette all'arancio* (orange bars) were invented with Italian autarky in mind. In addition to absorbing a larger proportion of waste chocolate (*scarti*) than the hand-dipped chocolates, the bars also featured a cheap, domestically sourced ingredient: Sicilian oranges, available for a song to northern industries that were willing to buy in bulk from the poverty-plagued south. In 1940, Perugina promoted an "autarkic week," featuring domestic ingredients like hazelnuts and chestnuts, as well as grapes, strawberries, cherries, pears, and lemons. In promotional materials like branded bags for carrying the candies, Perugina's Sicilian orange sat closest to the key word "Autarchica," reminding shoppers of the company's long-standing promotion of this celebrated Italian fruit (Fig. 3.11).

But rapid development came with growing pains. A series of strikes rocked the factory, as did the departure of several members of the original board, including Andreani, Ascoli, and, most notably, Annibale Spagnoli. His portion of the business devolved to Luisa, and by extension to their son Mario, by then the technical director of the company. These changes ultimately consolidated control in the hands of Giovanni Buitoni,

3.11. Paper bag for Perugina fruit and nut candy, designed by Mirko, "Settimana Autarchica del dolce Perugina," Perugia, Italy, 1940. Permission by concession of the Ministero per i beni e le attività culturali e per il Turismo. (Museo Nazionale Collezione Salce, Direzione regionale Musei Veneto, Venice, Italy)

a long-time worker and purportedly Luisa's lover (Fig. 3.12). Buitoni himself held 73.1 per cent control, Luisa Spagnoli had 18.6 per cent, and Societa Buitoni had 8.3 per cent.

For Perugina, 1923 was not only the year of the Bacio and the Spagnoli breakup, it was also the year of Mussolini. The year prior, the city of Perugia served as the staging ground for declaration of the start of Fascist rule. The night of 26 October 1922, the Perugian Hotel Brufani provided the urban stage set where Italo Balbo (aviator and future governor of the colonies), Emilio De Bono (future minister of colonial affairs), Cesare Maria De Vecchi (secretary of the Ministry of Finance), and Michele Bianchi (secretary of the Party and long-time Mussolini loyalist) declared the official start of Fascist rule, even before the March on Rome reached its destination. One year after the March, Mussolini returned to Perugia for its anniversary and visited the Perugina company on 30 October 1923 (Fig. 3.13). Female factory workers in uniform white aprons and hair kerchiefs lined up for inspection in the factory's interior courtyard, their arms raised high in the Roman salute.[26] Giovanni Buitoni and son appear to have accompanied Mussolini through every stage of the visit, while Luisa appears in more of the posed photographs of the major personnel outside of the factory walls. At the factory visit, she greeted him with a flower that he unenthusiastically holds in the formal photos. For the most part, the regime and Perugina maintained cordial ties: the minister of finance, Volpi di Misurata, paid a subsequent governmental visit to the factory in 1927. But although Perugina sustained ties with the regime, and in particular with its financial arm, that does not mean Spagnoli always toed the party line.

The relationship between Luisa Spagnoli and Benito Mussolini shifted in accordance with her entrepreneurialism. She acted to move her business forward, forcing

3.12. Photograph of Luisa Spagnoli and Giovanni Buitoni in an automobile, Perugia, Italy, 1924. Photo accession number GBB-F-005147–0000. (Archivio Alinari, Florence, Italy)

him to react. One of the niceties communicated by Mussolini during his 1923 visit – "Vi dico, e vi autorizzo a ripeterlo che il vostro cioccolato è veramente squisito!" (I tell you, and I authorize you to repeat it, that your chocolate is truly exquisite!) – was greeted with her appreciative laughter. Mere weeks later, she used this exchange as the foundation for a marketing blitz so intense that the regime had to outlaw Perugina's use of Mussolini's testimonial or risk losing authority. Moreover, Perugina commissioned provocative posters that evoked racial mixing at a time when the Fascist Party was increasingly concerned with framing whiteness as a sign of prestige. In 1925, Federico Seneca caused a scandal with his advertisement for Perugina milk chocolate, wherein a white woman represented milk and a racist caricature of a black

3.13. Benito Mussolini's official visit to the Perugina factory. Photographed by Adolfo Porry Pastorel. 30 October 1923, Perugia, Italy. (Footage supplied by Istituto LUCE Cinecittà. Fondo Pastorel: Celebrazioni del primo anniversario della marcia su Roma a Perugia e nella capitale del regno. Photo code FP00001476.)

man represented chocolate (Fig. 3.14). The two dance partners, the man nude and the woman in a transparent dress, nuzzle together. He cups her breast, and she smiles. Although the image was decried as indecent by the Fascist press for its implied portrayal of interracial sex, there were no legal or financial consequences for the company.

The general pattern of Perugina's interaction with the Fascist government was one of pushing the bounds through advertising as far as possible and only retreating when the regime said "enough." This was certainly the case with the *concorsi* advertising campaign. Perugina produced collectible *figurine* and albums, with the chance to win great prizes for kids and adults alike, like dolls, toy guns, refrigerators, or even a Fiat 500 Topolino. Each *concorso* had a theme, with the Three Musketeers being especially popular. The "Il feroce saladino" line ran for two years and included a radio show and publicity stunts like three costumed performers descending from a hot-air balloon at the Milan trade fair. To calm the ensuing furore, Mussolini stopped the campaign after two years because the media circus had clogged the airwaves. The third season never appeared. But apparently Mussolini objected to the marketing frenzy rather than the content: he was a Perugina Three Musketeers collector himself.[27]

3.14. Poster advertisement for Perugina Milk Chocolate, designed by Federico Seneca,
"Cioccolato al latte Perugina," Perugia, Italy, 1925. Permission by concession of the Ministero
per i beni e le attività culturali e per il Turismo. (Museo Nazionale Collezione Salce, Direzione
regionale Musei Veneto, Venice, Italy)

The Perugina Factory I: Rationalized Production

Early and undeniable success meant that Perugina's management helped to define
later Fascist-period models for women's factory work. During the late 1920s and
early 1930s, Perugina stood at the vanguard of industrial innovation with over 500
employees. Through streamlining and rationalization, the company transformed work
patterns. Rationalization, Perry Willson notes, "resulted in a factory that seemed to
function almost as if by clockwork, where the work many employees had to do was
specialized and simplified."[28] At Perugina, Mario Spagnoli helmed these efforts as
the technical director, a role that drew inspiration from his mother's approach to
personnel oversight.[29] At the same time, industry was also becoming more closely
affiliated with government.

The Ente Nazionale Italiano per l'Organizzazione Scientifica del Lavoro (ENIOS), a government office established to promote scientific management in Italian business enterprises, was founded in October 1925. The very same month, the association signed the Pact of Palazzo Vidoni with the regime and charted a course towards Fascist corporatism. Gino Olivetti, the typewriter magnate, became the ENIOS general secretary. He began to give courses on scientific management in Rome and later helped create an institute of industrial psychology in partnership with ENIOS.[30] Two years later, Mario Spagnoli applied for and received the Premio Enios for scientific management, a subset of government funds managed by ENIOS.[31] The *concorso* prize win demonstrates the government's admiration for and approval of Perugina's approach to factory work and personnel. With this additional financial backing from the regime, Mario further transformed the plant and its work methods, ultimately making the Fontivegge factory "the most mechanized in Europe."[32]

In 1929, Mario wrote, "Do not give orders without reason, do not give advice that is not useful, do not give unwarranted punishments, and people will do what you want with zeal."[33] He published this advice in *L'organizzazione scientifica del lavoro nella grande industria alimentare*, a manual that shared the Perugina approach to factory administration with fellow technical directors. Edizioni dell'Enios, the series in which Mario's manual appeared, promoted rationalism as a general project across urban, rural, and domestic realms. Mario's contribution focused on the application of streamlined management to industrial food production (Fig. 3.15).

By implementing rationalization, Perugina's leadership set out to control each moment of the workday. At 7:40 a.m., the whistle blew and the big door to the factory swung open, along with a second set of small courtyard doors leading to the different departments of the plant. At 7:55 a.m., a second whistle signalled that the doors were closing. Employees received a fine if they were late for work, which began at 8:00 a.m. sharp. At 1:00 p.m., work stopped and all employees were to proceed to the cafeteria. Doors reopened at 1:50 p.m. and closed promptly once more at 2:00 p.m., with more whistles providing auditory signals of the time. At 5:00 p.m., work ended, and employees punched out and went to change their clothes in the locker rooms. To exit, they had to pass through a small electric machine called "L'imparziale," a machine meant to discourage chocolate theft. Each of the 500 workers pulled its lever to leave, and eight times out of one hundred a red light would flash, signalling random selection for a full search of bags and pockets.

Machines like "L'imparziale" marked the plant as modern. Additional technological innovations included the Adrema address printing machine, the Kardex order management machine (which stored and retrieved customer orders and shipments), and the Macchina Burroughs adding machine. Perhaps most notably, the Kardex machine marked employees' base pay as well as any money that they owed to the company, such as their cafeteria lunches or fines for tardy arrivals on the factory floor. Here, the application of rationalist principles to women's factory work splits along classed lines. When speaking of female factory workers, management advocated

3.15. Photograph of chocolate sorting, 1928, Perugia, Italy. Photo accession number
APA-F-011729–0000. (Archivio Alinari, Florence, Italy)

streamlining chocolate making and packaging by controlling the movements of the
human body. But in the context of middle-class bookkeeping, the role of the machines was underscored as the source of speeding progress. The savings earned for
the company by replacing bookkeepers with the new Burroughs machines sets the
importance of this issue in italics. Prior to the Burroughs, Perugina needed four employees to manage the company paybook, whereas now they only had to pay for one.

Mario set out to measure, compensate, and control factory work by combining Taylorism with technology.[34] He advocated the Bedaux system, which tabulated the exact
movements necessary to carry out a single task. The normal eight-hour day equated
to sixty Bedaux per hour, with a base pay of 1.50 lire per hour. To incentivize quick
work, additional output over this base rate meant that each worker received a bonus.
Accounts payable worked from the top down to calculate workers' earnings: every day,
each department filled out a card with the date, the names and the number of workers,
the base Bedaux hours of the worker, the base pay of the worker, the type of the work

3.16. Photograph of factory workers wrapping chocolate Easter eggs, Perugia, Italy, 1928. Photo accession number APA-F-011730–0000. (Archivio Alinari, Florence, Italy)

done, and the number of actions, giving the Bedaux value for operations done. The new system included both dictatorial surveillance and care. Every employee had a file kept on them, including their application materials: their municipal police record, Italian citizenship, and a medical certificate of health. The company also automatically generated a checking account and insurance for the employees. By the start of the 1930s, Perugina had introduced the Bedaux system into four major departments, including bonbon making (*bomboneria*), candy wrapping (*incarto caramelle*), chocolate egg wrapping (*incarto uova*) (Fig. 3.16), and hand-wrapped chocolates (*incarto cioccolato a mano*).

The fact that Perugina rationalized the packaging sections of the plant before chocolate-making sections like candy making, mixing, decoration, and miniaturization highlights the importance of the visual impact of chocolates during this period. Elegant packaging for Perugina's products went hand in hand with their identity as a luxury product. Bolognese artist and industrial designer Emma Bonazzi created the majority of Perugina's boxes, window displays, and in-store promotions. Their fame is underscored by Mario's nod to Perugina's "elegant boxes" in the introduction to his

3.17. Photograph of chocolate boxing, 1928, Perugia, Italy. Photo accession number APA-F-011731–0000. (Archivio Alinari, Florence, Italy)

book, and by the company's period ads in *Domus* as well. During the 1920s and early 1930s, Perugina's brand identity worked in concert with Bonazzi's designs. Visual presentation mattered just as much as delicious flavour, because a beautiful box provided the in-store selling point.[35] Massive production of decorative cardboard, tissue paper, and lithograph notecards also speaks to the fact that Perugina was not only a chocolate factory. It could also be considered a paper company, another central form of women's factory work during the period. The chocolate trade was bound up with paper production. Perugina went so far as to produce its own cardboard boxes in a dedicated "reparto scatolificio e lavorazione cartonaggi" (Fig. 3.17).

The Perugina Factory II: Nurseries and Cafeterias

Packaging department notwithstanding, the cafeteria might have been the most thoroughly rationalist space in the Perugina factory. Starting in 1915, the factory provided

3.18. Perugina factory women's cafeteria, 1928, Perugia, Italy. Photo accession number
APA-F-011732–0000. (Archivio Alinari, Florence, Italy)

separate cafeterias for female and male workers. In the 1920s, Luisa updated the model,
introducing folding chairs and tables to make entrance and exit easier. Seats for the 300
women and 100 men were assigned in advance. Oddly, in the new model, all diners
faced forward, as if in a movie theatre. Daily lunch evoked *The Last Supper* (Fig. 3.18).

Streamlined service also invented new culinary roles in the factory. The employee
who presided over the head of the table (*capotavola*) grabbed four autarkic aluminium
bowls at a time, with thirty-two bowls per table. After lunch, bowls were returned
the same way. Positions like the *capotavola* turned low-ranking positions of service
into high-status roles, while at the same time shifting labour from paid waiters, who
were summarily fired, onto factory employees, who were not compensated for this
additional work. A parallel reduction of culinary employment halved the kitchen staff.
To prepare the 550 portions of lunch each day, Perugina added new technologies and
autarkic materials to reduce the original crew by half, from four women to two. New
stoves ran on lignite, domestically sourced brown coal. Marble sinks included hot
water and vapour jets for dish sterilization. The overall effect created "un ambiente

3.19. Photograph of Perugina factory nursery, 1931, Perugia, Italy, in "Condizioni di vita e di lavoro nelle maggiori industrie cittadine: Fabbrica di cioccolato Perugina," *Perusia: Rassegna mensile dell'attività culturale ed amministrativa del commune di Perugia*, A. 3 fasc. 5. PER.I. E 59. (Biblioteca Augusta, Perugia, Italy)

sano e decoroso" (a healthy and decorous environment).[36] Each meal cost 2.25 lire and provided bread, wine, soup or pasta, and meat. For the price and time period, Perugina offered an excellent deal, as evidenced by the fact that the majority of employees – 350 workers out of a total of 400 – elected to purchase a hot meal on a daily basis. The remaining fifty employees reheated their homemade lunches in the kitchen's bain-marie (*un grande armadio a bagnomaria*).

In addition to rationalizing the factory cafeteria, Perugina created Italy's first large-scale breastfeeding rooms and nurseries in a private industrial setting. The *nido materno* dated from the 1920s, well before Mussolini and the state's interventions into female industrial work and breastfeeding (Fig. 3.19). The company paid for it in its entirety. This social service included stipends for its management: two female pueri-culture specialists who looked after female employees' children during factory work hours. Newborns could be placed there until age one, and nursing mothers employed on the chocolate lines could visit the room every three hours to breastfeed. After weaning, toddlers were fed "pure Buitoni products," a form of company advertisement that drew attention to the *pastina* miniature pasta line for children in the broader

Italian marketplace. Providing Buitoni pasta also meant that the children of factory workers grew up eating foods produced by the factory next door, adopting early preferences that could remain for a lifetime.[37] There was even a "scuola del buon governo della casa" (a school of good household management), where workers got advice and "ammaestramenti practici non solo sul modo di curare la casa ma anche e sopratutto sul razionale allevamento dei bambini" (practical mastery not only on how to take care of the house but above all on rational childcare).[38]

In 1927, the Direzione Tecnica at Perugina developed their successful breastfeeding room and the nursery model further, in hopes of expanding its use from Perugina factory workers to all women in the town of Fontivegge. It was at this point that Luisa Spagnoli first approached ONMI to assume part of the financial development but had to put off the project until fatter times. In the 1930s, however, the Ufficio di Assistenza Sociale expanded to include the Cassa Mutua Malattie. This program provided female employees with daily pay while sick, free medication and doctors' visits, as well as "all things necessary" for childbirth. In a truly progressive measure, the fund provided funeral expenses that included a small stipend for the female employee's surviving husband.

Perugina's factory innovations such as the breastfeeding room and the nursing breaks later entered into national law through the Fascist government's maternal welfare arm, La Cassa Nazionale Maternità, on 26 September 1941.[39] According to internal company documents, Perugina factory social welfare was done in the name of modernity and continual innovation. In other words, modernity didn't just mean machines at work, it also meant bodies after work. The Opera Nazionale Dopolavoro after-work activities were part of what made Perugina a forward-looking company during the Fascist period.[40]

Industrial Artisans: The Paradox of Cottage Industry

Apparently unlikely industries merged: throughout the 1920s and 1930s, women were chiefly working in factories that produced food, paper, and textiles. Luisa Spagnoli's projects touched all three of these industries. In addition to chocolate production and its decorative wrapping, Luisa participated in the fashion world as well. By reinvesting funds from her Perugina empire in agricultural projects and rabbit raising at her Santa Lucia villa, she founded the Azienda Agraria Spagnoli. Mario raised chickens on the property and developed new standards for *pollicoltura*. Mother and son foresaw the two key autarkic meats that would gain popularity under the sanctions. That said, Luisa's rabbit raising focused on the value of fur, not flesh. Originally, she kept the rabbits as pets, along with a monkey. As for Spagnoli's villa, located just outside of Perugia, the land continues produce agricultural foodstuffs associated with the new autarky: organic extra virgin olive oil.[41]

As early as the late 1920s, Luisa Spagnoli had already begun to breed Angora rabbits, an animal not found in Italy before her own keen interest. She worked to select and cross the different breeds and developed a particular spinning technique to wind the rabbit fur into yarn, obtaining a soft and homogenous fabric. But her true innovations were kindled from social insight: first, she understood the potential for a new type of yarn in the autarkic economy of the time. And second, she realized that, in terms of production, place and experience mattered. Spagnoli knew that rural women were accustomed to doing piecemeal work at home and that they already knew how to raise small courtyard animals to feed their families. Instead of hiring women to come to a factory every day like her urban workers, Luisa arranged for countrywomen to raise rabbits, brush their fur, and spin it into yarn in their own homes. The organization launched a cottage industry: Luisa guaranteed that rural women would have a buyer for all of the *Angora lana* they could produce, and she benefited by saving on overhead. Her economic strategy decoupled textile work from its association with urban factories and instead placed it in rural homes.

Mario Spagnoli celebrated the rabbit wool as a country product, an expression of "nostra gente rurale" (our rural people). But to be more precise, this yarn was produced by applying international industrial acumen to a country setting.[42] First, neither Angora rabbits nor their fur production methods were autochthonous to Italy. Luisa employed the French method that replaced razors with combs: instead of shaving, the rabbits were simply brushed every day. Second, to instruct countrywomen in the foreign approach to fur and yarn production, she asked among the Perugina factory workers for six or seven volunteers to travel the countryside in small groups to share the new technique.[43] In truth, both chocolate and textile production were intertwined from the start through working-class women's labour spanning city and country. We might describe this type of textile production with a paradox: they were industrial artisans.

Her artisanal lab, Angora Luisa Spagnoli, began knitting sweaters to present at expos and fairs like the eighteenth Fiera di Milano and soon attracted the interest of the government. Angora sweaters were a frequent prize in the Perugina *concorsi*. She even put angora baby bonnets and baby socks in as surprises for Perugina's chocolate Easter eggs. This one gift combined major themes: chocolate and rabbit fur promoted pronatalism under the aegis of a Catholic holiday. In fact, Spagnoli's early and influential enthusiasm for rabbit raising in the 1920s may have inspired the Fascist regime's later push for a nationwide embrace of *conigliatura* as a source of autarkic food and fabric in the 1930s.

The search for new fabrics was part of autarky. With the onset of the sanctions, many Italian companies began using organic materials – rather than less-prevalent silks and wools – to develop textiles. Artificial fabrics, a market in which Italy was dominant, ruled the runways. Rabbits were one way around this. Unlike laboratory creations like rayon or lanital, rabbits met more than one bodily need. They could be either worn or eaten. Moreover, they multiplied. By the time the regime had realized the utility of rabbits as an autarkic source of both food and fabric, Luisa had not only already commercialized her creations but had also moved ahead in her workers' assistance projects with a plan for "La casa dell'angora" ("The House of Rabbits"), a factory town with houses for workers, a nursery, a pool, and recreational structures. After Luisa's death, Mario carried forward into the clothing business. The fashion house boasted over 200 employees by 1939. They had 8,000 rabbits by 1940, enough to open the first Angora Spagnoli fashion house in Perugia that same year. Angora Spagnoli expanded rapidly, with a second location opening in Florence in 1941, then a third in Rome in 1943. Using the American chain model that Buitoni instituted at Perugina, all three stores looked alike inside, making this one of the first Italian commercial chains.[44]

Entrepreneurism in the Time of Fascism

Urban food production and rural textile production implicated a common factory model. Women did both types of work and required working conditions that created space for the reproductive female body. This could mean either adding nurseries and breastfeeding rooms in a factory or simply allowing women to work from home. To be a successful female entrepreneur in early twentieth-century Italy was indeed exceptional. Perugina and Luisa Spagnoli – like Delia Notari and others to come – are case studies in how one could succeed under such conditions. Spagnoli, for her part, was an exceptional entrepreneur who invested in her personnel. She also invited Benito Mussolini to visit Perugina. There is quite a bit of Fascist history here: After Mussolini visited the chocolate factory, it benefited from rationing in the army, while rabbits seized on the autarkic moment. The Perugina archive does not hide these details – indeed, it does an excellent job in demonstrating how the time period informed company history. It is Luisa Spagnoli's relationship with Fascism that makes her such a complex figure. An entrepreneur and an opportunist, she identified the move towards alimentary autarky and addressed it with her chocolate products. She used pronatalism as a means to pitch social services for her personnel. She cultivated Mussolini as a company advocate. Put broadly, she interpreted the regime's ideology and then used those insights to promote her company. In other words, she was a scholar of Fascism. What's more, in some cases she may have anticipated the regime's goals, in creating social programs for breastfeeding and supporting industrial women workers' needs before they became Fascist projects. It is even quite possible that Mussolini borrowed and then modified some of her ideas during his 1923 visit to the factory before introducing them in his famous 1927 Ascension Day speech.

This chapter has examined Luisa Spagnoli's industrial innovations within their historical context to reveal the full political complexity and ambiguity of the actions necessary both to become and then to remain a successful female entrepreneur during the Fascist period. As the sole woman to ascend to such entrepreneurial heights, she was assumed to have an insider's perspective on the female mind and body. After her death, Luisa's idea of women's production as being framed within their reproduction lived on. First her son Mario and then her grandson Lino were able to bring all of her plans to fruition. Many of Luisa Spagnoli's early, factory-based models for breast-feeding rooms and industrial-scale maternal care were modified to increase state control over the reproductive female body.

Luisa and Perugina are emblematic of how industrializing and rationalizing took the country in a corporatocratic direction and led to more state policing of the body, both industrially and domestically. Luisa's work married the two when she introduced mutually beneficial programs for the mothers in her factories, making her a figure that's easy to exalt from both a progressive and a Fascist point of view. Under Fascism, urban female workers fed the nation through their factory work, not only by producing food but also by producing breastmilk. This was true even beyond food factories. With no temporal or spatial interval between its production and consumption, breastmilk appears to be that rare food that lies beyond the reach of government interference. Yet the powerful biological exchange inherent in breastfeeding proved too enticing for the regime to ignore. All foods shape the body, but ONMI films, newsreels, and periodicals insisted that breastmilk possessed the unique capacity to create the mind and spirit of the developing infant as well.

More and better breastmilk promised to minimize infant mortality while fortifying the national body, a key plank in the regime's platform for demographic control of the Italian populous. Recognizing how this food could promote their party's pronatalist goals, the Fascist regime approached breastmilk with economic, autarkic, and biopolitical considerations in mind. But the physical closeness of breastfeeding posed a problem. With no space between breast and mouth, there appeared to be no room for government inference. To resolve this paradox, the regime elected to work around, rather than inside, the nutritional exchange between mother and infant. Specifically, the Fascist state assumed control of breastfeeding's location, its physical context within the built environment. In the end, ONMI propaganda served to naturalize a factory-like vision of women's healthcare by casting breastfeeding and childbirth as forms of mass production belonging to the state. By framing their interference as support for working-class women, Fascism found an insidiously overarching way to control bodies and their growth through breastfeeding.

CHAPTER FOUR

RECIPES FOR EXCEPTIONAL TIMES

As middle-class women began to take on more of the cooking work that had previously been associated with the working class, the need to mediate and define the public and private zones of the home became increasingly acute. During this period, a servant crisis appeared to pull all classed labour in the home downward: middle-class women became working-class cooks, and working-class cooks were replaced by appliances. As Mark Mazower quipped, "Between the wars, middle-class homes in much of Europe still had maid's quarters to house the dishwasher."[1] The resulting class anxiety caused by the threatened drop in middle-class women's social status led to new types of furniture that promised to define and defend the border zone between a homemaker's working-class kitchen labour and her middle-class dinner conversations with her family.

The very title of Lidia Morelli's text, *Dalla Cucina al Salotto* (*From the Kitchen to the Salon*), encapsulates a dynamic narrative insofar as it evokes movement from one state to another, from the vulgarity of the private kitchen to the urbanity of the relatively more public salon. Morelli begins her consideration of the household in the kitchen before moving into the dining room and elsewhere. This order is counterintuitive given her acknowledgment of the relative social esteem accorded to both spaces, the salon being "un luogo ridente, pulito, elegante" (a laughing, clean, elegant place) and the kitchen being "semibuio, grigio, e disordinato" (half-darkened, grey, and disorganized). She goes on to describe the horror of sitting in the parlour, catching the nauseating admixture of the sweet vanilla scent of a charlotte tart with cabbage, cauliflower, and fried onions. For Morelli, it is not just the smell of fried onions, that most universal and humble of foods, but rather the fact that their odour contaminates the upper-class food smells of French pastry and expensive vanilla. More importantly, these foods call attention to the shared tastes of the upper and working class: even the elegant *signora* enjoyed cabbage, cauliflower, and other vegetables associated with *la cucina povera*.[2]

In addition to smells, sounds threatened these distinctions due to their ability to travel across architectural borders. As Morelli's tone indicates, the stink of garlic and the

4.1. Passapiatti by Ignazio Gardella, with Albini, Camus,
Clausetti, Mazzoleni, Minoletti, Mucchi, Palanti, and
Romano. In Ignazio Gardella's "I servizi della casa: La
cucina," *Domus*, January 1939: 56–9.

clatter of dishes were a threat because
they travelled easily across the physical
boundaries between the kitchen and
the salon, revealing the permeability
of social separations in the home. Morelli characterizes both the kitchen and
cooking as inherently dirty and thus in
need of surveillance to maintain a suit-
able level of hygiene. Morelli goes so
far as to recommend that women wear
"una tunica simile a quella d'infermiera,
che la guerra fece entrare quasi in ogni
casa" (a tunic like those worn by nurses,
that the war pushed into almost every
house). This garment, accompanied by a
white cap also modelled on nurses' garb,
promoted hygiene by dint of being
easily washable and because its odour-
absorbing capacity protected one from
nausea. Using the colour white also en-
abled an instant, material surveillance
of the kitchen's cleanliness. This move
suggests that the kitchen functioned as
a sort of clinic, where self-surveillance
could monitor and sterilize cooking
work.

The greatest architectural minds of the day came together to confront kitchen
smells and noise. At the Mosta dell'Abitazione alla VI Triennale in Milan, they finally unveiled their solution. A bi-fronted storage wall between kitchen and dining
room provided a newly reimagined form of architectural border work: the *passapiatti*
(Fig. 4.1).

For the remainder of the 1930s, interior designers mediated the tension of the
kitchen/salon divide with a new focus on the older furniture form of the *passapiatti*.[3]
As its name suggests, the *passapiatti* originally served as an intermediate semi-open
shelving unit where plated meals would be passed from the kitchen to the salon and
dirty dishes would be passed back from the salon to the kitchen. In other words,
the *passapiatti* is a furniture form specifically designed to mediate the social separations and labour-based connections of different genders and classes within the home.
Nineteenth-century *passapiatti* acted as lazy Susans: finished products came out of
the kitchen, but the cook and the sounds and smells created as by-products stayed
in. This early version separated different social groups almost completely, save for the

direct results of food production (cooked meals) and consumption (dirty dishes). But what to do when the cook belongs in the salon as well as the kitchen, as with the new housewife's role?

As articles in the architecture magazine *Domus* indicate, designers believed that redesigning the *passapiatti* would provide an architectural solution to the perceived problem of middle-class women's drop in social status within the home as they began to take on working-class cooking work. In an early attempt at creating a new form of *passapiatti*, the writers of *Domus* actually suggested placing the breakfast table, as well as the traditional semi-open shelving unit, across the kitchen and the dining room:

> Nel mobile divisorio è praticata un'apertura la quale i due locali, all'ora di pranzo, comunicano: ma non si tratta di un commune passapiatti. Sul basso dell'apertura corre il piano del tavolo, che resta metà in cucina e metà nel soggiorno. La disposizione è opportunissima perchè consente alla signora di sorvegliare i fornelli senza doversi continuamente alzare e restando in compagnia col resto della famiglia come se fossero tutti nella stessa stanza. Finita la colazione, l'apertura vien chiusa e il soggiorno è completamente libero.

> Part of the dividing furniture consists of an opening in which the two spaces, at dinner time, communicate: but this is not a normal *passapiatti*. Below the opening runs a tabletop, which rests half in the kitchen and half in the living room. The arrangement is very advantageous because it allows the lady to monitor the burners without her having to continuously get up and staying in the company of the rest of the family as though they were all in the same room. When lunch is finished, the opening is closed and the living room is completely free.[4]

But of course, communicating across the invisible wall between kitchen and salon is not the same as sitting together in the same room. As the article's photo (Fig. 4.2) demonstrates, this *passapiatti* seats the family together at the same table but divides its members across two rooms: the woman eats in the kitchen and her family in the living room. Even in its celebration of this new "dividing furniture," the authors admit that, at best, the family eats together "as though" they were in the same room. In other words, this *passapiatti* responded to the problem of middle-class women's newly unclear social status by dividing a single family into two different social classes, effectively demoting the middle-class woman to working-class status. Granted, the boundary-spanning table does allow her to eat with her family. But could husband and wife have looked each other in the eyes? Dishes seem to block the way – the *piatti* of the *passapiatti* block all possible communication, relegating the middle-class woman to a new working-class space (the kitchen) and role (the cook).

4.2. "Un tipico ambiente utilitario" (A typical utilitarian environment), kitchen photograph. Gio Ponti, *Domus*, January 1936: 70. The caption reads "La cucina. Si osservi la sistemazione del tavolo."

Merging Home and Home Front

Peeping through the *passapiatti* demonstrates how entrepreneurial domestic experts like Lidia Morelli manoeuvred through the tabletop politics of the Fascist period. Against the backdrop of Domus's and Bemporad's publishing house dramas, this nimble author successfully negotiated the competing calls of the regime (for autarkic promotion), their publishers (for numerous editions), their advertisers (for product placements), and their audience (for practical advice). Her media contributions extended across newspapers (*La Stampa*), magazines (*La Casa Bella*, which later became *Casabella*), cookbooks, and almanacs. She even had her own radio show, the ironically titled Florentine program "Abbassa la tua radio, per favore" (Turn down your radio, please). So why did Morelli become as popular as a movie star right after Mussolini marched on Rome? Why did the trajectory of public interest in these kitchen experts so closely mirror a darker trend, that of the population's cresting enthusiasm for the Fascist regime?

Over the arc of the *ventennio*, Morelli developed her blend of industry interests and government policy into a personal brand, allying herself with alimentary autarky with titles like *Le Massaie Contro le Sanzioni* (1935), *Le Massaie e l'autarchia* (1937), and *La Vita Sobria* (1941). Financial and political benefits fused: Morelli's publications for Cirio used the rhetoric of patriotism to promote the tinned tomato company that paid her bills. Cirio and other food-canning companies flourished during the 1930s.[5] But Morelli also continued to promote Cirio in government-financed

4.3. Cover of Lidia Morelli's *Dalla Cucina al Salotto: Enciclopedia della Vita Domestica* (Turin: S. Lattes, 1935).

publications, such as her household guides for the Società Reale Mutua di Assicurazione, the Fascist government insurance provider. In addition to the Cirio cookbook, Morelli produced multiple editions of *Cirio per la casa*, Cirio's annual almanac, which was meant to instruct both middle- and working-class women in household management while promoting Cirio's canned vegetables.

To promote autarkic eating, Morelli introduced the 1935 reprint of her popular housekeeping manual *Dalla Cucina al Salotto: Enciclopedia della Vita Domestica* (Fig. 4.3) by addressing how the sanctions affected the vocabulary she could and couldn't use in her book. Speaking to "the readers of today" in a note dated 18 November 1935, she asserts that words such as *marmitta norvegese, salsa ginevrina, sformato inglese, pagnottine scozzesi,* baking powder, bridge, and *tè alle cinque* were perfectly permissible "quando un vocabolario estero non voleva dire 'appartenente a Stato ostile e sanzionista'" (when foreign words didn't mean "belonging to a hostile, sanctionist

State"). In other words, Morelli classified all foreign elements of cookery, from phrases to habits to foods, as outdated. Her stance towards this attitudinal change is one of consent: she casts the situation as one of moral choice for the housewife, thus elevating the stakes of Italian food purchases ("Questo tempo di 'sanzioni' ha veramente un alto valore morale, del quale dobbiamo compiacerci" [This time of "sanctions" has a high moral value, of which we must satisfy].). Directly connecting linguistic autarky with autarkic cooking, Morelli claims to be pleased ("sono la prima a rallegrarmi che questo abbia fine" [I am the first to delight in the fact that this has happened]) that these types of linguistic shifts not only resulted in the "innocent rebaptizing" of certain food terms but also led to newly positive attitudes towards Italian products, like tomatoes, and the farming, canning, and metal industries that surrounded them.

Morelli was not alone: an adroit cookbook cohort comprising Ada Boni and Amalia Moretti Foggia, along with lesser-known writers like Erminia Macerati, Vanna Piccini, and Maria Diez Gasca, personalized national struggles to fit into everyday practices of autarkic cooking. These authors, as well as magazine editors like Delia Notari (*La Cucina Italiana*) and architects like Piero Bottoni and Ignazio Gardella, turned abstract ideas like economy and productivity into concrete cooking actions such as frying onions, sifting flour, and stirring a bubbling pot of polenta. Here, we see how authors translated autarky into Italian foods and recipes. In the next chapter, "Model Fascist Kitchens," we will see how architects translated autarky into Italian materials and design forms. In both cases, not only the object but also the method had to be Italian to qualify as autarkic. For example, Foggia's 1942 *Ricette di Petronilla per tempi eccezionali* (*Petronilla's Recipes for Exceptional Times*) notes the shift from English to Italian terms: "Una volta si chiamava roast beef, ma che ora venne italianamente battezzato in arrosto al sangue" (Once it was called roast beef but now it has been rebaptized in an Italian way as roast blood-style).

Turning the constraints of the sanctions into a personal challenge for her readers, Morelli notes her regret that certain recipes do not evoke the recent turn towards autarky in the kitchen:

Meglio sarebbero se più adatte ai tempi, se semplificate o cambiate, secondo un regime fatto più severo. Ma confido nel buon senso, nell'ingegnosità delle lettrici per una scelta sensata, per una sostituzione razionale … e razionata.

It would be better if [these recipes were] more adapted to the times, simplified or changed, according to a regime that has become stricter. But I rely on the good sense, on the ingenuity of the readers for a sensible choice, for a rational, and rationed, substitution.[6]

Whether these were truly Morelli's opinions or she merely felt compelled to perform obeisance in this public text matters less than the fact of this text's overwhelming popularity. Morelli's articulation of linguistic questions delineates them as less important than kitchen methods and market choices; this action casts autarky for the *massaia* as a set of practices grounded in the material world. Linguistic changes from *sandwich* to *tramezzino* merely herald the more substantive decision to prepare the sandwich with chicken rather than prosciutto.

Ada Boni goes so far as to open her book by framing the promotion of Italian cuisine as a form of culinary nation-building. Immediately following her letter to her readers, Boni provides an "Elogio alla Cucina Italiana," an essay framing international French and regional Italian cookery as a contested culinary binary. While the French have been, she claims, more successful at exporting their cuisine, Italian regional specialties rival the French in their exquisite flavours and variety. A rhapsody to the geese of Northern Italy and a paean to the pheasants, turkeys, pigeons, and poultry of Tuscany pave the way for her critique: we do not lament the Bresse chickens or capons of Mans. Like Morelli and Foggia, Boni suggests that any disparity between Italian food and the more celebrated French cuisine arose from the traditions of culinary language. To raise Italy's culinary status, she argues that women must list ingredients in Italian, and not in other languages: "In Italia si deve cucinare dappertutto all'italiana e ci si deve adoperare a far conoscere questo nostro patrimonio agli italiani prima, e poi agli stranieri" (In Italy one must cook first in an Italian style, and one must set oneself to introducing our patrimony to Italians first, and then to foreigners). They seem to be much in need of her advice, for not only had the French more successfully exported their cuisine, but Americans had begun to cook Italian food … badly. In American houses, she confesses, they prepare spaghetti in sauce already cooked and preserved in cans and boxes – "cibo da non augurarsi neanche al peggior nemico!" (food not to wish even on your worst enemy!).

Boni promoted De Cecco pasta as part of her larger regional preferences for Central Italian ingredients, recipes, and even food companies. She did not receive any pay from the company. In these recipes, pairing promotion of autarky, a Fascist policy, with private food companies like Cirio and De Cecco buttressed arguments for cooking with domestically, and in some cases locally, farmed and manufactured foods. By contrast, Morelli's motives in supporting alimentary autarky did include financial considerations. Still other authors came to the same conclusions for personal reasons. Italian foods, Italian words, and Italian preparations: Boni's culinary project fully supports domestic economic policy, without a single utterance of the word "autarky."

But in this celebration of domestic meats and vegetables, what is missing? As this chapter demonstrates, reading cookbooks against the grain teaches as much about the social history of the Fascist kitchens as it does about their political history. Morelli, Notari, and Macerati recommend raising chickens and rabbits, and they provide numerous recipes. But not one of them describes the outdoors work involved, such as how to build henhouses or hutches.[7] Although all three celebrate kitchen garden produce and the virtues of gardening, none explain how to sow a plot. Perhaps they did not know how, given their urban middle- and upper-class backgrounds. Writers, editors, and educators like Morelli, Notari, and Macerati may have focused on and elevated the importance of cooking and eating because of their familiarity with these realms, occluding the working-class women's work in gardens, courtyards, and fields that produced their ingredients.[8]

What united this disparate group of domestic experts was a common belief: all drew a conceptual connection between the kitchen and the domestic economy, a narrative strategy that elevated individual actions to the national stage. In this space, housekeeping manuals and shelter magazines framed home as the home front. The cookbook authors took different paths to the same destination. Autarky provided Morelli, Boni, and Macerati with convenient labels for their project. In other words, they used political trends to argue for culinary ideas, rather than the other way around. In fact, Morelli's constant negotiation and renegotiation with politics lies at the heart of the tabletop politics of the Fascist kitchen. Morelli was a public figure under the dictatorship, and her career reveals the types of dilemmas and choices that middle-class professional women made under Fascism. Her politics, like her recipes, reveal a practical and culinary bent, one that uses politics when convenient. By understanding both her assertions and her compromises, we can better glean the mechanisms – the daily sayings, jokes, assertions, and denials – that people used to deal with the Fascist environment.

The writers' range of attitudes towards autarky and their audience, itself a mix of classes and political affiliations, demonstrates that almost no publication found cooking autarkically to be a worthy project for patriotic motives alone. National service through cooking had to be coupled with a personal motive. Although these authors employ the rhetoric of the state, their domestic tips deviate from directly supporting its policies. Hygiene becomes cleanliness. Rationalism becomes practicality. But more often, we see that middle-class female cookbook authors' celebration of autarky evokes the recital of a Fascist script. Consequences, rather than intentionality, matter most to these authors: they made strident claims for their support of Fascist food policy in theory, an effective defence for deflecting regime interference in the private sphere of their practice. At first glance these cookbooks appear to bow to the regime's policies through what gender historian Andrea Newlyn has termed "explicit emblems of women's relegation to the domestic sphere."[9] But at the same time, they often convey ambivalence to Fascist politics. These sections undermine the propagandistic claim that women were filled with desire to adopt autarkic cooking to aid the national economy. What we see could be more specifically termed performative consent, in that the writers perform a somewhat unconvincing obeisance to regime dictates. These authors employ the rhetoric of autarky more as a rhetorical flourish or stylistic move to introduce or conclude recipes than as a justification for creating such dishes. Building on the work of previous scholars of Fascist cooking practices who have depicted productive work as the "cooking of consent," we might refer to this as the "cooking of convenience."[10]

To illuminate how these different voices coalesced as an ongoing conversation across different types of publications, this chapter examines the professional trajectories of three authors and the narrative structures of their cookbooks and housekeeping guides: Lidia Morelli's *Dalla Cucina al Salotto: Enciclopedia dalla Vita Domestica* and *La casa che vorrei avere*, Amalia Moretti Foggia's *Ricette di Petronilla* series, and Ada Boni's encyclopedic *Il Talismano della Felicità* (*The Talisman of Happiness*, 1928).[11] Writ broadly, the group could also include Maria Diez Gasca (*Cucine di ieri e cucine di domani* [Kitchens of Yesterday and Tomorrow], 1928), Elisabetta Randi (*La cucina autarchica* [Autarkic Cooking], 1942, and *A cucina del tempo di Guerra* [Cooking in the Time of War], 1943), and Erminia Macerati (*Casa Nostra* [Our House], 1942). But Morelli, Foggia, and Boni composed the core trinity: they were the most influential homemaking experts of the Fascist period and stood at the forefront of the larger group of authors and educators. Morelli's publication record alone topped thirty titles by the time of Italy's entry into the Second World War. Boni's *Il Talismano della Felicità* remains in print today: the seventh and most recent edition appeared in 1999. Petronilla, Foggia's pseudonym, has become a byword for Fascist-period cookery at large.[12] Undeterred by the League of Nations sanctions, these women produced an immensely popular body of work on practical homemaking, one that exemplified the home economics interests of a larger group of urban middle-class female writers in Italy.[13]

Paths to Professionalization for Cookbook Authors

In terms of professional backgrounds, academic interests, and approaches to both their own celebrity and publication, this group shared a number of commonalities. Early in their publishing careers, many women used pen names to sign the first, turn-of-the-century editions of their housekeeping guides. It was at the height of the Fascist period that their writings on household management rose in popularity and prominence: only then did Doctor Amal and Petronilla reveal herself to be one, female author, Amalia Moretti Foggia, Lunella de Seta admit to being Elisabetta Randi, and Donna Clara unveil her given name of Lidia Morelli. That said, while the women's popularity might be directly linked to the rise of Fascism, their use of pseudonyms can likely be explained by gender-related professionalism issues operating independently of Fascism; likewise, their decision to drop their pseudonyms is primarily indicative of their increased authority once popular. Cookbook authors' shift from pseudonymous attribution to given names spoke to a larger shift in professional identity: the timing of this change typically coincided with a decision to leave their former careers behind to devote their full energies to writing and journalism. Many taught in primary and secondary schools while writing and cooking in the evenings before becoming full-time authors.[14]

What did the path to professionalization look like for popular female writers in Fascist Italy? Reformers, male and female alike, constantly had to contend with and were often frustrated by the Fascist hierarchy, as Victoria De Grazia has observed. So how did these authors manage their highly public writing in the dangerously politicized realms of publishing and journalism? How did the cohort climb against and through government dictates?

Both Morelli and Macerati took a circuitous route to cookbook writing, beginning their careers in education: Erminia Macerati was a home economics teacher working in the tiny Alpine town of Vergeletto in the Valle Orsenone and a proponent for obligatory home economics courses for female students. She began her career at age twenty-one as an elementary school teacher in Brissago, where she worked from 1892 until 1901. In 1902, supported by the Department of Public Education and the Società Demopedeutica, she attended the school of home economics in Neuchâtel and began independent explorations into other home economics schools throughout Switzerland. She helped to found the Associazione "La Scuola," a group of liberal educators. Then, in 1903, she organized her first home economics course in Ticino, work that later qualified her to be the *docente superiore* of home economics in the Scuola Professionale Femminile of Lugano.

Similarly, Morelli worked as a secondary school instructor of linguistics and literature until the popularity of her columns made it possible for her to stop teaching part-time in order to write full-time. She soon became a public personality in her own right. Boni taught cooking classes in Rome and founded the magazine *Preziosa* in 1915 to share her lessons with a wider readership. Long afterward, this professional background in education continued to shape Foggia's, Boni's, and Morelli's publishing choices in a politically meaningful way: in addition to their cookbooks, they also generated a broad body of home economics materials aimed at working-class girls. Morelli wrote numerous pedagogical titles for use in public middle schools, including *Massaie di domani: Conversazioni di economia domestica per le scuole secondarie di avviamento professionale a tipo industriale femminile* (*Housewives of Tomorrow: Conversations in Home Economics for Secondary Schools for Professional Development for Women's Industrial Work*, 1942) and *Case e bambini: Conversazioni di economia domestica per le alunne della terza classe della scuola media* (*Homes and Children: Conversations in Home Economics for Third-Year Middle School Students*, 1943).[15] Maria Diez Gasca also wrote a number of textbooks for home economics courses in public schools, including her 1930 magnum opus, *Le donne e la casa: Le scuole di educazione e di economia domestica in Italia e all'estero, a cura di un comitato promotore per le scuole operaie femminili di educazione e di economia domestica nelle fabbriche*, which focused on the role and teaching of home economics in the larger context of Italian industry.

Diez Gasca's work was so successful, both in Italy and in Switzerland, that Swiss National Exhibition for Women's Work (known by the acronym SAFA) requested a presentation of her findings and named her to the directors' commission of Educatore della Svizzera Italiana in 1929. A single copy of *Le donne e la casa* would be used to teach a class of up to forty students. So although these authors' books for the middle class have been heralded for their popularity, publishing statistics alone cannot capture the massive extent of these writers' influence. Put simply, we must consider not only how many books were published in total but also how widely each individual copy was circulated.

At stake in this common background in education, and in home economics specifically, lay intersecting issues of bids for liberal social movements for domestic reform addressed through Fascist policies of *risanamento* (reclamation) and hyperproductivity. In other words, home economics, born of the political Left, took on a series of socially conservative characteristics by dint of the surrounding political climate. With a closer look, Italian home economics reveals bids by middle- and upper-class women for greater influence and power in a time of gendered suppression.

As with Margarete Schütte-Lihotzky's Frankfurt kitchens, Morelli and her cohort promoted laudable goals through practical means, like reusing coffee grounds to fertilize home gardens or saving chicken bones to decrease waste and make a better broth. But at the same time, these domestic guides also reveal that in many cases women took on additional power not by arguing with their male counterparts but by barging into working-class women's homes. Through prescriptive texts, pedagogical courses, and state-sanctioned visits, many of these women gained influence by compounding the oppression of those with even less power than themselves rather than by fighting with those above them. These types of exploitation are typical of class, but I contend that they are also politically inflected. Domestic interventions, couched in the liberal rhetoric of home economics, intensified under Fascism because the regime supported increased surveillance of the working class. Moreover, these writers used home economics as a means to promote the Fascist goal of domestic hyperproductivity. By studying the exploitative applications of liberal domestic reform in a Fascist climate, we can better understand how good intentions were applied to grim purposes and avoid repeating such errors.

Home economics and Fascism politics paralleled one another in popularity at least partially due to their common concerns. In both cases, dictating how to perform cooking and cleaning in the kitchen promised to promote autarky and class control by working through the private sphere. This is not to say, however, that all household management booklets were really Fascist tracts in disguise. Correlation, not causation, bound the two. And this link was not limited to Italy: Fascism rose in Spain and Nazism in Germany, and, less obviously, home economics rose internationally as well.

Domestic science began as an American specialty. It emerged as a formal discipline with the Morrill Act of 1862, which created new departments, courses, and syllabi at American land-grant colleges and universities, most famously at Cornell University, to educate farm wives in running their households while their husbands were being educated in agricultural methods and processes. While this trend began in the United States, it quickly moved outward thanks to Catharine Beecher's courses and publications on the science of running a household. Beecher's popularity, and that of home economics, crossed national boundaries as well: although she published her landmark readers in the mid- to late-1800s, her books were published in German, French, and Spanish during the 1930s and 1940s.

Home economics rose not in response to Fascism but in response to a series of broader social changes: working-class women began to leave domestic service for higher-paying factory work, leading to what was popularly known as the "servant crisis." The women who remained engaged in these forms of labour were poor indeed. As Victoria De Grazia has observed, "Domestic work was so ill-reputed for its harshness, isolation, and humiliations that few went into service if they could find other work." Middle-class women now had to cook and clean their own kitchens for the first time, creating a market for domestic how-to manuals. For these women, this change created class anxiety: If they had to work in the kitchen when their mothers did not, were they the new working class? Home economics provided one possible solution, raising the social status of feminine cooking by classifying it as masculine science.

That said, despite the cookbook cohort's frequent references to the servant crisis, in Italy, female domestic workers remained cheap and abundant during the Fascist period. Even at the lowest edge of the middle class, the wives of minor bureaucrats would still hire women at hourly rates (*donne a ore*) to help on laundry day. Willson notes the difficulty in determining the total number of women in domestic service at any given time, due to the high rate of turnover and the changing definitions of which occupations are defined as domestic service, but she puts the number at 482,080 total workers, 83.2 per cent of them female, in 1901. Yet, across Europe, and in Italy too, many bourgeois women complained that industrialization was creating a shortage of servants, inflating the wages of those who remained in service.[16] Government censuses held their ranks to have increased from 381,100 in 1921 to 585,000 in 1936 due to rural exodus and the scarcity of factory and clerical jobs.[17]

Shared interest in spreading the gospel of home economics through recipe writing and kitchen management brought Italian educators like Diez Gasca, Morelli, Foggia, and Macerati together, ultimately transforming them into popular writers and cultural figures. Several friendships bloomed out of reading: one woman would read another's work and then write an admiring letter, sparking an ongoing exchange of ideas. After an extended written conversation, they began to collaborate by contributing small pieces to each other's collections or by editing one another's books. Morelli and Macerati followed this exact order of social connection, establishing a friendly professional rapport that supported the publication of Macerati's *Casa Nostra: Trattato di economia domestica*, for which Morelli served as both a secondary editor and content contributor.

The example of Morelli and Macerati's developing relationship as friends and colleagues reveals how culinary ideas travelled not only from pen to paper but from woman to woman. These authors enjoyed warm professional relationships with established men as well. As I will discuss in the next chapter, Morelli regularly worked with male-dominated architectural periodicals like *Domus* and *La bella casa*. She used kitchen plans and layouts from their architects and designers in her domestic guides, and they in turn published her essays and financed her almanacs for working-class women. In her expansive work across *Domus*'s masthead, from their pricey architectural periodicals to their thrifty almanacs, Morelli exemplified how many kitchen thinkers worked at the time and how pervasive their influence was. It also demonstrates how middle-class women served as gatekeepers for upper-class men's ideas: Morelli's star power enhanced Ignazio Gardella's fame among middle- and working-class women. His articles for *Domus* and *La bella casa* often reached women via Morelli's media savvy and her omnipresence in almanacs and radio programs. Looking at Morelli, Gardella, and Piero Bottoni as members of a common kitchen conversation reveals which domestic designs emerged during the 1930s and how they evoke the period's evolving inter-class relations. But even more interestingly, this also shows how trends travelled across different social groups during the Fascist period. The theme of kitchens and cooking united authors across publishing genre boundaries, both at the level of the publication and at the level of individual authors.

La Cucina Italiana published articles on kitchen architecture, and *Domus* published recipes. Starting in 1935, *Domus* ran a recurring feature on regional cooking so as to provide a "gustoso giro d'Italia" (a delicious tour of Italy). As *Domus*'s offices were in Milan, it is perhaps unsurprising that the inaugural column opened with the rice- and cream-based dishes of the north, like risotto alla milanesa and il riso in cagnon. Recipes assumed a family of six and an autarkic diet largely based on rice and vegetables. Although couched as an elegant recipe due to its garnishes (truffle, parmesan cheese) and spices (saffron), risotto alla milanesa could also find a place on a working-class Sunday table. The main ingredients needed – rice, onions, cream, white wine, beef extract – were widely accessible, as were the dishes and tools required: a casserole dish, a wooden spoon, and a ladle. The next recipe, il riso in cagnon, is even more economical, consisting of rice, salt, and butter. And the third recipe in the article features a cheap protein from the "fifth quarter." Two kilograms of tripe, prepared with onion, clove, celery, carrot, pork cheek, tomatoes, beans, cabbage, potatoes, pepper, and breadcrumbs in butter, would be a very economical dish for a family of six, as one could add more vegetables to compensate for a lack of meat. The fourth dish presented is minestrone: once again, we return to rice and vegetables. Granted, the article does go on to describe more expensive meat dishes like costoletta alla milanese and ossobuco alla gremolata and pricey pastry like panettone, but the article's order deemphasizes these costly dishes. Cheap autarkic ingredients like rice and vegetables predominate.[18]

In a similar example of brilliant networking across industry lines, Foggia obtained her post at *La Domenica del Corriere* thanks to the invitation of the newspaper's director, Carlo Zanicotti. Foggia's dedication of her second cookbook to Zanicotti suggests that he mentored her turn towards journalism even as she continued to practise medicine. The frontispiece to *Altre ricette di Petronilla* presents Zanicotti and Foggia in miniature, questing across the newsroom-cum-stovetop, moving forward through the flames. "Per Carlo Zanicotti, che mi ha battezzata e che mi guida 'tra i fornelli' della *Domenica del Corriere*" (For Carlo Zanicotti, who baptized me and who guides me "between the burners" of the *Domenica del Corriere*). This metaphor blends the biblical and the lyrical, casting Zanicotti as the Virgil to Foggia's Dante. As this allusion suggests, these cookbooks contained vibrant literary worlds that defied the categories of high and low culture: we need look no further than Foggia's female doctor Dante, braving the hellfires of Milanese journalism. Her path from the Bunsen burners of the University of Padua to her recipe column "Tra i Fornelli" (Between the burners) at *La Domenica del Corriere* is noteworthy as it highlights the astounding professional acumen that these women executed to bring their visions of food, health, and cooking to the Italian public.

Amalia Moretti Foggia came from a long line of Mantovese pharmacists, but she graduated with a science degree in 1895 and then continued her studies in the esteemed school of medicine at the University of Bologna, funded by a 1,000 lire scholarship. She successfully defended her degree with a dissertation on women's reproductive health, focusing on her clinical research seeking the cure for peritonitis of the ovaries. Foggia then briefly moved to Florence to practise in a paediatric clinic before settling in Milan.

Arriving in Milan with only 500 lire to her name, she found professional and social support amongst a group of fellow feminists: Alessandrina Ravizza, Paolina Schiff, Linda Malnati, and Ersilia Maino.[19] Maino was critical to Foggia's success, as she helped her to secure a position in medicine at the Società Operaia femminile. Here, Foggia worked on a number of hygiene initiatives, including the fight against tuberculosis.

In 1902, she was hired as a doctor for the hospital Poliambulanza di Porta Venezia, where she would work for the next forty years. That year, she also married her husband, fellow doctor and Venetian citizen Domenico Della Rovere, whose presence peeps through her many culinary publications. In a lovely and consistent detail, Foggia's treatment of Venetian recipes consistently evokes, but never names, her husband and the cuisine of his regional origins in northeastern Italy. No other recipes ally geography with matrimony. But across all four of her major cookbooks, Foggia always opens the Veneto recipes in the same way: she professes a personal ignorance of the area's cuisine but then complements its economy and its good taste. In a nod to marriage that both hides and highlights her own, she goes on to say, "If you have a husband from the Veneto, here is a dish for risi e bisi that will delight." In this cyclical narrative introduction to the northeastern recipes, one can almost hear Foggia and Della Rovere at the table together, slurping their peas and rice.

Midway through her medical career, during the 1920s, Foggia also began to write a medical advice column for the popular illustrated newspaper *La Domenica del Corriere*, under the male pseudonym Doctor Amal. She soon took on other columns under other pseudonyms: "La massaia scrupulosa" (the scrupulous housewife) offered advice in home economics, and, most famously, the column on cooking for health that provided the recipe base for her future books, "Tra i Fornelli," she penned as "Petronilla."

As newspaper columns were collected into cookbooks, they seemed to presage a larger trend towards incorporating home economics into daily meal planning. But their scientific modernity obscured the inner workings of the home: in reality, most Italian bourgeois households maintained nineteenth-century patterns of domestic labour well into the late 1930s and early 1940s. Urban kitchens were the most common female workspace by far, and they had their own forms and norms of labour practices and payment for processing raw goods for consumption. An entire sub-economy revolved around cooks' salaries and housewives' invisible labour. After all, the majority of the family budget went towards food. In *Dalla Cucina al Salotto*, Lidia Morelli provides an intriguing illustration that divides middle-class household costs by months of work required for their payment. Food requires four and a half months of the yearly salary, whereas the second-most expensive bill, rent, requires only two.

In Italy, the swelling population of city centres did not keep pace with desirable job opportunities, and this dearth meant that a middle-class Italian woman could hire a full-time servant fairly easily. Wealthier *signore* could create a more elegant impression by hiring two women, a cook and a maid, rather than one *tutto fare* (woman of all trades). The poor labour market meant that employers could largely dictate the terms of work contracts with domestic workers, or with their fathers in the case of very young women. These factors were notably not in play in the United States and Great Britain, two nations where the servant crisis did assume measurable demographic significance with the onset of industrialization. However, because Macerati, Diez Gasca, and other members of the cookbook cohort took their cues from Anglophone home economics experts, they may have directly translated these foreign problems into their domestic manuals and then later simply continued with the party line because a perceived servant crisis provided a great push for their middle-class readership to buy cookbooks.

Narrating the Food Sanctions

This next section shifts from the professional trajectories of cookbook authors to the content of the cookbooks they wrote to investigate how different women felt about cooking, and about one another, against the politicized backdrop of the first wave of patriotic food sanctions and then later under the darkening clouds of wartime. From the early 1920s, fear of social class shifts and the mere perception of a servant crisis were sufficient to create a market for cookbooks amongst the middle class, who previously had not considered cooking.

Examining the introductory sections of Morelli's, Boni's, and Foggia's cookbooks reveals the complexity of the employer-employee relationship within the framework of these larger social changes. Through their housekeeping guides, Morelli, Boni, and Foggia defined class boundaries even as they crossed them. This is true not only in terms of their middle- and working-class book audiences but also in terms of how they collected the recipes that composed the majority of their books' pages. Morelli and these other writers were wildly prolific. During the late 1930s, Morelli regularly published over 600 new recipes per year every year. But no one can annually invent, test, and publish twice as many recipes as there are days without daily assistance. Who provided that help?

Ironically, at the very moment that working-class women stopped working in middle-class women's kitchens for more lucrative factory work, they began to send in recipes to middle-class women authors and private food company recipe contests, even with no expectation of financial remuneration. Occasionally they received a minor form of recognition, such as having their first names published near the recipe heading. But they never received any share of book profits generated by their culinary inventions and expertise.

Ada Boni's famous *Il Talismano* was derived from her *Preziosa* recipes, but those in turn were culled from working-class readers who sent in recipes in hopes of seeing their name in a national magazine. Boni was known for privileging reader recipes from her native Lazio and, more generally, from Central Italy. This preference also shows up in her cookbooks, *La cucina regionale italiana* and *La cucina romana*. In 1929, Boni published a compendium of 882 recipes from her columns. Subsequent editions grew to over 2,000 recipes. These appropriative trends intensified under Fascism, but they did not originate under it. By contrast, Pellegrino Artusi, writing thirty years earlier, came up with a mere 600 recipes. Artusi solicited the nucleus of his original recipes from Marietta Sabatini, his much-celebrated, but unnamed, cook. Subsequent recipes came from working-class women's letters sent from across Italy. In many ways, Boni's class-based culinary appropriation follows Artusi's.

Lidia Morelli's crossover projects with Italy's processed food companies like Cirio heralded such connections explicitly in commercial publications like *Nuovi orrizonti per la vostra mensa: 300 ricette scelte tra le 1224 premiate su 18000 inviate al concorso pomodoro pelati Cirio da 3000 concorrenti (New Horizons for Your Meals: 300 Recipes Selected from the 1224 Prize-Winners out of the 18000 Entries to the Cirio Peeled Tomatoes Competition of 3000 Entrants)*.[20] Although it would be tempting to read the Cirio publication and others like it as evidence of an exploiter-exploited relationship between urban middle-class female authors and urban or migrant peasant working-class female cooks, the truth is not so simple. Although they did not receive financial and authorial acknowledgment for their food work, they did exercise considerable agency in shaping the nation's culinary canon. Further, although middle-class women actively solicited recipe submissions, working-class women voluntarily provided them. And once printed, the recipes travelled across the peninsula, where other women recreated them in their own kitchens. Through these semi-exploitative means, working-class women shaped Italy's national cuisine from the bottom up.

Cookbook production, circulation, and material properties changed during the Fascist period as well; as household guides shifted from working- to middle-class status, their paper and cover quality rose. They also gained weight: books went from cheap tablets to leather-bound tomes. Perhaps most significantly, the books began to cross the threshold from public publishing to private homes in new ways. Previously, ladies bought these documents for their working-class cooks at the start of employment. All of these new household guides, but *Il Talismano* in particular, signalled a break in the social order. By the mid-1930s, wedding bells and Boni's book went hand in hand. As Lidia Bastianich recalled, the mother-in-law would present *Il Talismano* to the bride in hopes that she would cook delicious meals for her son through the years of marriage to come. From that point on, the book would move from mother to daughter as an heirloom, crossing the threshold on each generation's wedding day.[21]

Additionally, middle-class women began to clip recipes from the culinary columns of newspapers and magazines to use in their kitchens. When splatters and splotches inevitably soiled the cheap paper, women wrote letters to the columnists, requesting the recipes anew. But as reprinting of the same recipe went against writers' contracts, women turned from journalism to book publishing and enlarged their work from individual columns to full compendiums. In a colourful narrative, Foggia's opening letter of *Ricette* and *Altre ricette* provides a window into the personal use of the material culture of newspaper recipes by middle-class women. She claims to have written this book because "mi avete sì spesso pregata di trascrivere e di mandarvi – giacchè (le sventate!) non riuscivate più a trovare il foglietto ritagliato dal giornale e … messo con tanta cura da parte!" (you have so often begged me to transcribe and to send to you – because [scatterbrains!] you can no longer find the little piece of paper cut out of the journal and … put aside with so much care!).

This is not to say, however, that the publishing companies acknowledged the value of these particular forms of culinary knowledge. An advertisement for cookbooks tucked midway through the meat section of Foggia's *Altre ricette* translates forms of culinary knowledge, and their authors' gender and nationality, into a sliding scale of monetary value. At the top of the economic food chain sat Paul Beboux's *Nuove regime*, at 7 lire. According to the advertisement, the cookbook contains over 300 recipes geared towards medical conditions like enteritis, diabetes, arthritis, rheumatism, and obesity. By contrast, the Sonzogno-published cookbooks on regional Italian cuisine and home economics, written by women, cost a mere 2 lire per copy during the 1930s. To put this ratio in context with the culinary costs of the day, Beboux's cookbook was worth one kilogram of sugar but Foggia's was valued in mere spoonfuls.[22] Legacy reverses these monetary values, however, as *Nuovi regime* has been consigned to a historical footnote, whereas *Ricette di Petronilla* remains in print today. In this way, these household management guides mark not only the emergence of the middle class but also its continued existence and women's more contoured understanding of their own social class, along with the types of foods that sustained it.

With the servants supposedly gone but with their recipes in hand, the cookbook cohort deployed tone and structure to rework these dishes in literary rather than culinary terms, and in doing so, they incorporated politicized tropes of the heroic domestic reformer into their books. Because they wrote for women who were learning to cook for the first time, these authors introduced new recipe formats geared towards beginners. First, on an emotive front, they used a warm, communal tone to assure women that they had not lost status by stepping into the kitchen. They also incorporated literary elements to their writing to make cooking more of an art form and less of a daily drudgery. On a more practical front, they added quantitative features to the recipes, like cooking times and measurements. Previously, cooks would have learned these ideas from another cook in a kitchen, who might have told them to "throw in some flour." Watching that cook would have clarified "some" to be either a handful or a teaspoon, depending on the recipe. Now, written measurements took the place of oral and visual prompts.

Recipes and cookbooks codified Italian cuisine for the middle class, temporarily fixing it in place with numbers and directives. But politics continued to move, impacting which recipes were possible to prepare. In the 1920s, the growth in cookbook publishing was launched by misplaced fears of a servant crisis and new enthusiasm for home economics, but business truly boomed in the 1930s, when nearly all Italian households were forced to confront the question of how to cook with less butter, oil, and flour.

As advertising and financial records have shown, Morelli's, Boni's, and Foggia's renowned cookery came from recipes sent into newspapers by working-class cooks. And yet, close readings show how the middle-class writers maintain an odd inter-class paradox: they deprecate their servants even as these women are clearly the masters of their craft. Let us consider some concrete examples of how cookbook writers wrote about cooks. Morelli, for instance, assumed that her readers would have had a maid but not a cook. Boni, by contrast, assumed that her readers had neither. And Foggia showed this social shift in action: in the introduction to *Ricette di Petronilla* (1938), she scoffs, "La servetta da un scarso aiuto (se poco mi rende, poco però anche mi costa!)" (The servant offers very little help [but although she gives me little, little as well she costs me!]). Foggia's frequent in-text dismissals of her *servetta*'s intelligence and ability, coupled with her low pay, cast the larger economic and social issues of domestic workers' choices to leave homes for factories in stark personal terms. A mere four years later, many of these *servette* have disappeared from the text. In cookbooks like *Ricette di Petronilla per tempi eccezionali* (1942), Foggia's well-to-do characters, always including the literary version of herself, still have both maids and cooks, but middle-class women lament their lack of help at home. Changes to recipe content and format in this generation of writers evidences these changes: in contrast to Pellegrino Artusi's cohort, these women did not assume that their audience would know the "requisite ingredients" for *besciamella* or how to prepare this sauce "in the typical manner," as a standard nineteenth-century Italian recipe published in *La Scienza in Cucina e L'Arte di Mangiar Bene* reads.[23] This distinction highlights the social change that the ladies of the house, and not their servants, had begun to cook.

And how did the lady of the house learn the culinary arts? In an uneasy division of social authority between upper-class taste and working-class experience and ability, middle-class women learned from books and cooks in tandem. Angst clouded the kitchen as women from different social rungs renegotiated their standing and its value. Inter-class sniping marks these moments of anxiety: Foggia, for instance, invokes the *servetta*'s supposed feeble-mindedness even as she suggests that the lady of the house learn to cook from her:

> Ricordate, però, che parlando del come io abbia istruita la mia servetta, vi ho accennato alla prova generale che la faccio sempre fare sul come si devono presentare i piatti delle portate e mutare i piatti personali. Ebbene; se ancora inesperte – forse quanto la mia sempliciotta servetta – voleste osare… Ascoltatemi: di un pranzo, fate anche voi la prova generale; fatela fra stretti parenti o intimi amici; e … se v i avvederete di qualche mancanza, di qualche lacuna, persino di qualche magagna nel pranzo … potreste, così, tosto provvedere e riparare. Non c'è che fare, per imparare!

> Remember, though, that in talking about how I instructed my servant, I have signalled to you the general test that I always have done on how one must present the dishes and move the personal plates. And then, if she is still not an expert – perhaps as much as my sweet and simple little servant – you must dare … Listen to me: give a lunch, you too must do a general test; do it with close relatives and close friends; and … if you notice some lack, some lacuna, even some problem with the lunch … you could, thus, promptly see to it and repair it. There's nothing like doing, for learning![24]

This brief introductory passage includes multiple textual strategies for establishing social hierarchy. First, Foggia casts herself as a teacher twice over: she tutors her readers in household management by describing how she instructs her servant. She defines her servant in the negative, by what she is not: an expert. In establishing what she is, Foggia encases her employee in diminutives and endearments, denigrating both her profession and her intelligence. She is not a *serva* but the feminized and minimized *servetta*, the sweet little servant. Moreover, she is not merely *semplice* (simple) but *sempliciotta*: sweet, little, and simple. But who is teaching whom? Although the first two sentences cast Foggia and her readers as the culinary experts, an ellipsis silently points to their unspeakable lack of cooking experience and ability. The final two phrases speak to this lacuna, as Foggia recommends that her readers experiment with new kitchen techniques in a low-stakes social setting. She does not say who they will learn from, but there is only one other person in the kitchen: the servant.

But more and more often, Boni pointed out, the lady of the house might look around the kitchen for aid in preparing a fancy lunch only to find herself alone.

> Voi risponderete che è molto facile trovare una cuoca e trarsi rapidamente d'imbarazzo. Ebbene no. Ciò poteva accadere molti anni addietro; ma adesso, credete, questi tempi felici son passati, e le cuoche si fanno sempre più rare. E in ogni caso, anche quando Voi per una fortunata combinazione foste riuscite a pescare questa perla rara, vi trovereste necessariamente costrette ad abdicare ad ogni Vostra autorità, a rinunziare a qualsiasi controllo e lasciare che una persona mercenaria faccia e disfaccia a suo talento, imponendovi le sue opinioni, il più delle volte interessate o illogiche, spendendo il Vostro danaro senza menomenete preoccuparsi di realizzare la più piccola economia. Inoltre le cuoche hanno i loro piatti di battaglia dai quali non ci si libera.

> You will respond that it is very easy to find a cook and to rapidly remove oneself from embarrassment. But no. That could happen many years past; by now, believe me, these happy times have passed and cooks make themselves ever more scarce. And in any case, even if by some happy coincidence you have managed to fish this rare pearl, you might find yourselves necessarily constrained to abdicate your authority, to renounce any control and to allow that a mercenary person does and undoes according to their talent, enforcing their opinions, which are often biased or illogical, spending your money without hardly bothering to attain the smallest savings. Moreover, cooks have their canon of dishes from which they will not part.[25]

Boni speaks to the double bind that this dilemma presented: the woman of the house needed either a cook or cooking skills, but the former were increasingly difficult to find. She compares the process of successfully employing a cook to "fishing this rare pearl" out of the oceanic depths. On the other hand, cooking knowledge marked one as working-class. How then to reassure her elegant readership that they could learn to cook while maintaining their high-class status?

Boni considered this last dilemma key to her book's success. She devotes most of her introduction to raising the social status of domestic activity, framing cooking as the gayest of arts and the most pleasant of sciences. Thousands of royals, artists, poets, and other *donne elette*, according to Boni, not only do not distain the culinary arts but brag about their knowledge of them. She goes on to directly confront her readers' fear of status loss: "E' sopratutto non temete di degradarvi, manipolando degli intingoli" (And above all, do not fear degrading yourself, handling the condiments). Boni went so far as to indicate where middle-class women ought to place *Il Talismano* when not in use: "Voi potrete accogliere liberamente il presente volume nella biblioteca e nei giorni di ricevimento mostrarlo, senza dovere arrossire, a tutte le Vostre amiche, siano esse, come Voi, dame di fine eleganza e di impeccabile buon gusto." (You can freely welcome this current volume into the library or show it on social visiting days, without having to blush, to all of your female friends, being these, like you, women of fine elegance and impeccable good taste.) Fumes of social anxiety waft off this assertion and suggest that although women may have felt they needed to learn how to cook, they also wanted to hide the evidence.

Close readings of cookbooks show how cooking changed over the course of the *ventennio*, but more importantly, they also show how women felt about cooking under Fascism. This next section approaches cookbooks as literary creations, with narratives, characters, and structure that develop in tandem with shifting political and social currents. As previously mentioned, a common conceit of Fascist-period cookbooks is to open with a letter to the readers from the author, written in a warm personal tone. Ada Boni's two-page opening letter, *Alle Gentili Lettrici*, frames social class in terms of pastimes and competencies.

> Di Voi, Signore e Signorine, molte sanno suonare bene il pianoforte o cantare con grazia squisita, molte altre hanno ambitissimi titoli di studi superiori, conoscono le lingue straniere, sono piacevoli letterate o fini pittrici, ed altre ancora sono esperte nel "tennis" o nel "golf," o guidano con salda mano il volante di una lussuosa automobile. Ma, ahimè, non certo tutte, facendo un piccolo esame di coscienza, potreste affermare di saper cuocere alla perfezione due uova al "guscio."

> Of you, Gentlewomen and Young Ladies, many know how to play the piano well, or sing with exquisite grace. Many others have very ambitious scholastic titles, know foreign languages, are pleasingly well-read or fine painters, and still others are experts in tennis or golf, or guide the steering wheel of a luxurious automobile with a steady hand. But, alas, certainly not all of you, doing a small examination of conscience, could attest to knowing how to perfectly hard boil two eggs.[26]

The very first words of this exhaustive tome of cookery, weighing in at over 2,000 recipes, contextualize the work of cooking as a necessary body of knowledge for women of all social classes. In brief: you may know how to drive a luxury car, but you can't boil an egg. Boni's gentle mockery of her readership affirms their high-class status even as they prepare to engage in working-class labour that might threaten their social standing.

Foggia takes a similar tack in her introductory letter. Once again poking fun at the upper class so as to reassure her readership that she and they share similar class status, she scoffs, "Oh, non pensatemi di professione cuoca; nè da mane a sera fra pignatte e padelle ad almanaccare nuove pietanzine e piatti ricercati!" (Oh, don't think of me as a professional cook, nor as someone who is from morning to evening among the pots and pans daily writing an almanac of new foods and sought-after dishes!) But if she is not a professional cook, or one who works from sunup to sundown amidst the clatter of pans, she is also not a professor of gastronomy. "Io non sono una professorona che parli dall'alto d'una cattedra culinaria" (I am not a professor who speaks from on high from a culinary pulpit). Rather, Foggia goes on to claim, she belongs to the same class as her readership: "Io sono semplicemente una 'qualunque donnetta' che della sua borghesissima cucina dice quali piatti ella riserbi per le sue colazioni e i suoi pranzetti" (I am simply a "little woman like any other," who from her very middle-class kitchen says which plates she sets aside for her lunches and little dinners).

Boni and Foggia take a similar tone; both poke fun at the upper class, and both mock a specific subset of women in this class – women in academia, be they those with lofty titles who speak foreign languages, as in Boni's text, or those who are chaired professors, as in Foggia's. Given that both Boni and Foggia were academic women themselves, with backgrounds in education and, in Foggia's case, a career in medicine, this mockery suggests some self-consciousness as to their own standing vis-à-vis their readership. But in a sense, Boni and Foggia are correct: they are neither haughty professors speaking down to their students nor beleaguered cooks preparing dishes for the dining room upstairs. They are – at their core – writers, chatting with other women of the same middle-class social standing.

But of course, it is the author who speaks, and the readers who listen. Some authors, like Boni, stop there. Her recipes evoke a lesson: she is the speaking instructor, and her reader is the silent learner. Imperative commands (Prepare ... Mix ... Fry ... Boil ...) and third-person descriptions (One prepares ... One mixes ... One fries ... One boils ...) predominate.[27] The recipes consist of an ingredient- and preparation-based title, like beccaccia farcita, *beccaccia* being woodcock, the main ingredient, and *farcita* being stuffed, the preparation. A paragraph-long narrative description provides the recipe in a conversational but largely instructional format, not unlike the American Fanny Farmer cookbooks written during the same period. The number of people served, the types and amounts of ingredients, and the cooking times and methods are never found above the text but must be mined from the body of the recipe. Even this empirical information is not always present. For instance, the recipe for zuppa inglese e chantilly indicates that it serves six and references measurements ranging from teaspoons to litres, but the charlotte romana recipe just one page before includes neither. Boni does, however, describe the shape and properties of the uncommon tools involved in the charlotte romana, including the charlotte mould, and indicates that it ought to hold roughly a litre of berries and batter.

This narrative format is much closer to oral transmission of recipes, in that it describes the cooking process chronologically without providing an overview at the start. Boni's treatment of measurement also reflects this moment of transition from oral to textual transmission of recipes: in addition to grams and litres, you also see more casual measurements, like two fingers of oil to put in a pan for the coniglio in padella. Often, sensory cues mark the dish's progress rather than the ticking of the clock's hand. In the case of the rabbit in a pan, Boni suggests that the reader pour half a cup of dry wine over the rabbit once the meat has fried to a rosy hue. The colour pink, rather than the five-minute warning, indicates the next step of the recipe. Only at that point should you "aggiungete un pochino d'acqua – non troppa – moderate il fuoco, coprite il recipente e lasciate che la cottura termini dolcemente, e la salsa possa bene addensarsi" (add a little bit of water – not too much – moderate the flame, cover the dish and let the cooking sweetly finish, and the sauce can nicely thicken).

Although this simple recipe is very short, it is also incredibly subjective. How should the novice cook know how much water is "a little bit" and when they have sloshed in "too much"? Further, in a move from everyday cooking to culinary history, Boni often concludes with a brief note on the recipe's regional history. She notes, for instance, that English pudding is, despite its nomenclature, a classic Roman dessert.

Moving from the level of the recipe to the level of the chapter structure, Boni, like Morelli and Foggia, organized these recipes to proceed in the order of a meal, with appetizers at the beginning and desserts at the end. This meal-mimicry format had the added pedagogical bonus of naturally moving from easy to difficult dishes. *Il Talismano* begins with basic concepts (like preparations for consommé, candies, etc.) before proceeding into sauces, cold appetizers, soups and pastas, fried dishes, eggs, fish, meat, cold dishes and salads, green sides, pastry, syrups and liquors, and conserves. Illustrations were few but provided aid for esoteric challenges. They showed how to assemble a vol au vent pastry, how to open a lobster, how prepare a fillet of sole, how to cut a cooked goose, how to truss, chop, and serve a chicken, and how to slice a dry peach and demonstrated which cuts of beef came from which parts of a cow. Illustrations, instructions, and recipes reflect a conversation. These feed into the larger book structure, which ultimately evokes the sociability of a family dinner.

Like Boni, Foggia embraced this moment of transition from oral to textual relation of cooking skills. But whereas Boni largely confined her creativity to the humorous tone of her opening letter, Foggia went further by playing on the literary traditions of textual storytelling. Continuing the precedent set by the introductory letter, she embraces the warm tone and choral format of an egalitarian conversation amongst female friends in the recipes themselves. Her first book, *Ricette di Petronilla* (1938), introduces a cast of characters drawn from Foggia's life. And just as these people stayed with Foggia throughout her life, so too do their characters persist across her cookbooks. We meet her butcher, Nene, and learn his recipe for beef roast. We meet Damia, a friend of Foggia's from elementary school, when she shares her low-cost recipe for veal and tuna (vitello tonnato all'economica). The dish promises elegance on a budget: Damia concludes the recipe with the impressive claim, "You will even see your dear mother-in-law, I swear, lick the point of her finger when she

4.4. Illustrated cover of Amalia Moretti Foggia's *Altre ricette di Petronilla* (Milan: Sonzogno, 1938).

thinks no one is looking." We wave goodbye to Damia in the dessert chapter, after she discusses the best way to prepare fried cream (crema fritta) with Foggia, but we greet her again the following year when she pops up in the introduction to Foggia's second cookbook, *Altre ricette di Petronilla* (1939; see Fig. 4.4). Characters like Nene and Damia populate and personify Foggia's recipes: Nene, a jocular butcher, provides meat recipes. Shrewd Damia, whose work pays little, offers recipes for stretching the family purse.

Cookbook authors like Foggia deftly incorporated literary elements like tone and character development to help their readership manage the supposed servant crisis, a historically specific social dilemma, through recipes. But Foggia wrote in the heart of the Fascist period. How did she wield her literary tools to negotiate the period's notorious political edicts? In her wartime cookbooks, when economics became a central concern, Foggia assigned different characters to personify different budgets, encouraging her readers to find their cookbook character corollary in her prescriptive literature and to then follow their recipes in real life.

In *Ricette di Petronilla per tempi eccezionali*, Foggia marks the shift between two similar fish recipes, one expensive and one economical, by shifting speakers, "Ben fortunate tu e l'Adalgisa che potete permettervi il lusso di piatti sopraffini (interrompe la cara Gemma). Io invece … io, per il pranzo d'oggi, ho comperato 800 gr. di economiche sardelle che in pescheria ho viste fresche." (How fortunate you and Adalgisa are that you can allow yourself the luxury of very fine dishes [interrupts dear Gemma]. I, however, … I, for lunch today, bought 800 grams of cheap sardines that I saw fresh at the fishmonger's.) In this cookbook, Foggia introduces and defines her ten female characters by traits that range from their regional origins, education, and families to their cooking proclivities. Readers could easily find a character similar to themselves, in terms of budget, tastes, and cooking style. Then they could follow that character's recipes throughout the books, creating another form of identification and connection between the reader and the cookbook text. Although Foggia typically defines her characters with three or fewer identifying traits, this minimalist personality palette allows her to shape each recipe as a dramatic tale, opening with a social problem and concluding with a culinary solution.

In "Angela's Ravioli," a mother is locally famous for her pasta. She becomes jealous of her neighbour Angela, a pasta expert in her own right, because her own son prefers Angela's ravioli. Angela kindly agrees to teach the mother her ravioli recipe, and the social order is restored. Foggia devotes equal space – one page apiece – to the recipe and to this tale, indicating the dual importance of food and story. Similarly, Foggia couches a recipe for boiled fish with mayonnaise dressing within the larger narrative of a woman chasing her, Foggia, across the town's central piazza to ask for advice on how to cook trout. Foggia invites the woman home, ties on an apron, and demonstrates how to make mayonnaise. The recipe narrative reads like the script for a contemporary cooking show. It even manages to convey a sense of closeness with Foggia, as if she were our friend or neighbour. These recipes speak to the rhythms of daily life in a small Italian town: each recipe is a short story that invites the reader to participate in communal life through cooking.

But of course, time matters as much as place. In Foggia's wartime cookbook, *Ricette di Petronilla per tempi eccezionali* (1942), the narrative shifts.[28] Once again, Foggia frames the book as a conversation among female friends, but silences indicated by ellipses mark all that they cannot bear to say. In the Sonzogno edition, the title even includes an ellipsis, and its placement points to a euphemism: *Ricette di Petronilla per tempi … eccezionali*. The times are not simply exceptional: they are bad. But Petronilla avoids putting such a direct indictment on her book cover. Instead, she self-censors with a trail of ellipses.

Further, the characters in her cookbooks consistently rely on the ellipses to avoid discussing the negative effects of war: absence, want, disease, and death. The daily battle

4.5. Interior illustration, "Sono dieci amiche che…" (There are ten friends who…). Amalia Moretti Foggia, *Ricette di Petronilla per tempi eccezionali* (Milan: Casa Editrice Sonzogno, 1942). (Harvard Schlesinger Library, Cambridge, MA)

for nourishment in wartime is the "eternal theme" of their discussions: they bend their brains to get more out of less, to get something out of nothing. They meet every day, "chiacchierando sugli … eventi" (chatting about the … events) of war while spinning wool, knitting socks, and repairing shoes (*sferruzzando*) (Fig. 4.5). An ellipsis aims a spyglass on the faraway battles won and lost, the lives of loved ones hanging in the balance. These women have gathered to talk – and here Foggia draws attention to her own lacuna: "Chiacchierando … chiacchierando … su che?" (To talk … to talk … about what?) They cook with "poco grasso, poco riso, poca pasta, poca farina e poco zucchero, spendendo pochetto ma … nutrendo però bastevolmente" (little fat, little rice, little pasta, little flour and little sugar, spending very little but … nourishing sufficiently). Six repetitions of the word "little" hammers in the nail: wartime cookery is defined by absences rather than presences.

The format also deviates from the courses of a typical cookbook. Because of shortages, it begins with filling pasta and bean dishes rather than bite-sized appetizers. Turn-taking between speakers occurs when one person wants to save gas for the oven but another wants to save her ration of flour. The group has gathered to discuss how women might use their culinary skills to manage the effects of war at home. They are, Foggia announces, a group of friends, gathered in a time of strife, to pass the time away by telling tales. Each day's recipes follow a single culinary theme, to be decided by the first speaker. Throughout, Foggia's ellipses wreathe each stoic understatement, conspicuously marking these lacunae. In Foggia's hands, the deprivations and deaths of 1940s Fascism echo the bubonic plague of fourteenth-century Italy. The Black Death levelled the European population and inspired satires of the corrupt authorities of church and state. The *Decameron*, by Giovanni Boccaccio, was the most masterful of these works. This canonical collection of novellas concerns a group of ten young people who flee pestilence-ridden Florence for the countryside, where they pass ten unsettled days by telling stories in the round. Cookbooks like Foggia's can be literary creations: *Ricette di Petronilla per tempi eccezionali* is not just a collection of recipes; it is Foggia's culinary *Decameron*.

Marginalia in older editions of the Petronilla series show that cooks frequently adjusted the ingredient amount or ratio in the case of shortages, or in accordance with

4.6. "Pranzo a casa di Bò" (lunch at Bò's house) in *Noi Quattro a Scuola e Altrove*, 1933–7. (Archivio Diaristico Nazionale, Pieve Santo Stefano, Italy)

family preferences. Moreover, diaries written by women during the 1930s suggest that many of them thought about cooking in the same way that Foggia describes in her cookbook. That is, they frame it as an evolving dialogue articulated by groups of women who spent many afternoons together. *Noi Quattro a Scuola e Altrove* (*The Four of Us at School and Elsewhere*) provides an example of the communal spirit that animated these conversations. Written in daily turns from 1933 to 1937 by Cacridobò, the war name (*nome di battaglia*) of four Roman girls (Leda Casalini, Lydia Cristina, Wanda Doniselli, Vittoria Boni – Ca, Cri, Do, and Bò, respectively), this diary covers their ambivalent reactions to Fascist foreign policy and home economics recipes alike. Drawn by the women themselves, the first of two colour pencil illustrations shows Vittoria Boni in a neat hat and jacket standing outside her house awaiting lunch guests (Fig. 4.6). The culinary theme of the day is marked by a pot, cut and pasted in from a magazine. The next drawing shows the four women as they cook lunch together in Bò's kitchen (Fig. 4.7). Asides to Ca and to Cri turn the diary into a play

4.7. "Torta di patata" (potato cake) recipe and cooking drawing in *Noi Quattro a Scuola e Altrove*, 1933–7. (Archivio Diaristico Nazionale, Pieve Santo Stefano, Italy)

and the kitchen a theatre set, echoing with the four voices engaged in conversation over how to prepare the torta di patata recipe, also included in the diary. Drawings and diaries demonstrate that women were interacting with these cookbooks and their recipes in a communal format similar to the one described in Foggia's text.

How Wartime Privation Shaped Cooking and Taste

Two of Foggia's final cookbooks, *Ricette di Petronilla per tempi eccezionali* (1942) and *Desinaretti per … questi tempi* (1943) (Fig. 4.8), offer a time-lapse microcosm of how women changed their cooking ingredients and preparations in response to autarky and wartime sanctions. But more broadly, they exemplify how women redefined the boundaries of acceptable ingredients, recipe preparations, and meal structure to manage extreme privation.

In her first wartime cookbook, Foggia evokes the ambient anxiety of the Italian home front, suffusing the text with the constant mental calculus of ingredient costs,

amounts, and availability. In her recipe for vegetable soup, which is not
an expensive dish to begin with, her
character Carla recommends adding six tablespoons of her rice ration
("il mio riso tesserato") but only "se
posso disporne" (if I can spare it).
In other words, women faced cupboards so lean that the decision to
use roughly one-third of a cup of rice
required serious deliberation and accounting against the other recipes
for the month. Selecting a cooking
method required the same fore-
thought: What if you want to serve
risotto but save propane? The next
woman addresses this question: "Io
che al pare non voglio tanto spendere
il gas per bollir verdure, io preparo
assai spesso minestre con fiocchi di
cereali che non sono tesserati" (I by
contrast do not want to spend gas to
boil vegetables, I frequently prepare
soups with grains that are not rationed).

4.8. Illustrated cover of Amalia Moretti Foggia's *Desinaretti
per ... questi tempi* (Milan: Sonzogno, 1943).

The Fascist regime introduced rationing fairly late compared to other European
governments, a decision that increased food scarcity and hoarding. The regime first
rationed extras like coffee and sugar in early 1940. Later that year, oils and fats joined
the list. By the following winter, rice and pasta were rationed as well, followed by
bread in early 1941. In this recipe and others, women constantly track the foods that
are and are not rationed (*tesserati*). The Italian term for "rationed" derives from the
card (*tessera*) used to obtain rationed goods. As scarcity increased, Foggia's characters
began to characterize their recipes by their ingredients, especially rationed ingredients
like oil, butter, and meat, and by items found in abundance, like cabbage and rabbits.
Ingredient quality became salient. For the first time, pasta was ranked: Foggia suggests
"qualità #2" in an early recipe. Eating formerly disregarded (or discarded) foods also
became newly acceptable. It took *tempi eccezionali* for Foggia to devote an entire chapter to cooking with innards. In addition, if punctuation like ellipses mark the abstract
absences and terrors of the times, then quantitative adjectives like *poco* (little) denote
the more concrete deprivations of cakes without sugar and meatballs without meat. A
recipe for spaghetti calls for "poco olio poco burro tanta verza" (little oil, little butter,
lots of cabbage).

Reflecting the growing importance of rationed foods, Foggia introduces exact measurements for the first time. This is an interesting contrast with Boni, who introduced measurements because her middle-class readership did not know how to cook and needed empirical guidelines. Wartime shortages forced women to reevaluate not only the boundaries of what was good to eat and what was edible but also where foods belonged in the course of a meal or in the context of a recipe. Rationing turned bread into a treat, a shift indicated by Foggia's reclassification of toasted bread from a formerly invisible supporting ingredient used to stretch meat-based dishes to a starring role as dessert. Foggia's inclusion of toasted bread in the dessert section speaks to just how much the traditional Italian meal forms and accepted tastes shifted. As might be expected, Foggia recommends sweet toppings for the bread, like conserves, but she recommends savoury ones like spicy tuna as well. This dish may look familiar – it is essentially crostini – but its placement in the dessert section suggests that wartime rationing vaulted this humble appetizer to new social heights. The crostini's unexpected flight to the end of the meal reveals a broader move to redefine the social meanings of food while maintaining a familiar recipe form with known ingredients and preparations.

But many recipes did change: with the onset of war, the quantity of non-rationed ingredients per recipe (for example, the amount of cabbage in a single minestrone recipe) and their frequency across recipes (the number of cabbage-centric recipes across the soup section) rose in tandem. This shift points to the additional steps that women began to take to obtain food prior to preparing it and a move away from urban markets and shops to rural hillsides and rivers. Foraging, hunting, fishing, and animal raising became typical even for town dwellers and involved considerable time investment before the cooking began. They might even be considered the first step to preparing these dishes. This is the first cookbook where Foggia assumes that her readers have a home garden. Modelling this new expectation, her character Carla brings a gift of homegrown cauliflower to Foggia's house on the day she hosts her ten guests. Wild game and vegetables ascended the culinary ladder, moved from side dishes to main courses. Foraged woodland finds like mushrooms, chestnuts, and chicory shifted from minor to main ingredients. Egg-based dishes proliferated: omelettes lay siege to the meat section, and the dessert chapter is covered in meringue.

In a similar shift from periphery to centre, Foggia recommended that women prepare regional recipes emphasizing these ingredients; though this was a move born of privation, it had the potential to nationalize cuisine. One woman at the table makes the argument for increasing reliance on recipes from the "muddy earth" of the Lombard rice fields during wartime. With only a spoonful of rationed goods, she claims, she was able to present "the most delicious dish" of boiled frogs. The recipe is fairly simple and begins at the marketplace rather than the marshes: buy two big, fat, decapitated, skinned frogs, and boil them for twenty minutes in salt water. Make a roux with a spoonful each of butter and flour. Add that to the frog broth, along with salt and pepper, plus three egg yolks mixed with the juice of two lemons. Combine the sauce with frogs and frog broth, then serve on a warm plate. Foggia's narrative indicates that women may have been more concerned about crossing boundaries of class than taste when considering this new recipe. "Siete piuttosto ... schizzinosette. Non sono io ... [essendo] della 'bassa,' cioè della grassa terra tutta acquitrini di risaie. E nell'acqua fangosa delle risaie, non gracidano le rane? Ebbene, ligia alle costumanze familiari e regionali, io stamane ho presentato in tavola un bel piatto di rane in salsa." (You are so ... snobby. Not I ... [being] from the "lowlands," that is from that fat earth, all marshland rice fields. And in the muddy water of the rice fields, do the frogs not croak? Well, faithful to the familial and regional customs, this morning I presented at the table a beautiful plate of frogs in sauce.)[29] Several recipes featuring *salamelle*, a Lombard sausage, follow, although rice figures more predominantly in their titles: risotto salamelle (risotto with sausage), arancette di riso (fried rice balls), and pasticci di riso (a big mess of rice). In this narrative and beyond, Foggia dangles regionality as bait for autarkic cookery: women could claim that their motive for cooking a dish was culinary exploration and a desire to try the ingredients and preparations of Lombardy, rather than economic privation.[30] This strategy reshaped what a typical dinner might consist of both at the level of a single Wednesday dinner and at the level of the Italian culinary canon.

Even when women cooked the same foods as before, they began to use more and different parts: in the case of meats, Foggia's chapter on innards (*frattaglie*) includes recipes that predate the Fascist period, with dishes such as zampone (Bolognese boiled pig's foot, often served for Christmas and New Year's) and ingredients like liver, tongue, and other sweetbreads, as in the recipe for lingua in gelatina (tongue in gelatin). However, the sheer predominance of head- and heart-based recipes departs from previous traditions. Foggia devotes many pages to *testina* and prominently features dishes like cuore in salsetta d'acciughe (heart in a little anchovy sauce) and cuore in padella (heart in a pan). For Foggia, the metaphorical potential of the head and the heart transcended their culinary value. As an ingredient and as a symbol, the heart in particular spoke to the emotional costs of wartime and of going from cooking with little to cooking with virtually nothing at all. In Foggia's final book, written in 1943 at the nadir of the war, she concludes every chapter with a pen-and-ink illustration. Recipe becomes augury. Her final cookbook ends with cuore grigliate: two hearts, skewered by sharp metal tines.

The literary and culinary elements in this cookbook, *200 Suggerimenti per ... questi tempi* (1943), speak to the lowest depths of wartime cookery. Gone are the chatty tales of wild piazza chases for trout recipes. Gone too are the round robins of women gathered together for solace. *200 Suggerimenti* shows a world without people: stories and dialogues give way to measurements and imperatives. Foggia's non-narrative treatment of the recipes suggests the elimination of all unnecessary expenditure, including the effort that it takes to speak. This text is terse. It reads like martial law.

Recipe format diverges as well. The header for "Zuppa per ... questi tempi" (Soup for ... these times) includes a conspicuous subheading with the absent ingredients.

In her previous 1942 publication, Foggia folded those missing foods into the recipe body. The header for Foggia's wartime soup recipe lists all of the rationed ingredients that you do not need to make this recipe rather than those that you do: "niente pasta, niente riso, niente grassi" (no pasta, no rice, no fats). Bare cupboards guide this cookbook's use. The highlighting of what is not necessary rather than what is shows a different focus on the way that women approached cooking in the late war years. The repeated *poco* of 1938 had dissolved into *niente* by 1943. Absences of people, and ingredients, are so vast that they balloon into presence.

While Foggia's instructions are terse, she still managed to embed soft touches to acknowledge her readership's worries. Foggia recommends this soup recipe for the end of the month, when the rice and pasta have been eaten and the oil has long since been poured. All you need are common garden vegetables (carrots, onions, cabbage, beets, potatoes, turnips, celery, and parsley), two or three cubes of bouillon, and cheese shavings ("but only if you have them," she kindly adds). Special versions of this soup, provided at the end, include adding old bread, or – luxury of luxuries – a bit of butter. She reassures her readership that they are not at fault and that they are not alone: "E' cosa che puo capitare a tante in questi tempi eccezionali" (It's something that can happen to many of us in these exceptional times).

Concern for absences impacts the cooking methods as well. Instead of describing culinary flourishes that might add to the dish, Foggia devotes a significant amount of space to cooking techniques to save gas: "Ma il contatore di gas corre sia per poca sia per tanta minestra, dunque ... preparate la zuppa in quantita bastante per due ed anche per tre pasti" (But the gas counter runs whether it's for a little or a lot of soup, so ... prepare the soup in sufficient quantities for two and even for three meals at once). These recipes reveal that rationing impacted ingredient use. But less obviously, they also demonstrate that cooking methods – and thus the Italian culinary canon – changed as a result of wartime gas shortages.

Along these lines, Foggia's 1943 recipes both continue and intensify many of the culinary shifts to ingredients, preparations, and meal forms begun in her 1942 cookbook. Garden vegetables, one of the few remaining food types still found in abundance, now appeared in every course, a shift that redefined where greens do and do not belong in the menu order. Potatoes, carrots, and beans now fill out cakes, pies, and puddings. When both the ingredients and the cooking style have changed due to shortages of sugar and gas, the original dish might be held in place by the title alone as in "a plum cake ... per questi tempi," which contains neither sugar nor butter, eggs, or even white flour.[31]

The comparative rarity of meats meant that women took a different tack to obtain the protein they needed. Here, the ingredient selection grows sylvan: wild bird eggs take the place of chicken eggs in some recipes, indicating that women ventured deeper into the swamps and forests to forage for food than they ever had before. Foggia began to assume that men hunted wild game and that women maintained rabbit hutches in addition to the gardens dug in 1942. Her recipes for innards devolve into alchemy. Across from the preparation for the grilled hearts, the canonical recipe of this text, sits a recipe for fried blood.[32]

Foggia's departure from the kitchen table to the abattoir finds a counterpart in the move from the culinary to the chemical. Bouillon cubes and Vegetine, faux foods with origins in labs rather than in the earth, can be found in every course. While most foods were rationed, these food substitutes were cheap and readily available. The dessert section features a Vegetine tart as well as a Vegetine pudding. Futuristic industrial products proliferate alongside the primordial blood and hearts.

Wartime pushed women to negotiate the boundaries of Italian cuisine to the outer limits of taste and edibility. But this does not mean that they engaged in such projects willingly. Perhaps Foggia's conclusion to her letter to the readers is most telling in this regard. Her final cookbook, and her work as an author, concludes with a plea for peace, even if it comes at the expense of her legacy. Above the image of the white dove with the olive branch in its beak, she expresses her wish for peace in terms of the future demise of this cookbook: "Questa opera mia (diventata vana) possiate metterla – e definitivamente – da parte" (that [having become done in vain] you may put my work – definitively – aside). May the war end, and may my work here become irrelevant, consigned forever to a dusty kitchen shelf.

Translating Domestic Policy into Recipes

How did women think and feel about cooking during the Fascist period? This chapter has interwoven a variety of sources to reveal how a specific group of writers dealt with questions like the many meanings of autarkic eating, the Fascistization of home economics, and what it meant to go from cooking with potatoes to cooking with their peels. The phenomena described here – the *passapiatti* (a semi-open wall set between the kitchen and dining room), the Liebig broth, the commercial tie-ins for domestic writing – pre- and post-date Fascism, but they take on different meanings and intensities during this particular period. Under Fascism, the rationalist drive to separate workspaces and workers so as to specialize and perfect the labour and bodies they housed meant that an apparently innocuous piece of furniture amplified social divisions in the home along gendered lines.

Lidia Morelli and her books hit peak popularity in tandem with Mussolini's influence. Exploring this correlation alongside that of fellow cookbook writers like Ada Boni and Amalia Moretti Foggia reveals what middle-class women's professionalization looked like during this period. It shows educated, liberal ideas like home economics wielded in the service of retrogressive purposes – in this case, for the social control of working-class women so as to raise middle-class women's social status. Female reformers and the Fascist Party shared the aim of granting middle-class women the power to dictate the activities that filled working-class women's days. The Fascist government wanted efficient, productive, hygienic bodies at work, and it ideally did not want to pay for it. By tracing writers' financial tie-ins with *Domus* and Cirio, we see how high design and private food industry were complicit in supporting the regime's alimentary push.

Ingredients and cooking methods matter under the sanctions because they give a feel for the privations of wartime. But narrative structure and character development matter as well. Foggia even assigns different characters to incarnate different food budgets, a critical help to women who would identify with and thus literally become their household resources. Cookbooks could change daily behaviour because recipes rely on procedural discourse, that is, on a series of commands.[33] Imperative-driven formats could prescribe culinary changes, like eating more rice and less pasta, to produce economic benefits for the Fascist state. Studying these documents is valuable for the portrait they paint of how the Fascist regime and major companies envisioned the participation of a discrete population in a broad economic policy. It also underlines cookbooks' unique capacity to serve as bearers of political symbolism.

Cookbooks and domestic manuals by Morelli, Boni, and Foggia show how popular female authors seized the political moment of Fascism and then used it towards different professional ends. Rationalization in industry inflected kitchen management, professionalizing food preparation. Suddenly, it was not enough to prepare the daily minestra. Autarkic onions, carrots, and celery with a home-raised chicken or rabbit had to be diced and measured. Clocks and scales quantified meal preparation. Food work was politicized under Fascism. To cook with autarkic ingredients using rationalist methods meant to prepare food patriotically. Moreover, these women all had to figure out how to make a career as professional women under a regime that advised them to work in the home. In many ways, Morelli, Boni, and Foggia did just that by reframing the home as a workplace. This shift did not valorize women's food work among the professional class or among men as much as it forcibly asserted middle-class women's power over working-class cooks. Cookbooks show how middle-class women used the rhetoric of hygiene to justify increased surveillance and interference in food work. Moreover, Fascist food policies filtered into private kitchens through these cookbooks. Some authors, like Morelli, embraced the regime and called on their readership to adopt these approaches to the kitchen as dynamic protagonists of the electric-appliance-driven age. Others, like Foggia, wished for the regime's end and counselled readers in how to manage Fascist food policy's deleterious effects on their monthly grocery budget. Cookbook authors advocated a range of political attitudes from enthusiastic consent to hard-bitten resistance. But regardless of their attitudes towards the regime, Morelli, Boni, and Foggia were all deeply affected by it. Cookbooks grappled with Fascist food policies in visceral terms. They translated domestic policy into recipes, providing Italians with instructions for how to cook and eat under Fascism.

CHAPTER FIVE

MODEL FASCIST KITCHENS

New, new, new: we hear the word repeated in the dedicatory letter that opens the 1936 edition of Lidia Morelli's domestic guide, *Dalla Cucina al Salotto*, the first to grapple with the onset of the sanctions. "Non sono laudatrice dei tempi antichi" (I'm not one to laud the old days), Morelli claims. She characterizes home life in 1936 in terms of newness and in terms of speed, invoking "questa vita nuova dal ritmo acceleratissimo" (this new life of very accelerated rhythm) to keep up with "nuove mode, nuove gusti, nuovi progressi, nuovi orientamenti" (new ways, new tastes, new progress, new orientations).[1]

So what precipitated all this emphasis on modernity? Home economics, an international movement, arrived relatively late in Italy. Here, home economics emerged as *massaismo*, literally translated as housewifery. That said, unlike the state and party services created to promote the Italian family, the drive to apply scientific management to the home predated Fascism by nearly a decade and drew support from both religious and social groups. On the conservative side, Catholic associations had offered home economics courses in working-class neighbourhoods since before the Great War to bourgeois feminist groups. Augusta Regiani Banfi (the head of the nationalist Italian Woman's Association) founded a mutual aid society to help middle-class women promote home-based businesses in 1921. Republican Teresa Avila Peruzzi founded the Needle Federation the following year.

On the liberal end of the spectrum stood Piedmontese Maria Diez Gasca, perhaps the most prominent advocate of home economics in Italy. An industrialist's daughter who trained as a doctor, Diez Gasca introduced *massaismo* to Italy at the Fourth International Congress of Home Economics in Rome in 1927. In 1929, ENIOS, the government office established the year before to promote scientific management in Italian business enterprises, founded a special monthly called *Casa e lavoro* dedicated to the promotion of rationalist principles in private homes. The assiduous Diez Gasca agreed to serve as the editor. In a parallel to Morelli's comprehensive approach to *Dalla Cucina al Salotto* contributors, Diez Gasca selected the *Casa e lavoro* columnists and freelancers from prominent architects, business managers, and industrialists, as well as fellow women writers characterized as having "a modern outlook," meaning egalitarian relationships with men and interests outside the home. In addition to her editorial work, Diez Gasca was a successful translator. She translated American home economics pioneer Christine Frederick's *The New Housekeeping: Efficiency Studies in Home Management* (1923) into Italian as *La casa moderna: Come risparmiare tempo, fatica e denaro* (1933).

When Christine Frederick and Lillian Gilbreth came to Rome, home economics theories finally took root; these were the early years of Fascism, but from that point, the ideas spread voraciously. Taylorism, the factory management system that divided production into a series of specialized repetitive tasks, now applied to homes. In manufacturing as in cooking, Taylorism aimed to increase efficiency. The Taylorist work triangle, with three different stations for cooking (the stove), cleaning (the sink), and preparation (the table) or storage (the cupboard) was a particularly popular model for rethinking the mechanics of kitchenwork. The very newness of the kitchen as a hygienic and rational space, as well as the reframing of cooking as science, dovetailed smoothly with Fascism's obsession with technology, speed, productivity, and all that was new. Fascism sought these abstract qualities across many realms: literature, film, architecture. Soon enough, new kitchen styles – and authors like Lidia Morelli – took advantage of the political moment, recasting what had been an international trend towards small spotless kitchens as a Fascist concept.

The kitchen and cooking both depend upon and impact spaces outside the home and actions in the public realm. More broadly still, the kitchen has a reciprocal relationship with food production in the factory and the field. This chapter aims to deprovincialize the kitchen through a careful accounting of the architectural history of lived space. Read within this larger context, the kitchen shows how daily actions fed Fascism.

The period's conception of an ideal kitchen reflected broader ideas about Fascist urban aesthetics. Fascist urban planning demolished slums in Rome to create broad avenues and imperial forums. *Sventramento* literally translated as the removal of the city's belly. The language of architectural gutting suggests that the regime was not only concerned with the metaphor of the social body at large but was genuinely and particularly concerned with the stomach and its processes. In other words, they saw the belly of the city as a problem to be solved. *Sventramento* also occurred at the level of the kitchen. In the new kitchen designs, furniture was cleared from the centre of the room to create paths and workspace. Similarly, the city digested its inhabitants by passing them along byways and out into open forums. Streamlined industrial design freed blockages in cities and in bodies, promoting biological efficiency for eugenic purposes, a move that Christina Cogdell has termed "smooth flow."[2]

Ideal Fascist kitchens matter because design inventions for this room parallel, and often magnify, the methods and goals marking Fascist urban planning projects deployed at the municipal scale. Improved urban hygiene promised to speed up human evolution by forcing science and urbanism into a shotgun marriage: it was time to birth a new race of men. Indeed, period publications use the language of vast Pontine Marshes reclamation projects to discuss individual houses in eugenic terms: ultrafunctional "ruralized," that is, decluttered, city apartments were considered "eugenic dwellings" (*casa eugenica*) that would contribute to a "human reclamation" (*bonifica umana*) by promoting their inhabitants' fertility.[3] Put simply, these writings conflated cluttered homes with crowded sterile cities. The open spaces of organized homes evoked the countryside's expansiveness and fertility.[4] This is why organization meant ruralization. Cleaning up made cramped city apartments look and feel more like roomy country houses, and this supposedly prompted a productive boost. The vast majority of the kitchens discussed in this chapter are idealized urban ones, which best evoke the rupture between regime ideology and lived history. I focus on the relatively more rapid and widespread interventions in urban kitchens and the highly variable degrees of success that the regime had in implementing these ideal designs.[5]

Most building projects can be attributed to the private kitchenware firms and designers who translated the state's broad calls for autarky into specific practices for their core consumers. Meaning can be gleaned from the extent and type of decoration, intended and actual use, materials, size, and heft of objects. Put broadly, architects' plans for how their buildings should be used mattered less than the politicized culture that surrounded their construction. Interwar urban planning was infused with Fascist hypotheses about how the world worked, like the fertile countryside and eugenic design. Domestic layout and organization absorbed these politicized concepts, which had consequences for the people who lived in those homes. Kitchens need not have been created with the conscious intention of exerting control over women to influence how women cooked and ate.

To wit, consider how the firms that built such projects were chosen. Industrial design successfully colludes with politics not only because it possesses the capacity to travel from the public sphere to the private, but also because it is a form of intervention in daily life that passes largely undetected by the object's user. Regime-affiliated groups ranging from the Istituto Nazionale Fascista della Previdenza Sociale to the regional Confederazione Fascista dei Professionisti e degli Artisti mobilized design to promote autarky through ideal Fascist kitchens that fused tradition and technology.

Not only did the regime run architectural competitions (*concorsi*) to select the architectural firms to design and construct new urban public housing units and their kitchens and canteens, but it also funded the ongoing maintenance and refurbishment for these projects. For example, the attendee list of the 1936 Lombard Convention, a key urbanism conference, suggests a mix of government and design professions. But the highest levels of influence distinctly emphasize direct political connection to the regime. The *presidenza generale* included Prof. Dante de Blasi, president of the Italian

Fascist Hygiene Association, Prof. Giuseppe Petragnani, general director for public health, Dr. Giuseppe de Capitani Arzago, state minister and president of the Lombard Bank, and Duke Marcello Visconti di Modrone, Milanese magistrate.[6] Moreover, they placed these kitchens under government surveillance, installing building managers to supervise their use by working-class populations in cities from Bari to Milan.[7]

On one hand, halting the spread of disease among the poor is a goal of democratic states and dictatorial states alike. But it is still noteworthy that the means used by the Fascist Italian government relied on authoritarian control of these spaces through surveillance. Frequency and intensity of punitive measures like internal confinement and prison sentences also characterized the Fascist Italian approach to daily life in the public housing projects. Moreover, this was the first time the state attempted to create public housing and to interfere in private life – and is thus highly noteworthy as a tipping point in this regard.[8] Suffice to say, traditional gender roles and technological innovations provided two planks to support the broader goal of hyperproductivity, but economic prudence and trendiness also played significant roles in shaping popular aesthetics. Within the general frame of obeisance to the regime via promotion of autarky, designers took variant approaches. In sum, Fascist politics deeply impacted the concept of the ideal kitchen during the 1930s, increasing the pressure to speed productivity.

The sign of success for the regime's productivity projects was a swollen female stomach. A big belly could indicate prosperity, pregnancy, or both. Eating forms the body from the inside out through the process of digestion: food contributes vitamins, fats, and proteins that form muscles, fire synapses, and power every heartbeat. In less obvious ways, cooking shapes the body from the outside in through the effects of repeated movements. Cooking can stoop backs or callus fingers through daily chopping while bent over a cutting board. The regime's promotion of regional foodstuffs extended beyond the celebration of Tuscan grapes and Piemontese rice. Autarky also encompassed actions associated with food: one could cook, eat, shop, and clean autarkically. Cooking autarkically, for example, meant using aluminium pots and pans. Aluminium was first mined as bauxite ore, then refined in plants, and finally designed and manufactured as cooking tools – all in Italy. Cooking autarkically also meant eschewing the authority of French cuisine by choosing a recipe invented by an Italian cookbook author, then written in the Italian language. Autarky in the kitchen was a total project: it involved the entire supply chain, spanning Italian mines and publishing houses as well as fields and farms.

With all of this in mind, the Fascist government recognized cooking as work, and intervened by introducing Taylorism and rationalism to the kitchen. Increased hygiene and productivity went hand in hand, as these projects were predicated upon the same underlying assumption: working-class women were dirty, wasteful, and generally unhealthy.[9] The daily work of chopping and mixing develops certain muscles; repeatedly hunching over a worktable or sitting straight creates bent backs or straight ones. And spending hours in a dark, cramped, and unwashed space or a light, open, antiseptic one can make a cook more or less susceptible to sickness. Autarky provided a stepping stone to reach a higher ambition: Fascist interventions into the home would cleanse the working-class female body, making her a model of health and strength. Her new vitality would attest to the regime's benevolence and to its power.

Mussolini called for rationalism and autarky in speeches and propaganda, but commercial publications translated these abstract policies into specific guidelines for kitchen management. These texts dictated kitchen spaces and cooking practices aimed at reforming the working-class female body. Incursions to kitchen design, like the implementation of the Taylorist work triangle and increased use of electricity/water flow/sunlight, aimed to sterilize and rationalize working-class female bodies directly. Rationalizing the cook provided the regime's means and its end as well. We might read it in terms of the Futurists' ambitions to adapt human bodies to suit the lightweight aluminium trains of the future.[10] The era's kitchen aesthetics can demonstrate Fascist aesthetics. They evoke a sterile, hyperproductive militarized nation with no need for homemade food or love. Such designs ultimately aimed to remove the cook from the kitchen. Taken to the extreme, model Fascist kitchens function automatically, with no human presence at all.

This chapter provides a case study of Lidia Morelli's *Dalla Cucina al Salotto: Enciclopedia dalla vita domestica* (*From the Kitchen to the Salon: Encyclopedia of Domestic Life*) and the utopic urban kitchens celebrated therein. Arguably the most popular housekeeping guide of the Fascist period, this book, in its content (kitchen plans), structure (opening letters), and tone (friendly and communal but also authoritative and classist), emblematizes the Fascist-period debates about why kitchens mattered and the cohesive nature of those discussions. First, I analyse Morelli's ideal kitchen layout in context with trends in architecture and design to understand the political and social significance of these changes. Reading these documents both with and against the grain illuminates the overlaps and gaps between ideal urban kitchens and actual kitchen use. Morelli's ideal kitchens reveal how middle-class women related to working-class cooks. But indirectly, the gaps, occlusions, and complaints in her texts also intimate how cooks might have felt about their employers. I also situate Morelli's ideal urban kitchen within the broader design and publication trends of the period, namely Piero Bottoni's design work for *La bella casa* (now *Casabella*) and *Domus*, the glossy architectural periodical edited by Gio Ponti during the Fascist period.[11] Model Fascist kitchens demonstrate how old spaces acquire new political meanings under Fascism. They also reveal the circumstantial and fractured nature of designers' personal politics. Taking an inductive approach, this chapter describes kitchen aesthetics in depth as a means to explain Fascist aesthetics at large.

Rationalist Architecture in the Home

Piero Bottoni was one of the leading practitioners of rationalism, serving from 1929 to 1949 as the Italian delegate to the International Congresses of Modern Architecture. *Domus* featured many of his kitchen designs in the mid-1930s. Educated at the Politecnico di Milano, he distanced himself from the institution in 1927 until 1937 for political reasons. Morelli often discusses Bottoni's architecture, layout, and design throughout her work. The 1936 edition of *Dalla Cucina al Salotto* included seventy-five illustrations and twelve tables, the majority of which were originally printed in *Domus*. Morelli opens "La cucina," her third chapter, with *Domus* photography of kitchens and worktables designed by both Piero Bottoni and Ignazio Gardella. In her discussion of stoves, fridges, and other appliances, she also uses photography from brands that advertised in *Domus*. For example, she shows an Algidus Radaelli fridge, its door open to reveal the stuffed shelves of eggs, milk bottles, and tempting paper-and-string packages within. Algidus used this image to hawk its products on *Domus*'s pages throughout the 1930s.

In other words, the characteristics of the ideal Fascist kitchen design and layout did not emerge fully formed from the minds of a handful of male Milanese architects. Rather, they emerged through a collaborative process involving multiple players, female and male, across a variety of disciplines. These sorts of citations between authors and designers also took place at local and global scales. In terms of the former, conversations could occur between authors and designers working at the same publication.

In his writings for *Domus*, Ignazio Gardella followed Morelli's lead. To describe ideal kitchens in his long-running domestic advice column, he often reproduced photos from earlier issues. And like Morelli, he frequently cited Bottoni as a kitchen expert. For instance, in his May 1939 article "Consigli tecnici per la casa," Gardella cites Bottoni both directly in the text and visually in images.[12] Specifically, he shows one of Bottoni's designs for a new type of kitchen worktable: the tabletop is autarkic linoleum, and the slide-open drawers (a ribalta) are rationally designed. Another kitchen table, also by Bottoni, features drawers that slide out to the side, as well as a pull-out natural wood board for pasta making. The placement and design of kitchen worktables were a key issue in the kitchen debates of the Fascist period. In the nineteenth century, kitchens typically placed a large table in the centre of the room. Bottoni's designs are typically of emerging twentieth-century designs that shrank the table and pushed it flush with the kitchen walls so as to rationalize the kitchen space by creating an open central space to promote more-efficient workflow. Similarly, the pull-out drawers reflect a new concern with eliminating unnecessary physical effort in the kitchen, as well as an emerging interest in organized storage. Late-1930s designs attempted to remove the worktable entirely.

Gardella's citation of Bottoni's fame in the kitchen debates serves to assure the *Domus* readership that Gardella understands the key figures in such discussions.

Therefore, his own counsel in this area ought to be taken seriously. In this same article, Gardella also moves from the hyper-local environment of the *Domus* offices to point to international developments in kitchen design. He unfavourably compares old-fashioned Italian kitchens with the modern ones emerging from Swedish and American architectural firms. He further notes the link between national industry and the aesthetics of appliances: for example, he mentions his jealousy of American factory standardization that allowed for matching appliances of the same colours and dimensions, lamenting the fact that Italian firms rarely produced fridges and ovens *in serie*. In sum, not only did these conversations occur vertically, across hierarchical lines of social value like class, gender, and their associated disciplines like architecture and cooking, but they also occurred horizontally, within firms and across oceans.

In particular, though, Bottoni and Morelli's model Fascist kitchens provided a united architectural design to elicit rationalist (re)productive work from working-class women. Analysis of these spaces suggests two key points: first, ideal kitchens should not be considered emblematic of all kitchens constructed or in use during the Fascist period. Many middle-class kitchens remained dirty, cluttered, or fusty. Many working-class kitchens resembled stables due to the presence of livestock for warmth. Second, women used these spaces in a variety of ways that designers did not intend. Nonetheless, the ideal kitchens discussed here do reveal much of how actual kitchens functioned. Here, I focus on middle- and working-class kitchens in the urban context because these spaces were particularly susceptible to forced regime kitchen changes: *Casabella Costruzione* provides a useful case study. Being protected by geographic distance, rural lodgings absorbed politicized design changes more slowly and in different ways.

Kitchens featured by Morelli and Bottoni aim for the smooth flow of water, electricity, and light for hygienic purposes; these material interventions encapsulate the larger trends in Fascist-period urbanism that lurch towards social control. Moreover, I focus on these two figures because their approach to Fascism exemplifies that of many private practitioners who were professionally successful during this period: both are ambiguously allied with the regime. As such, their kitchens showcase an array of design interventions that range from the merely political to the fully politicized. They are, additionally, embedded in transnational conversations of social control in the kitchen that involved Axis and Allied powers alike.

I investigate the origins and trajectories of Morelli and Bottoni's Italian translations of Germanic concepts like the Frankfurt kitchen, as well as American ones like the Taylorist work triangle. These discussions reveal how these noted authors and designers listened to each other's ideas, debated and developed them, and then offered new possibilities for rationalist cooking in a global context. For instance, Morelli and Bottoni often use the same images of kitchen layouts and descriptive text in their books and articles for *Domus*, *La bella casa*, and household guides and almanacs, but each writer focuses on different elements of the same spaces. Morelli may note the fact that her ideal kitchen's white tiles reveal dirt and are easy to clean, whereas Bottoni might focus on how their brightness connotes a modern aesthetic. Tone varies as well: to return to the example above, Morelli often takes an inclusive tack by addressing her readers as a collective *noi*, a move that equalizes author and audience by placing them in the same social category of middle-class women. By contrast, Bottoni addresses his audience with commands in the *voi*, leaning on his expert status to impress the importance of his views upon the readership. In tone as well as content, these documents typify the cross-pollination of Fascist ideas common to domestic publications of the period. This complexity also breaks down many assumptions regarding gender and class in the kitchen. An architecture magazine will feature glossy photos, whereas a household manual will offer practical tips for scrubbing floors and serving soup. But while both magazines and manuals include these instructions and illustrations, they also include some unexpected enthusiasms. Morelli's housekeeping guide discusses rational design at length. Like Bottoni, Morelli regularly contributed to architectural magazines, such as *Casabella*. The feminized arenas of textiles and interior design, rather than the masculine realm of architecture, characterize her contributions here.[13] *Domus* also breaks the mould: architect Ignazio Gardella wrote a regular column on proper kitchen use, including distinctly unglamorous details such as how to conserve stale breadcrumbs and where to store a soaked mop. Eliminating puddles on floor tiles spoke directly to national concerns of the time, like decreasing infant mortality through hygienic child-rearing. By examining each of these documents in terms of content, financing, production, circulation, and use, we see how different people manoeuvred through the kitchen's complex political landscape.

Morelli and Bottoni do not only establish the qualities of the ideal kitchen; they also include instructions for its construction and use. This prescriptive approach to the kitchen characterizes both *Dalla Cucina al Salotto* and *Domus*. They are how-to books, providing the upper, middle, and working class with different scripts for daily, repeated actions in the private sphere. Morelli assumed an audience of middle-class women with a working-class cook in their employ. From the very first page of the 1936 edition of *Dalla Cucina al Salotto*, she frames the importance of rationalist kitchens and autarkic cooking. Indeed, she uses the League of Nations sanctions and her platform as a writer as a springboard to launch one of the main points of the book: to combat the sanctions at home, middle-class women ought to adopt practices to increase productivity and to decrease waste.

Morelli was a rationalist of the first hour. She anticipated the application of rationalism to the private sphere as early as 1921: she had already translated the rationalism of industrial and factory settings into a series of culinary practices and plans for kitchen design in that edition of her book, nearly a decade before *Domus* and *Casabella* began to explore the topic in detail. Fascism's affinity for exploiting working-class women's labour through a series of projects centred on autarky, hygiene, and productivity provided Morelli with a politically salient framework to argue a point that she had made from the beginning: autarkic materials and hygienic practices met through kitchen floors and walls. For instance, she recommends Italian-produced linoleum as a covering for the kitchen table, as it is both impermeable and washable. White walls and cupboards provide a "metodo più moderno e igienico" (a more modern and hygienic method) to "impedire un viavai ingombrante e un perditempo in cucina" (prevent awkward comings and goings and a waste of time in the kitchen). She engaged her readers in this project as active subjects. Each woman was to be "an agent of reform who restores an otherwise marred domestic landscape."[14]

Morelli's titular movement from the *cucina* to the *salotto* illuminates the shifting trajectory between public and private within the Fascist domestic sphere. The kitchen houses productive work behind the scenes. It is an area that supports the semi-public meetings of the salon, a space of social display. Solitary cooking and cleaning took place in the kitchen, whereas the social rituals of afternoon tea were held in the salon. But these definitions of private and public within the house are predicated on a middle-class perspective of the home. For the working-class women employed in the kitchen, this was a semi-public space of employment. Many of these women worked in more than one kitchen each day: they would have cooked for their own families in the tiny kitchens of the *case popolari* in the nascent urban exurbs before travelling into town to work in the kitchens of the middle and upper class.

For urban working-class women, even their own kitchens cannot be considered entirely private. State interventions constructed the kitchens of the *case popolari* with Fascist goals in mind: by introducing the Taylorist work triangle, regime-affiliated architects attempted to rationalize *case popolari* kitchens so as to increase the hygiene and productivity of female working-class spaces and bodies. In addition to architectural interventions, the regime entered these kitchens with prescriptive literature like household guides and almanacs. These interventions underscore the fact that Morelli's movement from the kitchen to the salon was not only a spatial progression but also a classed passage.

How did Morelli characterize the titular *cucina* of her famous housekeeping guide? And more broadly, what can her work tell us about the ideal Fascist kitchen, about the political concepts expressed through Securit glasswork tables and tiled walls of bright white and celestial blue? Using a warm collective address, she walks us through the house: "Cammina cammina, traverseremo il vestibolo, infileremo un corridoio o una serie di stanze, e senza lasciarci distrarre o incuriosare, punteremo dritto sulla cucina" (Walking, walking, we will cross the vestibule, pass through a hallway or a flight of stairs, and, without letting ourselves get distracted or curious, we'll head straight to the kitchen). From her dedicatory letter describing the sanctions as a motive for rationalist housekeeping, Morelli proceeds into "la casa nel suo insieme" (the house in its entirety) before zooming in to focus on the kitchen in chapter three. Pausing with her at the threshold, what do we see?

Standing at the kitchen entrance, we see a small, white room with a black floor with four discrete zones: a work area (a table), a storage area (a cabinet), a cooking area (a stove), and a cleaning area (a sink). Moving clockwise from the left, we begin with the work area, composed of a preparation table with a chair. An apple crostata appears to be in preparation: on the tabletop is a black ceramic mixing bowl filled with flour. A half-peeled apple posed on a napkin sits beside a small, serrated knife and a white ceramic plate. This first zone is the cook's primary workspace, where she would sit to peel and chop apples, to sift flour, and to mould the pastry for baking. Moving a bit to the right, we enter the storage area. Here, a cabinet twice as tall as the worktable stands flush with the back wall. Glass cabinets open to reveal white tea and coffee cups. Just below, the counter provides a space to set the ingredients and machines for preparing afternoon coffee: sugar, coffee, and a coffee grinder, a new appliance for the period. A black cord snakes between the grinder and the wall, marking a key modern innovation that would otherwise be invisible: this kitchen is wired for electricity.

Although we cannot see the contents of the pull-out drawers and swing-open cabinets below, Morelli's chapter "Fabbisogno" (Tools) states the drawers might contain flatware and kitchen tools like ladles, with the pots and pans neatly stacked in the cabinets below. At the centre of the image, we see the two most important elements of the kitchen, both in the cooking area: the clock and the stove. This photo appears to have been shot at an angle so as to place the clock at the kitchen's hub to mark its beating heart. The effort that the photographer put into centring the clock suggests that time ruled women's cooking work. It is a quarter to two, and the three-burner stove bears a double boiler, perhaps gently simmering a soup for a late lunch. Below the burners, the oven awaits the apple crostata in progress. Although no wires are visible, four circular dials mark the oven as electric. Finally, in the cleaning zone, we see two white towels hung from dedicated hooks, ready for use above a sink filled with dishes. Tubes and pipes mark the modernity of the kitchen, rendering hidden hydraulics conspicuously visible. From top to bottom, we see a water tank, the external pipes, the faucet, the sink itself, and the release pipes below.

Morelli's ideal kitchen thus includes every element described by Ignazio Gardella in his ideal kitchen list for *Domus*: in order of importance, he recommends that every working-class kitchen have an electric clock, appliances "for coffee grinding, potato mashing, meat grinding, etc.," a trashcan (*vuotatutto*) that "must be emptied often to keep flies away, and a hydraulic set-up: an instant water heater and a water softener" (*addolcitore d'acqua*). Rather than use the more common *bidone* or *cestino*, Gardella invents a two-part neologism, the *vuotatutto*, or "empty-all," a linguistic invention that evokes F.T. Marinetti's bid for linguistic autarky as described in *La cucina futurista*. That new culinary lexicon had promised to banish French and English import words from the Italian kitchen: the maître d'hotel would become a *guidopalato* (palate guide), and a sandwich would be a *traidue* ("between two [slides of bread]").[15] Gardella appends these two final suggestions, noting the need for a water supply where no hydraulic set-up is available and explaining the need for the water softener in terms of the effects of excessive calcium on cooking times and food taste. These two concessions to the minimal hydraulics in the *case popolari* shows that he is one of few *Domus* writers with an awareness for the reality of working-class kitchens.[16]

Morelli couches this new kitchen design as a remedy to the "alloggio insufficiente e mal congegnato" (insufficient and badly designed lodgings) of public housing developments. Her treatment of the kitchen in chapter three demonstrates how middle- and working-class women negotiated the challenges of modernity. Class disruption, the discovery of germs, and the spread of electricity all played out through objects like swivelling stools, linoleum floors, and aluminium toasters. Granted, many different motives fed into these domestic trends. The fervour for hygiene that swept Italy in the 1930s was due as much to scientific advancements as to Fascist eugenic planning. But it is only by analysing the resulting admixture – the kitchen – that we can understand how everyday spaces become politicized under the dictatorship and, conversely, the limits of the regime's control over women's food work. To examine these issues, let us follow Morelli's chapter structure. In her guide, Morelli discusses the space, the materials, the oven, the sink, the tools (*fabbisogno*, etymologically derived from "fa bisogno," basic needs), and the governance of the kitchen. If these chapters promised solutions to her readership, then they also pose a question to historians. What problems was she trying to solve?

Shrinking Kitchens, Expanding Living Rooms

Morelli's ideal kitchen in figure 5.2 emblematizes the Fascist-period trend towards shrinking kitchens. Her caption for this ideal kitchen conflates small dimensions with an organized workflow, "L'insieme di questa cucina, tutt'altro che grande e ingombro, provvede in tutto alla sua funzione" (This kitchen set-up, anything but large and awkward, arranges everything according to its function). As her contrastive phrasing suggests, examples of modern twentieth-century kitchens were continually juxtaposed against the old-fashioned nineteenth-century designs: "large and awkward" spaces where function did not follow form.

"Intolerable Kitchens," a 1910 prefect's report from Udine, lists the characteristics that public housing planners for the regime would later deem unacceptably old-fashioned: Prior to the nineteenth century, the majority of Italian homes consisted of one large multipurpose room (Fig. 5.1). The kitchen served as a workspace and a communal bedroom. People, cows, chickens, dogs, and cats – all gathered together around the hearth fire. Before central heating, warmth, rather than specialization of purpose or division of inhabitants, was the key concern for kitchen design and use. Because kitchens housed many bodies, both animal and human, they held negative associations as dark, dirty spaces.

5.1. "Visioni di Sardegna: Interno rustico" (Visions of Sardinia: Rustic interior) postcard. Photo taken in Laconi, Sardinia, by Ditta G. Dessi (Cagliari). Photo printed as postcard by Fotocelere in Turin, Italy, in 1925. (ACS, MRF, b. 90, f. 151 sf 6–10, Rome, Italy)

The petite dimensions of Morelli's ideal kitchen react against these qualities: its small size squeezes out everyone but the cook, confining the room's purpose to cooking only (Fig. 5.2). While these twinned trends reached an apex in the kitchen, they also emblematized two broad shifts in 1920s and 1930s domestic design in Italy: rooms became specialized in their use and in their inhabitants. In the case of the kitchen, it became a space for food preparation only, to be used by a single, female worker. Two key factors drove the fashion for diminishing kitchens: first, rising domestic labour costs led to fewer workers in the kitchen. In middle-class households, the former lady of the house often became the de facto cook. Second, and relatedly, the rise of the home economics movement aimed to rationalize and sterilize food preparation. Smaller workstations with continuous countertops saved time, and proper lighting and ventilation improved hygiene, remodelling the large and cumbersome kitchen of the past into a small, sanitary laboratory.

Morelli's ideal kitchen can thus be seen as part of the Fascist-period attempts at socially engineering the working class. *Domus* advocated a specific form of family-level social control in the private sphere: as kitchens shrank, living rooms grew. For example, Gardella suggested that the apartments in the new Milanese apartment blocks be built with kitchens in the smallest possible dimensions "per *impedire* che la famiglia si raccolga a vivere e a mangiare in cucina" (to *impede* the family from coming

5.2. Kitchen photograph, *Dalla Cucina al Salotto: Enciclopedia della Vita Domestica* (1935), 24a.

together to live and eat in the kitchen [emphasis Gardella's]).[17] Put another way, architects shrank kitchens not only to keep working-class women in but also to keep their families out, nudging them into different rooms of the house. Specifically, Gardella urged working-class families to spend more time actually living in their living rooms, though, in reality, many families preferred to treat these spaces like upper-class salons, cordoning them off except for formal display to visiting guests.[18]

Public housing for the working class set these ideas in cement: the cheapest available housing in a new Milanese apartment complex laid out in the November 1939 issue of *Casabella Costruzione* listed the specialized rooms it contained according to their size: the living room, 9.35 metres squared; the bedroom, 8.37; the bathroom, 2.77; and finally the kitchen, 2.25 metres squared. A semi-public entrance added 1.26 metres squared for a total of 24 metres squared in this *alloggio minimo*. The living room is the largest room in the house, almost three times the size of the smallest room, which is the kitchen. Consider this in contrast to nineteenth-century homes, where the kitchen and living room were one and composed the largest (if not the only) room in the house. The relatively large size of the new living room almost seems like overcompensation, an acknowledgment that this was a contested space. For working-class Italians in the Fascist period, the living room and the leisure that it implied were not yet viewed as necessary or useful. While the middle-class women of

Morelli's text were gently ushered from the *cucina* to the *salotto*, working-class families were actively squeezed out of the kitchen and into the living room by *Domus*. In
doing so, a statement was made about who was supposed to spend how much time in
which room of the house. The kitchen went from being a space for everyone to being
a space exclusively associated with women. Gardella mused,

> Mi pare si possano raggruppare i servizi di cucina delle normali abitazioni, soprattuto
> per quanto riguarda la loro disposizione nell'alloggio in due categorie: servizi di cucina
> per appartamenti popolari-economici, dove il lavoro di cucina è svolto direttamente
> dalla padrona di casa; e servizi di cucina per appartamenti dove il lavoro di cucina è
> svolto da una persona di servizio.

> It seems to me that one can group the kitchen services of normal homes, especially in
> terms of their placement in the lodging, in two categories: kitchen services for popu-
> lar-economic apartments, where the kitchen work is undertaken directly by the woman
> of the house; and kitchen services for apartments where the work of the kitchen is
> undertaken by a service person.[19]

Of course, Gardella's differentiation between the "woman of the house" in the *case
popolari* apartment and the "service person" of the middle-class kitchen obscures the
fact that these two people were often the same woman. A working-class woman's
identity shifted from woman of the house in the morning, when she prepared breakfast at dawn for her own family, to service person at her place of employment in
another woman's kitchen for most of the day, and then back to woman of the house
again when she returned home in the evening. The same woman would work in more
than one kitchen per day. Although she stayed the same, the kitchens she worked in
would have been very different. For this reason, Morelli presented not one but two
ideal kitchens to solve this social paradox.

Whereas the clock dominated Morelli's first ideal kitchen, gleam – sunlight from
the window bouncing off linoleum shelves and aluminium appliances – characterizes
her second kitchen (Fig. 5.3). Moving from left to right, this kitchen is a hall of mirrors:
a large shelving unit's spotless metal backsplash reflects another open shelving unit and
its drawer pull – the cleanliness of the room allows us to see invisible parts of the kitchen
that are obscured by the camera angle. A large pot with an inexplicable number of handles casts shadows against the shelves. At the centre of the photograph, a large horizontal window provides the all-important natural light source that animates this space. Also
central to this scene are the five domestic trophies – new appliances – arrayed on the
worktable and electric stove below. A stand mixer with its bulbous balloon whisk, an orange juicer, and a coffee grinder are all poised at the ready. Both the mixer and the juicer
flaunt their status as electric rather than hand-powered tools. Like the coffee grinder
in Morelli's first ideal kitchen, their black cords twirl ostentatiously frontward. These

electric wires and the modernity they
display trump rationalist injunctions to
keep the cooking workspace clear and
unencumbered. On the four-burner
electric stove, a pot and a Moka await
the cook's attentions. Here, the cook
can choose from three different cooking
zones: the stovetop, the upper oven for
broiling meat and vegetables, and the
lower oven for baking bread and cakes.
As with Morelli's first ideal kitchen, this
major appliance sits front and centre,
indicating its importance. Sun from the
window signals that it's morning and
that we are approaching breakfast time.
But come sundown, an electric light on
the right wall of the room will illuminate

5.3. Piero Bottoni, kitchen photograph. *Dalla Cucina al Salotto: Enciclopedia della Vita Domestica*, 24b.

dinner preparations. Is that a *tabella dietica* (nutritional table) that we see above the sink?
That dinner will be sure to uphold the latest nutritional studies. Sunlight and electric
light reveal kitchen cleanliness by showing gleam on wiped surfaces and by evoking a
dull reflection on dirty ones. A new emphasis on glass and metal intensifies this effect.
Appliances minimize or eliminate cooking actions where the cook's hands touch the
food, as in whipping cream, squeezing oranges, and grinding coffee.

This focus on the importance of washable materials and sterile machines is purely
Morelli's: this ideal kitchen photograph appeared in other publications, including on
the pages of *Domus*, but the values ascribed to this space are hers alone, as evinced by
the characterization of the space in her figure citation: "Arch. Piero Bottoni. Cucina,
questa, più grande e completa, dove dalle pareti in materiale gommato lavabile ai mo-
bili di vetro e metallo, agli scaffali in linoleum, tutto è perfetta espressione di igiene."
(Arch. Piero Bottoni. Kitchen, this one, larger and more complete, where from the
walls in washable rubberized material to the glass and metal furniture to the shelves
in linoleum, everything is the perfect expression of hygiene.) But when we speak of
the ideal Fascist kitchen, what is the significance of this perfect hygiene? In other
words, what does gleam really mean?

Hygiene: The Meaning of Gleam

Designing for cleanliness carried a moral and, as we shall soon see, a political charge;
it was not just the frequent washing of these materials that marked a housewife as
good but her selection of these materials in her kitchen's construction in the first

place. Bacteria had only recently been discovered to be the origin of tuberculosis, the eradication of which obsessed the Fascist regime.[20] In 1927, Mussolini launched the Battle Against Tuberculosis, which he characterized as a "social disease." Citing ISTAT statistics, he levelled the charge that tuberculosis cost Italy 1,315 lives in 1925, a disturbing rise from the 664 deaths caused by the disease in 1922.

The meaning of sanitation spread from the microbial to the political. Tuberculosis passes from person to person via microscopic water droplets sprayed by coughing, sneezing, or spitting, but also by laughing or singing. Meanwhile, regime organs for hygienic urbanism like *Architettura* and *Difesa Sociale*, as well as key actors like Dr. Elena Fambri, director of L'Istituto Fascista di Medicina Sociale, suggested that ideas move like germs do, jumping from person to person more readily in neighbourhoods with high population density.[21] By logical extension, working-class apartment blocks provided the dangerously crowded conditions necessary for not one but two problems: rapid tuberculosis transmission and potential political instability. Scholars of Fascist urbanism like Claudia Lazzaro and Roger Crum have noted that the massive guttings that followed demolished whole city neighbourhoods with the aim of increasing the flow of air and light to mitigate poor hygiene.[22] But few historians have noted that working-class restaurants, and the liberal political conversations they sheltered, played a key role in these larger interventions.

Osterie and cheap public restaurants, according to the regime, needed to be the first targets of the war on tuberculosis and its concurrent *risanamento* projects. The regime moved legislatively to diminish public food and drink consumption in the city by increasing the ratio of inhabitants to public bars from 500:1 to 1000:1 and limited hours for the sale of alcoholic beverages, a move that resulted in the closure of 25,000 osterie after the law's passage in June 1926.[23] Improving hygiene to fight tuberculosis excused the politicized gutting of the public restaurants. As Mussolini sarcastically noted in his Ascension Day speech, "Since we [Fascists] probably will not have the opportunity to solicit votes from bar owners and their clients, as happened during the democratic-liberal Middle Ages, we can afford ourselves the luxury of closing these dispensaries of cheap, ruinous happiness."[24]

Clearing the air by design became a Fascist principle at the level of both the urban block and each apartment. In her description of the ideal outfitting for the model kitchen, Morelli deems materials the foremost consideration for hygiene. Colours transcend workaday cleanliness and seem to aspire to celestial purity: she recommends clear glass tabletops, white linoleum floors, sky-blue tiled walls, chrome backsplashes, and silver aluminium pots and pans. *Domus*'s editorial staff echoed Morelli's focus on colour, opening a collectively authored article on ideal kitchens with the injunction that "tutt'è bianco, o meglio, azzurro celeste" (everything is white, or better, sky blue).[25] In Morelli's photo, everything shines in the clear, silver, white, and blue colours of the sky, indicating that a woman has recently wiped every surface: the gleam of the stove's chrome-plated nickel reflects in the spotless linoleum floor. The materials for the kitchen floors and walls, as well as the kitchen furniture like shelving and tables, marked and promoted hygiene by being easily washable and by revealing dirt on their light-coloured surfaces. Brightly coloured foods, like the red tomato, the orange, or the tuft of parsley, reflected across these mirrored planes, rendering the kitchen "vivo ed adorno" (alive and adorned).[26] But the constant wiping necessary to maintain these shining surfaces would have been impossible without the new hydraulic capacity behind these sinks and the electric (and gas) connections behind the stoves and appliances.

This new attention to kitchen cleanliness became possible during the Fascist period due to improvements in electricity, ventilation, and hydraulics in private homes. Consider the attention that *Domus* paid to sinks: they specify that each sink should have two basins and two faucets (*rubinetti*) with hot and cold water, as well as, ideally, two draining spaces (*sgocciolatoi*). Sinks were novelties: a generation before, indoor plumbing was rare. This set-up provided a linear workflow: first, one placed the dirty dishes in the left drainage space, washed them in the first sink in hot water, rinsed them in the second, and then left them to dry on the right drainage space. Underneath the sink, cleaning products like soda and pumice stones (*pomice*) stood ready to help.[27] The hydraulic capacity of the working-class Italian kitchen could even conjure the glories of Roman aqueducts, the ultimate Fascist realization of Romanità. As architect and *Casabella Costruzione* editor Giuseppe Pagano put it, "Quando la percentuale dei bagni nelle abitazioni italiane sara salita da 9 a 25% sara una bella tappa nella riconquista della civilta e ci saremo avvicinati alle tradizioni romane ben più che con la scimmiesca imitazione degli anacronistici colonati" (When the percentage of bathrooms in Italian homes has risen from 9 per cent to 25 per cent it will be a great step in the reconquest of civilization, and we will have come closer to Roman traditions, much more than with the apelike imitation of anachronistic columns).[28] It was significant to designers that the invisible kitchen infrastructure of pipes, tubes, cables, wires, and ducts in each individual kitchen connected with larger water mains, generators, and exhaust valves at the level of the apartment complex. Such infrastructure, in middle-class and working-class homes, was quite new during the Fascist period and was celebrated in luxurious advertisements in *Domus* (Fig. 5.4). Faceless and with one arm obscured by a towel held behind her head, standing at a three-quarter turn, the nude female figure here evokes an ancient Roman sculpture. Little wonder then that the appliances wear their wires with the pomp and pageantry of a beauty queen's sash: their invisible flows and currents indicated a new domestic modernity, one marked by hygienic appliances – *elettrodomestici*, the new electric servants.

Electric Servants for the Modern Hostess

Chief among the new cast of "electric servants" for the modern hostess is the stove: as Morelli affirms, this appliance "tiene – è evidente – il primo posto" (has, it's evident,

5.4. Advertising illustration opposite "Note di economia domestica," in *Domus*, July 1937.

the first place). Electric stoves, like this 1935 American model (Fig. 5.5), cooked food faster and with less effort. They also made cooking a cleaner process: whereas wood and even gas create ash, smoke, and fumes, electricity burns without a trace. And perhaps most centrally, they replaced the female working-class cook with a sleek and sexless metal box: What could be more modern? Morelli intimates all three of these benefits to the electric stove. First, she suggests that electricity's inherent hygiene is reason enough to convert from another type of hearth. Next, she further characterizes electricity as practical and easy to adopt. And finally, Morelli suggests that form indicates function in the context of stoves, in that solid materials and construction could ensure a more consistent temperature thanks to a steady flame. Whereas a cook necessitated constant supervision, governing an electric stove meant simply turning a dial. In middle-class kitchens, middle-class women took on working-class cooking, and the cook became a stove. People turned to machines, realizing a Futurist dream.

5.5. Magic Chef stove. American Stove Company, manufactured in Missouri, 1935. Enamelled steel, chromium-plated steel, cast iron, stainless steel, plastic. Author's photo. (Wolfsonian Institute, Miami, XX1989.245)

But what of upper-class kitchens that maintained a cook and a stove? Morelli treats those cooks and appliances differently, promoting the status of both: the cook is described as an army officer and the appliances serve as her foot soldiers, or, at the very least, as her weaponry. "Così preparata ad attaccare l'ignobile lotta contro l'unto, la servetta – o la massaia – si accinge coraggiosamente e con l'ausilio di armi adatte, a debellare il nemico" (Thus prepared to attack the ignoble struggle against grease, the maid – or the housewife – courageously prepares herself, with the auxiliary of appropriate weapons, to defeat the enemy).[29] This narrative casts both cook and housewife in a heroic light and lends gravity to their work. Morelli frequently invokes this analogy in the context of providing the necessary tools for a cook to do her job, be they the proper garments or utensils: "Allo stesso modo che non si può esigere da un soldato che ben combatta se lo si lascia senza armi, non si potrà pretendere da una cuoca che estrinsechi le sue abilità, se non avrà sottomano le efficacissime armi per la lotta contro la fame" (In the same way that one cannot expect a soldier to fight well if you leave him without weapons, one cannot expect a cook to express her abilities if she does not have very effective weapons for the fight against hunger).[30] Because many families had a soldier at the front, emotional ties stretched from the kitchen to the battlefield. Inter-class suspicion colours domestic manuals like Lidia Morelli's. Recommendations to middle-class women include peeping into the kitchen every so often to ensure that the working-class cook is keeping the wall and floor tiles freshly washed. Periodic checks also supposedly ensured that the cook was busy cooking, not wasting time by smoking a cigarette. Cooks were not trusted to maintain good kitchen hygiene if left to their own devices, suggesting that middle-class women viewed cooks, and food work, as inherently dirty. In contrast to the unpredictability of living cooks, the domestic manuals frame electric appliances as more reliable and hygienic helpers. They could be trusted to cook meals quickly and healthfully every time. Writ broadly, such manuals recommended trusting machines over people. As this rhetoric shows, Morelli's characterization of the inter-class relationships in the kitchen was highly influenced by Fascism and by the mounting bellicosity in the years leading up to World War II.

Dirt and mess in the kitchen supposedly led to sickness and death in the family. Morelli characterizes the cook as a soldier who fights these abstract foes through hygienic products that just so happen to be made of autarkic materials that support domestic industry. It is no coincidence that every material presented here is not only washable but also made in Italy. Man-made domestic materials reign: glass, stainless steel, linoleum, and aluminium were all major Italian industries that took off under Fascism. New, scientific-sounding material names – like Securit and Temperit[31] – proliferated. Because the majority of these new materials shone, light came to signify autarky: an ideal kitchen photo published in *Domus* the same year as Morelli's text reflects this connection. Here, sunbeams bounce off shining tiles, lacquered furniture, chrome metal finishes, and Securit glass tables.[32] In Morelli's text, aluminium receives a soliloquy for its hygiene: "Più conveniente … privo d'ogni pericolo, di cui si spiega il grandissimo attuale favore … e si pulisce con la massima facilità" (More convenient … and without any danger, which explains its current great favour … and one can clean it with the greatest of ease).[33] Morelli's passion for aluminium is rivalled only by her love of linoleum, which she suggests as a covering for the floor ("so much easier to clean than old-fashioned stone floors!"), as well as the walls and even the tabletops. Again, hygiene – now conflated with modernity too – provides the justification for selecting autarkic materials.

Morelli used science to suggest the superiority of Italian materials. She notes that laboratory tests demonstrated that no food can alter aluminium utensils. Broadly speaking, Morelli's emphasis on these easy-to-clean materials speaks to the Fascist period's obsession with hygiene and to the recent discovery of microbes and germs. But it also speaks to the strengthening links between national chemical, plastics, and glass industries and the home. Hygiene under Fascism can be considered slippery: the period's associations with soap and water slide from the Catholic morality of cleanliness to washable autarkic materials.

Architect Giuseppe Pagano went so far as to decry antiquated architecture – not its construction, but the building itself, as immoral. Conflating the unhygienic (*malsana*) with the immoral (*male*), he argued that "malsana e immorale architettura" (unhealthy and immoral architecture) created an unhealthy home (*casa malsana*). The idea of the *casa malsana* was not Pagano's own: architects, doctors, and social scientists in the 1920s and 1930s widely blamed the unhealthy dwelling for depressing the national birth rate.[34] This negative model, perhaps the opposite of the ideal kitchens examined here, was characterized by poor construction, faulty electric wiring, and excessive decoration ("male illuminata, male costruita," "false decorazioni") which combined to produce a "fabbrica di malattie infettive," the dark shadow of these bright Taylorist dreams.[35]

By contrast, cooking with machines made from autarkic materials (aluminium and chrome) and presenting food in dishware cast in the characteristic hues of these metals (shades of silver) imbued cooks with the modern aesthetic that Fascism took pains to associate with these metals.[36] Materials matter in kitchen object use, and so does physical form: ladles and cups act as extensions of the body, safely and artfully conveying hot liquids from tureen to bowl or kitchen to dining room when hands cannot. Because cooks handled these objects every day, they began to feel like body parts. After endless chopping, it is hard to say where the arm ends and the knife begins. Calluses hardened on the outsides of hands, and muscles knotted on the insides of shoulders. Kitchen tools not only guided women's motions; they also altered their bodies, inside and out.

As industrial design historian Donald Norman has observed, different types of materials prompt people to use objects in specific ways, an idea he refers to as "affordances" – glass invites delicate movements, while wood suggests rusticity.[37] Using a toaster rather than an open fireplace, for example, created an upper-class body. Metalwork signals a shift from old cooking methods, such as heating food over an open hearth, to new ones, such as toasting bread with electricity in a chrome-plated appliance. With an open fireplace, one would need to lean over the flames, possibly while manipulating a heavy iron grill, which would redden and roughen the servant's face, hands, and arms over time. It would also build out her arm muscles. With a toaster, the lady of the house just pushes a button, allowing body parts to stay delicate, white, and unmuscled – the markers of female upper-class status in Northern Italy at this

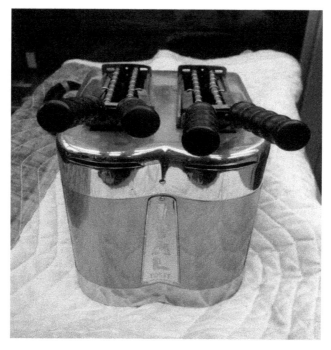

5.6. Toaster, Milan, manufactured by ItalToast, chrome. (Wolfsonian Institute, Miami, xx1990.393)

time. In addition, electric cooking used far less of the body than cooking with fire did. Meanwhile, showing an ease with machines such as airplanes or automobiles was a mark of masculine modernity during this period. It was very chic to know how to drive a car. Showing off an ease with electric appliances served a similar function for middle-class Italian women.

Foreign products had previously reigned as the height of fashion for these objects, casting an aura of modernity and style over Italian designs for coffee makers and tea-cups that aided the autarkic cause. With this idea in mind, we can glean the meaning of style and construction from the perceived and actual properties of an ItalToast toaster, a popular kitchen appliance.

Designed in Milan, this electric ItalToast chrome toaster (Fig. 5.6) features two sets of adjustable heat-level controls. The construction allows the cook to minutely control multiple facets of the cooking process by turning dials and pushing buttons. A flashing red alert light takes on the attending work previously required of the servant. In addition to being composed of autarkic materials, metal-based electric appliances such as the ItalToast toaster decreased the time and toil necessary to feed a family. By automating these elements, the toaster abstracts the cooking process from the original combination of fire, pan, and bread into a Taylorist succession of easy hand movements, rather than difficult full-body operations. Moreover, cooking faster and with less effort meant cooking in a modern way. This object's physical aesthetics signal modernity with its streamlined curves and metallic shine; so does its function.

To echo Norman's terminology, metal affords electric work in a way that other materials do not, as it conducts and withstands high heat without melting, cracking, or exploding. Speed and hygiene mark the object in its design and in its use. This toaster suggests that increasing the speed of cooking while diminishing the effort involved was a positive practice that marked the lady of the house as fashionably modern. By accelerating the toasting of bread, this kitchen appliance translates Taylorism into a daily practice for the domestic sphere. Appliances were still fairly uncommon at this point, but small ones like this toaster were far more accessible than large ones like refrigerators, meaning that autarky could be practised by more than just the upper class. Small appliances like toasters typically cost less than 300 lire. This was at a time when a pair of women's shoes cost 48 lire, and a bus ticket or a stamp for a letter cost 0.50 lire. A car, like the Fiat 500 Topolino, would cost 10,800 lire.[38]

Like the *passapiatti*, this toaster would have helped women negotiate class boundaries between the kitchen and the salon. One might expect a toaster to sit on a counter in the working-class space of the kitchen. This is because most contemporary Americans associate toast with breakfast in one's kitchen, but in the social context of the 1930s, toast was served in salons for afternoon tea. This chic object served social wants, not bodily needs. A *Domus* column providing advice on new electric appliances echoed this idea in their coverage of the *tostapane elettrico*: "Eccovi ora un apparecchietto di importanza certo non vitale, ma tuttavia utilissimo a tutte le nostre donnine di casa: il tostapane elettrico" (Now here is a little device certainly of non-vital importance, but nonetheless very useful to our little ladies of the house: the electric toaster).

Here, we see modern appliances cast as stars in the breaking news.[39] The Elettrodomestico notes page was structured like a series of small bulletins and updates. This format uses the associated speed of news tickers to connote the modernity of Italian technology: inventions proliferate so fast that they require news bulletins. As the introduction explains, this recurring section is about new objects and useful, practical appliances for "donnine" (little women), another diminutive for the middle-class woman who cooked. The advertising copy extends the decorative – as opposed to utilitarian – characterization of the toaster from the electric servant to its master, the woman who used it; repeated diminutives for the toaster and the woman raise their class status but do so by reducing their utility to that of "non-vital importance."

Looks matter more than function: the article turns on aesthetics, focusing on the toaster (and presumably the *donnina*'s) "aspetto elegante" (elegant look) and the associated social benefits the object can provide. A sexy toaster lets the signora (emphatically not the cook) prepare toast "senza allontanarsi dal salotto, e, quello che forse più importa, senza interompere la conversazione con le amiche" (without leaving the salon, and, perhaps even more importantly, without interrupting the conversation with friends). Two levels of meaning mobilize here. Literally, owning a toaster meant that the lady of the house did not have to physically leave the salon to go to the kitchen. Figuratively, it also speaks to the fact that she would not have to leave the middle-class social environment and the conversation with other women of the same stature to become a working-class cook, even for the three minutes necessary to toast a piece of bread. In sum, the class status of food (toast) and people (cook vs. signora) is not fixed: as this toaster ad copy proves, their class status could fall – or rise – as they moved, as in Morelli's title, *Dalla Cucina al Salotto*.

The visually apparent characteristics of metal, such as its shine, smoothness, and association with machines, imply modernity, even when found in other materials. Gleam emanates from a ceramic coffee set glazed in bright primary colours as well as black and white. Stark colour or material differentiates between discrete functional parts of objects, such as an aluminium coffee maker with wooden handles. So while all these different materials (metal, wood, and clay) were produced in Italy by Italian designers, the aesthetic of modernity unites them, as does their physical destination – the kitchen. All of these utensils take on further meanings depending on their intended physical context, on a stove or in a drawer, or more broadly, in the kitchen or in the living room. For example, a bread plate on the kitchen table could be considered functional, but that same object could be considered decorative if it were mounted on the dining room wall. By asking what role these objects played in context, we can better understand how they shaped daily life in private homes.

Kitchen objects also absorb cultural meanings from their associated foods. Definitionally, a teacup holds tea. And just as tea can stain a teacup, tea's meaning can colour the cup as well. In this particular case, the relationship between the tea and the teacup evokes a larger question: What characteristics defined a product or an object as Italian? Not only is afternoon tea a foreign ritual, but tea itself is also a foreign product. How then to reinscribe tea, as well as coffee, sugar, and chocolate, as domestic and thus autarkic? At stake in these two issues were the tabletop politics of Fascist imperialism and alimentary autarky. A visually dazzling Italian teacup heralded a cultural shift – it signalled the beginning of the end of France's and England's monopoly over style in Italian homes. But how do these associations of tea – energy, expense, and above all colonialism – stain a teacup? A simple tea set exemplifies how kitchen object design negotiated politicized questions of autarky and how women used these aesthetics for patriotic self-presentation at tea time.

Aesthetics of smooth flow emerge in a ceramic tea set by the designer Galvani (based in Friuli-Venezia Giulia), produced in Pordenone around 1935 (Fig. 5.7). Jet black and gleaming, this tea set evokes modernity using two of the same elements as the ItalToast toaster: gleam and novel form. Although ceramic, the tea set's black glaze and smooth texture cast off light. Sharp colour contrast between the matte orange on the oval-shaped handles and knob finials energizes the visual composition. Brightness draws attention to the rendering of the cup handles: while traditional in that it allows for a modified handgrip of the cup, the ovoid form departs from the

5.7. Galvani, tea set, Pordenone, c. mid-1930s, ceramic. (Wolfsonian Institute, Miami, 84.7.27.9)

formerly diffuse English teacup handle style: a dainty ear-shaped curve. Form (novel), material (clay), and aesthetics (modern) mark this tea set as conceived and manufactured in Italy, making it an autarkic product.

What would this object have meant in physical context? Tea also embodied the paradox of a stimulant drunk slowly. As such, tea embodied what Jeffrey Schnapp refers to modernity's double logic of speed and speed limits. Modernity evokes a constant sense of urgency due to the pressures of quantifiable productivity. At the same time, this "tempo and complexity give rise to distinctive forms of slowness: distractions, bureaucratic delays, traffic jams."[40] While the beverage is quickly prepared, one spends a languid afternoon taking part in tea's ritualized consumption.

In Italy, tea drinking never attained the popularity of coffee consumption. And in the 1930s, the beverage went from vaguely unpopular to potentially seditious. To enact this well-known British culinary tradition in sanction-bound Italy was politically risky, if not downright unpatriotic. In the 1935 edition of *Dalla Cucina al Salotto* Lidia Morelli went so far as to add an introductory letter to claim regret that her publishers had not had time to edit her description of té alle cinque to comply with linguistic autarky. It was the gendered, classed, and foreign associations of tea drinking, rather than the product itself, that became problematic under the sanctions. Yet design offered a powerful and politically expedient mode to redefine afternoon tea as properly modern and autarkic, as well as Fascist and Italian. Being both decorative and functional, this tea set beautifies the table. We see the products prior to consumption; in contrast to the ItalToast toaster, these objects do not attempt to modernize, sterilize, or accelerate the cooking process. Instead, these objects act as diplomats, translating foreign rituals and products into domestic ones. By serving tea to guests with this explicitly Italian service, the lady of the house could mark herself as patriotic, or even chic, with her up-to-the-moment awareness of the Fascist political climate.

By examining kitchen objects like this tea set against their larger political context, we can better understand how some women displayed status during the Fascist
period. Morelli's final chapter, "Governance: The Cook in Action," concerns the relationships between the working-class cook, the middle-class lady, the kitchen, and
cooking. To demonstrate the ideal interactions for these two actors, the space they oc-
cupy, and the actions they undertake, Morelli advocates that middle- and upper-class
women install Frankfurt kitchens in their apartments so as to place cooks within the
Taylorist work triangle. Both of the ideal kitchens visited thus far exemplify both of
these terms, but let us examine what each meant in the transnational context of the
interwar period.[41]

Taylorist Work Triangles in Frankfurt Kitchens

Austrian architect and domestic economist Margarete ("Grette") Schütte-Lihotzky
was one of the first European designers to translate modern theories about efficiency,
hygiene, and workflow from the factory to the kitchen. Unlike her Italian counterparts, Schütte-Lihotzky did not support the ascendant social conservatism of the
day. She was not only a Communist but an agitator active in the German resistance
to Nazism.[42] As such, the story of her professional success provides a fascinating
counterexample to that of the more politically acquiescent Lidia Morelli and Piero
Bottoni. The divergent degrees of consent to Fascism expressed by Morelli and Bottoni in Italy and Schütte-Lihotzky in Germany demonstrate the potential political
paths to success in the architecture world for the nations that would later form the
Axis powers.

During the interwar period, Schütte-Lihotzky's original research, consisting of
time-motion studies and interviews with housewives and women's groups, proliferated across upper-class shelter magazines and working-class housewifery guides alike.
In Germany, inflation destabilized housing costs in nearly all German cities, including Frankfurt. But there, the ambitious New Frankfurt housing initiative aimed to
construct affordable public housing and modern amenities for the German working
class – including 10,000 kitchens designed by Schütte-Lihotzky, more than 10 per
cent of Frankfurt's total population at the time.

For Italian designers, Schütte-Lihotzky's expertise lent an aura of authority to
German home economics in general. The following quotation from a *Domus* article
typifies this attitude: "E qui c'è una cosa interessante da osservare per noi Italiani: tutti
i libri tedeschi (e in questo genere di studi i tedeschi sono all'avanguardia) parlano
della cassetta di cottura" (And here there is an interesting thing to observe for us Italians: all the German books (and in this area of study the Germans are the vanguards)
speak of the oven). This same article also cites "La *Bauentwurfslehre*" (*Architects' Data*)
from Prof. Ernst Neufert as expert testimony to the fact that the ideal dimensions of

a kitchen should be 1.90 by 2.30 metres squared – dimensions identical to those of Schütte-Lihotzky's Frankfurt kitchen.[43]

Spatial and temporal organization mark the Frankfurt kitchen. Each specialized workspace proceeds in a logical order: the cook moves from preparation at the work-table to cooking at the stove to cleaning at the sink to placing the plated meals at the final counter under the cupboards. Like in a factory, the timepiece set high on the wall marks the rate at which the cook completes her daily work. And indeed, the kitchen is set up like a small factory, complete with a Taylorist work triangle: the preparation space, the cooking space, and the cleaning space. In an assembly that would later rematerialize in Morelli's text and Bottoni's designs, each of Schütte-Lihotzky's Frankfurt kitchens came complete with a swivel stool, a gas stove, built-in storage, a fold-down ironing board, an adjustable ceiling light, and a removable garbage drawer. Labelled aluminium storage bins provided tidy organization for staples like sugar and rice and allowed easy pouring. Careful thought was given to materials for specific functions, such as oak-wood flour containers to repel mealworms and beech-wood cutting surfaces to resist staining and knife marks.[44]

Although she does not use this term specifically, Morelli evokes the Taylorist work triangle in her text, advocating *scienza pratica* as a key element of modernity in the kitchen. Likewise, Bottoni's new rationalist kitchen designs, derived from Schütte-Lihotzky's Frankfurt model, allow for "minore spreco di fatica e di salute" (less waste of effort and health).[45] Morelli and Bottoni were not alone in their enthusiastic application of Schütte-Lihotzky's kitchen designs, and the ideas about gendered and class-based food work were reinforced by organized cupboards and spinning stools. *Domus* writers in general, and Ignazio Gardella in particular, played an outsize role in translating the Frankfurt kitchen and the Taylorist work triangle into the Fascist urban context and further disseminated these designs to the Italian middle class via *Domus* photographs, layouts, plans, and even free carpentry guides.

Domus heralded the Frankfurt kitchen and the Taylorist work triangle in a long-running series of articles by Gardella. Hailing from a family of architects, Gardella graduated in engineering from the Politecnico di Milano in 1928. Together with university acquaintances, he took part in creating the Italian modern movement before turning to rationalism. Interest in medical structures and Fascist social hygiene marks his construction projects of the mid- to late 1930s, such as the Dispensario Antitubercolare in 1934–8 and the Laboratorio Provinciale di igiene e profilassi, both built in Alessandria in Piedmont. His work in this realm featured autarkic building materials and regularly won the regime's architectural competitions, fostering ongoing financial as well as conceptual links with the regime.

Like Bottoni, Gardella was among a number of social experts who proposed courses for housewives on furnishing, maintaining, and managing the home according to rationalist principles. These courses were to be particularly directed at recent immigrants to the city arriving from rural areas.[46] He characterizes how designers envisioned a kitchen layout suited to working-class women's labour. Some of these themes we have already seen: Gardella, like Morelli, argues for the shrinking kitchen to decrease the number of people who spend time in this space. He states that the kitchen should only be large enough to allow one person to work, dimensions that he fixes at three to seven metres squared. Yet he also concedes that even a much smaller kitchen could accommodate two cooks if they were determined to work together. Reducing the number of bodies has a direct correlation to increasing the number of machines: he suggests that all appliances ought to be purchased in series for design consistency and placed along the walls. He proposes clearing the nineteenth-century worktable out of the centre of the kitchen and pushing it up against a wall to create space for movement; this also creates the top point for the triangle, the focal point of the new kitchen.

But how would these principles have worked in action? People (the cook), objects (food, pots, pans, mops, and brooms), and energy (sunlight, air, water, gas) moved through this space. And matter transformed as well: from raw to cooked and from cooked to waste. A floor plan from *Domus* reveals how a cook was intended to manage the flow of work and facilitate hygienic practices (Fig. 5.8). First, in the numerous *piani girevoli* (lazy Susans) and pipes, we see a bid to organize food and waste movement. Space K, a lazy Susan with access to both the kitchen and the dining room, allows the cook to place finished dishes on the wheel for dining room service, moving food from one room to another without being seen. This architectural inclusion occludes the cook and the kitchen space: the diners may consume their meals with no hint as to the messy production involved. Space C contains trash prior to moving through space D, composed of *tubazione* (tubes or pipes) to move garbage out of the kitchen. With these two spaces, the kitchen's design suggests a body performing the invisible digestive work of eliminating waste.

Eliminating waste also occurs on the metaphorical level of diminishing effort through rationalist movements. Every space contains a minutely specified type of kitchen work: space A and A' hold the prep table and a small recess for recipe ingredients, while a dish-drying rack on top of the refrigerator constitutes space G. In each space, architecture supports the particular type of work involved. The architect notes, for example, that the table topping space C's trash receptacle stands at the same height as all other work surfaces, an American innovation in kitchen design inspired by Taylorism. Concern for hygiene also influences each space. The trash features a hermetic seal. Space B, a cupboard, contains lazy Susans for easy ingredient access to avoid spills as well as ventilation to decrease spoilage. This plan suggests that directed, hygienic flows of material and labour render the kitchen modern and rational. Similarly and more explicitly, Ignazio Gardella articulates this conception of the kitchen in his inaugural January 1939 column on home economics, "I Servizi della Casa." He echoes the sentiment that the kitchen serves as a place of work, "di un determinato lavoro, importantissimo nell'economia della famiglia" (of a specific work,

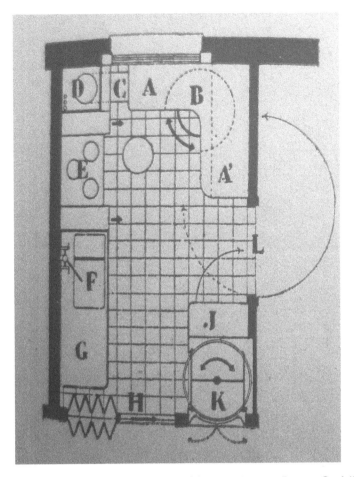

5.8. André Hermant, Rational Kitchen Floor Plan. The plan illustrates Ignazio Gardella's article "I servizi di casa" (House services), *Domus*, January 1939: 59.

extremely important in the family economy).[47] This phrasing means more than just money. Family economy can also refer to the functionality of the family unit. In this article, Gardella treats the two definitions as inseparable, in that improving one necessarily benefits the other. Gardella's ideas in this realm were not new: they derived from home economics.[48] In this holistic view, rational kitchen design, coupled with rational cooking methods, benefits the family purse.

The accompanying article caption to the model kitchen photo (Fig. 5.9) reads,

Architetto A. Hermant. – Vista della cucina modello dalla porta H. Questa cucina ha una superficie di circa 6 mq. Comprende due centri ben distinti: uno di preparazione e cottura verso il pranzo. Il lavoro è facilitato al massimo. La tavola di preparazione nell'angolo sotto la finestra è ben studiata, con l'armadio per casseruole, spezierie, ecc.

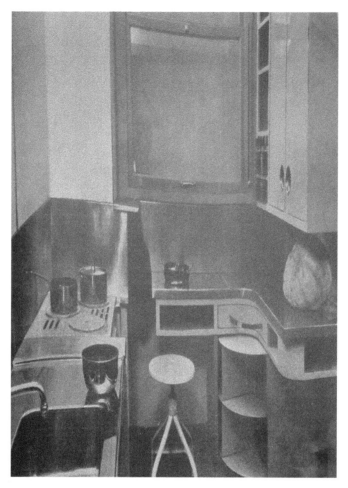

5.9. "I servizi della casa: La cucina," photograph of A. Hermant's kitchen. Article by Ignazio
Gardella, *Domus*, January 1939: 59.

sospeso a muro, alla destra, e la cucina elettrica a sinistra. Si può preparare e cuocere
comodamente le vivande senza muoversi dallo sgabello. Va notato in particolare l'arma-
dio-dispensa girevole (utilizzazione dell'angolo sotto il tavolo) ventilato direttamente
dall'estero. Al disopra un cassetto per posate, pure girevole. In primo piano, il centro di
lavaggio e servizio con a sinistra l'acquaio. A destra (non visibile in fotografia) un armadio alto, girevole, per stoviglie. Utilizza un altro angolo della cucina, e consente una
grande superficie di ripiani accessibili. La parte di mezzo serve da passapiatti.

Architect A. Hermant – View of the model kitchen from door H. This kitchen has a
floor area of roughly 6 metres squared. It includes two distinct centres: one for preparation and cooking for lunch. The work is eased to the maximum. The preparation
table in the corner under the window is carefully placed, with a closet for casserole

dishes, spices, etc. hung from the wall, on the right, and the electric oven on the left. One can prepare and cook the same food without moving from the stool. It should be noted in particular the revolving closet-storage space (using the angle under the table) ventilated directly from the outside. On top a drawer for silverware, also revolving. In the foreground, the wash centre and services with a sink on the left. On the right (not visible in the photograph) is a cupboard, revolving, for dishes. It uses another corner of the kitchen, and allows for a greater surface area of accessible shelves. The part in the middle serves as a *passapiatti*.

This caption reveals two key aspects of the Frankfurt kitchen in the Italian context: first, Gardella's decision to highlight the work of a French architect speaks to the international dimension of this project. He reprints a photo and a kitchen plan taken directly from the pages of the French shelter magazine *Décor d'aujourd'hui* and explicitly cites this source not once but twice, in captions.[49]

To trace the Frankfurt kitchen's development from its conceptual origins to its appearance in this photo, we must cross oceans as well as Axis and Allied lines: American home economics inspired a German designer – at this point, all of the creators in question are women. From here, a French architect adopted the Frankfurt kitchen: André Hermant worked as an architect, furniture and lighting designer, and editor on projects ranging from museum design in the 1930s to town reconstruction the postwar years. Alone in his Paris office, he continued to publish the noted trade journal *L'Architecture* during the German occupation of France. In yet another crossing of international home economics, the article cites French home economics expert Mlle Bernège, the author of *La Methode Menagère* (*The Housekeeping Method*), and applauds her call to "classificare gli oggetti per categorie, definirne le funzioni" (classify the objects by category and define their functions) before cooking. Bernège further states that each cooking task must be "preparato intellettualmente prima di essere eseguito materialmente" (intellectually prepared before being materially enacted). In the end, an Italian architect and writer interpreted and disseminated, but did not conceive, this ideal Fascist-period kitchen on the pages of *Domus*.

Although new ideas in kitchen architecture placed the cook in a central position, physically at the hub of the kitchen on her rotating stool, with all room and appliance dimensions tailored to her body, the goal of this design is to facilitate the efficiency and ease of her movements. This characterization of the work triangle and its use exemplifies the broader body of articles on the cook and her use of the kitchen in *Domus*. For example, note the commonalities of phrasing in this collectively authored article, "Parliamo un po' della cucina … razionalmente":

La cuciniera stando seduta su uno sgabello rotante ha a portata di mano la tavola per la preparazione, la cucina, l'acquaio, non solo, ha riunite in un solo armadio grande tutti gli utensili, gli alimenti, le droghe, ecc. che le sono necessarie, senza possibilità, data la

grande specializzazione di ciascun scompartamento, di creare alcun disordine o confu-
sione tra le cose contenute. Ciò permette di organizzare razionalmente, direi quasi sci-
entificamente il lavoro, dando così anche a chi si deve occupare di queste funzioni che
fino ad oggi sono state considerate esclusivamente pratiche, la possibilità di giungere al
loro perfezionamento attraverso un'organizzazione di pensiero piuttosto che attraverso
un semplice e meccanico lavoro manuale.

The cook, being seated on a rotating stool, has at hand the table for preparation, the
oven, the sink, and that's not all – all together in one cabinet she has all the utensils,
the foods, the spices, etc. that are necessary, without any possibility, given the great specialization of each compartment, to create any disorder or confusion of the things contained. This permits rational organization, I would say almost scientific organization,
of work, given also that the person who must manage these functions that until today
were considered only practices, the possibility to achieve their perfection through the
organization of thought rather than through a simple and mechanical manual work.[50]

"These *functions* that until today were considered only *practices*" (emphasis mine).
This phrasing underlines a key shift in designers' understanding of food preparation
work during the Fascist period. Gardella's caption evokes how *Domus* architects
viewed the role of the cook within the broader context of the kitchen: she is a
worker, with tools at the ready, stationed at centre of the workspace. And the workspace, according to Gardella, must be specialized so that she cannot create disorder
or confusion.

The kitchen of "Parliamo un po' della cucina" offers a plan to support maximum
economy of space, time, and effort in cooking and cleaning. The dimensions and layout of the kitchen and everything in it focus on the cook's body, but on a part-by-part
basis. In focusing on activities over persons, this process quarters the body into parts.
For example, table heights mention leaving space for human legs, rather than for the
cook herself. Reconceptualizing cooking work in this way signals a shift from cooking
as physical practice ("simple and mechanical manual work") to mental function ("the
organization of thought") thanks to the "rational ... almost scientific" organization.
In other words, the "perfection" of work proceeds along Darwinist corridors, moving
from the hand to the mind.

And last, we see how the specificity of the Taylorist work triangle translates into
more general principles of hygiene, modernism, and rationalism through the management of motion. Everything spins: the cook at her stool, the revolving closet-storage
space, the silverware drawer, and the dish cupboard. Drawers move in and out on runners, and tables glide forward and back on casters. Bottoni's new designs for kitchen
worktables (Fig. 5.10) found fame due to their in-drawer runners alone. Whereas a
large worktable stood at the centre of the nineteenth-century kitchen, empty space for
bodily movement between workstations (in large kitchens) and the famous spinning

stool (in small kitchens) characterized the twentieth-century kitchen.

What does this new emphasis on glide mean for kitchens, and for daily life, during the *ventennio*? Historians of the Fascist period have generally agreed that acceleration, speed, mechanization, and new forms of movement characterized Italian modernity. In providing exemplars, most have turned to new transportation technologies like airplanes, trains, and cars, and more generally to the aviation developments, rail lines, and highways that spread across the country to support them. But there is more than one way to move a human body. In addition to the overwhelmingly

5.10. Photograph of Piero Bottoni kitchen table in Ignazio Gardella's "Consigli tecnici per la Casa," *Domus*, May 1939: 23–4.

male realms of Futurism, *aeropittura*, and the Tripoli car races, we ought to examine the subtle ways that daily life accelerated during the Fascist period. Not every social change of the Fascist period exploded into existence. For working-class women, the embodied experience of modernism arrived as quickly and quietly as the spin of a stool or a drawer sliding open.

Storage Space and the Meaning of Mess

In a way, storage was to the kitchen what the kitchen was to the entire apartment. Both constituted the hidden, unruly mess of the domestic sphere. They were to be organized, rationalized, and sterilized with architecture and design. Drawer contents mattered: during the Fascist period, domestic economists and designers alike placed a new emphasis on the importance of kitchen storage. Adding cupboards and closets to the kitchen moved food, tools, silverware, plates, linens, and cleaning from visible spaces on tabletops and counters to invisible spaces inside of drawers. Along with this "disappearing" of kitchen clutter by adding additional storage space, designers also moved to specialize the storage that was already there. *Domus* specified storage by food type: perishable foods went in a small electric refrigerator, and dry foods went in high cabinets, complete with "little drawers for spices." Low cabinets held pots and pans and used internal divides to discourage messy piles. A cupboard held the kitchen linens, rags, and dish towels, and the kitchen worktable offered a drawer for knives and a small cutting board, as well as a specialized section for the rolling pin. Even the

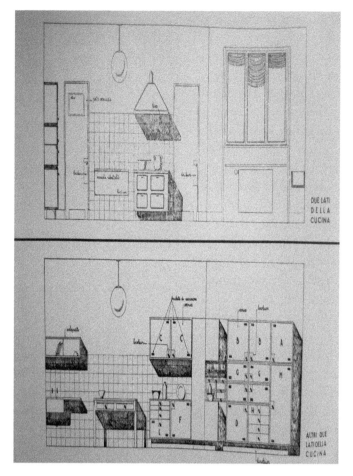

5.11. "Un esempio di composizione," kitchen plan. Gio Ponti, *Domus*, January 1936: 54.

electric oven provides a form of specialized storage: a shelf directly over the three to four burners took advantage of ambient heat and provided a holding space to keep food warm before service.[51]

In fact, *Domus* placed so much importance on storage that it provided carpentry plans (Fig. 5.11) for kitchens and pantry storage in hopes of wide adoption by the middle class, both upon marriage and as families grew. Accompanying text clarifies the meaning of the gift.

> Disegni per il falegname che deve costruire la vosta cucina: alcuni elementi che si possono aggiunge man mano che la famiglia aumenta. Domus dà ai suoi lettori delle idée e il modo di tradurle in pratica. Con questi disegni, un bravo falegname vi può costruire quella cucina che a voi serve meglio, componendola con gli elementi che sceglierete. Questa cucina può essere poi arrico.

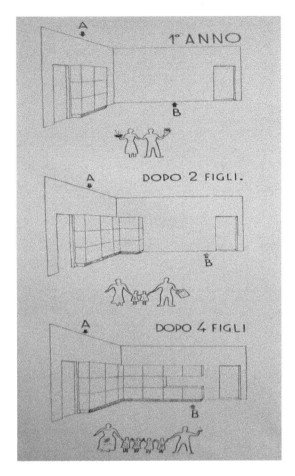

5.12. "Un esempio di composizione," expansion of family and kitchen storage. Gio Ponti, *Domus*, January 1936: 56.

> Drawings for the carpenter who must construct your kitchen: some elements that one can slowly add as the family grows. Domus gives to its readers the ideas and the means to translate them into practice. With these designs, a good carpenter can construct that kitchen which works best for you, composing it with the elements that you will choose. This kitchen can then be enriched.[52]

Normally, *Domus* articles celebrated aspirational images of ideal kitchens designed by famous architects. This inclusion of carpentry plans for middle-class family kitchens stands out for its rarity: these kitchen plans were pedagogical, or even propagandistic, forms of design work.

Further, the article's treatment of storage tells us that the ideal kitchen was an ongoing process rather than a completed state. In figure 5.12, the rising number of children marks the passage of time and indicates the need for expanding storage.

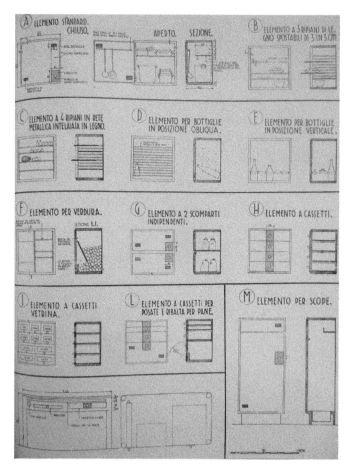

5.13. "Un esempio di composizione," kitchen storage. Gio Ponti, *Domus*, January 1936: 55.

We also see the physical changes that accompany courtship, birth, and parent-hood. Over the course of the images, the wife gains weight and the husband exchanges his bouquet of flowers for a pipe. Ample hips and pipe tobacco suggest that the family can afford plenty of food, as well as some small luxuries. But worn clothes, marked by patches and scratches, imply limits to their prosperity. Perhaps the family income could not always keep pace with their increasing number of children. Storage physically dwarfs the tiny family. Some of these new organizational objects and techniques – like convertible chair/ladders and horizontally mounting wine bottles neck-to-neck – did in fact save space and time, and perhaps even money. But adding and specializing storage space in the kitchen could also create clutter rather than remove it. Many new types of storage were designed to house a single product; for example, *Domus* advertised specialized drawers with holes to balance eggs, as well as "dedicated potato closets" (Fig. 5.13).

This article names the typical kitchen storage needs as one closet for pots, pans, and ladles; two closets for fruit; two closets for bottles – a vertical one for milk, and a horizontal one for wine; a vegetable drawer; a glass-fronted closet for flatware; a bread storage area; a vertical space for brooms; and a table with a pull-out cutting board.[53] Nearly every tool and ingredient now had a specialized storage space. But while storing potatoes, onions, and peppers in separate drawers rather than a single one may have created visual harmony in the kitchen, it also wasted space. With so many new containers dedicated to specific purposes, storage could clutter the space it meant to clear.

And if we were to open those kitchen drawers, what might we see? Perhaps knives, specialized tomato slicers (*affetta-pomodori*), universal cheese/bread/meat/potato grinders (*tritatutto-universale*), egg cutters (*taglia-uova*), apple corers (*leva-torsoli*), pear seeders (*togli-semi*), citrus zesters (*coltellino per agrumi e per dolci*), and fish scalers (*paletta per togliere le scagli dei pesci*). Drawings and explanations for each of these objects appear in the advice-column-style advertisement – "La Rinascente presenta: delle novità per il servizio razionale della cucina e della casa" (La Rinascente presents: the latest products for rational service in the kitchen and the home) – which appeared on page three of *Domus*'s June 1940 issue. Here, the famous department store La Rinascente hawked these grinders, corers, and peelers by deploying the rhetoric of rationalism and hygiene. All of the objects for sale are touted for their ability to regularize and sterilize kitchen work. In the text, rationalism translates as the vegetable knife's ability to cut zucchini and peppers with increased regularity and precision, evoking factory output more than human work. Hygiene comes to the fore in the copy advertising the universal grinder: "E' un utensile della massima praticità ed igiene, poiché evita di toccare con le mani le cibarie (es. il formaggio sulla grattuggia). E' completamente smontabile e può essere lavato in ogni sua parte." (It is a utensil of the maximum practicality and hygiene, because it prevents one from touching crumbs (ex. cheese on the grater) with one's hands. It can be completely disassembled and each part can be washed.) Like rationalism, hygiene promises to replace human hands with metal planes. In the first case, rationalist knives diminish human variation in chopping movements to promote a more regularized end product: identical vegetable slices. In the second case, hygienic grinders separate bits of cheese from human hands in the first place and allow for easy washing if such contamination does occur. Taking these kitchen tools out of the drawer and considering them within the greater historical context of the period reveals that different groups, from cookbook authors to architects to ad men, made use of the Fascist rhetoric of rationalism and hygiene. Banal commercial aims were interwoven with these political concerns. Apple corers and fish scalers, reimagined as innovative tools for scientific homekeeping, provided the paraphernalia to mark modernity in the model Fascist kitchen.

Cooking Fire Protests in Public Housing Projects

But these model kitchens are depopulated – no cooks, no food, and no mess disrupts their perfect form and prescribed function. How then shall we understand the kitchen's actual use? This concluding analysis leaves the idealized kitchens of the middle-class neighbourhoods to examine the design and use of working-class kitchens in the outer rings of urban centres.[54] Major trends of diminishing and partitioning this space, including the shifts from big kitchens to small ones, the division of large living spaces into separate rooms for cooking and sleeping, and the division of humans from animals, women from men, and parents from children, show that, in the context of Fascist kitchen interventions, aesthetic goals united kitchens more than urban geography separated them. Architectural plans and articles in *Casabella Costruzione* depict the cook as a worker and the kitchen as a workspace. Comparisons to public, regime-controlled workspaces, such as factories and offices, predominate descriptions of this domestic space. But these kitchen designs contain a key difference: dimensions, layout, and building materials all work to hide, contain, and obscure the messy bodies and disordered labour of female and lower-class workers.

Comparisons between old and new urban kitchens associate antiquated models with the feminine and with the working classes via the assumed shared traits of disorder and mess: chaotic workflows, time- and energy-wasting practices, and lack of air circulation and light were evidence of the old-fashioned nineteenth-century kitchen's unsuitability, and the need for intervention. The structure and use of the ideal kitchen (according to the regime and these leading architectural publications), by contrast, exemplifies hygiene-inflected attributes; the designs obscured and hermetically sealed the women's work. Hygiene, rather than autarky, reveals itself as the chief concern.

Paradoxically, the writers and architects with the closest ties to the regime appear to have been the least interested in changing private kitchens to support alimentary autarky. In the rare references to autarky in the kitchen, these cultural creators treat it as an abstract aesthetic of thrift and sobriety rather than a concrete means to preserve the domestic economy. In other words, their key goals were saving time, space, and effort, rather than money or food.[55]

To conclude this chapter, I provide a case study on how one Rome-based group of mothers refused to eat in communal cafeterias; they cooked meals for their families outdoors instead, a decision that profoundly shaped the urban landscape outside of many northern cities, including Milan and Turin. Changes came from the bottom up as well as from the top down. And in both cases, those upsets focused on the kitchen. Before now, our analysis has zoomed in, moving from kitchen layout to use to contents. We will now reverse this order by zooming out from the kitchen to the apartment and to the surrounding urban neighbourhood, ultimately establishing the stakes for individual kitchen designs and use in the context of Fascist city planning and social control. *Casabella*'s trade journal for industrial architects, *Costruzioni*, demonstrates how architects and engineers translated kitchen ideals into built structures. Examining this document, alongside conference proceedings from the 1936 Convegno Lombardo and letter exchanges between city prefects and regime bursars for the financing, construction, and refurbishment of urban kitchens, reveals how working-class women actually used these structures. Through intentional misuses and fiery rejections of these new models for domestic bliss, they changed the face of Italy's urban exurbs.

A plan for the kitchen is a map of the city: *Casabella Costruzione*'s December 1939 "Relazione tecnica" shows how the right angles of rectangles, squares, and grids attempted to impose order on unruly spaces from the kitchen to the working-class quartiere.[56] Here, the new Milanese neighbourhood appears from a geometric bird's-eye view of the new quarter as 177.92 by 80.15, for a total of 14,264 metres squared, on a north-south axis. For Fascist-period architects, quantification overpowered explanation. As Pagano put it, "Per toccare la realtà della situazione non valgono le parole, ma le cifre" (To understand the reality of the situation not words, but numbers, count).[57] The plan, a kaleidoscope of rectangles and squares, shows that modernity connoted specific architectural forms. Rationalist geometry ruled neighbourhoods and private homes alike. Every civilized living space had to have four sides.[58] Large windows, electric bulbs, and shining surfaces brought hygienic light into the private kitchen. The kitchen-apartment relationship and its design solutions discussed in *Dalla Cucina al Salotto*, *Domus*, and *Casabella Costruzione* translated far beyond single-family dwellings, however, as articles scaled the kitchen-apartment relationship to the apartment-neighbourhood relationship and up to the neighbourhood-city relationship. In other words, architects applied many of the domestic design shifts for the promotion of hygiene, rationalism, and autarky from model kitchens all the way up to the municipal scale.

A *Casabella Costruzione* article on the new Milanese *case popolari* on Via Illirico and Via Biscioia suggests that the conflation of light and hygiene applies to this design at the level of the apartment block through the conversion of attics to solariums, and at the level of the city block by planning building distances to ensure that sunlight could fall between the buildings, even in winter when the angle of light is low.[59] Whereas smoke-sucking oven hoods promoted hygiene through ventilation in private kitchens, courtyards and parks provided lungs for the apartment block and the city block to breathe. The same concepts underlie kitchen, apartment, and city planning: air and light combat wetness and odours and promote cleaner living. And at all three levels, architects were guilty of conflating literal and moral cleanliness. On Via Biscioia, all washing, of people and of clothes, took place in showers and laundries in the basement. In other words, this apartment block design emphasized the metaphorical lowness of washing by placing it underground.

The design and use of the *case popolari* can be read as an ongoing conversation (and, from time to time, a heated argument) between the builders and inhabitants of low-cost, urban apartment blocks and their kitchens. And just as home economics constituted an international conversation during this period, so too did the role of the kitchen in new public housing projects from Siena to Stockholm. *Casabella Costruzione* regularly ran comparative articles examining the public housing in northern European countries. This means not only that Italian Fascist city planners were looking abroad for architectural inspiration, but also that in doing so it implied Italians had much to learn from northern Europeans. They believed that ideal public housing plans increased productivity in industrial sectors. They admired the "perfetta organizzazione che esiste in Svezia come in tutti i paesi scandinavi, organizzazione che consente in maggiore rapita e minor prezzo di lavoro" (perfect organization that exists in Sweden as in all Scandinavian countries, organization that allows for greater speed and lower price of work). This article takes the Coperativa Foruendet's public housing as its ideal and scales its lessons up to the working-class neighbourhoods of Söder and Norr Mälastrand. In another social conflation, it admires how these blocks intermingle the middle and working classes by placing blue-collar workers and white-collar employees (*operai e impiegati*) side-by-side.[60] In Italy at the time, this degree of mixing inside of a single high-rise was uncommon, being viewed as distasteful for all apartment dwellers regardless of their social standing.[61]

Architect and *Casabella Costruzione* editor Giuseppe Pagano dedicated a full issue (November 1939) to the theme of the *case popolari*.[62] In the introductory article, "Case per il popolo," Pagano frames the issue of the *case popolari* as a problem of national hygiene to be solved by architecture.[63] To prove his point, he relies heavily on statistics: 21.6 per cent of Italian dwellings possessed no kitchen, 43.3 per cent no drinking water, 29.5 per cent no bathroom, 42 per cent no electricity. Pagano's passion for statistics is apparent not only in the high ratio of numbers to words per page but also in his passionate evaluation of the power of ISTAT's government statistics, which he refers to as "quelle preziose informazioni che ci può offrire l'Istituto Centrale di Statistica" (that precious information that the Central Statistics Institute can offer us).[64] These particular numbers are trumpeted in the article headline and repeat throughout the article, suggesting that Pagano's equation of national hygiene with domestic architecture carried an additional nuance: the importance of space specialization according to activity.

Hygiene referred not only to cleanliness but to social organization within the home as well. Pagano believed that ideally each apartment in the *case popolari* ought to house multiple rooms, each dedicated to specific purposes, outfitted with the proper hydraulics and wiring. More statistics march in to defend his line of reasoning: out of 100 inhabitants, 9 have a bathroom, 5 have central heating (*termosifone*), 13 have a garden. What use are the 4,255 apartments that the Istituto delle Case Popolari di Milano expects to build next year when there are 40,000 requests for housing, of which 15,435 are urgent requests? Why are the Istituti delle Assicurazioni headquarters made of "mountains of marble" when there are 28,212 couples who cannot marry because they are not yet financially ready to buy a home? But quantification is not the same as explanation, and numbers can act as black boxes, obscuring the information that they contain. For example, Pagano claims that 65 per cent of Southern Italian homes consisted of a single, unspecialized room, when in fact this statistic comes from a single city: Matera stands for the entire Mezzogiorno. Pagano uses statistics the way that the Fascist government used them: to cast a halo of rationality over subjective argumentation.

Despite the paternalistic rhetoric of *case popolari* serving as a direct regime provision for the poor, most of their construction funding resulted from prickly and protracted negotiations between regional and state authorities. Numerous regime-affiliated groups collaborated in this process, including the Istituto fascista autonomo case popolari (IFACP), Istituzioni pubbliche di assistenza e beneficienza (IPAB), Istituto nazionale fascista previdenza sociale (INFPS), and the Ente Opere Assistenziali (EOA), as well as many other aid groups.

Financial requests tended to come from the bottom up, from relatives and friends of minor officials, to prefects or to state government, rather than downward from the regime. A letter exchange between a Florentine prefect and regime officials exemplifies these communications. Both here, and in other cases, the town prefect would write a letter to the Segretario Particolare del Duce outlining city construction work to be done in order of descending urgency. Most frequently prefects requested *case popolari* and specified the building type. Our Florentine prefect, for instance, appealed to the segretario for "Case popolari – semi rurali" (Public housing – semi-rural). Requests for nurseries, hospitals, and other social services also fill such letters. Separate letters list requests for public works projects (*opere di pubblica utilità*) such as aqueducts, electricity, and sewers. Other requests pertain to the rooms in the *case popolari*, specifying their dimensions and supporting infrastructure (often running water and sometimes electricity). These letters almost always listed the projected cost for each project.[65] From here, the regime and the prefect would negotiate the specifics of the proposal through a series of national, regional, and local funding sources before finally coming to an agreement regarding the finances.

Successful proposals tended to take up to a year of negotiations.[66] The vast majority of requests, however, remained unanswered and unfunded.[67] Further reinforcing the piecemeal nature of this process, female family members of officials played a surprisingly significant role in selecting which building projects received funding. First-hand knowledge of community needs and a supposed natural social consciousness attached to femininity lent them authority to make suggestions in this arena. Officials heeded their word – in a striking example of motherly influence at work, Achille Starace sent 200,000 lire to refurbish an Istituto Serafico per sordo-muti (Institute for the Deaf and Dumb). Official letters repeatedly stated that the project's urgency stemmed from "segnalazione forte della mamma" (the strong recommendation of his mom). Her friendship with the local priest alerted her to the building project's existence, demonstrating how local social and religious ties could drive regime-sponsored construction work.[68]

Once financing was achieved, a patchwork collection of nationally revered and locally cherished architects, engineers, and *geometri* (surveyors) designed and built the *case popolari* and the kitchens within. Regime-run, commercially sponsored conventions brought these professionals together to determine the ideal form and function for *case popolari* kitchens.[69] Their votes decided which ideals would become industry norms, dictating what the kitchens looked like aesthetically and their construction process, in terms of materials, dimensions, ventilation, plumbing, electricity, and the types of building contractors that would be involved at each step of the process. Many of these motions concern the number and type of bodies permissible in different lodging types. For example, one architect at the Lombard Convention of 1936 suggested that childless couples be confined to single-room apartments to lessen crowding for families. Another put forth the motion that apartment dimensions be directly proportional to the number of inhabitants. Attendees unanimously approved both measures.[70] At the higher levels, many of these men held multiple posts, writing for architectural magazines and journals, teaching at technical universities, and planning *case popolari* on behalf of the regime.

Piero Bottoni, for instance, not only espoused the rationalist ideal for kitchens on the pages of *Domus* and contributed photographs to Lidia Morelli's housekeeping manual, but also helped create design norms promoting hygienic kitchen work for *case popolari* throughout Lombardy.[71] Bottoni's presence at the Lombard conference, his design suggestions, votes for *case popolari* kitchen norms, and construction work on behalf of the regime demonstrate that individual architects materially influenced how denizens of the *case popolari* lived. Bottoni's communications to Mussolini further evidence both professional practicality and public alliance with the regime. To wit, Bottoni sent Mussolini a free copy of his book *Urbanistica* along with an explanatory telegram in November 1937.[72] The following year, Bottoni wrote to Mussolini requesting a dust-jacket recommendation of his book.[73] He must have had considerable confidence in his influence and stature to do so.

But while Bottoni and others advocated for the division of activities by room, originally, family apartments in the *case popolari* did not have private kitchens at all. Large communal refectories predominated, partially due to the social history of working-class apartment blocks.[74] Exurban *case popolari* initially grew out of the Catholic Church's welfare tradition of financing, constructing, and managing *alberghi per sfrattati*, literally, "hotels for the homeless."[75] At these *alberghi per sfrattati*, run primarily as soup kitchens and secondarily as homeless shelters, priests and nuns supervised all refectory meals as part of their larger commitment to public welfare and to promote Catholic social norms in lay society. Beyond this communal dining space in the *alberghi*, private eating and cooking in the smaller apartments were forbidden. This rule was both practical and social – practical, in that it discouraged vermin, and social, in that it allowed the clergy to impress Catholic codes of commensality onto the *alberghi* residents three times a day.

During the 1910s and 1920s, many architects familiar with the refectory model applied it to the *case popolari*, with one key difference. Soup kitchens could not charge their destitute clients for food: the *sfrattati* had no choice but to "eat this soup or jump out the window," to quote a common proverb of the time. By contrast, the *case popolari* refectories could extract a monthly fee for these collective meals. Working-class women who were used to deciding how to compose a food budget protested this encroachment on their preferred meal content, cost, timing, and location.[76] They used a spectrum of more and less direct methods to protest the refectory format. Some ate in their private apartments, while others built fires to cook in the courtyard.[77] In the specific and characteristic case of the Alberghi Luzzatti building complex in Garbatella, women protested the financial imposition of the refectory, but railed most strongly against the social effects of being forced to eat en masse, disparaging the refectory for eliminating "una sorta di pudore morale" (a sort of moral respect).[78] In other words, more than just economics were at stake in the kitchen question – for the female residents of the Alberghi Luzzatti, cooking was a question of dignity and humanity. Having their own kitchens meant having the right to choose which foods they preferred. It gave them the right to sustenance but also the right to taste.

The "ostinazione" of these women forced the Alberghi Luzzatti to close the communal kitchens and repurpose them for other uses.[79] In one case, the refectory became a small theatre; in another, the refectory was sanctified as a chapel. Meanwhile, the kitchen protests continued to spread beyond Garbatella: women rebelled across the capital. Protesters from Pietralata, Tor Marancia, Gordiani, and the other newly built Fascist *borgate* (working-class suburbs) assembled en masse before Mussolini's balcony at the Campidoglio in 1928 and again in 1931. Between these two mass demonstrations, open-air cooking fires increasingly lit up the *borgate*, suggesting that cooking outdoors might be considered act of culinary civil disobedience.[80] Regime architects soon dropped refectories from *case popolari* plans and began to construct the first private family kitchens for the urban working class.

Early models appeared in miniature at 4 by 2.85 square metres, a plan that accorded just enough space for a countertop (*bancone*) with two cast-iron burners in the stonework (*fornelli di ghisa in muratura*).[81] The changes quickly spread – a 1933 article in the newspaper *Messaggero* notes that the regime donated a total of eighty-two such homes, each consisting of either one or two generalized rooms, plus one kitchen, to *famiglie numerose* for the Natale di Roma, the celebration marking the legendary founding of Rome by twins known as Romulus and Remus, who were raised by a she-wolf. The article neglects to mention that this was hardly a free gift. Families paid 11,000 lire for the first type of home and 17,000 lire for the second.[82] The largest families were not necessarily the ones most in need of housing. This meant that a well-off family with eight children would be more likely to receive housing than a poor family with six children. The supposed donation shows how regime concerns dovetailed – families that supported pronatalism by having many children were selected for public housing, and in those houses, the regime introduced gas, and later water, to support hygiene and productivity. Additionally, the fact that gas preceded water in the utilities servicing of most homes underscores the importance of cooking over other daily activities, including even washing and using the toilet. Further, the introduction of gas may have also paved the way for the introduction of water. Although small, the addition of the kitchen to private apartments for the working class marked the first of many different specialized private rooms to come: after the kitchen, the next room to emerge across multiple building projects for the working class was the bathroom.

Of course, the addition of kitchens to private apartments did not indicate that architects, food industry officials, and Fascist officials meant to relinquish social control over this domestic space to the families living in these apartments. Far from it: a raft of new pedagogical literature instructed working-class women in rationalist housework. These cheap and often free booklets provided regime-approved methods for actions as specific as chopping and dicing and as general as sitting and standing in the new public housing kitchens.

Domus's almanac, *Il Libro di casa 1938*, proved particularly popular. In many ways, the booklet's production emblematizes the Fascist-period approaches to kitchen design and use that we have seen thus far: First, its production crossed national and industry lines. Like the magazine, the almanac embraced northern European trends in home economics, with a particular emphasis on German time-motion studies in the kitchen. The majority of authors and editors involved also wrote for *Domus*'s magazine and had further publishing ties with the company's affiliated publishing house. What's more, *Domus* crossed into the private food industry to fund this project, and that move influenced its content. As a matter of fact, Cirio, the tinned food company, was the sole sponsor of *Il Libro di casa*'s publication. Product placements for canned tomatoes, beans, and peas fill the almanac's recipe sections, alongside more obvious print advertisements, with open can images repeating like a Warhol print.

It perhaps bears mentioning that Francesco Cirio founded his namesake company in Turin in 1856 while still in his twenties. More than food, his firm sold technology. Tinned peas, corn, and the famous Cirio tomatoes drew on canning techniques first developed by Nicolas Appert. By eliminating air and introducing a hot-water bath, Cirio applied and perfected the French inventor's conservation techniques. Just as Appert's business benefited from war (Napoleon Bonaparte requested long-lasting foods to feed soldiers on the march), so too did Cirio, who exported canned tomatoes to East Africa during the first waves of Mussolini's imperial campaign. The company base then spread southward, opening satellite factories across the Mezzogiorno with a regional base in the San Giovanni a Teduccio quarter of Naples. Cirio's status as a domestic Italian food company also complicates the almanac's stance towards alimentary autarky; after all, where did the *Domus* writers' financial interests end, and where did their government interests begin?

We can observe how rationalism and autarky bifurcated: they appeared in two separated book sections, with rationalism as the topic for articles and autarky as an incidental inclusion in the menus proposed by the daily calendar. Whereas *Il Libro di casa* treats autarky as subsidiary, a culinary practice that takes the unobtrusive form of vegetarian recipes and an emphasis on rice and rabbit over bread and steak, it centres rationalism as a new kitchen practice. Whereas alimentary autarky evoked the dreary cuisine of the poor, rationalist kitchen work was aspirational. Rationalism carried associations of professionalism, because it was first and foremost the realm of architects and scientists. In a series of inspirational guides and cautionary tales, *Il Libro di casa* defined what *Domus* meant by rationalist kitchen work. The article "Il lavoro quotidiano di casa" takes a businesslike tone: to avoid the "malattia fisica e mentale" (physical and mental sickness) caused by unsystematic housework, the article contends that working rationally amounts to the "normalizzazione dei procedimenti essenziali" (normalization of essential processes). To this end, the article temporally divides housework into annual, monthly, weekly, and daily tasks.

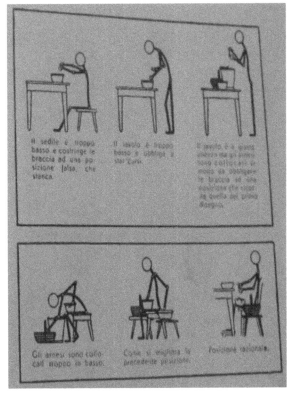

5.14. Illustration for "Il lavoro quotidiano in casa" (Daily housework), published by *Domus* in *Il libro di casa 1938*, 20 by 15 centimetres. (Museo della Figurina, Modena, Italy)

At the daily level, a sample calendar dictates tasks down to the hour. Unofficial duties begin even before the morning's work. The schedule dictates the *massaia* to "procedere alla prima pulizia personale, in modo che alle sette si sia pronte a cominciare il lavoro casalingo" (proceed to personal cleanliness, so that at seven you will be ready to begin the housework). When the workday officially begins at 7 a.m., the *massaia* must clean the dining room, make and serve breakfast, clean and put away the dishes, clean the rooms, harvest the garden, prepare lunch, and set the table for the family lunch at noon. Similar activities fill the afternoon. Rationalist kitchen practices chopped the day into ordered, predictable time segments that mapped bodies onto time and space. Moreover, illustrated schedules showed when and where to find the *massaia*'s body and what type of work she will be engaged in when you find her. To this end, graphics depicted Taylorist positions and movements to save time and effort in housework. Among these images (such as those in Fig. 5.14), we see stick figures engaged in cooking and cleaning.[83]

Like a Taylorist version of Goldilocks, tables and tools are either too low or too high before proceeding to the "rational position" – just right. The captions read, "Gli

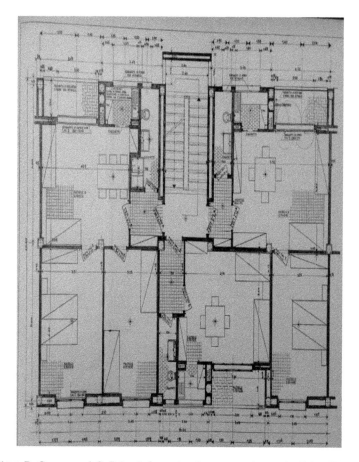

5.15. F. Albini, R. Camus, and G. Palanti, floor plan for *case popolari* in the Fabio Filzi neighbourhood of Milan, illustrating G. Pagano's article "Un'oasi di ordine" (An oasis of order), *Costruzioni Casabella*, December 1939: 385.

arnesi sono collocati troppo in basso" (The tools are positioned too low), "Come si migliora la posizione precedente" (How one improves the preceding position), "Posizione rationale" (Rational position).[84] These images suggest that Taylorism and rationalism were not static sets of practices and aesthetics: during the Fascist period, they took on new functions and meanings when they moved from factories to kitchens. Architects translated and reworked Taylorism and rationalism as types of intervention and improvement in cooking and cleaning that ultimately amounted to forms of social control. By controlling her body and its movements through architecture, a cook would self-discipline, ultimately reaching what the regime considered to be a "rational" state.

Moreover, the typical working-class kitchens' petite dimensions render the room unfit for relaxation or sleep, confining its functional purpose to food-related work (see Fig. 5.15). Typical dimensions and design suggested a separate 4-by-4-square-metre room outfitted with a sink (explicitly including running water and multiple taps, plus

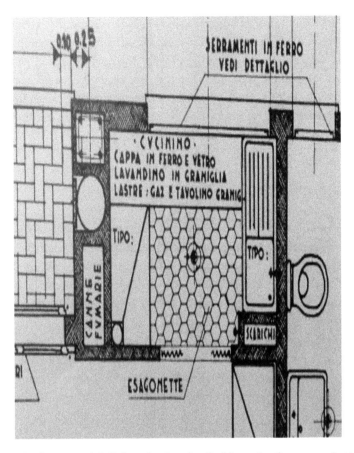

5.16. F. Albini, R. Camus, and G. Palanti, kitchen detail of floor plan for *case popolari* in the Fabio Filzi neighbourhood of Milan. The small kitchen (*cucinino*) features an iron and glass oven hood and a small, faux-marble chip sink. The floor is done in hexagon tiles, and the door features iron closures. Pagano, "Un'oasi di ordine," 385.

a drain pipe) and a dish-drying rack.[85] Smaller alcove kitchens, a less common model, were situated in the corner of a combined dining and living room. They measured a total of 2.47 metres squared – a tiny space even in a petite 14-square-metre apartment. Further, their dimensions allowed only one person to work at the centre of this flow. The rectangular form crowned by a sink and flanked by longer walls for storage create a work triangle, effectively separating preparation, cooking, and cleaning into three successive activities. The room is built for efficiency, reducing the cook's movements to a minimum (Fig. 5.16). Kitchen organization constitutes a bid at social engineering, in that it uses sink and storage placement to induce the cook to work in a particular physical position, one that she might not choose without architectural encouragement.

While the spread of these apartments and their private (but regimented) kitchens cannot be read as a pure triumph of women over Fascist officials, it can be read as part of a larger ebb and flow of power between individuals and the regime. It demonstrates that women had the power to protest. By lighting a thousand cooking fires, they changed the face of public housing in Italy. The open design of alcove kitchens also demonstrates that *case popolari* architects occasionally lost sight of their goal for improving hygiene. In this case, noise and cooking odours freely circulated throughout the apartment, effectively transforming the main room in the house into the maligned old-fashioned kitchen.

The Problem with Rationalism

Case popolari architects, along with Morelli, *Domus*, and other kitchen thinkers, prescribed rationalism as social medicine. But the problem with medicine is that it tastes terrible: whether middle-class or working-class, no one wanted to work in these new Frankfurt kitchens with their Taylorist work triangles and rationalist tools. Because of these women's churlish attachment to lowbrow concerns like warmth and comfort, they failed to appreciate what Ignazio Gardella exalted as the "lyrical incandescence" of modernist style. At most, homeowners approved rationalist kitchens and bathrooms. Rationalism may have improved these functional rooms, but it certainly did not enhance the pleasures of dining room or salons. Homeowners seemed to believe that rationalism would freeze conviviality.[86]

> Il signore che amava ardentissimamente il nero "buffet" intarsiato della sua sala a pranzo collo specchio decorativo a due metri dal pavimento, le zampe di leone e il baldacchino polveroso del letto, pure ammette con un sorriso serio e compassionevole: "Oh sì, lo stile razionale è buono per i bagni e le cucine."

> The gentleman who so ardently loves the black inlaid "buffet" in his dining room with a decorative mirror reaching two metres from the floor, the lions' feet and the dusty bed canopy, still admits with a serious and compassionate smile: "Oh yes, the rational style is good for bathrooms and kitchens."[87]

Gardella's characterization in *Domus* suggests two things: First, people preferred not to dwell in the cold, functional spaces so beloved by rationalist architects. Both the working class, due to financial need, and the bourgeois, due to taste, occupied spaces associated with time periods that Fascism decried. Regardless of their social class, homeowners and renters alike favoured old-fashioned interior design. This persistent and widespread preference for decorative elements like large mirrors and lions' feet conflicts substantially with the Fascist period's denigration of the nineteenth-century Giolittian liberal elite. The elite were painted by Fascists as excessive, as well as feminine and foreign, yet it would appear that most people continued to identify with their design aesthetics.

> Per quell'equivoco, c'è chi, quando si occupa dell'arredamento della propria casa, accetta magari per il bagno, la cucina, e gli altri servizi, un arredamento moderno (che sarà sempre un brutto moderno di maniera), ma vuole poi per il "salotto" e la "camera da letto" un arredamento un po' "meno moderno" se non "antico" del tutto. E nascono quei zoppicanti, borghesissimi, tristi appartamenti che tutti conosciamo e che deprimono, invece di esaltare, le nostra possibilità di vita.

> Because of this misunderstanding, there are those who, when it comes to the furnishing of their own house, accept perhaps for the bathroom, the kitchen, and the other service rooms, a modern furnishing (which will always be an ugly modern style) but who then wants for the "salon" and the "bedroom" furnishings that are a bit "less modern" if not entirely "old-fashioned." And this gives birth to those limping, very bourgeois, sad apartments that we all know and that depress, rather than exalt, our possibility of life.[88]

Gardella notes this tendency among upper-class male signore and decries their tendency to apply rationalism only to functional rooms (*servizi*) like kitchens and bathrooms.[89] To his mind, working rooms like kitchens and bathrooms receive modern treatment because, unlike living rooms and bedrooms, they are meant to improve work rather than to promote enjoyment. They simply serve different purposes. As far as style and its emotional effect on the room's inhabitants, functional and decorative rooms are framed as opposites – which he saw no problem with. Gardella suggests that denigrating the modern is a "mistake," in that modernism too can offer aesthetic pleasure. But the fact that he must address this issue suggests that many homeowners disagreed.

Modernist style and rationalist layouts attacked the nineteenth-century aesthetics, promising to rehabilitate leisure rooms and to change them into workspaces. The August 1937 *Domus* article "Parliamo un po' della cucina razionalmente," written by the magazine staff, suggests that rationalism serves as an antidote to abject spaces in the house. In this article and in others, Gardella, along with Delia Notari, Vanna Piccini, and others writing on the kitchen explored in the previous chapter, conflates rationalism with modernism. Saving time and energy through more-efficient food work was not only innovative, it was also nationalistic in that it promised to boost the economy. This conflation of domestic cooking and domestic affairs suggested that each kitchen metonymically figured the national larder, a synecdoche that imbued cooking actions like stirring a pot of risotto with the patriotic significance of supporting soldiers on the front.

When speaking of food and the kitchen between the world wars, the significance of the connection between the personal body and the national body assumes heightened importance. Fascist Italy held that repetitive, daily practices were productive of particular types of bodies and minds, and in this context, the kitchen offered a potent material dimension for governing private lives. This construction appeared to valorize the socially denigrated work of cooking, but with a Fascist, not socially progressive, goal in mind: to open up food preparation to regime intervention. From bodies (the bend of the back over the risotto pot on the electric stove) to activities (the number of stirs per minute, the time of day of the meal preparation) to spaces (the washable linoleum floor beneath the cook's feet, the aluminium of the risotto pot), this was fertile ground. Change the kitchen, the cooking method, or the recipe, the thinking goes, and you will see the effects of these changes in the national economy.

For the regime, intervening at the level of everyday practices allowed for intervention in private lives. Rationalism, this time accompanied by practicality, once again promised to discipline unruly gendered and classed bodies, activities, and spaces to render them productive, efficient, and hygienic. Prescriptions of science and modernity countered the supposedly inherent messiness of the cook, cooking, and the kitchen. Hygiene functioned not as a trait but as a set of practices held in place by regular washing and wiping. The kitchen, being inherently dirty, thus required constant cleaning. Zeno's paradox became Cinderella's: the shining surfaces could forever approach cleanliness, but they would never be completely clean and thus required diligence and a regimented approach.[90] National economics enter the private sphere through mass-produced texts and objects, that is, through narrative and also through design. This shift to rationalism contributed to a new definition of autarky that was specific to women and defined as a set of daily, primarily culinary, practices. But more broadly, it also supported governmental efforts to institutionalize the kitchen, to control this productive space through the form and function of both objects and people.

The gleaming white surfaces of ideal Fascist kitchens reflect the material connections between autarky and design. Specifically, these architectural plans and their proposed use illuminate how Lidia Morelli, Piero Bottoni, and Ignazio Gardella translated abstract Fascist principles into concrete kitchen features. Hygiene converted into electric currents, air circulation, and running water. Productivity flowed through Taylorist work triangles, introduced by German counterpart Margarete Schütte-Lihotzky. And autarky became commonplace through the pervasive use of domestically sourced and produced building materials like aluminium, tiling, and glass. These currents in rationalist kitchens design informed the new *case popolari*, aiming to increase the productivity of women's domestic labour.

But as the case of the Garbatella housing blocks demonstrates, not every Taylorist kitchen fed a Fascist family. Architectural ideals did not always equate to peaceful ends in the politicized context of Fascist domesticity. Taken in sum, these kitchens – ideal and real – illustrate three characteristics of how national politics operated in these supposedly apolitical spaces: First, Fascist projects that appeared to be distinct in policy actually overlapped in practice. When rendered through cooking practices, autarky and productivity mutually reinforced one another within the same object and its associated activity. For example, linoleum floors supported Italian industry as well as kitchen cleanliness. Second, debates over modern versus old-fashioned kitchen styles show rationalism to be an aesthetic marker of productivity and hygiene in the home. Rationalist cooking instructions, if followed, would provide visible evidence of how closely working-class women were adhering to the regime's goals for improving the efficiency and hygiene of their food work. And finally, experiments, both successful (tiny kitchens, lunch canteens) and unsuccessful (no kitchens, dinner canteens), reveal the possibility of a world without women cooking and what this would mean for Italian conviviality. Fascist housing reforms aimed to bring working-class women's food work into closer alignment with the state ideology of familial togetherness, a concept forged of paternal authority and female dedication – what Victoria De Grazia has termed "Fascist familism." Model Fascist kitchens reveal that this family togetherness was often accomplished by physically isolating working-class women and their food work, as opposed to actually bringing the family members all together. At stake in these kitchens is a profound reckoning with class boundaries and what it means to feed the family. The regime did not invent these ideals anew. Rather, it centred and sanctified them, dictating domesticity through kitchen architecture.

FROM FEEDING FASCISM TO EATING MUSSOLINI

"What did you expect to eat when you came to Italy? The corpse of Mussolini?" In his post-war novel *The Skin*, Curzio Malaparte taunts a dinner party of American army generals, mocking their horror upon being served what appears to be a "poor boiled child" on an enormous silver tray – a baby manatee.[1] Here, Malaparte (pseudonym of Kurt Erich Suckert) tells the lurid tale of a dinner party held in Naples in 1943 wherein American army generals dined on the remaining stock of the city aquarium. The menu includes a variety of fish and crustaceans, as well as the famous sea cow-cum–siren. By equating military occupation with cannibalism, Malaparte stages a hyperbolic offensive against the horrors of World War II. To do so, he pushes Fascist food policy to its logical extreme: in this scene, food and politics have blended to such a degree that the Allied presence in Naples signifies Il Duce's bodily consumption by the Americans, and by Malaparte himself in his semi-autobiographical role as the Italian war correspondent. But Malaparte's dark joke also poses a serious question: What does one eat when war has blasted away the normal parameters of edibility?

The January 1943 issue of *La Cucina Italiana* suggests some possible answers to this question. First, wartime cooks turned towards the medicinal qualities of food, largely eschewing concerns for flavour. In this sixteen-page issue, one of the last produced before the magazine's wartime pause from August 1943 to January 1952, *La Cucina Italiana*'s resident herbalist Rosi Brisighello devoted a full page to the preparation of curative teas and poultices based on foraged wormwood. These recipes for fever, indigestion, and infant deworming consisted of little more than boiled wild herbs and reflect the widespread ailments caused by poverty and malnutrition. Repeated shortages in shops and astronomical prices on the black market led women to fields and forests to stock their cupboards. In line with Amalia Moretti Foggia's cookbooks, they further suggest a reconceptualization of food's possible effects on the body beyond its pleasant ability to fill the belly. In another reflection of the period's austerity, *La Cucina Italiana*'s January 1943 recipes indicate a desire to maintain culinary traditions by advocating traditional preparations even in the absence of defining ingredients, as in "zuppa di riso al brodo di pollo … senza pollo!" (rice soup with chicken broth … without chicken!). The implied disappearance of even autarkic animals like chicken and rabbit speaks to the increasing meat scarcity of the times.

But despite attempts to approach food as medicine, to maintain former recipes without key ingredients, and to explore new foodstuffs, subscriber letters to *La Cucina Italiana* that same month show that hunger rumbled through the background of readers' lives and stomachs. One subscriber, Marsalesina Bella, wrote to the magazine to ask how to help her ailing brother: at eighteen years old, he stood 1.60 metres tall and weighed only 40 kilograms. Marsalesina recounted that the skin on his face was dry, his cheeks were hollow, and his hair was continually falling out. The editors of *La Cucina Italiana* featured this desperate situation as their first letter on the response page, a space typically reserved for the problems deemed most salient to the maga- zine's readership. Recall that the magazine's founding editors, Delia and Umberto Notari, openly supported the Fascist regime by promoting Mussolini's autarkic cam- paigns with reader contests and letters to the editor. The issue, the editors wrote, was simple: Marsalesina's brother weighed 16 kilograms less than he should. To help him gain weight, they advised Marsalesina to prepare foods with butter, milk, fats, and flour – the very foods under strictest rationing by the Fascist regime. In a conspicuous lacuna, the article refrains from connecting their contentious alimentary advice to the wartime circumstances that caused malnourishment. By 1943, *La Cucina Italiana* covers and articles had moved so far into politics that cooking advice became an afterthought.

As food supplies dwindled and rations shrank, citizens increasingly blamed the regime and Mussolini, who they accused of starving the national body. World leaders went even further, connecting the Italian body politic to Il Duce through gastro- intestinal metaphor. At a Kremlin meeting with Churchill in October 1944, Stalin sputtered, "It was the Italian people who had vomited up Mussolini."[2] He blamed the Italian body politic for the existence of their leader, suggesting that the Italian people's bout with political indigestion had vomited Mussolini into the world. In this sense, vomiting represents unsuccessful consumption. Instead of assimilating food into the body, vomiting produces something vile, in this case, a political regime that pushed food prices up and calorie consumption down. As Carol Helstosky notes, during the early 1940s, each social class's diet fell to the level of the nutritive levels of the one below.[3]

Schoolteachers, pensioners, and government employees sought charity and fre- quented soup kitchens. When contrasted against those living in urban environments, women in the countryside experienced wartime deprivation as less dire. Some women planted home gardens and raised their own animals for meat or foraged for additional sustenance. However, the fortitude of these women should not be conflated with access to more or better foods: rather, these stoic attitudes and practical responses merely reflected the fact that hunger had always been a nagging presence in Italian peasant life, and many adopted strategies accordingly. One can also see these strategies on display in the inventive preparations of non-standard ingredients which mark *la cucina povera*. Feeding Fascism not only threw up Mussolini, it also starved its countrywomen, the beating heart of the body politic.

Americanization and the Economic Boom

Long after Fascism was discredited as a movement and Mussolini had met his end, the architectural and social legacy of these ideas lives on. Housing remained scarce immediately after the war, and utilities were often quite rudimentary. In 1951, only 7.4 per cent of households possessed electricity, running water, and an indoor toilet.[4] The building industry provided a key engine for Italy's economic growth during the 1950s and 1960s, alongside exports.[5] The suburban building boom that accompanied the so-called "economic miracle" of the late 1950s and early 1960s harked back to the Garden City ideals espoused in New Town literature of the Fascist period. Situated within the broader Fascist perception of the city as a barren, diseased body and the countryside as a fertile and healthy zone, these towns simply shifted the Taylorist objective of the factory from maximized production of goods to maximized production of healthy children. Similar preoccupations figured in the city planning of the New Towns in the Pontine Marshes. The accompanying population jump that followed leaves one with the uneasy realization that the Fascist-period union of rationalism and pronatalism continued to shape Italy's urban landscape, particularly in ever-expanding *periferie*, the outer rings of Milan, Turin, Naples, and Rome.

Migration, both internal and external, rose concurrently: many Italians moved from the countryside to the city and from the south to the north, filling the new suburban housing developments in and around the burgeoning industrial centres. Illegal building and wild real estate speculation, together with corrupt landlords and indifferent city officials, soon led to crowding and crime in the Fascist *borgate*, urban enclaves built on the periphery of large cities as part of Fascist urban planning and social control of the leftist working class.[6] Others moved abroad, to the United States, to Canada, and to Argentina. In these new locales, the majority of Italians owned their own homes, and, subsequently, their own kitchens, for the first time.

Ironically, the Fascist fantasy of hyperproductive, streamlined, and hygienic kitchen work promoted by Ignazio Gardella and other architects of rationalist domesticity materialized after the fall of the regime, during the economic boom. Small dimensions, gleaming white tiled walls, and preparation spaces organized in the Taylorist work triangle emerged as the ideal standard kitchen design in magazines. Concurrently, new forms of advertising hawked novel products, particularly appliances, to fill these homes. New domestic habits (more frequent washing) and expectations (whiter laundry) arrived with them. Instead of decreasing the amount of women's labour in the household, these products increased the social expectations for the quality of product that their labour should produce.[7]

Fascist legacies in the kitchen also included the celebration of a woman's place being in the home, where her role was managing the household through hygienic, rational, modern means. During the 1950s, the woman of the house was celebrated for her caring work on behalf of the family breadwinner, under the assumption that her savvy purchases improved the husband's earning power; this in turn allowed the family to purchase even more modern goods, creating a virtuous cycle of consumption.

Two Shifts: Industrial Food Products, Domestic Workforce

Thanks to workers' movements in the late 1960s and early 1970s, expectations for safe and clean working conditions rose in parallel with new apartment blocks and refurbished industrial plants. At Perugina chocolates, workers' strikes rocked the company from the early 1950s, almost as soon as the plant was rebuilt from World War II bombardments. Labour action continued well into the 1970s and did not quiet until the brand's sale to the global, American-based chain Nestlé. Because of Nestlé's product emphasis on baby formula, this merger paradoxically regressed Spagnoli's progressive emphasis on breastfeeding at the factory. The current factory also eliminated the original breastfeeding rooms.

Reorganizing Perugina under Nestlé's aegis raises additional questions regarding how archival organization shapes historical narratives of the Fascist period. Film coverage of Perugina has been widespread and universally positive in tone. This body includes "Luisa, le Operaie e gli Altri, la donna che inventò il Bacio," a documentary film directed by Aldo Zappalà and produced by Rai Tre's educational series, "La storia siamo noi."[8] In celebration, the town of Perugia screened the film at its Morlacchi di Peru theatre. Attending the opening night were Nicoletta Spagnoli, the delegate of Luisa Spagnoli S.p.A; Manuela Kron, director of corporate affairs for Nestlé Italia; and Piero Corsini, the head of Rai Educational and "La storia siamo noi." In addition to the local industrial heirs to Spagnoli's empire, an entire balcony was reserved for former employees to attend the opening. The evening's attendants speak to the enduring influence of female leadership: Luisa Spagnoli, both by her model and by the gender-inflected policies that she put into place, created a factory that emphasizes female leadership even to this day. The story of how Spagnoli founded Perugina continues to draw broad media interest as well.[9] In part, this enthusiasm is due to contemporary gender politics. While the tendency to celebrate female entrepreneurs provides a critical counterbalance until we reach gender parity in historical accounts, we must also be careful not to diminish women's full complexity down to heroic archetypes. Spagnoli profited from Fascist policies like alimentary autarky. She also used Mussolini's complimentary evaluation of Perugina chocolates to promote the company. Analysis of the company's daily operations reveals a series of innovations and compromises in its daily operation. It is this uncomfortable interweaving that best characterizes the Fascist-period history of Perugina, a rare and successful female-run food company.

Perugina's sale to Nestlé also speaks to a broader post-war trend: the Americanization of Italian foodways. For two reasons, Madison Avenue's enticements frequently succeeded where Fascist propaganda had failed. First, advertising now appeared less artistic but more realistic. Instead of the "punch in the eye" aesthetic of the 1930s, advertisers of the 1950s and 1960s used realism. This style encouraged consumers to imagine themselves interacting with new products. Under the general ethos of modernization through consumption, industry and advertising assumed the task of instructors in everyday life that had been previously occupied by the Fascist government. Second, when advertising took on this pedagogical role, it made following instructions appealing by promising glamour as a reward. Television, in particular the popular evening show *Carosello*, spread American advertising tropes across the peninsula. Concurrently, print advertisements in magazines, such as the newly reinstated *La Cucina Italiana*, introduced readers to American food products like Coca-Cola, Ritz crackers, and Kraft cheese.[10] Early-1950s ads for these products suggested aspirational class status through convivial context, showing elegant couples sipping Coke from wine goblets at parties, fashionable ladies nibbling on Ritz crackers at afternoon tea in salons, and manicured fingertips delicately placing Kraft cheese singles on margherita pizzas (Fig. C.1).

American modernity and plenty resituated within an Italian context also informed one of the most popular themes in this period's advertising: full refrigerators, opened to the viewer's gaze. During Italy's economic boom period, refrigerators lagged behind only television sets as the most frequently purchased major appliance.[11] As part of what Stephen Gundle has called "the Americanization of everyday life," refrigerators changed Italian cooking in two key ways: they altered national foodways by allowing for increased consumption of expensive perishable goods such as meat and dairy products and also shifted household work patterns by decreasing the necessity of regular market trips. In numerous refrigerator ads, chic young couples gaze in satisfaction at the interior array of goods, always exploding with expensive products like meat and cheese, as well as new American treats like Coca-Cola (Fig. C.2). A celebratory array of French Champagnes typically beckoned from the open door (Figs. C.2 and C.3). But the incongruity of placing mass-produced foods in chic Italian surroundings also evoked the relative underdevelopment of the domestic economy. In a holdover from Fascist food history, the foreignness of goods like tea, coffee, and sugar equated to modernity, luxury, sweetness, and energy. Such positivity problematically cast local versions of these goods as inferior in quality and in associated class

C.1. Magazine advertisement for Kraft cheese. "Kraft cheese singles: the secret to the successful pizza." *La Cucina Italiana*, March 1955.

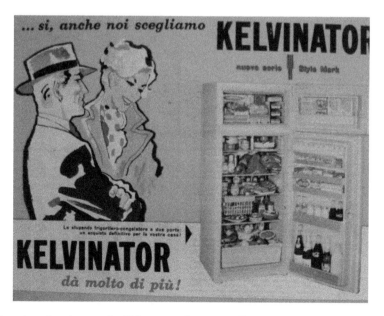

C.2. Magazine advertisement for Kelvinator refrigerators: "Yes, we too chose Kelvinator." *La Cucina Italiana*, April 1953.

C.3. Magazine advertisement for Ignis refrigerators: "Nelle ore liete" (In the happy hours). *La Cucina Italiana*, April 1953.

status. Thus, American soda and crackers, generally coded as middle-class foods in the United States during the 1950s, rose to high-class status when they crossed the Atlantic.

Despite the geographic divergence in prestige, prices for American foods in Italy and in the United States remained nearly identical throughout the economic boom period. As early as 1950, journalists noted that the five-cent twelve-ounce bottle of Coca-Cola remained "one of the most staunchly held price lines in U.S. economic history," a cost that nearly equated to Italian-manufactured Coca-Cola, sold in 1938 for 1 lira in 200 cubic centimetre bottles.[12] After the war, however, higher production costs drove up both soda prices and soda sizes.

Emphasis on appliances, including refrigerators, continued the Fascist-period trend that celebrated technology in the kitchen. In both the 1930s and the 1960s, machines increasingly did the cooking. But in a divergence between the periods, domestic workers reentered the kitchen. Whereas the 1930s saw a servant crisis, the late twentieth century saw a rise in migration. Many women from Eastern European countries (Albania, Ukraine), South East Asia (Philippines), and the former East African colony of Eritrea have come to Italy for work, assuming household tasks like the care of the very young and the very old.[13] Cooking and cleaning often form a subset of these women's paid labours. In terms of the latter, the emphasis of domestic work shifted, focusing more on cleaning during the 1950s, rather than on cooking, due to the prevalence of new frozen and pre-prepared products as well as appliances. Cristina Lombardi-Diop has argued convincingly that the constant pursuit of ever more limpid whiteness for dishes, laundry, floors, and appliances in the 1950s derived from Fascist racial policy privileging whiteness.[14] In many ways, race displaced class as a marker of who engages in domestic labour in other people's homes.

Agricultural Labour from Neorealism to Eataly

But where did those foods come from in the post-Fascist years? Moving from consumption in the home to production in the field, interwar divisions between reality and representations of women's agricultural work continued to diverge during the economic boom. In the aftermath of the Fascist period, the *mondine* continued to interest a range of political, media, and academic groups.

The neorealist film *Riso Amaro* (*Bitter Rice*, 1949) was both a critical and a commercial success. Driven by the star power of Silvana Mangano and Doris Dowling, the film turns the rice fields into a stage for drama and tragedy. The plot centres on the rice-weeding season in the Po valley. Two petty thieves, Francesca (Doris Dowling) and Walter (Vittorio Gassman), are on the run from the law and hide themselves amongst the trainloads of *mondine* as they head north to the rice fields. Francesca befriends one of the *mondine*, Silvana (Silvana Mangano), who introduces her to rice-weeding work. Towards the end of the *monda*, Walter arrives at the fields, planning to steal a large quantity of rice. Silvana falls for Walter and creates a diversion to help him carry out the heist, only to be stopped by Francesca. The two women face each other, armed with pistols; Francesca reveals Walter's duplicity to Silvana. Silvana shoots him and then kills herself in remorse. As the other rice workers depart, they pay tribute to Silvana, showering her body with rice.

Many former *mondine* noted their appreciation of Silvana Mangano's powerful performance and the ensuing media attention that her glamorous portrayal of a crafty *mondina* brought to their work. Former *mondina* Milena Lavagnini recalled,

Se ricordate il film meraviglioso RISO AMARO, la vita della mondina era vissuta e descritta con una tale verità che ha sempre fatto grande onore alle mondina il REGISTA perché solo chi veramente l'ha vissuta in prima persona, essere lontana di casa, fare otto ore con i piedi e le mani dentro l'acqua, la schiena piegata, intonare cori per comunicare e lavorare, lavorare con il corporale che controllava se solo ti fermavi un minuto erano guai.

If you remember the marvellous film BITTER RICE, the life of the rice weeder was experienced and described with such truth that the DIRECTOR always greatly honoured the rice weeder because only one who had experienced it in person, being far from home, doing eight hours with feet and hands in the water, back bent, singing choruses to communicate and work, working with the corporal who would check [and] if you stopped even for a moment there would be trouble.[15]

For Lavagnini, the film's neorealist aesthetic communicates respect for the *mondine* by accurately portraying the physical and emotional demands of rice weeding. Thanks to the domestic and international appeal of *Riso Amaro*, the image of the *mondina* remained culturally salient into the economic boom period and beyond. Migrant agricultural labourers and strikers were reimagined for rice packaging as buxom beauties who weeded golden fields while dressed in black thigh-highs (Fig. C.4). This packaging marketed food based on an idealized national past by obscuring labour and its physical toll on the female body. Contemporary American marketing takes a reverse tack, using archival film stills of real *mondine*, albeit attractive ones, to evoke the begone world of rural work that is less often associated with Italian rice today (Fig. C.5).

Former *mondine* writing in the present day almost universally recall this forty-day period as powerfully formative of their identity, political stances, and awareness of social class. While weeding, women voiced the corporeal experience of working conditions in the rice fields through musical creation, using call-and-response work songs to express the emotional and physical agony of migrant agricultural work. They framed this pain as communal, affecting workers from China to Russia to Italy. Liberation, they believed, would come with the global rise of leftist politics.

Because historians have tended to focus on women's role as consumers with regard to the national political picture, this book has endeavoured to instead demonstrate how women's role as producers of food fits into national questions of foodways and political identity. Further, it has attempted to put the predominantly leftist politics of these women into dialogue with their role as producers for a far right state. The heart of this analysis beats with the sayings, habits, and movements of the Northern Italian women who worked as *mondine* during the Fascist period. Their testimonials and work songs position female family members at the centre of their narrative construction. They also emphasize early sensory impressions of everyday life and their lasting effect on the women's conception of themselves as gendered and classed subjects. Ultimately, in both their diversity and their harmony, this chorus evokes the range of women's voices raised in resistance to Fascism.

risotto

RADICCHIO
from Treviso
NET WT. 12 OZ · 340 GRAMS

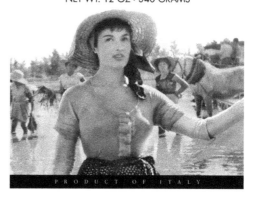

C.4. Curtiriso Arborio rice packaging   C.5. Italian Harvest rice packaging design, 2017,
design, 2015, Milan, Italy.   Eataly, Boston, United States.

Debates in Italian Food and Politics

Wartime austerity made a political virtue of economic necessity. By suggesting that
citizens follow simple preparations, maintain regional foodways, and emphasize
grains, legumes, and produce over meat and fats, the regime created the appearance
of consent by ordering its citizens to cook in the same way that they had for hundreds of years. What had been traditional became patriotic overnight. After the fall
of Fascism, however, the terms reversed: what had been known as Fascist foodways
returned to being understood as traditional Italian foodways. This conservatism illustrates a broader theme in Italian food history: Italian cuisine is itself conservative,
resisting drastic change to its core ingredients and preparations. But while Italian
food and foodways remained largely the same, the rhetoric surrounding them shifted
dramatically.

   Moreover, while the regime's political goals of pronatalism, rationalism, and autarky
ultimately failed, the means that the regime used to achieve such goals persisted.[16]
This was likely due to the regime's deep infiltration of everyday life. Although the
justifications for activities like double weighing and eating locally grown vegetables

changed, the activities themselves did not, likely due to their daily repetition and connections to the material world. To put it telegraphically, the *why* of these activities shifted in accordance with new political, cultural, and social trends, but the *what* and the *how* of everyday life stayed the same.

As this book has asserted, food politics are hashed out at the kitchen table in a constant negotiation between individuals and the regime. Tabletop politics can be characterized as an ongoing conversation between the national and the local, rather than as a set of top-down directives and bottom-up responses. Current Italian politics, economics, and social mores have moved away from the Fascist dictatorship of the 1930s, but the issue of feeding political ideologies remains salient.

In contemporary Italy, most people have plenty to eat. There is greater food quantity and quality than ever before. Many Italian women work outside the home, so either someone else must take on the cooking or the family meals must not be labour- or time-intensive. Migration has introduced new persons undertaking domestic labour in Italian households, as well as new types of food and food traditions, like the post-discotheque kebab enjoyed by Italian millennials, known as the *generazione mille euro* for their €1,000 monthly salaries and the precarious lifestyles that accompany such baseline earnings. And this brings us back to the question of tabletop politics.

Food provides a concrete way to translate abstract ideas about gendered work, family structures, and national traditions into a set of concrete actions oriented around preparation and consumption. As such, food companies must responsibly consider questions of messaging in their advertising. The way that consumers engage with these images illuminates the relative popularity of the social norms they infer at any given time. This book brings these themes to the fore. It has investigated the overlap between rationalizing kitchens and rationalizing working-class women's bodies. Ultimately, these interventions aimed to increase autarkic production of Italian foods and children. Hanging in the balance of Fascism's approach to feeding work is the social class disparity between what different women's labour in the kitchen can look like – and how isolated she might be from the rest of her family (or social class) as a result.

This work also signals the need for more research to answer certain questions about the role of food in social relations and national culture: How does control of food production, distribution, and consumption establish gender roles and gendered work in both the public and the private sphere? How does food symbolically connote femininity and masculinity and establish the social value of gendered work? And how do women's and men's attitudes towards their bodies affect the object and perceived legitimacy of their appetites? This book has approached Italian culture and family life as mutually constitutive entities: we cannot say where politics and industry end and everyday life begins because they mutually reflect and affect one other. For these reasons, it is absolutely critical that we use culinary ephemera, such as the types introduced in this book, to investigate how women perform, negotiate, and transform social relationships through daily habits and rituals, ultimately reconstructing the history of everyday life.

The body of evidence examined here not only leads to new conclusions regarding the nature and extent of women's involvement in national political projects; it also attempts to reframe current historiographic debates by demonstrating that contemporary conversations regarding feminist food justice (the idea that women ought to lead food-related social reform), migratory food work, and the relationship between individual consumers and the food industry have a gendered history that informs their modern incarnations. In many ways, my work here is an attempt to use an integrated archive to evaluate the real effects of Fascist alimentary policy. This book has opened the cupboards of Fascist Italy to investigate how the regime leveraged women's food work, changing what people ate so as to reform the national body. Many popular books on Italian food culture have explored elite sources from the Renaissance and the early modern period, creating a romantic mythology of Italian cuisine. But far fewer studies examine what, when, and where ordinary women cooked during the modern period, much less how they ate and why.

A NOTE TO FUTURE RESEARCHERS

Scholars of Italian Fascist culture often visit and revisit the same sites: the Roman Archivio Centrale dello Stato and Biblioteca Nazionale, along with the library's northern counterpart in Florence. Even the Napoletano Biblioteca Nazionale receives fewer and more specialized visitors than these three sites, despite its accessible location at the heart of a major Southern Italian city. Visibility, accessibility, and prestige partially account for their popularity, and their holdings are indeed excellent. But because government archives contain government voices, their overuse can skew the historical record. Overemphasizing these sites means that, without care, scholars can unintentionally recreate Fascist-period narratives of order and control, accidentally enshrining propagandistic messages like working-class women's widespread approval of and consent to the regime as historical fact.

Scholars should consider different archives as specialized tools and choose the most appropriate tool for the task. Private food companies and private citizens are not innocent, but they had different motives from the government; these countervailing voices create a more cohesive picture of life under Fascism. Regional museums tell regional stories: if you want to study history from below, you need to think about who cared about the people involved while they were still alive, where they might have lived and travelled, and what social resources they would have had to preserve their stories before they aged into histories.

I use these archives and their collections to answer questions about the places explored in this book. Women remade apartment blocks by living in them, shifting the contents of entire rooms according to their own designs. Architectural journals like *Casabella*, *Domus*, and *Costruzione* detail emerging building plans and developing debates. Unpublished financial contracts and building plans that went through government offices demonstrate that buildings are never truly finished and rarely have a single author. Studying buildings as processes – that is, over time – demonstrates how these structures changed as a result of constant negotiations between different social groups. Embracing this double focus can reconstruct the interactions between the creators and (re)creators of lived spaces like public housing projects, zooming in to bring family apartments and their kitchens into focus.

In many cases, the archival materials detail the Fascist-period histories of the buildings in which they are housed. For example, the Ministero della Salute manages a health archive in the EUR district of Rome. This collection contains a massive repository of materials related to women's nutrition and its effects on sexuality and reproduction, such as medical conference proceedings complete with records of audience interactions like whoops and whistles. Second, another collection of Italian state archives is oriented around media type. This too is a direct inheritance from Fascism, as these archives typically came from government bodies producing radio or film. Radio archives, for example, include the Ente Italiano per le Audizioni Radiofoniche (EIAR), now housed in three locations: the government library of the Ministero delle Comunicazione per la Stampa e la Propaganda in Rome and in the two core Rai Teche in Rome and Milan. For film, consider the Cineteca Nationale (under the aegis of the Centro sperimentale di Cinematografia) and Archivio LUCE, both in Rome. The vastness of these holdings allows the careful researcher to spot internal inconsistencies in the Fascist building projects, and then use these cracks in the regime edifice to identify arenas for further study. For instance, LUCE documentaries for ONMI used newly built rationalist clinics as architectural proof to herald the modernity of their healthcare system. But LUCE newsreels promoting the regime's rail lines and roads reveal a different view in their scenic pan shots from the train cars and inadvertently show the reality of regional country clinics in disrepair. This type of discrepancy provides a point of entry to study the regime's claims in relation to women's experiences of Fascist-period healthcare. But the LUCE archive is now almost entirely digital: original reels would have provided critical provenance information that has since been lost as part of the digitization project. Material traces hold worlds.

To value regional archives should not mean to disparage state archives. Major archives and libraries such as the Archivio Centrale dello Stato di Roma (ACS) and the Biblioteca Nazionale di Firenze provide critical context for any historical study with their collections of traditional historical materials. These sites demonstrate the nature of the connection between cookbook authors and Fascist officials. Dry cascades of government and industry paperwork – the endless bulletins and memos that provide the names, dates, and numbers – ultimately prove that private food companies enacted government policies on behalf of the Fascist regime to reap personal and financial benefits.

At the state archives, you can read women's letters to the regime both with and against the grain, seeking contradictions and occlusions as you psychologize the text. But these records, however valid, are incomplete. The contemporary ACS preserved and organized this collection, but the Fascist-period government selected the materials to be saved. We cannot know how many angry letters they threw away. This is why we need to expand our reading of Italian Fascist culture to include more than one set of collectors. Historical inclusivity means hearing from the person affected by the policy, not just the supposed expert who put the law on the books.

Rarely consulted archives were hidden in plain sight, as unadvertised sections of larger institutions. The state archive system contains two types of specialized sites for the study of Fascist-period culture. These categories provide different ways of thinking about how the history of private life is contained in the government files. First, one subset of state archives has a thematic structure, which is great if you want to learn about tourism, or health, or the colonies. This thematic approach to historical collections is a direct inheritance from Fascist governmental structure. Many former Fascist ministries, such as the Ministero della Salute and the Ministero dell'Agricoltura, now house libraries and archives with historical periodicals and propaganda.

Who would have had the money and the motive to conserve such quotidian ephemera? The Musei delle Aziende group, and more specifically the food industry archives, provided stunning original materials for this research. The Musei delle Aziende developed out of the earlier Musei Artisici Industriali Italiani group established with the onset of Italian industrialization in the mid-1850s. Locations of these archives follow the pulse of Italian industry: as of 2001, 75 per cent of the total museums in the group were located in Northern Italy. Moreover, 80 per cent of the total ownership remained in private rather than public structures, and 73 per cent of all museums employed a dedicated curator. Today, these museums span themes ranging from buttons (Collezione Marangoni in Milan) to bells (Museo delle Campane Marinelli in Agnone) to beer (Archivio Peroni in Rome).[1] The company archives held by Barilla and Buitoni-Perugina, respectively located at the outskirts of Parma and Perugia, provide an excellent example of these types of sites and their holdings. The Barilla archive and its associated Gastronomic Library provided an impressive collection of menus for the project. All are lavishly decorated, from the expensive hand-painted watercolours gracing the menus of society banquets to the cheap but no less beautiful mass-produced colour lithographs enlivening cocktail menus for local bars. Splotches and stains attested to the ghosts of puttanescas past – and the markings on the menus suggest that many of these items were frequently used.

The Barilla archive also contains culinary magazines like *La Cucina Italiana*, autarkic and wartime cookbooks, and numerous almanacs and household manuals, all written for and by middle-class Italian women. Both live and local, the Peroni Beer Museum combines a working factory with a private archive. This site traces craft brewing history and then uses those lessons to inform the contemporary factory layout and use. The architecture for production and bottling plants demonstrates how female workers moved through their workdays; changing beer recipe formulations point to new national tastes for bitter and herbal flavours; and evolving bottle dimensions, colours, and designs speak to changing habits in drinking with women's family and friends. It is worth noting, however, that working sites like the Peroni Beer Museum require an integrated and inclusive approach to organizing interviews.

It is absolutely critical to establish, build, and maintain collegial relationships with everyone at and around the site, from financial officers and box packers to curators and librarians. This approach not only helps to create an interwoven narrative of the brewery but also provides the groundwork for future collaborations with the people who populate the neighbourhood surrounding the brewery.

Museum founder Mitchell ("Micky") Wolfson took a similarly democratic approach to deciding what history ought to consist of. The Wolfsonian-FIU collected and preserved Fascist-period women's almanacs, along with propagandistic recipe pamphlets, colonial board games for children, and a copy of *Mein Kampf* written in Braille. His puckish delight in the subversive kitsch of dictatorial culture informs which items are selected. Included in this book are bread plates painted with Fascist food poetry and a streamlined aluminium toaster modelled after Italian race cars. But how do those items get to the Wolfsonian Museum? Tracing object provenance leads to another network of antiquarians and collectors. Scholars who want to purchase materials for study and use might consider tracing these back. All five senses engage in such materials: reading diaries, listening to songs, and sniffing the bits of chocolate left in the corner of a century-old wrapper can collapse time, creating a temporal free-fall between present and past.[2]

Regional sites offer colourful and original materials to research, but smallness alone does not cast a moral halo. Like the major government sites, the ACS and the ministry archives, food industry archives are financed and maintained by company interests. The Barilla factory, for example, yields a Barilla archive, and the narratives it contains are invested with supporting the business right next door. Emphasis on the company story tends to come through via relative accessibility and the emphasis on different types of information. The easily accessible Barilla Gastronomic Library in the Parma historic town centre holds menus and cookbooks not associated with the company. The more distant Archivio Barilla, off the *autostrada* and beyond the *tangenzienale* towards Pedrignano and Chiozzolo, contains relatively more sensitive materials, such as Fascist-period calendars depicting the civilizing myth of Italians teaching Ethiopians how to cultivate and harvest wheat, the main ingredient in Barilla pasta. The materials at these sites, especially financial records, factory photographs, and executive interviews, still need to be contextualized and read against the grain in the same way as government memos and propaganda. That said, the private food industry archives included in this book were forthcoming in sharing the breadth of their Fascist-period materials, including those that risked damaging the company reputation, in a way that government archives were not.

In a second parallel to the state archive system, many smaller archives mirror the state archives in their material culture emphasis. The Museo della Figurina in Modena maintains a huge collection of illustrated food packaging and labels, as well as rare promotional ephemera like scented pocket calendars (used to advertise colognes and perfumes) and illustrated matchbook covers. The Archivio della Communicazione in

Parma has original artists' studies for food advertisements. These colourful charcoal renderings, collages, and paintings reveal the individual artists' decision-making process that led up to the creation of the stereotypical culinary images that papered city walls and illustrated everyday life during the 1920s and 1930s.

In Italy, used cookbooks and culinary ephemera from this problematic historical period occasionally resurface from grandmothers' attics only to be discarded as soon as they are found. They do not appear valuable and typically provoke familial embarrassment thanks to the unpopular politics they contain. As well, the Harvard Schlesinger Library's cookbook collection provides materials that can be difficult to find in Italian institutions. Two pioneers created the former collection, Barbara Haber and Barbara Ketcham Wheaton. Both librarians at the Harvard Schlesinger Library, they made an early commitment to the then controversial idea that food could open working-class women's history. Their democratic approach to women's history means that Schlesinger Library now houses more female-authored interwar Italian cookbooks and almanacs than can be found at the Biblioteca Nazionale di Roma. In other words, studying the provenance and organization of archive holdings matters as much as the materials themselves.

Researching Women's Experiences of Fascism: The Power of the Small

This book examines how the social threads connecting cookbook authors and regime officials wove together in co-authorship at newspaper meetings and created financial bonds. Because female food workers have often been treated as minor characters in the larger narrative of Fascist history, the information could not be found in any archive. Illuminating a social web involves cross-comparison and triangulation of many sources over a long period of research. Deep patience unlocks small archives to such a considerable extent that this frame of mind serves as a methodological approach. It takes time to learn where these archives are and what they contain.

Planning a research trip focused on small archives should therefore include three budget items, which will cost you little money but much time. First, you will need to budget for the many macchiati to be consumed in museum cafeterias, because the value of a research site lies in its people even more than its materials. Ask open-ended questions. Be interested. Be kind. Learn one thing from everyone. Do not rush: you are having coffee with the institutional memory. Expert advice comes from curators and librarians and also from neighbourhood residents. Plan for many coffees in small-town bars. During these visits, you may learn that your research sites will need to expand beyond small archives and museums to include non-traditional locations, like second-hand markets or abandoned factories. For this reason, it is also helpful to plan the research locations for only 50 per cent of your trip. Explore! Leave the second half unplanned so that you have the time to follow up on these valuable site recommendations. This should be your second budget item: the time to travel down the unexpected research paths that these conversations will open. This includes time to spend on unexpected materials as well as places. If your hand stops over a particular map or menu, ask why. Finally, budget for burnout. If you feel frustrated or stuck, pause before choosing your next far-flung research site or opening the next folder of yellowed correspondence. You will ultimately save time by pausing to carefully choose your next move, instead of rushing ahead down the wrong path. This holds true for drawing conclusions from apparently opaque historical documents as well. Stalls and dead ends are the shadows revealing the central form. In other words, repetition and half-truths illuminate by outlining verifiable histories. Ultimately, they frame the central story.

The small, the regional, and the concrete realms of Fascist cultural history mark the point at which the dictatorship touched the individual through the physical conditions of daily life – that is, through food and shelter. Food history necessarily involves the people who did the cooking. To amplify the voices of these rural and urban working-class women, *Feeding Fascism* introduces a vivid selection of culinary ephemera gathered from a large collection of regional sites. This out-of-the-way element constitutes a methodological theme: I purposely look for archives that are small, isolated, and difficult to find, not simply because they have received few visits from scholars and little academic notice of their holdings, but also because they have proven to be more likely to hold the types of regional, everyday culinary ephemera of women's lives.

Italian food – like Italian women – holds a cherished symbolic status that does not translate into physical centrality or financial remuneration. In archives as in society, food occupied a lower cultural status compared with other arts. Consider the opera. Nearly every major Italian city boasting an opera house – including Rome, Milan, Turin, Verona, and Venice – also boasts a well-furnished archive located in the historic city centre. This accessibility coupled with greater funding for digitization of the holdings and visiting fellowships eases the study of their subjects and spreads these materials further than those in underfunded regional archives. This ease in turn impacts historiography, creating a false sense of the ubiquity of high culture by dint of the number of contemporary scholars who focus on these materials. By contrast, the history of food and farming is cast to the urban periphery. Understanding agricultural history and food-supply chains has clear merit and significance for economics. The Archivio Centrale dello Stato houses large collections on the history of rural life and agriculture, with valuable photographs and statistics gathered from nineteenth- and twentieth-century state inquests. But government endowments for the preservation of material culture produced by peasants are scant. Both matter, and they provide the greatest richness when read in tandem. By contrast, archives devoted to elite histories and pursuits, such as economics and diplomacy, opera and architecture, are comparatively central to their respective Italian cityscapes. They are also well funded. Put another way, archives look like their subjects: the geographic location and relative size of an archive hints at whose records – and whose interests – it contains.

By first dismantling the idea that we can speak of Italian women as one cohesive population, we can then begin to reconstruct individual women's lived experiences of the Fascist regime. Although the low literacy rates and general poverty of the women who worked in the fields and factories during the Fascist period would seem to indicate a lack of written records for study, the economic boom lifted many of these women out of the working class and allowed them to obtain advanced education later in life. Many wrote and illustrated testimonials to record their lives under Fascism. These documents can be found at the out-of-the-way Archivio Diaristico Nazionale in Pieve Santo Stefano, outside of the city of Arezzo in Tuscany.[3] The archive not only contains first-hand accounts from formerly illiterate labourers but also includes ephemera from the time period, like their school workbooks and their artistic productions, such as poems, drawings, and paintings. Many testimonials intermix the mediums and thus function as heavily mediated scrapbooks, with photos, picture cards, and art produced by the women. These first-hand written and visual accounts intertwine with audio materials. Workers' archives, like those organized by the Confederazione Generale Italiana del Lavoro (CGIL), can be found in small towns as well as large cities across Northern Italy. CGIL archives contain troves of interviews and work songs that attest to the variety of women's political opinions.

To get at the feel of women's experiences of Fascism, we need to rummage through the dented cheese graters, crumpled chocolate wrappers, and scratched matchbooks that they touched every day. Fascist interventions in foodways examine how these forms of bodily control extended into less overt but more pervasive forms of daily life. Following a Galvani teacup's trajectory from kiln to kitchen accomplishes two goals: it contextualizes the teacup in relation to broader patterns of ceramic manufacturing and tea distribution, and it reveals how the teacup's physical properties, like small size and light weight, encouraged different forms of packaging and handling at each step of its journey.

Examining kitchen objects from creation to disposal reveals how industrial design colludes with Fascist politics. Like cookbooks, cooking tools appear to be apolitical. As such, no alarms sound when they carry public politics to the private sphere. Once there, they prompt politicized behaviours in daily life that often pass undetected by the object's user. In this case, propaganda travels not through textual dictates but through material details. These meanings are so subtle, yet so ubiquitous, that even the designers themselves may be unaware of their presence. I treat these objects as "scriptive things," to use Robin Bernstein's useful term. That is, I approach cups and plates as items of material culture that prompt, but do not dictate, feelings and actions.[4] Scentscapes and soundscapes matter to the history of the gendered body. They flesh its bones, creating muscle and scars through that daily denting, crumpling, and scratching. In taking this holistic approach to the archive, I anchor my work in the power of the small.

NOTES

Introduction: Tabletop Politics

1 Recent debates have focused on Fascism's origins and spread in a global context. Madeleine Albright defines a Fascist as a person "who claims to speak for a whole nation or group, but is utterly unconcerned with the rights of others, and is willing to use violence and whatever other means are necessary to achieve the goals he or she might have." She compares strategies used by Vladimir Putin, Kim Jong-un, and other contemporary leaders with those employed by Fascists in the 1920s and 1930s. Albright, *Fascism: A Warning*, 28. Stanley Payne (*How Fascism Works*) also takes a transnational approach to Fascism, providing examples from Europe, Africa, and Asia to argue that Fascism wreaks havoc not through hyperbole but through normalization. Enzo Traverso studies "Islamic Fascism," an idea promoted by the European radical right, in *New Faces of Fascism*.

2 "What is the significance of a twenty-year parenthesis in Italian history?" Benedetto Croce cast Fascism as a parenthesis, a metaphor suggesting that Italy should be praised for having defeated Fascism rather than blamed for aiding in its rise and rule (*Croce Reader*, 56–7). The parenthesis also reinforced Croce's appeal to the Allied powers for clemency. Similarly apologist in approach are the Fascist-period biographies and histories of Renzo De Felice, *Interpretations of Fascism*. On the idea of a set of criteria without which Fascism could not exist, see Roger Griffin, *Modernism and Fascism*. Griffin defines the Fascist minimum as an enumeration of common traits as broad as brutality and as specific as a preceding decade of neoliberal decadence. If the regime meets a sufficient number of these conditions, then it is said to be Fascist. Robert Paxton argues for the Five Stages of Fascism, consisting of intellectual exploration, rooting, arrival to power, exercise of power, and radicalization or entropy. Paxton, *Anatomy of Fascism*.

3 Arendt, *Origins of Totalitarianism*.

4 Food studies scholarship frequently invokes the idea of foodways: the culture surrounding food as well as food itself. The centrality of foodways to food studies scholarship is evoked by the title of one of the field's leading journals, *Food and Foodways*, which is devoted to the history and culture of human nourishment. This examination of Fascist foodways builds on Arjun Appadurai's approach. His seminal research relies on cookbooks to investigate the creation of national, politically inflected foodways in the context of modern India in "How to Make a National Cuisine." More recent foodways research has focused on national identity: Jeffrey Pilcher, *¡Que vivan los tamales! Food and the Making of Mexican Identity* (Albuquerque:

University of New Mexico Press, 1998); Warren Belasco and Philip Scranton, eds., *Food Nations: Selling Taste in Consumer Societies* (New York: Routledge, 2002). I build on this work by exploring political foodways in the context of European nationalism in the interwar period.

5 See interviews by Revelli, *L'anello forte*. Two hundred sixty interviews with women living outside Cuneo tell the stories of the traditional farming province.

6 Treitel, *Eating Nature in Modern Germany*.

7 Comparing Fascist Italy with Nazi Germany, one sees just how distinct the two approaches were. Germany, if it was going to continue to expand, needed to tighten its belt. Following this reasoning, the Nazi Party pursed both demographic numbers and *Lebensraum* settler colonialism in tandem with rapid efficiency. By contrast, the Italian Fascist regime favoured massive resettlement schemes of ethnic Italians who worked the land in North and East Africa, establishing Italianità at home through their agricultural labour abroad. The regime seems to have thought that increasing the population at home would somehow lead to a self-sustaining empire in Libya, Ethiopia, Eritrea, and Somalia, one that would soon send surplus goods to Italy. But the Fascist Italian plan proved inviable: Italy's North and East African colonies were never self-sustaining. In fact, colonists depended on Italian exports for survival. For details, see Roberta Pergher, *Mussolini's Nation-Empire: Sovereignty and Settlement in Italy's Borderlands, 1922–1943* (Cambridge: Cambridge University Press, 2018).

8 Birke, "Bodies and Biology," 48.

9 Wazana Tompkins, *Racial Indigestion*, 7.

10 Hodder, *Entangled*.

11 Appadurai, "How to Make a National Cuisine."

12 See Chang's *The Crisis-Woman*; Pinkus's *Bodily Regimes*; Gundle's *Bellissima*; Landy's *Fascism in Film*; Marcus's *Italian Film in the Light of Neorealism*; and Pickering-Iazzi's *Mothers of Invention*.

13 Victoria De Grazia has noted, "The story that Mussolini made the trains run on time arose in the late '20s and gained credence abroad mainly because of well-heeled British tourists who considered the hopelessly refractory Italians governable only by dictatorial means. His regime built magnificent central stations and upgraded the main lines on which businessmen, politicians and comfort-minded tourists sped between Milan and Rome." See "Will Il Duce's Successors Make the Facts Run on Time?" Although it is true that World War I had left the Italian rail network in poor repair, the rebuilding process was already well under way by the time the Fascists came to power. Mussolini took credit for these improvements after the fact.

14 For many years, Italian colonial studies were blinkered by lack of access to historical materials. In the 1990s, Italy's main colonial archive, the Archivio Diplomatico in Rome, finally opened its doors to scholars rather than only former government officials. Cultural historians of Italy and Ethiopia such as Tekeste Negash, Haile Larebo, Mia Fuller, Ruth Ben-Ghiat, and Richard Pankhurst have since traced the cultural, racial, and economic legacies of the Fascist period into modern-day East Africa. Scholars are now turning their attention to tracing the contours of everyday life in the colonies. More recently, Cristina Lombardi-Diop, Gaia Giuliani, Sandra Ponzanesi, Ruth Iyob, Barbara Sòrgoni, Giulia Barrera, Patrizia Palumbo, and Irma Taddia have also produced transnational Italian histories of race and racism, as well as new feminist ethnographies and oral history work.

15 Antonio Gramsci argued that discord between the north and south originally derived from Alfredo Niceforo's suggestion that the answer to the southern problem was northern nationalism and Fascism. Gramsci, "Il Mezzogiorno e il Fascismo," *L'Ordine Nuovo*, 15 March 1924. Reprinted in *La questione meridionale 1935* (Rome: Editori Riuniti, 1966). The regime installed Northern politician Cesare Mori, the so-called Iron Prefect, to defeat the mafia.

Connections between the Fascists and the mafia emerged soon after, and the regime removed Mori amidst a hail of propaganda declaring the Fascist defeat of the mafia. John Dickie, *Darkest Italy: The Nation and Stereotypes of the Mezzogiorno, 1860–1900* (New York: St. Martin's Press, 1999).

16 In many ways, the Southern Question in Italy predated the nation itself. Northern Italy existed in an economic organization similar to that of other states of Europe, whereas Southern Italy had limited industry and infrastructure, largely due to the fatherly administrations of Spain and the Bourbons. Italian Unification was known as the Piedmontization of Italy, for the resurgent power of the north over southern land and people. It split the nation in two even as it claimed to cohere divergent regions into one country. Mediterranean climate purportedly degenerated culture, thereby eliminating the possibility for self-rule in the Mezzogiorno. Massimo Montanari and Alberto Capatti have observed that regional cuisines composed national Italian cuisine in Pellegrino Artusi's *La scienza in cucina e l'arte di mangier bene*, arguably Italy's first nationalist cookbook. But as Dickie notes, they did so unevenly. Sicily, Calabria, Campania, and Puglia are represented by less than 10 per cent of the total recipes in the book, despite containing almost half of the Italian population when the book was first published in 1891. The largest number of recipes came from Emilia-Romagna, the natal region of Artusi and, later, Mussolini. For further history see Nelson Moe, *The View from Vesuvius: Italian Culture and the Southern Question* (Los Angeles: University of California Press, 2002).

17 On schools, see "Growing Up" in De Grazia's *How Fascism Ruled Women*, McLean's *Mussolini's Children*, and Paluello's seminal *Education in Fascist Italy*. On the church, see Kertzer's *The Pope and Mussolini* and Zuccotti's *Under His Very Windows*. On the piazza, see Berezin's *Making the Fascist Self* and Lasansky's *Renaissance Perfected*.

Chapter One: Towards an Autarkic Italy

1 In this context, the *ventennio* refers to the span of Italy's Fascist dictatorship, beginning with the March on Rome of 28 October 1922 and ending with the death of Benito Mussolini on 28 April 1945.

2 Weinreb, "'For the Hungry Have No Past,'" 53–4.

3 Just as historical periodicity reflects the authorial perspective rather than broad truth, so too does subject selection and material analysis. Joan Kelly's foundational argument, "Did Women Have a Renaissance?," in *Becoming Visible: Women in European History*, edited by Renate Bridenthal and Claudia Koonz (New York: Houghton Mifflin, 1977), 175–201. Antoinette Burton signals, "It's not just women who are secondary, it's our materials." *Dwelling in the Archive: Women Writing House, Home, and History in Late Colonial India* (New York: Oxford University Press, 2003).

4 Carl Ipsen has convincingly argued that Mussolini "equated declining fertility with moral decadence and cited statistics that demonstrated Italy's decline. Mussolini blamed two basic causes for this decline: industrial urbanism, as borne out by the low fertility of Italy's most industrial cities (Turin, Milan, Genoa); and small property holdings, which gave rise to the fear that having several children would lead to the eventual division of an already small holding." *Dictating Demography*, 66.

5 Like rationalism, pronatalism was an international phenomenon. However, as with the architectural aesthetic, pronatalism's expression in Italy possesses unique characteristics. For instance, the negative attention paid by the regime to traditional midwives appears far greater in Italy than in other countries. See Triolo, "Fascist Unionization and the Professionalization of Midwives."

6 As part of a larger demographic project, pronatalist policies worked in concert with other strategies for population control, such as re-routing external emigration to the United States,

Canada, and Argentina into internal immigration to the Fascist New Towns in the Pontine Marshes. See Caprotti, "Internal Colonization, Hegemony, and Coercion."

7 This is the standard English translation for ONMI used by scholars of Fascist maternal policy, such as Elizabeth Dixon Whitaker, David Horn, and Maurizio Bettini. Translations are the author's own unless otherwise specified.

8 On the regime's legislative and financial support of ONMI, see Cioccetti, "Il finanziamento," in *Esperienze e prospettive dell'ONMI*, 38–60.

9 Anthropologist Penny Van Esterik is one of few academics to argue for the inclusion of breastmilk in food studies scholarship. She has called attention to international discussions of the relative merits of breast- versus bottle-feeding. See *Beyond the Breast-Bottle Controversy* (New Brunswick, NJ: Rutgers University Press, 1989). Since the publication of her ground-breaking book, international debates over milk and formula have intensified. Debates swirl around La Leche League's staunch pro-breastfeeding stance, and Nestlé's infant formula scandals across Asia and in China in particular. See Yanzhong Huang, "The 2008 Milk Scandal Revisited," *Forbes*, 16 July 2014; and Jill Krasny, "Every Parent Should Know the Scandalous History of Infant Formula," *Business Insider*, 25 June 2012.

10 For an example of how such scholarship might address the female body both within the built environment and as a lived space, see Stormer, "Mediating Biopower and the Case of Prenatal Space."

11 For the effects of the scientific discovery of the calorie on interwar diplomacy in Europe, see Cullather, "Foreign Policy of the Calorie."

12 For the Fascist demographic campaigns focused on mothers and soldiers, see Horn, *Social Bodies*.

13 For regime control over the insides of homes via prescriptive domestic literature, see L'organizzazione scientifica del lavoro, "Note di economia domestica"; *Domus*, August 1939 (Milan: Editoriale Domus Società Anonima), xvi–xxx; and Domus, ed., *Il libro di casa 1938*. For regime control over the insides of bodies via foodways and maternal care via didactic newsreels, see *La Protezione della Stirpe* and *Alle Madri d'Italia*.

14 For example, see Boccasile, *Mangiate Riso*.

15 Horn, *Social Bodies*, 40.

16 For example, the November 1935 cover illustration heralded the *Giornata della Fede*, the Day of Faith, wherein women gifted their gold wedding rings to the Fascist Party to raise capital for the East African campaign.

17 Virgilio Retrosi studied at the Regia Accademia di Belli Arti in Rome before working for the manufacturers Rosati and Sprovieri. He provided articles, designs, and vignettes for *La Casa*. Beginning in 1925, he also produced many plates featuring Fascist propagandistic content for the Fabbrica Ceramiche d'Arte Roma. In the mid-1930s, he abandoned ceramics to work with graphic design. Fabbrica Ceramiche d'Arte produced this glazed ceramic plate in Rome in 1927. For many years, it was attributed to Ferruccio Palazzi. Palazzi published the manual *Tecnologia della ceramica* in 1932 and edited the monthly bulletin *Centro Studi Ceramici* (C.S.C.) from 1934 to 1937. Economic difficulties led him to close his ceramics studio in 1937, at which point he assumed a government post as a minerals researcher in Italian East Africa. While in Ethiopia, he also founded a ceramics school.

18 Helstosky, *Garlic and Oil*, 15. For a global analysis of the relationship between fatness and food security, see Forth and Carden-Coyne, *Cultures of the Abdomen*.

19 Pietro Cavallo observes this visual theme across pro-Fascist political posters and leaflets. See *Italiani in guerra* and *La storia attraverso i media*. For negative portrayals of this image, see Angelo Ventrone's interpretation of Socialist, Communist, and Anarchist cartoons, "Vogliam del

pane per i bambini o la testa di Mussolini" and "Abbasso la guerra imperialista," in *Il nemico interno: Immagini, parole e simboli della lotta politica nell'Italia del Novecento* (Rome: Donzelli, 2005), 132–5.

20 Ben-Ghiat, "Envisioning Modernity."

21 This culinary trend periodically resurfaces, most recently in the early 2000s, with Spanish Catalan chef Ferran Adrià's restaurant El Bulli in Bilbao. Along with British chef Heston Blumenthal, Adrià is often associated with molecular gastronomy, although neither formally associates their cuisine with the category. Adrià, for instance, refers to his cooking as deconstructivist. He defines the term as "taking a dish that is well known and transforming all its ingredients, or part of them; then modifying the dish's texture, form and/or its temperature. Deconstructed, such a dish will preserve its essence … but its appearance will be radically different from the original's." The goal is to "provide unexpected contrasts of flavour, temperature and texture. Nothing is what it seems. The idea is to provoke, surprise and delight the diner." Interview in Katy McLaughlin, "Portrait of the Artist as a Chef," *Wall Street Journal*, 31 October 2008.

22 Marinetti, *The Futurist Cookbook*, 11.

23 Baron Justus von Liebig founded Liebig's Extract of Meat Company in Germany in 1847 based on the development and promotion of a method for industrial production of beef extract and stock cubes. By 1924, the company's assets included more than 2 million hectares of farmland and herds of cattle in Argentina, Uruguay, Paraguay, Rhodesia, Kenya, and South Africa. Because Italian factories produced this originally German brand on peninsular soil, they were considered an autarkic food by the regime. See Brock, *Justus von Liebig*.

24 Marinetti and Fillìa, "Manifesto of Futurist Cooking."

25 Funding for this periodical and the sugar advertisements contained therein came from Banca Commerciale Italiana, Banco di Sicilia, Credito Italiano, Istituto Nazionale delle Assicurazioni, Officine Villar Perosa, and R.A.S. Breda. For further information, see Valentina Pisanty, *La difesa della razza: Antologia 1938–1943* (Milan: Tascabili Bompiani, 2006).

26 See Cullather, "Foreign Policy of the Calorie."

27 Clinicians frequently recommended clean kitchens as part of the antidote to infant mortality due to tuberculosis specifically. See notes from the Congresso Nazionale di Medicina del lavoro, held in Florence, 11–14 June 1922, published by Istituto Italiano di Igiene, *Organizzazione e Medicina Pubblica* (Prato: M. Martini, 1922).

28 Cullather, "Foreign Policy of the Calorie."

29 Italian nutritional science appeared in scientific tracts and popular books as well as the military cookbooks cited here. For examples drawn from soup kitchens, factory cafeterias, and summer camps, see Alessandra Olivi, "Mangiare 'per due' o mangiare 'quel che c'è': Regimi alimentari della madre in Romagna (1930–1950)," in *Donne e microcosmi culturali*, ed. Adriana Destro (Bologna: Patron, 1997), 77–106.

30 Fornari, *Il cuciniere militare*.

31 Zamarra, *La Cucina Italiana della Resistenza*. She also wrote *Almanacco della cucina per la famiglia Italiana 1939* (Milan: Sonzogno, 1939).

32 "The U.S. government first made the calorie during the Progressive Era, as a gauge of social and industrial efficiency … The current world pattern of humanitarianism, exchange, and subsidized dumping began to emerge only after the Anglo-American allies recaptured the calorie among the spoils of World War II." Cullather, "Foreign Policy of the Calorie," 339.

33 Way, "Wheat Crisis of the 1930s."

34 Scarpellini, *Material Nation*, 110.

35 By 1943, Massaie Rurali had mobilized three million farm women to rationalize agricultural work and increase output.

36 Images of the winners of these competitions travelled further south as propagandistic images for the Mostra della Rivoluzione Fascista, as demonstrated by the large unfinished catalogue of Massaie Rurali competition photos from whence these three examples come. ACS, MRF, 1934–6, b. 90, f. 151 sf 6–12, 407–34.

37 Giovanni Pascoli, "Risotto Romagnolo," *La Cucina Italiana*, 15 June 1930; Ada Negri, "Il companatico dell'illusione," *La Cucina Italiana*, 15 August 1930; Margherita Sarfatti, "Zuppa d'aragosta," *La Cucina Italiana*, 15 October 1930, and "La botte piena e la moglie ubriaca," *La Cucina Italiana*, 15 April 1931.

38 Scarola, "Le riviste gastronomiche."

39 Helstosky, *Garlic and Oil*, 65.

40 Most Italians ate autarkically, but they did so due to economic necessity rather than political affiliation. See "Unification through Monotony: Italy 1861–1914" and "The Great War and the Rise of State Intervention, Italy 1915–1922," in Helstosky, *Garlic and Oil*.

41 Griffin argues that this characteristic combination of palingenesis and ultranationalism differentiates Fascism from other authoritarian regimes. It is, in his phrasing, the "fascist minimum" without which a regime cannot be called "Fascist." See "Staging the Nation's Rebirth," 2.

42 Although it was first electrolytically synthesized in 1854, the large-scale industrial production of aluminium during Italy's interwar period derives from its use in World War I for light, strong airframes in shipbuilding and aviation. Though naturally soft and light, this ductile metal easily forms alloys, which can increase its hardness while preserving its light weight. It could then be used to make flexible bands, sheets, and wire to make everyday items like eyeglass frames and aluminium foil. Aluminium tableware emerged from this industrial boom and gradually supplanted copper and cast iron. For a history of the topic, see Mimi Sheller, *Aluminum Dreams: The Making of a Light Modernity* (Cambridge, MA: MIT Press, 2014). On the specifics of aluminium in the Italian context, see Schnapp, "Romance of Caffeine and Aluminum."

43 This bread plate is part of the Wolfsonian Museum collections. Lino Berzoini, Bread Plate, Milan, c. mid-1930s, designed for Calderoni and manufactured by Motta, patinated tin, 25.5 centimetres diameter (Wolfsonian Institute, Miami, 84.9.12).

44 Photographs of Fascist events show regime officials awarding women decorative plates like these, most commonly in recognition of prolific motherhood. For an example of these award ceremonies, see "Il folto gruppo delle madri più prolifiche d'Italia posa sulla scalinata d'ingresso della Mostra della Rivoluzione Fascista" (The dense group of the most prolific mothers of Italy posed on the stairs of the entrance to the Exhibit of the Fascist Revolution). Photo by LUCE, 23 December 1933, Rome, Italy (Archivio LUCE: photo code A00052074).

45 See Dennis P. Doordan, "In the Shadow of the Fasces: Political Design in Fascist Italy," *Design Issues* 13, no. 1 (1997): 39–52; and Marianne Lamonaca, "A 'Return to Order': Issues of the Vernacular and the Classical in Italian Inter-War Design," in Kaplan, *Designing Modernity*, 194–221.

46 Diaries attest to the placement of these plates. See Baldi, Testimony.

47 Eugenio Colmo went by the pseudonym "Golia" at the time of this bowl's production. He began using Golia as a pen name while writing satirical cartoons for various publications, such as *Frigidarium* and *La Donna*. For over ten years, he also produced graphic design for the latter magazine. In the 1920s, he wrote many anti-war pieces for this journal, so the propagandistic content of this plate is quite surprising, especially as his work in ceramics began in this same period, starting in 1922. He produced over 2,000 pieces before bombardments in Turin destroyed his studio in 1941. This coupled with the death of his first wife, Lia Tregnaghi, and artistic partner in the same year resulted in a period of inactivity that lasted until 1944, when he assumed work for *Gazzetta del popolo* and married his second wife, Alda Besso.

48 See Willson, *Peasant Women and Politics in Fascist Italy.*
49 See Whitaker, *Measuring Mamma's Milk.*
50 See Anderson, *Control and Resistance.*
51 See Pine's "Food in Nazi Germany."
52 *Pravda*, 10 May 1936, cited in Neary's "Mothering Socialist Society," 403.
53 Treitel, *Eating Nature in Modern Germany.*
54 See Richards, *Time of Silence.*
55 In June 1941, Nazi officers Herberte Backe and Hermanne Göring outlined the Hunger Plan in a series of documents collectively known as "Göring's Green Folder." These foodways manipulations planned to use starvation as a weapon as part of the military preparations for Operation Barbarossa, the Nazi invasion of the Soviet Union.
56 Collingham, *Taste of War.*
57 Here I use Michel Foucault's definition of biopower, "an explosion of numerous and diverse techniques for achieving the subjugations of bodies and the control of populations" (*History of Sexuality*, 140).
58 Architecture provides a spatial case study of how the Italian Fascist urban planning highlighted certain time periods by erasing others. Medina Lasansky has shown that the regime scrubbed building facades of Baroque details to privilege Renaissance features. Lasansky, *Renaissance Perfected.*
59 Scholars of totalitarianism have examined the Fascist myth of national rebirth and the related projects of nationalizing the regional. Roger Griffin defines Fascism as "palingenetic ultra-nationalism." The crux of this theory is the belief that Fascism is defined by its core myth, the promise of national rebirth (palingenesis). See Griffin, "Staging the Nation's Rebirth."
60 Historians of the Italian Southern Question have noted the persistent elision of women with landscape in the *popolo donna* narrative, wherein Southern citizens of all genders are figured as being more female than Northern Italians. Franco Cassano, *Il pensiero meridiano* (Rome: Laterza, 1996); Dickie, *Darkest Italy*; Robert Lumley and Jonathan Morris, eds., *The New History of the Italian South: The Mezzogiorno Revisited* (Exeter, UK: University of Exeter Press, 1997); Moe, *View from Vesuvius.*

Chapter Two: Agricultural Labour and the Fight for Taste

1 Serpieri, *La Guerra e le classi rurali italiane.*
2 Scott, *Weapons of the Weak*, xvi.
3 Scott, *Weapons of the Weak*, 29.
4 Tracing the propagandistic turn in country almanacs reveals this seizure to be corporatist in nature, often accomplished through private publishers. Particularly in the 1920s, publishers' adherence to state doctrine should be considered more a matter of practicality than of ideology. Only later, with the institutionalization of Fascism in the 1930s, did the regime install dedicated editors that truly toed the party line. See annual memos from Enrico Bemporad to Mussolini (ACS, SPD, CO, b. 509, f. 230).
5 Turrini, "'L'Almanacco della donna italiana.'"
6 Guidalestro, "L'Italia cambia viso," in *Almanacco della Donna Italiana 1936*, 91.
7 Rhetoric soars in these comparisons, as in Guidalestro's characterization of the sanctions as "un tentativo di paralizzare l'Italia, di impedirle, non solo di conquistare ciò che le spetta, il diritto di respirare, di dare lavoro e pane a tutti i suoi figli; ma addirittura di portare in Abissinia la civiltà, di distribuire al mondo le richezze che quel paese possiede e che rimangono inutilizzate" (an attempt to paralyse Italy, to prevent it, not only from conquering what it's entitled to,

the right to breathe, to give work and bread to all of its children, but even to bring civility to Abissinia, to distribute to the world the riches that country possesses and which remain unutilized). "L'Italia cambia viso," in *Almanacco della Donna Italiana 1936*.

8 Nina Milla, "La donna e le sanzioni," in *Almanacco della Donna Italiana 1936*, 358.

9 In this almanac, articles promoting medicalized approaches to children's nutrition emblematize this tendency, as in "Maternita e infanzia" by Ida Lodi and "Parassiti intestinali dei bambini" by Prof. Vittorio Vani, docent of Medicine and Parasitology at the University of Rome.

10 For a comparative example, contrast *Almanacco della donna italiana 1936* with Zamarra's *Almanacco della cucina per la famiglia Italiana 1939* or *Almanacco della donna italiana 1941*.

11 Rodolfo De Angelis, "Sanzionami questo" (Cristallo 15562; Columbia Records, DQ 1783).

12 Castelli, Jona, and Lovatto, *Senti le rane che cantano*.

13 This powerful phrasing continues to resonate, as scholars Elisabetta Palumbo, Marco Scavino, and Elda Zappi have all used this lyric to title their respective works on the *mondine*. For example, see Palumbo, *Se otto ore vi sembran poche*; Scavino, *Se otto ore vi sembran poche*; and Zappi, *If Eight Hours Seem Too Few*.

14 Scarpellini, *Material Nation: A Consumer's History of Modern Italy*, trans. Daphne Hughes and Andrew Newton (Oxford: Oxford University Press, 2011), 62–4.

15 LUCE produced and disseminated propagandistic and didactic films, as well as entertainment films, on behalf of the Fascist regime. See Forgac's *Italian Culture in the Industrial Era* and Forgacs and Gundle's *Mass Culture and Italian Society from Fascism to the Cold War*.

16 Helstosky, "Cooking of Consent, Italy 1925–35," in *Garlic and Oil*.

17 Goody, "Recipe, the Prescription, and the Experiment."

18 Antagonistic facial expressions abound in LUCE photographs of the *mondine*. Accompanying letter exchanges between local public officials and the regime attest to the careful decision-making involved in selecting appropriately positive photographs for propaganda. See folder *Milano: Ente Nazionale del Riso, Contributi del Duce per l'assistenza alle Mondariso* (ACS, PCM, 1934–6, b. 509.488, f. 2).

19 For a characteristic example, see the 1935–6 letter and memo exchange between Novarese prefect Aldo Rossini and Benito Mussolini (ACS, PCM, 1934–6, b. 509.488, f. 2).

20 Molinari, "Mondine," 155.

21 Zappi, *If Eight Hours Seem Too Few*, 10.

22 Willson, *Peasant Women and Politics in Fascist Italy*, 18.

23 Divided by work site, Vercelli hosted 24,200 *mondine*, Novara 14,000, Pavia 22,900, and Milan 1,400, as cited by the Confederazione Fascista Lavoratori Agricola, *Campagna Monda del Riso 1938*.

24 "Il riso italiano: Per il vantaggio della nazione," in Boccasile, *Mangiate Riso*.

25 This 1934 labour law set the value of women's work at 60 per cent of a man's. See Serpieri, *La Guerra e le classi rurali italiane*.

26 Istituto Centrale di Statistica del Regno d'Italia, *Compendio Statistico Italiano 1939*.

27 Minardi, *La fatica delle donne*, 29.

28 Chiozzi, Testimony, 8.

29 Zappi, *If Eight Hours Seem Too Few*, 13.

30 Scalabrini, Testimony, 1.

31 Confederazione Fascista Lavoratori Agricola, "Le disposizioni delle Conferazioni," in *Campagna Monda del Riso 1938*, 21.

32 Baldi, Testimony; Chiozzi, Testimony; Cipolli, Testimony; Scalabrini, Testimony; Verzani, Testimony.

33 Chierici, Testimony, 13.

34 The song catalogue of the *mondine* is little analysed but remarkably well preserved thanks to extensive archivization of the *mondine*'s music by media libraries in Northern Italian towns, as well as Confederazione Generale Italiana del Lavoro (CGIL) workers' archives across the former Rice Belt. In the 1960s and 1970s, song corps offered a natural fit for the mood of agitation and social change that lit the workers' and students' protests in the Hot Autumn of 1968. Young students on strike then wanted to learn how older workers had used similar tactics to win labour rights in the past. Mutual sympathy between academic and workers' groups developed and continued into the early 1970s. A number of former *mondine* created choirs after retirement, and they continue to sing today.

35 Taddei, "Il cibo nell'Italia mezzadrile."

36 L. Betri and S. Uggeri, "Or son passati quaranta giorni," *E la partenza per me la s'avvicina*, liner notes for disc *Sorelle Bettinelli* (1972), p. 45. Cited in Castelli, Jona, and Lovatto, *Senti le rane che cantano*, 181.

37 M.A. Arrigoni and M. Savini, "Trenta giorni di polenta," *Nel paese di Ogh e Magogh: Storia, folklore, dialetto a Cozzo Lomellina* (Amminstrazione provinciale di Pavia, Guardamagna, Varzi, 1991), 383. The last section also appears in S. Mantovani, *La cultura della cascina cremasca: Le sorelle Bettinelli* (Cremona, 1979), 25–195. Cited in Castelli, Jona, and Lovatto, *Senti le rane che cantano*, 181.

38 "Da ber ci dan dell'acqua," *La nostalgica avventura delle mondine*, supplement to 2 (3) of "La Piazzetta delle Catene: Storia cultura tradizionali di Pieve di Cento," October 2004, p. 9. Cited in Castelli, Jona, and Lovatto, *Senti le rane che cantano*, 181.

39 Betri and Uggeri, "Or son passati quaranta giorni," 45. Cited in Castelli, Jona, and Lovatto, *Senti le rane che cantano*, 181.

40 "Non più riso e fagioli," *La nostalgica avventura delle mondine*, supplement to 2 (3) of "La Piazzetta delle Catene: Storia cultura tradizionali di Pieve di Cento," October 2004, p. 4. Cited in Castelli, Jona, and Lovatto, *Senti le rane che cantano*, 181.

41 See Palumbo, *Se otto ore vi sembran poche*; Scavino, *Se otto ore vi sembran poche*; and Zappi, *If Eight Hours Seem Too Few*.

42 Castelli, Jona, and Lovatto, *Senti le rane che cantano*, 183.

43 Of course, it is extremely unlikely that this dream menu would come to pass: meat dishes served with a glass of good wine would have been rare for the working classes, even if it were for Sunday lunch.

44 According to testimonials written by former rice workers, "Son la mondina, son la sfruttata" (I am the rice weeder, I am the exploited) and "La Lega" (The union) were the most widely dispersed, frequently sung, and dearly beloved of the extensive *mondine* song catalogue. Common political themes unite "Son la mondina" and "La Lega": both songs commemorate successful anti-government action by working-class women in early twentieth-century Italy, Russia, and China. Moreover, the songs' strident Socialist and Communist themes underscore the rice workers' defiant commitment to liberal politics and the international working class in the mid- to late 1930s, that is, at the height of the Fascist regime's popularity. Zappi, *If Eight Hours Seem Too Few*.

45 Lavagnini, Testimony, 8.

46 For an extended discussion of "La Lega," see Garvin, "Singing Truth to Power."

47 Chierici, Testimony, 4.

48 Scalabrini, Testimony, 1.

49 Lavagnini, Testimony, 5.

50 De Grazia, *How Fascism Ruled Women*, and Ipsen, *Dictating Demography*.

51 Scalabrini, Testimony, 21.

52 Verzani, Testimony, 4.

53 Scalabrini, Testimony, 4 (capitalization in original).

54 Minardi, *La fatica delle donne*, 22.

55 Chierici, Testimony, 3.

56 Castelli, Jona, and Lovatto, *Senti le rane che cantano*, 47.

57 Staro, *Lasciateci passare siamo le donne*, 43.

58 Staro, *Lasciateci passare siamo le donne*, 40.

59 Castelli, Jona, and Lovatto, *Senti le rane che cantano*, 209.

60 Staro, *Lasciateci passare siamo le donne*, 40.

61 Castelli, Jona, and Lovatto, *Senti le rane che cantano*, 215.

62 Molinari, "Mondine," 155.

63 Confederazione Fascista Lavoratori Agricola, *Campagna Monda del Riso 1938*, 32.

64 "Contratto collettivo di lavoro per i lavoratori forestieri da adibirsi alle operazioni di monda e trapianto del riso nell'anno 1938," in Confederazione Fascista Lavoratori Agricola, *Campagna Monda del Riso 1938*, 47.

Chapter Three: Raising Children on the Factory Line

1 As of 3 April 1926, 327,978 women workers could be counted in Italy, 15 per cent of the total workforce of 2,116,960. Women made up 25 per cent of all agricultural workers (158,458 female workers) and 17.5 per cent of the industrial sector (155,355). Additional sectors with a sizeable group of women workers included commerce (14.5 per cent with 7,721 workers), the oddly titled "intellectuals" (11.2 per cent with 4,002 workers), banking (7.8 per cent with 1,940), and transport (1.7 per cent with 1,002 workers). *La donna operaia e lo stato fascista: I quaderni delle corporazioni*, no. 14, 2nd ed. (Rome: Edizioni del Diritto del Lavoro, 1928), 16.

2 Between 1921 and 1931 male employment in Italy rose while female employment fell. Conversely, in the period 1931–6, women's employment rose while men's fell, probably due to women taking over some men's jobs in the Ethiopian war. See P. Sabbatucci Severini and A. Trento, "Alcuni cenni sul mercato di lavoro durante il fascismo," in *Quaderni storici*, 29–30 (1975), cited in Willson, *Clockwork Factory*.

3 Of those employed in agriculture, the most economically precarious category "seasonal arms for hire" (*braccianti avvertizie*), that is, the Northern Italian *mondine* and threshers, comprised the vast majority of rural female workers, with 148,833 represented. Other groups included the *mondine*'s equally precarious Mezzogiorno counterparts who worked the large Southern plantations (*mezzadre e colone* with 2,256 workers), as well as the far luckier fixed-salary workers (*salario fisso*, 7,350) and a tiny group of agricultural experts and consultants (*perite in agraria*, 29). *La donna operaia e lo stato fascista*, 16.

4 Rossella Ropa and Cinzia Venturoli, *Donne e lavoro* (Bologna: Editrice Compositori, 2010), 35. In terms of the specifics, textiles had the vast majority of 81,993 workers. Relatedly, clothing employed 17,461 female workers. This group was followed by paper and printing with 6,472 female workers. Other large industrial sectors with female employment included construction (*edilizia*) with 4,290 workers, the vast majority of whom built ovens (3,137 *fornaciaie*); chemistry employed 12,647; furniture-making (*ammobiliamento*) employed 212; metal work employed 5,911; glass work 2,517; water, gas, and electricity 1,330; and mining employed 813. Ropa and Venturoli, *Donne e lavoro*, 35.

5 Business (*commercia*) included hotel personnel (2,350), sales clerks (1,881), insurance employees (*impiegate di assicurazioni*, 1,089), restaurant personnel (473), and bar and café personnel (192). Ropa and Venturoli, *Donne e lavoro*, 35.

6 *La donna operaia e lo stato fascista*, 27–8.

7 Benito Mussolini, "Macchina e donna," in *Il popolo d'Italia*, 31 August 1934, p. 206. Cited in Willson, *Clockwork Factory*, 2.

8 In the later years of the regime, thousands of women who sought an abortion were deemed "asocial," as controlling fertility was considered inappropriate to a woman's role in Nazi society. Punishment meant extradition to concentration camps or murder in the T-4 ("Euthanasia") program.

9 See Aprile, *La protezione della maternità e dell'infanzia*.

10 See Zuccotti, *Under His Very Windows*.

11 "Nessun dubbio che la donna durante la gravidanza e l'allattamento ha esigenze alimentari qualitative e quantitative del tutto speciali e variabilissime in rapporto al mutare del suo stato di salute e della sua attività lavorativa con consequenze notevoli sulla gestazione, sul feto e sull'infante" (No doubt that the pregnant or breastfeeding woman has alimentary needs that are special and variable in relation to differences in the state of her health and work activities with notable consequences for gestation, for the fetus, and for the infant). "I Refettori materni ... vogliono sopratutto proteggere e favorire lo sviluppo numerico e qualitative della razza attraverso il benessere attuale procacciato alla donna come madre e al fanciullo in quanto energia potenziale" (The Mother's Refectories want above all to protect and benefit the numeric and qualitative development of the race through the current well-being provided for the woman as mother and the child as potential energy). See "I refettori Materni," *Maternità e Infanzia*, May 1935: 5.

12 See Landy, *Fascism in Film*.

13 For in-depth analysis of this term, see Garvin, "Taylorist Breastfeeding in Rationalist Clinics."

14 Cassa nazionale di maternità, Memorandum del dattore di lavoro, Article 47 (Rome: Libri di Matricola e di Paga USILA, 1925), p. 5.

15 Willson, *Clockwork Factory*, 5–6.

16 See *La donna operaia e lo stato fascista*. This series was part of a paired initiative between the Centri di Cultura and the Propaganda Corporativa.

17 Maria Guidi, "Le nostre industrie: La 'Perugina,'" *Il Giornale della Donna*, 1 May 1931: 6.

18 She was particularly active in the early 1920s in terms of invention and entrepreneurship, and these interwar years were the years of the consolidation of the financial and management for Giovanni Buitoni's company. Perugina ended up being the sweets sector of that larger company. Buitoni, in his autobiography, recalls Luisa's business acumen: "mente brilliante che sapeva abbracciare tutti i complessi problemi dell'azienda" (a brilliant mind that knew how to embrace all the complex problems of the business) and "molto apprezzata ed amata dal personale" (much appreciated and beloved by the personnel) as the "fabbricante delle caramelle e dei cioccolatini" (maker of candies and chocolates). Giovanni Buitoni, *Storia di un imprenditore* (Rome: Longanesi, 1972), cited in Curli p. 199.

19 After his mother's death, Mario Spagnoli converted the *buoni* into a specific fund bearing her name. The Fondi di beneficenza Luisa Spagnoli then provided financial coverage in the event of workplace accidents and also provided female employees with a dowry if they decided to marry.

20 Luisa Spagnoli's son Mario seems to have taken his mother's ideas and continued to develop them as the Fascist years wore on. He began this initiative in 1936, right after Luisa's death. See Covino, *Perugina*.

21 Curli, "Dalla Perugina all'Angora: Luisa Spagnoli."

22 For the purposes of this chapter I use Francis Galton's definition of eugenics: "the science which deals with all influences that improve the inborn qualities of a race; also with those that develop them to the utmost advantage." See "Eugenics: Its Definition, Scope, and Aims," 1.

23 "18° Fiera di Milano," dir. Arnaldo Ricotti, 21 April 1937, duration 00:02:15 (Archivio LUCE, Giornale LUCE B/B1079, film code B107908). This newsreel was one of four produced by Ricotti on behalf of the Ministero della cultura popolare to highlight different industrial sectors, including transportation (Archivio LUCE, Giornale LUCE B/B1078, film code B107808), textiles (Archivio LUCE, Giornale LUCE B/B1081, film code B108108), and mechanics (Archivio LUCE, Giornale LUCE B/B1080, film code B108008).

24 See Perry Willson's in-depth examination of the women's industrial work in the Magneti Marelli factory – a light engineering firm – in Sesto San Giovanni outside of Milan. Willson, "Flashes and Glows," in *Clockwork Factory*, 9.

25 *Cioccolato militare* remains a strong memory of military service for many Italians, which may explain the March 2018 relaunch of this product in Florence. It is wrapped in the original packaging and made according to a secret recipe. Difesa Servizi Spa, the financing arm of the Italian defence department, and the Agenzia Industria Difesa, which manages its industrial plants, has tasked the Calenzano-based organic chocolate manufacturer Fonderia del Cacao to produce and sell the Cioccolato Militare range. Part of the proceeds will go to Florence's Stabilimento Chimico Farmaceutico Militare, which manufactures "orphan drugs" (commercially underdeveloped pharmaceuticals), as well as providing a quick response service for Italy's armed forces. Cioccolato Militare contains 70 per cent cocoa solids and is available as a 50 g or a 100 g cube, a 200 g bar, 5 g individual chocolates, and a spreadable cream. It was used by the Italian army as part of the daily rations until 1937. The United States was the first country to introduce chocolate to the armed forces, with the dual goal of providing a quick source of emergency energy and raising morale. The range is retailed in Italian shops and via the Italian armed forces.

26 At the Perugina Museo Storico, tourists can browse an exhibit of historical photographs, including a panel dedicated to the stages of Mussolini's trip to the factory. See the 30 October 1923 exhibit photos, "Visita allo stabilimento Perugina di Fontivegge tra Francesco Buitoni e Giovanni Buitoni" and "Mussolini in visita allo stabilimento Perugina." Photographic plates courtesy of Archivio Storico Buitoni, Sezione fotographica, b. 4, f. 42–3.

27 Covino, "Perugina: Crescita e sviluppo."

28 Willson, "Organization of the Work Process," in *Clockwork Factory*, 62.

29 Armando and Aldo, Luisa and Annibale's two younger sons, also remain employed at Perugina after Annibale's departure from the firm. However, they played smaller roles than Mario and as a result are rarely mentioned.

30 *Organizazzione Industriale*, Nov. 15, 1932.

31 This was not Mario's first publication: in 1926, he published the first Italian manual on chocolate making.

32 He cites "an American magazine" for this compliment. Spagnoli, *L'organizzazione scientifica del lavoro*, 8.

33 Spagnoli, *L'organizzazione scientifica del lavoro*, 9.

34 Spagnoli, *L'organizzazione scientifica del lavoro*, 9.

35 Spagnoli, *L'organizzazione scientifica del lavoro*, 4.

36 Spagnoli, *L'organizzazione scientifica del lavoro*, 4.

37 "La nostra Società non ha neppure trascurato questo importante elemento di assistenza per le operaie che hanno avuto la gioia della maternità. Due assistenti, esperte in materia di puericultura, custodiscono con molto zelo, in un ambiente appositamente attrezzato, i piccoli che le mamme affidano loro durante le ore di lavoro. Ogni tre ore le madri possono sospendere il lavoro e recarsi ad allattare il loro bambino. I neonati, ospitati fino ad un anno di età, sono nutriti con alimenti sanissimi ed appropriati, quali: farine di cereali diastasate, pastine glutinate

Buitoni, latte, ecc. Le spese di funzionamento del nido materno sono a carico completo della Ditta." (Our Company has not left behind this important element of assistance for the female workers who have had the joy of maternity. Two assistants, experts in the subject of puericulture, watch with much zeal, in a specifically appointed environment, the little ones who their moms have left to them during the work hours. Every three hours the mothers can suspend their work and come to breastfeed their children. The newborns, held until one year of age, are fed with very healthy and appropriate products, such as: desiccated grain flour, Buitoni pasta glutinate, milk, etc. Nursery costs are completely covered by the Company.) "Nell'anno, luglio 1935 – giugno 1936, sono stati allevati 15 neonati con ottimo esito." "Relazione sui provvedimenti assistenziali attuati a favore della maestranza della S.A. Perugina" 29 August 1936.

38   Perugina *relazione* cited in Chiapparino and Covino, *La fabbrica di Perugina,* 279.

39   "La Cassa Nazionale Maternità dispone che per il periodo di allattamento, le Aziende che occupano complessivamente 50 o più donne, tra operaie ed impiegate, hanno l'obbligo di mettere a disposizione delle madri una camera di allattamento, consentendo alle medesime DUE periodi di riposo di MEZZ'ORA ciascuno. L'Azienda è in regola, ma le madri approfittano di tale concessione per portare i periodi di riposo a 3 ed anche 4" (Viene citato l'esempio di un' impiegata che si assenta troppo spesso accumulando 4 periodi di riposo per circa due ore al giorno). "Le altre madri ne approfittano un po' meno. Tanto comunico perché la Direzione sia al corrente di quanto succede, e, se ritenuto opportuno, prendere i necessari provvedimenti." ("The National Office of Motherhood allows for a breastfeeding period, the Businesses that employ 50 or more women, between laborers and employees, have the obligation to provide mothers with a breastfeeding room, allowing these same [women] TWO breaks of HALF AN HOUR each. The business is standard, but the mothers take advantage of such concessions, taking three and even four breaks" [The example was noted of an employee who is too frequently absent, accumulating four breaks for almost two hours per day]. "The other mothers take advantage of it less. I communicate this so that the Direction is up to date with the state of affairs, and, so if convenient, they can take the necessary measures.") Nota sull'applicazione delle disposizioni sull'allattamento secondo la Cassa Nazionale Maternità, 26 September 1941.

40   Consegna all'Ente Nazionale Italiano per l'Organizzazione Scientifica del Lavoro (ENIOS), drawings and various descriptions of the organization and work systems by Technical Director Mario Spagnoli, 30 June 1927.

41   Pietro Cuccaro, "L'olio di Luisa Spagnoli, storia di un sogno," *AgoraVox,* 6 October 2014, https://www.agoravox.it/L-olio-di-Luisa-Spagnoli-storia-di-1.html.

42   Mario Spagnoli, *Norme pratiche sull'allevamento del coniglio angora per il potenziamento della conigliatura nazionale.*

43   Assunta Cappuccini, a former Perugina factory worker, recalled these details from her work as a volunteer leader for spinning lessons. Aldo Zappalà, director, "La storia siamo noi: Luisa, le Operaie e gli Altri, la donna che inventò il Bacio," Rai Tre, Rai Educational, 2009, https://web.archive.org/web/20160206193424/http://www.lastoriasiamonoi.rai.it/puntate/luisa-spagnoli-le-operaie-e-gli-altri/941/default.aspx.

44   That business is still in the family: Mario left it with his son Annibale (Lino), who passed the management to his daughter Nicoletta, the current Spagnoli in charge of the fashion house.

Chapter Four: Recipes for Exceptional Times

1   Mazower, *Dark Continent,* 23.

2   Morelli, *Dalla Cucina al Salotto,* 26.

3 *Passapiatti* can only be placed in a specific type of apartment layout, wherein the kitchen and the salon are adjacent. However, Italian architects of the period almost universally designed homes in this manner, as noted by Gardella in "I servizi della casa: La cucina."

4 "Un tipico ambiente utilitario," kitchen photograph, *Domus*, January 1936: 70.

5 Gino Boccasile parodied their financial success and the dubious flavour of their products by equating plastic fruit and fruit in a can in a 1939 cartoon "Moda e pubblicità" (Fashion and advertising). A woman reads an advertisment, "Comprate la squisita marmellata Za! E' proprio buona." In a comic turn, she wears a large hat decorated with cans, the subject of three women's conversation in the background: "E' la moglie di un grosso industriale; invece di mettersi la frutta finta sul cappello, si mette i barattoli di frutta in conserva fabbricati dal marito" (She's the wife of a big industrialist; instead of putting fake fruit on her hat, she puts the cans of conserved fruit that her husband makes). Cartoon originally featured in *Settebello*, 1939, reproduced in Gianeri, *La donna la moda l'amore*, 17. For an in-depth study of tomatoes in Italian food history, see Gentilcore, *Pomodoro!*

6 Morelli, *Dalla Cucina al Salotto*, 2.

7 This type of information could be found in technical manuals for farmers, such as F. Maiocco's *Il coniglio* (Rome: Ramo Editoriale degli agricoltori, 1937). The cover, designed and signed by a certain Martinatio, featured two oversized black rabbits cuddling in front of a fashionable red-headed woman shown in profile, flaunting a green V-neck dress with a white rabbit-fur-trimmed collar. The Biblioteca per l'insegnamento agrario professionale (the Library for the Instruction of Professional Agriculture) published a series of these instructional booklets, at the affordable price of 3 lire apiece.

8 Although the Fascist Massaie Rurali group conducted courses in gardening and rabbit- and poultry-raising, along with silkworm farming and beekeeping, mass media and household manuals tend to emphasize a later stage of food preparation and consumption rather than the early stages of production. The national and local directors of the Massaie Rurali as well as teachers at Sant'Alessio College, the training school for these leaders, came from wealthy, urban backgrounds. Many of these middle-class urban women were ill prepared to advise countrywomen in matters of rural productivity. Throughout the 1930s and early 1940s, the Massaie Rurali struggled to find qualified technical leaders to provide courses. See Willson, *Peasant Women and Politics in Fascist Italy*.

9 Newlyn, "Challenging Contemporary Narrative Theory," 37.

10 See Helstosky, "Cooking of Consent."

11 The exact dates of Amalia Moretti Foggia's wartime publications are as follows: *Ricette di Petronilla per i tempi eccezionali*, 1941; *Ricettario per i tempi difficili*, 1942, *200 suggerimenti per … questi tempi difficili*, 1943; *Desinaretti per … questi tempi*, 1943.

12 Petronilla's work not only is historical but also has been the recent subject of interest amongst contemporary Italian food blogs like *Massaie Moderne*. Food appliance groups cite her influence as well. She even has a cooking tool named for her: in Italy, pressure cookers are known as Petronilla *pentola* (the Petronilla pot) or as the *forno elettrico* Petronilla (the electric Petronilla oven) and are produced by major appliance companies like Agnelli.

13 Maria Diez Gasca was particularly influential in this regard. In addition to editing a home economics magazine, she also published across numerous Fascist hygiene and industry journals. See, for example, "L'organizzazione moderna della casa per la contadina svizzera" and "Un consultorio per l'economia domestica a Roma."

14 Ada Boni's most famous cookbook, *Il talismano della felicità*, was the fruit of her prior publishing projects. In 1915 Boni founded *Prezioso*, a monthly home economics magazine that she would continue to run until 1959. By the mid-1930s, this magazine had collected, tested, and published over 800 recipes that eventually comprised the *Talismano*.

15 In a further reflection of Morelli's collaboration with other kitchen experts, she worked with Giovanni Battista Allari to co-author this book and with Enrico Montalto di Fragnito to illustrate it. *Case e bambini: Conversazioni di economia domestica per le alunne della terza classe della scuola media* (Turin: Editrice Libraria Italiana, 1943).

16 Perry Willson observes that this chorus of complaints predates Fascism. She cites a 1907 commentator who observed that "half the worries of middle-class ladies were about this 'servant crisis.'" Willson, *Women in Twentieth-Century Italy* (New York: Palgrave Macmillan, 2009), 19. But, as Willson and De Grazia note, domestic service in Italy persisted throughout the Fascist period.

17 Cited in De Grazia, *How Fascism Ruled Women*, 102.

18 See "La Cucina Elegante: Specialità di Milano."

19 Journalist Roberta Schira reads the broader narrative of Foggia's friendships with feminists like Anna Kuliscioff, Sibilla Aleramo, and Ada Negri as "una sorta di suora laica: il suo modo di essere donna, di essere femminista era quello di aiutare le altre donne" (a sort of lay sister-hood: her way of being a woman, of being feminist was that of helping other women). She contextualizes Foggia's professional life and personal friendships within the broader frame-work of contemporary feminist practice: "Il suo era un femminismo moderno, che ancora oggi è attualissimo" (Hers was a modern feminism, that even today is very current). See Roberta Schira and Alessandra De Vizzi's *Le Voci di Petronilla: Storia di una modernissima donna d'altri tempi, uno scorcio di vita femminile italiana dal 1872 al 1947* (Milan: Salani Editori, 2010). Also see Antonella Scutiero, "La Storia: Petronilla, Femminista Ante Litteram," *Lettera D*, for *Elle It*, 5 March 2015.

20 *Nuovi orizzonti per la vostra mensa: 300 ricette scelta tra le 1224 premiate su 18000 inviate al concorso pomodoro pelati cirio da 3000 concorrenti*, introduction by Lidia Morelli (Portici: Tip. E. Della Torre, 1937). Subsequent editions were published in 1939 and 1940.

21 Bastianich observes, "Ada was a feminist, if you will, but in a very nonthreatening way to the Italian male. She said, 'Cook a home meal,' but at the same time there was a message, 'You can do other things, and I'll help you with the recipes.'" Bill Daley, Interview with Lidia Bastianich, "Culinary Giant: Ada Boni," *Chicago Tribune*, 15 May 2013.

22 To put this monetary ratio in terms of carbohydrates rather than sweetener, Foggia's book would have been worth only one kilogram of bread, while Beboux's was worth five or six loaves. Emanuela Scarpellini traces the relative monetary values of different foods across time in a useful chart in *Material Nation*, 110–11.

23 See Rina Simonetta's interview of Marietta Sabatini in *La Cucina Italiana*, February 1932. Sabatini served as Artusi's chef for over forty years. As Artusi notes, all of his recipes are really Sabatini's – she invented them, tested them, and codified them. As he states in his introduc-tion, he collected and published these results under his own name. See Pellegrino Artusi, in-troduction to *La scienza in cucina e l'arte di mangiar bene* (Florence: Landi, 1891).

24 Foggia, *Altre ricette di Petronilla*, 56.

25 Boni, *Il talismano della felicità*, 9–10.

26 Boni, *Il talismano della felicità*, 2.

27 For an example of a recipe dominated by imperative commands like "Preparate una pasta à choux, infornate tutto" (Prepare a choux pastry dough, put everything in the oven), see bombe alle uova in Boni, *Il talismano della felicità*, 223. For an example of a recipe dominated by third-person descriptions like "Si spiuma la salsa, si fiammeggia e si sventra la beccaccia" (One foams the sauce, one singes and removes the innards of the woodcock), see beccaccia farcita (423).

28 Foggia, *Ricette di Petronilla per tempi eccezionali*, 1941.

29 Foggia, *Desinaretti per … questi tempi*, 23.

30 Even in her first cookbook, Foggia uses regionality to frame atypical ingredients. Her earliest version of risotto with *salamelle* opens with multiple markers of Northernness: "Questo risotto ... da noi, donne d'Alta Italia, nelle nostre cucine, vien fatto così: Si toglie alle salamelle (1 ogni 2 persone) la pelle; se ne versa il sapido contenuto, con poco burro" (This risotto, at our house, the [houses of the] women of Northern Italy, in our kitchens, is made like this: Skin two sausages (1 for every 2 people); pour the savoury contents into a pan with a little butter) (*Ricette di Petronilla*, 92).

31 Despite their title, Italian plum cakes do not contain plums. This curiosity predates Fascism and in fact stretches at least as far back as the Unification. Pellegrino Artusi commented that plum cake is a "mentitore ... del nome suo," (liar of its own name) (*La scienza in cucina e l'arte di mangiar bene*, 1053).

32 Foggia, *Desinaretti per ... questi tempi*, 86–7.

33 Linguist Tim Wharton's application of the term "procedural discourse" to twenty-first-century American, British, and French recipes informs this analysis. In "Recipes: Beyond the Words," Wharton argues that cookbook content must be convincing, be credible, and offer a reward.

Chapter Five: Model Fascist Kitchens

1 Morelli, *Dalla Cucina al Salotto*, 2.

2 Cogdell, "Smooth Flow."

3 Piccoli, *La bonifica umana e la casa*. The concept of *bonifica*, or reclamation, centred Fascist modernization discourses on subjects as far-ranging as agricultural reclamation (*bonifica agricola*), human reclamation (*bonifica umana*), and cultural reclamation (*bonifica culturale*). Collectively, these variegated projects aimed to radically reengineer Italian society by "pulling up the bad weeds and cleaning up the soil." "Bonifica libraria," *Critica fascista* (1 January 1939), cited in Ben-Ghiat, *Fascist Modernities*, 4. The agricultural *bonifiche* and the creation of the Fascist New Towns are discussed in Diane Ghirardo, *Building New Communities* (Princeton, NJ: Princeton University Press, 1989).

4 Horn, "Sterile City," in *Social Bodies*, 108–9 and 120–1.

5 Although the regime hoped to intervene in rural kitchens as well, they were largely unsuccessful in changing the domestic landscape in the countryside. For more information on rural kitchens and the regime's unrealized plans for their refurbishment, see Cerletti, "Il problema della casa rurale"; Gestri, *Il problema della Casa Rurale dal punto di vista medico-sociale*; and *Le Case Rurali in Provincia di Mantova*.

6 See *Convegno Lombardo per la casa popolare*, v.

7 Bottoni, "Determinare i criteri della casa di Oggi"; Fraticelli, "Parva sed apta mihi."

8 Although the Liberal government conducted enquiries as to the quality of life of the Northern urban working class in the early 1900s, they did not build as a result or respond to the reported misery in any way. See Nick Carter, "Rethinking the Italian Liberal State," *Bulletin of Italian Politics* 3, no. 2 (2011): 225–45.

9 As Mary Douglas famously observed, dirt is in the eye of the beholder: "If we can abstract pathogenicity and hygiene from our notion of dirt, we are left with the old definition of dirt as matter out of place. This is a very suggestive approach. It implies two conditions: a set of ordered relations and a contravention of that order. Dirt then, is never a unique, isolated event. Where there is dirt there is a system. Dirt is the by-product of a systemic ordering and classification of matter, in so far as ordering involves rejecting inappropriate elements." *Purity and Danger*, 35.

10 In the culinary invective "Against Pasta," F.T. Marinetti writes, "Let us make our Italian bodies agile, ready for the featherweight aluminium trains which will replace the present heavy ones of wood iron steel." *Futurist Cookbook*, 32.

11 As an architect, industrial designer, teacher, and publisher, Gio Ponti's prolific production rendered him a towering figure in the field. He founded *Domus* in 1928 and served as editor until 1941, when he left to establish and serve as editor for *Stile*, where he stayed until 1947. He then returned to serve as editor of *Domus* in 1948, remaining in the post until his death in 1979. While many of its contributors heralded the Fascist regime, it would be an oversimplification to characterize *Domus* as a Fascist periodical: debate, rather than consensus, characterized its mood. Working as a professor on the permanent staff of the Faculty of Architecture at the Politecnico di Milano from 1936 until 1961 allowed Ponti to mentor young designers and thus influence emergent building initiatives both directly and indirectly. His architectural contributions also helped form the modern skylines of Turin and Milan. Smaller in scale but broader in scope, Ponti's product designs could be found in many high-style stores.

12 Gardella, "Consigli tecnici per la Casa."

13 See Morelli, "Mèzari tessuti e mèzari stampati," "Una mostra d'arte applicata," "La raplina," "L'alloggio a crescenza," "Piccoli problemi nella decorazione della villeggiatura," "Il punto cavandoli," "Elogio del cotone da calza," and "Arte paesana."

14 Morelli, *Dalla Cucina al Salotto*, 30.

15 Marinetti, "Piccolo dizionario della cucina futurista," in *La cucina futurista*, 247–52.

16 See Gardella, "Consigli tecnici per la Casa."

17 Gardella, "I servizi della casa."

18 In his article, Gardella specifically suggests shifting the locus of working-class family life from the kitchen to the living room. In addition to hectoring families for gathering in the kitchen, he also decries their avoidance of the living room due to decorum: "lasciando il soggiorno a funzioni solamente 'rappresentative' per quello *sbagliato* senso di 'decoro'" (leaving the living room only to "representative" functions for a *mistaken* sense of "decorum"). Gardella, "I servizi della casa."

19 Gardella, "I servizi della casa."

20 Horn, "Sterile City," 108–9 and 120–1.

21 Elena Fambri published not one but two articles on this topic in a single issue of *Difesa Sociale* in 1938. "La casa e il problema demográfico I" and "La casa e il problema demográfico II," *Difesa sociale* (1938): 273–9 and 963–71.

22 Lazzaro and Crum have shown that the Lazio prefecture razed medieval structures to showcase ancient Roman buildings (*Donatello Among the Blackshirts*).

23 Gaetano Zingali, "I provvedimenti mussoliniani per lo sviluppo quantitative e qualitative della popolazione," in *Atti del Congresso internazionale per gli studi sulla popolazione* (Rome, 7–10 September 1931), vol. 7, ed. Corrado Gini (Rome: Istituto Poligrafico dello Stato, 1931), 585–604.

24 Benito Mussolini, "Il discorso dell'Ascensione [Address to the Chamber of Deputies]," 26 May 1927, in *Opera omnia di Benito Mussolini*, vol. 22, ed. Edoardo Susmel and Duilio Susmel (Florence: La Fenice, 1951), 363.

25 "Parliamo un po' della cucina razionalmente."

26 "Parliamo un po' della cucina razionalmente."

27 "Parliamo un po' della cucina razionalmente."

28 Giuseppe Pagano, "Case per il popolo," *Casabella Costruzioni* 143, November 1939: 3–6.

29 Morelli, *Dalla Cucina al Salotto*, 56.

30 Morelli, *Dalla Cucina al Salotto*, 56.

31 "Casa M.: Cucina," *Domus*, January 1937, heralded the invention of Temperit with a photographic feature showcasing a series of shining black tabletops (9).

32 "Parliamo un po' della cucina razionalmente."

33 In "Romance of Caffeine and Aluminum," Jeffrey Schnapp points to the 1930s as the "golden era of aluminum designs for the kitchen and the beginning of Fascist Italy's pursuit of domestic autarky" (245). He further notes how aluminium kitchen products evoked abstract concepts of "lightness, speed, mobility, strength, energy, and electricity" (245).

34 As David Horn notes of the *casa malsana*, it "operated to reduce *fertility*: by threatening the reproductive health of women (Coruzzi 1933) and by 'alienating' men from the home and their conjugal duties (Ilvento 1925: iv)." "Sterile City," 110.

35 Pagano, "Case per il popolo."

36 Writers and artists of the day such as Filippo Tommaso Marinetti and Mario Sironi also conflated the physical properties of metal with the idea of modernity. See Schnapp, "Romance of Caffeine and Aluminum."

37 Donald Norman's concept of "affordance" helps to unlock the significance of the toaster's materials: "The term *affordance* refers to the perceived and actual properties of the thing, primarily those functional properties that determine just how the thing could possibly be used. A chair affords ('is for') support and, therefore, affords sitting. A chair can also be carried. Glass is for seeing through, and for breaking." *Design of Everyday Things*, 9.

38 ACS, Pubblica Sicurezza, Ispettorato Generale di Pubblica Sicurezza, Servizi Annonari, b. 36. Also see Scarpellini, *Material Nation*, 110–15.

39 See "Elettrodomestico" advice column, *Domus*, September 1935: 21.

40 Schnapp, *Speed Limits*, 31.

41 On the Frankfurt kitchen, see Jerram, "Kitchen Sink Dramas"; Henderson, "Housing the Single Woman"; and Schütte-Lihotzky and Noever, *Die Frankfurter Küche Von Margarete Schütte-Lihotzky*.

42 Charles S. Chiu relates this history: "In 1939 Schütte-Lihotzky joined the Austrian Communist Party (KPÖ) and in December 1940, travelling back to Vienna to secretly contact the Austrian Communist resistance movement. She agreed to meet a leading Resistance member nicknamed 'Gerber' and help set up a communications line with Istanbul, but when she met her fellow resistor at the Cafe Viktoria on January 22, 1941, they were surprised and arrested by the Gestapo. While her fellow architect, co-resistor and friend Herbert Eichholzer was seized by the Volksgerichtstof and summarily executed in 1943, Schütte-Lihotzky was sentenced to 15 years of imprisonment and brought to a prison in Aichhach Bavaria where she was eventually liberated by U.S. troops on April 29, 1945." Women in the Shadows, 155–6.

43 "Parliamo un po' della cucina razionalmente."

44 Design notes from "The Frankfurt Kitchen," in Counterspace: Design + the Modern Kitchen, The Museum of Modern Art, 15 September 2010–2 May 2011.

45 Morelli, *Dalla Cucina al Salotto*, 60.

46 Piero Bottoni, "Per l'educazione al vivere nella casa popolare," in *Convegno Lombardo per la casa popolare*, 142–5.

47 Gardella, "I servizi della casa," 56.

48 Although primarily led by women, Domus chose to primarily publish articles by male authors on this topic. See, for instance, Domus's publication of Prof. Ernesto Romagnoli's adaptation of the Organizzazione Scienfiica del Lavoro's domestic studies in "Il valore economico e morale delle attività casalinghe delle donne" (The economic and moral value of women's housework).

49 See "Parliamo un po' della cucina razionalmente," kitchen photograph and plan, 30.

50 "Parliamo un po' della cucina razionalmente" was a landmark article on the ideal kitchen. Although the article was authorless, Ignazio Gardella likely contributed, along with other staff writers at *Domus* specializing in Frankfurt kitchens. In his capacity as editor, Gio Ponti would have influenced the tone and content of this article as well. See Linda Zanolla, ed., *Volumi in Cucina: Storia del progetto cucina* (Milan: Archeo, 2010).

51 "Parliamo un po' della cucina razionalmente."

52 Ponti, "Un esempio di composizione."

53 Other articles generally agreed with these storage needs. Gardella, for instance, suggested that every kitchen possess: a fridge; storage space for perishable and semi-perishable foods; storage space for pots, casseroles, linens, utensils, dry goods; storage space for dirty utensils, rags, and brooms; and chairs (small kitchen – one spinning stool; larger kitchen – spinning stool, plus one or two collapsible chairs). Gardella, "Consigli tecnici per la Casa."

54 For more information on Fascist interventions in rural kitchen design, see Romano Gestri's *Il problema della Casa Rurale dal punto di vista medico-sociale*; Arcangelo Ilvento (pseudonym), "Il problema della casa rurale," *Difesa Sociale* 5 (May 1935): 254–5, and Bice Crova, *L'abitazione nei suoi riflessi sociali* (Rome: Istituto di Medicina Sociale, 1937).

55 See Vinaccia, *Per le Città di Domani*; and Vidoni, "Il problema della casa."

56 Giuseppe Pagano, "Relazione tecnica: Anno di costruzione: del primo lotto 1936–1937, del rimanente 1937–1939," *Casabella Costruzioni* 144 (December 1939): 4–5.

57 Pagano, "Case per il popolo."

58 This contrast of civilized squares and barbarous circles applied to imperial architecture and urbanism as well. Mia Fuller, for instance, has noted that LUCE used the circular huts of East Africa (actually created by the Italians themselves) to connote primitivism (*Moderns Abroad*). Similarly, Heyaw Terefe's examination of Addis Ababa's shift from a circular garrison town to a Fascist grid system evokes this concept in "Contested Space." Once again, the same design concept scales from apartment to city.

59 Pagano suggests that light itself cleans the attic space: "assai più puliti che non i soliti sotto-tetto" (much more clean than the normal attics). Pagano, "Relazione tecnica," 4.

60 Attilio Podesta, "Case Popolari a Stoccolma e a Praga," *Casabella Costruzioni* 147 (March 1940): 4.

61 Ghirardo, "Architecture and Culture in Fascist Italy," 66.

62 Two key articles introduce this issue: "Case per il popolo" by Giuseppe Pagano the volume, followed by "Case Popolari per Aosta" by Bernascioni and Lauro. The theme returned in the December 1939 issue with an extended "Relazione tecnica."

63 Pagano, "Case per il popolo."

64 Pagano, "Case per il popolo."

65 For example, see the 11 November 1940 letter, ACS, SPD, CO b. 208, f. 596.

66 See letters and telegrams, ACS, SPD, CO b. 181, f. 789.

67 The regime generally did not grant requests that collapsed projected expenses into a single category, such as a Sienese prefect's appeal for "Opere di Risanamento Igienico (Contributo statale)" (Hygienic Reclamation Works [State Contribution]). The term *risanamento* often implied demolition projects, aimed at clearing working-class living spaces for replacement with modern apartment blocks. The rhetoric of health provides a euphemistic cover for these class-inflected architectural projects (ACS, PCM, 1934–6, b. 7.I.2, f. 4131).

68 See ACS, SPD, CO, b. 501, f. 034/3. Also see public works construction requests from women addressed to Rachele Mussolini, ACS, SPD, CO, b. 109005, f. 2.

69 Four banks and three insurance companies sponsored the Lombard Convention of 1936, along with the Milan municipality and the Committee for Model Rural Living (Comitato per l'abitazione rurale modello).

70　See "Ordini del giorno," *Convegno Lombardo per la casa popolare*, 28–35.

71　See Bottoni, "Per l'educazione al vivere nella casa popolare."

72　See 23 November 1938 letter, ACS, SPD, CO, b. 522884.

73　Bottoni makes this request in an 8 October 1941 letter. He goes on to suggest that the regime offer social security for residents in the *case popolari* that he designed. Specifically, he recommends that workers "get," but do not "own," their residence after a certain number of years of paying insurance. ACS, SPD, CO, b. 522884.

74　P. Angeletti, "La periferia e le case popolari," in *Case romane*, ed. P. Angeletti, L. Ciancarelli, M. Ricci, and G. Vallifuoco (Rome: Clear, 1984), 13–15.

75　E. Bonfanti and M. Scolari, *La vicenda urbanistica e edilizia dell'Istituto case popolari di Milano dagli esordi alla seconda guerra mondiale*, ed. L. Scacchietti (Milan: Club, 1982).

76　F. Albini, R. Camus, and G. Palanti, "Una casa per famiglie numerose," *Casabella* 78 (1934): 12–15. Also see Associazione culturale Tufello, *Dal giardino in città alla città in campagna*, ed. Tufello and Montesacro (Rome: Fratelli Palombi, 1999).

77　Calza Bini, "La sistemazione dei Borghi a Roma," *La Casa*, 1936: 357–60; and "Il piano regolatore e le abitazioni in Roma," *Quaderni della Roma di Mussolini* 11 (1942): 4–19.

78　"Case popolari e corporazione edilizia," *Concessioni e costruzioni*, 1935-II, p. 671; "Case rurali," *Concessioni e costruzioni*, 1935-II, pp. 672–3; and "Casette modello costruite dall'Istituto per le Case Popolari di Roma alla Borgata-Giardino Garbatella," *Architettura e arti decorative* (1930), fasc. V–VI, pp. 254–75.

79　Cesp-Cobas, Alberone, *"Questa città ribelle …": L'altra Resistenza dagli anni '20 alla Liberazione* (Rome: Viterbo, 2007).

80　Borden W. Painter, *Mussolini's Rome: Rebuilding the Eternal City* (New York: Palgrave Macmillan, 2005); Angeletti, "La periferia e le case popolari."

81　G. Brunelli, "La casa per tutti: Programma generale," *Casabella* 73 (1934): 46–7; A. Calza Bini, "La sistemazione dei Borghi a Roma"; "Il piano regolatore e le abitazioni in Roma."

82　See "La lotta contro l'accattonaggio in Roma," *Il Messaggero*, 24 October 1928.

83　Both text and images suggest that German and American movements heavily influenced the Italian call for rationalist housework. This article, for example, cites "illustri scrittrici di scienza domestica" (illustrious writers of home economics) and German household picture workbooks such as *Reichkuratorium fur wirtschaftlichkeit* (*Fordism and Organized Capitalism*) as inspiration. Figure 5.14 originally appeared in this source.

84　The top image captions read, "Il sedile è troppa basso e costringe le braccia ad una posizione falsa, che stanca" (The seat is too low and constrains the arms in a false position that tires [the cook]), "Il tavolo è troppo basso e obbliga a star curvi" (The table is too low and forces one to bend), "Il tavolo è a giusta altezza ma gli arnesi sono collocati in modo da obbligare le braccia ad una posizione che ricorda quella del primo disegno" (The table is the right height but the tools are positioned so as to force the arms into a position like that shown in the first drawing).

85　See *Convegno Lombardo per la casa popolare*. Note that several apartment blocks in Rome's Pietralata neighbourhood still feature these designs.

86　Gardella, "I servizi della casa."

87　Kitchen photograph and plan from "Parliamo un po' della cucina razionalmente," 30.

88　Gardella, "I servizi della casa."

89　Interestingly, Gardella reserves his ire for those who fail to introduce modern design in living rooms and bedrooms rather than the kitchen, which, for many authors, was the first domestic arena targeted for rationalist intervention. As he states, "Antiche cucine rurali o vecchie ville di campagna hanno invece una loro simpaticissima anima" (old-fashioned rural kitchens or old country villas have however their own very sweet spirit). Gardella, "I servizi della casa," 58.

90 This characterization fits into the regime's treatment of the social body with regard to hygiene. In *Social Bodies*, David Horn notes that "social bodies, like physiological bodies, could be cured, defended, and made objects of an ongoing prophylaxis ... the medicalized metaphor of the social body served not only as a basis for political characterizations but also as a framework for specific interventions" (23).

Conclusion: From Feeding Fascism to Eating Mussolini

1 Writer and journalist Malaparte inserted a version of himself in many of his semi-fictionalized wartime novels, including *The Skin* and *Kaputt*. See David Moore's introduction to Malaparte's *The Skin*.

2 Quotation cited in Ginsborg's *History of Contemporary Italy*, 39.

3 See "Austerity and Decline, 1935–1945" in Helstosky, *Garlic and Oil*, 110–11.

4 Comparison cited in Ginsborg, *History of Contemporary Italy*, 210.

5 Italy's GDP practically doubled between 1951 and 1963, growing by 86 per cent. Arvidsson, *Marketing Modernity*, 80. This increase was in line with the economic golden age experienced by other developed capitalist countries during the 1950s and 1960s. The United States, for instance, increased its GNP by two-thirds during this same period, as noted by Mazower, *Dark Continent*, 258.

6 Primavalle, one of the twelve Roman *borgate* built under Fascism, exemplifies this type of overdevelopment. Today, this neighbourhood still lacks basic services and entertainment options despite being home to over 200,000 inhabitants. See Trabalzi's "Primavalle: Urban Reservation in Rome." On the development and legacy of the Fascist *borgate* across the peninsula, see Villani's *Le borgate del fascismo*.

7 This point builds on Ruth Schwartz Cowan's thesis that technological innovation in the American context unevenly targeted women's, men's, and children's household labour. She convincingly argues that technology largely decreased or eliminated men's and children's traditional forms of housework, such as chopping logs and carrying water, while raising the standards, and thereby increasing the total labour, for women's housework, such as cooking. See *More Work for Mother*.

8 Zappalà, "La storia siamo noi."

9 Roberto Sabatini, "Luisa Spagnoli: Orgoglio di una città," *Perugia Corriere*, 17 November 2009.

10 While this export boom temporally corresponds with Marshall Plan projects to promote American food industry in Europe, politicians declined to promote these brands due to their status as luxury products. Speaking on behalf of Congress's Economic Cooperation Administration (ECA), Dennis A. Fitzgerald, director of the Food and Agriculture Division of the ECA, rebuffed Coca-Cola's repeated petitions, stating that the point of the Marshall Plan was to insure private investment in reconstruction projects. Coca-Cola was not an essential, but perhaps even a luxury. See Elmore, *Citizen Coke*, 163.

11 Data cited by De Grazia and Furlough, *Sex of Things*.

12 Purdy and Thurber, "Nickel Soda Pop," 1.

13 For a sociological examination of the connections between Eritrean women's domestic work in Italian homesteads in colonial East Africa and in Italian homes in contemporary Europe, see Marchetti, *Black Girls*.

14 Giuliani and Lombardi-Diop, *Bianco e nero*.

15 Lavagnini, "Le mie prigioni," 28.

16 On the legacies of Fascist maternal healthcare amongst working-class women, see Maurizio Bettini's *Stato e Assistenza Sociale in Italia*.

A Note to Future Researchers

1 For further history of the Musei delle Aziende, see Monica Amari, *I Musei delle Aziende: La cultura della tecnica tra arte e storia* (Milan: FrancoAngeli, 1997).

2 This piece of 100-year-old chocolate can be found in the Wolfsonian library's collection of *figurine*. See the collectable picture card, "Un mercado en los alrededores de la capital" (A market in the outskirts of the capital) in "La Guerra entre Italia y Abisinia" (The War between Italy and Abyssinia) series. Printed by Manuel Oríí Roca Benicarló Chocolates Company, 1939, Barcelona, Spain. Card 20 of 23-card set (Wolfsonian Museum, XC2014.12.12.40.15, Miami, United States).

3 Christopher Duggan is one of few scholars to have worked extensively with their holdings. Whereas Duggan analyses short sections from diaries and letters written primarily (though not exclusively) by middle- and upper-class men, I investigate the experiences of working- and middle-class women, focusing on extended close readings of female perspectives to trace the individual eddies and larger currents of women's political thinking during the Fascist period.

4 For example, this approach considers how the handle of an aluminium Moka coffee maker will prompt cooking actions like pouring water for coffee preparation and then finished coffee while serving. As Bernstein clarifies, "The set of prompts does not reveal a performance, but it does reveal a *script* for a performance. That script is itself a historical artifact. Examination of that artifact can produce new knowledge about the past." Bernstein, *Racial Innocence*, 71–2.

BIBLIOGRAPHY

Abba, Francesco. "Pane e riso." *La difesa sociale: Rivista mensile d'igiene, previdenza ed assistenza* 2, no. 11 (1935): 671–2.

Adamson, Walter. "Strapaese." In *Dizionario del fascismo: L–Z*, edited by Victoria De Grazia and Sergio Luzzatto, 703–6. Turin: Einaudi, 2003.

Albini, Franco, Renato Camus, and Giuseppe Palanti. "Una casa per famiglie numerose." *Casabella* 78 (1934): 12–15.

Albright, Madeleine. *Fascism: A Warning.* New York: Harper Collins, 2018.

Allardyce, Gilbert. "What Fascism Is Not: Thoughts on the Deflation of a Concept." *American Historical Review* 84, no. 2 (1979): 367–88.

Allaria, G.B. "I liquidi per preparare la pappa." *Maternità ed Infanzia*, February 1936: 9–11.

Alle Madri d'Italia. Directed by Pietro Francisci. Rome: Istituto Nazionale LUCE, 1935.

"Alle Madri d'Italia." *Maternità ed Infanzia*, April 1936: 19.

Almanacco della donna italiana 1936. Rome: Bemporad, 1936.

Almanacco della donna italiana 1941. Florence: Marzocco, 1941.

Amari, Monica. *I Musei delle Aziende: La cultura della tecnica tra arte e storia.* Milan: FrancoAngeli, 1997.

Ambasz, Emilio. *Italy: The New Domestic Landscape; Achievements and Problems of Italian Design.* New York: New York Graphic Society, 1972.

Anderson, Lara. *Control and Resistance: Food Discourse in Franco Spain.* Toronto: University of Toronto Press, 2020.

Angeletti, Paolo, Luca Ciancarelli, Marcello Ricci, and Giuseppe Vallifuoco, eds. *Case romane.* Rome: Clear, 1984.

Appadurai, Arjun. "How to Make a National Cuisine: Cookbooks in Contemporary India." *Comparative Studies in Society and History* 30, no. 1 (1988): 3–24.

Aprile, Attilio Lo Monaco. *La protezione della maternità e dell'infanzia.* Rome: Istituto nazionale fascista di cultura, 1934.

Arendt, Hannah. *The Origins of Totalitarianism.* New York: Harcourt, Brace, and Company, 1951.

Arrigoni, Maria Antonietta, and Marco Savini. "Trenta giorni di polenta." In *Nel paese di Ogh e Magogh: Storia, folklore, dialetto a Cozzo Lomellina.* Amminstrazione provinciale di Pavia: Guardamagna, Varzi, 1991.

Artusi, Pellegrino. *La scienza in cucina e l'arte di mangiar bene.* Edited by Piero Camporesi. Turin: Einaudi, 2001.

Arvidsson, Adam. *Marketing Modernity: Italian Advertising from Fascism to Postmodernity.* London: Routledge, 2003.

Associazione culturale Tufello. *Dal giardino in città alla città in campagna.* Edited by Tufello and Montesacro. Rome: Fratelli Palombi, 1999.

Azzarita, Fantasio. "L'autarchia alimentare e l'opera nazionale maternità ed infanzia (intervista con S.E. Marino Mutinelli." *L'Autarchia Alimentare,* January 1939: 7–9.

Baldi, Angela. Testimony of Angela Baldi, 1903–82. Transcript of manuscript MP/T 01087, Archivio Diaristico Nazionale, Pieve Santo Stefano, Italy, 1997.

Baranowski, Shelley. *Strength through Joy: Consumerism and Mass Tourism in the Third Reich.* Cambridge: Cambridge University Press, 2004.

Bartetzky, Arnold, and Marc Schalenberg. *Urban Planning and the Pursuit of Happiness: European Variations on a Universal Theme (18th–21st Centuries).* Berlin: Jovis Diskurs, 2009.

Bassi, Alberto. *Design anonimo in Italia: Oggetti comuni e progetto incognito.* Milan: Electa, 2007.

Baxa, Paul. "Capturing the Fascist Moment: Hitler's Visit to Italy in 1938 and the Radicalization of Fascist Italy." *Journal of Contemporary History* 42, no. 2 (2007): 227–42.

Belasco, Warren, and Philip Scranton. *Food Nations: Selling Taste in Consumer Societies.* New York: Routledge, 2002.

Ben-Ghiat, Ruth. "Envisioning Modernity: Desire and Discipline in the Italian Fascist Film." *Critical Inquiry* 23, no. 1 (1996): 109–44.

– *Fascist Modernities: Italy 1922–1945.* Berkeley: University of California Press, 2001.

– *Strongmen: Mussolini to the Present.* New York: W.W. Norton, 2020.

Ben-Ghiat, Ruth, and Mia Fuller. *Italian Colonialism.* New York: Palgrave Macmillan, 2005.

Bentley, Amy. *Eating for Victory: Food Rationing and the Politics of Domesticity.* Urbana: University of Illinois Press, 1998.

Berezin, Mabel. *Making the Fascist Self: The Political Culture of Interwar Italy.* Ithaca, NY: Cornell University Press, 1997.

Bernstein, Robin. *Racial Innocence: Performing American Childhood from Slavery to Civil Rights.* New York: New York University Press, 2011.

Berrino, Stefania. *Casa di donna: Analisi dello spazio domestico tra le due guerre.* Edited by Michela Rosso. Diss., Politecnico di Torino, Facoltà di Architettura, 2006.

Bettini, Maurizio. *Stato e Assistenza Sociale in Italia: L'Opera Nazionale Maternità ed Infanzia 1925–1975.* Livorno: Edizioni Erasmo, 2008.

Bice, Crova. *L'abitazione nei suoi riflessi sociali.* Rome: Istituto di Medicina Sociale, 1937.

Birke, Lynda. "Bodies and Biology." In *Feminist Theory and the Body: A Reader,* edited by Janet Price and Margrit Shildrick, 42–9. New York: Routledge, 1999.

Black, Rachel. "Acqua minerale di Sangemini: The Italian Mineral Water Industry Finds a Place at the Table." *Journal of Modern Italian Studies* 14, no. 2 (2009): 184–98.

– *Porta Palazzo: The Anthropology of an Italian Market.* Philadelphia: University of Pennsylvania Press, 2012.

Boccasile, Gino. *Mangiate Riso.* Milan: Ente Nazionale Risi, 1935.

Bocchetti, Federigo, ed. "I Problemi della Maternità e dell'Infanzia: Atti dei Congressi Scientifici." In *Problemi Assistenziali della Maternità e dell'Infanzia,* vol. 13. Rome: Partito Nazionale Fascista.

Bonfanti, Eziio, and Massimo Scolari. *La vicenda urbanistica e edilizia dell'Istituto case popolari di Milano dagli esordi alla seconda guerra mondiale.* Edited by Luca Scacchietti. Milan: Club, 1982.

Boni, Ada. *Il talismano della felicità.* Rome: Colombo, 1929.

Bordo, Susan. *Unbearable Weight: Feminism, Western Culture, and the Body.* Berkeley: University of California Press, 1993.

Borgatti, Mario. *Canti popolari emiliani: Raccolti a cento.* Florence: L.S. Olschki, 1962.

Bottoni, Piero. "Determinare i criteri della casa di oggi." *Domus* 145 (1940): 23–4.

Bourdieu, Pierre. *Distinction: A Social Critique of the Judgment of Taste.* Cambridge, MA: Harvard University Press, 1984.

Boym, Svetlana. *Common Places: Mythologies of Everyday Life in Russia.* Cambridge, MA: Harvard University Press, 1994.

Brin, Irene. *Usi e costumi: 1920–1940.* Rome: Donatello di Luigi, 1944.

Brock, William. *Justus von Liebig: The Chemical Gatekeeper.* Cambridge: Cambridge University Press, 1997.

Brunelli, G. "La casa per tutti: Programma generale." *Casabella* 73 (1934): 46–7.

Buitoni, Giovanni. *Storia di un imprenditore.* Milan: Longanesi, 1972.

Burton, Antoinette. *Dwelling in the Archive: Women Writing House, Home, and History in Late Colonial India.* New York: Oxford University Press, 2003.

Bytwerk, Randall. *Bending Spines: The Propagandas of Nazi Germany and the German Democratic Republic.* East Lansing: Michigan State University Press, 2004.

Butler, Judith. *Bodies That Matter: On the Discursive Limits of "Sex."* New York: Routledge, 1993.

– *Gender Trouble: Feminism and the Subversion of Identity.* New York: Routledge, 1990.

Caldwell, Lesley. "*Madri d'Italia*: Film and Fascist Concern with Motherhood." In *Women and Italy: Essays on Gender, Culture and History*, edited by Zygmunt G. Barański and Shirley W. Vinall, 43–63. New York: St. Martin's Press, 1991.

Calza Bini, Alberto. "Il piano regolatore e le abitazioni in Roma." *Quaderni della Roma di Mussolini* 11 (1942): 4–19.

– "La sistemazione dei Borghi a Roma." *La Casa* (1936): 357–60.

Caprotti, Federico. "Internal Colonization, Hegemony, and Coercion: Investigating Migration to Southern Lazio, Italy in the 1930s." *Geoforum* 39, no. 2 (2008): 942–57.

Carter, Nick. "Rethinking the Italian Liberal State." *Bulletin of Italian Politics* 3, no. 2 (2011): 225–45.

"Casa dell'ONMI." *Casabella*, October 1935.

"Casa della madre e del bambino, a Trieste." *Casabella*, November 1935.

"Case popolari e corporazione edilizia." *Concessioni e costruzioni* (1935): 671.

"Case rurali." *Concessioni e costruzioni* (1935): 672–3.

"Casette modello costruite dall'Istituto per le Case Popolari di Roma alla Borgata-Giardino Garbatella." *Architettura e arti decorative* (1930): 254–75.

Cassa nazionale di maternità, Memorandum del dattore di lavoro, Article 47. Rome: Libri di Matricola e di Paga USILA, 1925.

Cassano, Franco. *Il pensiero meridiano.* Rome: Laterza, 1996.

Cassata, Francesco. *Building the New Man: Eugenics, Racial Science and Genetics in Twentieth-Century Italy.* Budapest: Central European University Press, 2011.

Castelli, Franco, Emilio Jona, and Alberto Lovatto. *Senti le rane che cantano: Canzoni e vissuti popolari della risaia.* Rome: Donzelli, 2005.

Cavallo, Pietro. *Italiani in guerra: Sentimenti e immagini dal 1940 al 1943.* Bologna: Mulino, 1997.

– *La storia attraverso i media: Immagini, propaganda e cultura in Italia dal fascismo alla Repubblica.* Naples: Liguori, 2002.

Cavallo, Pietro, and Pasquale Iaccio. *L'immagine riflessa: Fare storia con i media.* Naples: Liguori, 1998.

Celli, Carlo. *Economic Fascism: Primary Sources on Mussolini's Crony Capitalism.* New York: Axios Press, 2013.

Cerletti, Ugo. "Il problema della casa rurale." *Difesa Sociale: Rivista Mensile d'Igiene, Previdenza ed Assistenza* 5 (May 1933): 200–1.

Chang, Natasha V. *The Crisis-Woman.* Toronto: University of Toronto Press, 2015.

Chiapparino, Francesco, and Renato Covino. *La fabbrica di Perugina: 1907–2007.* Perugia: ICSIM, 2008.

Chierici, Antonietta. Testimony of Antonietta Chierici, "Mia madre: Una donna dell'Emilia," 1920–60. Transcript of manuscript MP/Adn2 05024, Archivio Diaristico Nazionale, Pieve Santo Stefano, Italy.

Chiozzi, Ermanna. Testimony of Ermanna Chiozzi, "Ermanna nella storia fra arte e racconti," 1933–46. Transcript of manuscript MP/Adn2 04629, Archivio Diaristico Nazionale, Pieve Santo Stefano, Italy.

Chiu, Charles S. *Women in the Shadows: Mileva Einstein-Marić, Margarete Jeanne Trakl, Lise Meitner, Milena Jesenská, and Margarete Schütte-Lihotzky.* New York: Peter Lang, 1994.

Cinotto, Simone. "Memories of the Italian Rice Belt, 1945–65: Work, Class Conflict and Intimacy during the 'Great Transformation.'" *Journal of Modern Italian Studies* 16, no. 4 (2011): 531–52.

Cioccetti, Urbano. *Esperienze e prospettive dell'ONMI.* Rome: Opera Nazionale Maternità ed Infanzia, 1956.

Cipolli, Ivana. Testimony of Ivana Cipolli, "Amici fino alla morte," 1944–2006. Transcript of manuscript MP/T2 05715, Archivio Diaristico Nazionale, Pieve Santo Stefano, Italy, 2006.

Clark, Martin. *Modern Italy, 1871–1995.* London: Longman, 1996.

Cogdell, Christina. "Smooth Flow: Biological Efficiency and Streamline Design." *Popular Eugenics: National Efficiency and American Mass Culture in the 1930s,* edited by Christina Cogdell and Susan Currell, 217–48. Athens: Ohio University Press, 2006.

Collingham, Lizzie. *The Taste of War: World War II and the Battle for Food.* New York: Penguin, 2012.

Colombi, Marchesa. *In risaia.* Milan: Piovan, 1878.

Conboy, Katie, Nadia Medina, and Sarah Stanbury. *Writing on the Body: Female Embodiment and Feminist Theory.* New York: Columbia University Press, 1997.

Confederazione Fascista Lavoratori Agricola. *Campagna Monda del Riso 1938.* Rome: Arte Stampa, 1939.

Congresso Nazionale di Medicina del lavoro, Istituto Italiano di Igiene. *Organizzazione e Medicina Pubblica.* Prato: M. Martini, 1922.

Convegno Lombardo per la casa popolare nei suoi aspetti igienico sociale: Protocollo e relazioni. Milan: Reale Società di Italiana di Igiene, 1936.

Coradeschi, Sergio, and Ippolite Rostagno. "The Novecento Style in Italy: Commercial and Graphic Design / Lo stile novecento italiano: Grafica di massa e design esclusivo." *Journal of Decorative and Propaganda Arts* 3 (1987): 66–83.

Corsi, Pietro. *La tutela della maternità e dell'infanzia in Italia.* Rome: Società Editrice di novissima, 1936.

Corvisieri, Valerio. *Luisa Spagnoli.* Perugia: Alino editrice, 2017.

Costa, Maria. "Pellicole specializzate per l'educazione e la profilassi." *Maternità ed Infanzia,* March 1936: 8–9.

Counihan, Carole. *Around the Tuscan Table: Food, Family, and Gender in Twentieth-Century Florence.* New York: Routledge, 2004.

Counihan, Carole, and Valeria Siniscalchi. *Food Activism: Agency, Democracy and Economy.* New York: A&C Black, 2013.

Counihan, Carole, and Penny Van Esterik. *Food and Culture: A Reader.* New York: Routledge, 1997.

Covino, Renato. "Perugina: Crescita e sviluppo." In *Perugia: Una storia d'azienda, ingegno, e passione.* Perugia: Amilcare, 1997.

Cowan, Ruth Schwartz. *More Work for Mother: The Ironies of Household Technology from the Open Hearth to the Microwave.* New York: Basic Books, 1983.

Croce, Benedetto. *A Croce Reader: Aesthetics, Philosophy, History, and Literary Criticism.* Edited and translated by Massimo Verdicchio. Toronto: University of Toronto Press, 2017.

Croci, Maria. "Al Pavillon de Marsan." *La casa bella* 3 (1929): 23–5.

– "Gli insieme decorativi di Eugène Prinz." *La casa bella* 9 (1929): 29–33.

– "Gli italiani al Salon d'Automne." *La casa bella* 12 (1929): 50–3.

– "Il ricamo bandera." *La casa bella* 3 (1928): 45–6.

– "La decorazione della tavola." *La casa bella* 7 (1929): 37–40.

– "La mostra parigina delle arti domestiche." *La casa bella* 3 (1928): 40.

– "Passaggi parigini." *La casa bella* 5 (1929): 38–40.

– "Stoffe d'arte francesi." *La casa bella* 6 (1929): 37–9.

– "Una mostra documentada a Parigi." *La casa bella* 2 (1929): 14–16.

Crova, Bice. *L'abitazione nei suoi riflessi sociali.* Rome: Istituto di Medicina Sociale, 1937.

Cuccaro, Pietro. "L'olio di Luisa Spagnoli, storia di un sogno." *AgoraVox*, 6 October 2014. https://www.agoravox.it/L-olio-di-Luisa-Spagnoli-storia-di.html.

Cullather, Nick. "The Foreign Policy of the Calorie." *American Historical Review* 112, no. 2 (2007): 337–64.

Curli, Barbara. "Dalla Perugina all'Angora: Luisa Spagnoli." In *Donne imprenditrici nella Storia dell'Umbria*, 198–207. Rome: FrancoAngeli, 2005.

Dahl, Robert A. "The Concept of Power." *Behavioral Science* 2, no. 3 (2007): 201–15.

Daley, Bill. "Culinary Giant: Ada Boni." *Chicago Tribune*, 15 May 2013.

Davidoff, Leonore. *Worlds Between: Historical Perspectives on Gender and Class.* New York: John Wiley & Sons, 2013.

Davis, Belinda. *Home Fires Burning: Food, Politics, and Everyday Life in World War I Berlin.* Chapel Hill: University of North Carolina Press, 2000.

De Beauvoir, Simone. *The Second Sex.* New York: Knopf, 1953.

De Certeau, Michel. *The Practice of Everyday Life.* Berkeley: University of California Press, 1984.

De Felice, Renzo. *Interpretations of Fascism.* Cambridge, MA: Harvard University Press, 1977.

De Fusco, Renato. *Made in Italy: Storia del design italiano.* Rome: Laterza, 2007.

De Grazia, Victoria. *How Fascism Ruled Women: Italy, 1922–1945.* Berkeley: University of California Press, 1992.

De Grazia, Victoria. *The Culture of Consent: Mass Organization of Leisure in Fascist Italy.* Cambridge: Cambridge University Press, 1981.

– "Will *Il Duce*'s Successors Make the Facts Run on Time?" *New York Times.* Opinion section. May 14, 1994.

De Grazia, Victoria, and Ellen Furlough. *The Sex of Things: Gender and Consumption in Historical Perspective.* Berkeley: University of California Press, 1996.

Di Paolo, Ennio. *Regio Trans Tiberium: Storia ed architettura della sede del Ministero della Salute in Lungotevere Ripa.* Rome: Ministero della Salute, 2011.

Dickie, John. *Darkest Italy: The Nation and Stereotypes of the Mezzogiorno, 1860–1900.* New York: St. Martin's, 1999.

– *Delizia! The Epic History of the Italians and Their Food.* New York: Free Press, 2008.

Diez Gasca, Maria. *Cucine di ieri e cucine di domani.* Rome: ENIOS, 1928.

– *Le donne e la casa: Le scuole di educazione e di economia domestica in Italia e all'estero, a cura di un comitato promotore per le scuole operaie femminili di educazione e di economia domestica nelle fabbriche.* Milan: L'Eroica, 1930.

- "L'organizzazione moderna della casa per la contadina svizzera." *L'Organizzazione Scientifica del Lavoro* 10 (1928): 654.
- "Un consultorio per l'economia domestica a Roma." *L'Organizzazione Scientifica del Lavoro* 5 (1928): 347.

Domus, ed. *Il libro di casa 1938*. Rome: Cirio, 1937.

—, ed. "Servizio razionale." *Domus*, October 1935: 24–5.

Doordan, Dennis P. "In the Shadow of the Fasces: Political Design in Fascist Italy." *Design Issues* 13, no. 1 (1997): 39–52.

Douglas, Mary. *Implicit Meanings: Essays in Anthropology*. London: Routledge & Paul, 1975.
- *Purity and Danger: An Analysis of Concepts of Pollution and Taboo*. New York: Praeger, 1966.

Duggan, Christopher. *Fascist Voices: An Intimate History of Mussolini's Italy*. London: Oxford University Press, 2013.

E.F. "Piccoli passatempi musicali che possono aiutare o impedire il lavoro." *La difesa sociale: Rivista mensile d'igiene, previdenza ed assistenza* 2, no. 11 (1935): 504–5.

"Elettrodomestico." *Domus*, September 1935: 21.

Elmore, Bartow J. *Citizen Coke: The Making of Coca-Cola Capitalism*. New York: W.W. Norton, 2014.

Fagioli, Giovanni. *Il bimbo al seno: Le grave conseguenze del baliatico mercenario*. Rome: Istituto Romano di Baliatico "La Nutrice," 1940.

Fella, Stefano, and Carlo Ruzza. *Re-Inventing the Italian Right: Territorial Politics, Populism and "Post-Fascism."* New York: Routledge, 2009.

Ferris, Kate. *Everyday Life in Fascist Venice, 1929–40*. New York: Palgrave Macmillan, 2012.
- "'Fare di ogni famiglia italiana un fortilizio': The League of Nations' Economic Sanctions and Everyday Life in Venice." *Journal of Modern Italian Studies* 11, no. 2 (2006): 117–42.

Foggia, Amalia Moretti. *Altre ricette di Petronilla*. Milan: Sonzogno, 1937.
- *Ricette di Petronilla*. Milan: Edizioni Olivini, 1938.
- *Ricette di Petronilla per tempi eccezionali*. Milan: Sonzogno, 1942.
- *Ricettario per i tempi difficili*. Milan: Sonzogno, 1942.
- *200 suggerimenti per … questi tempi difficili*. Milan: Sonzogno, 1943.
- *Desinaretti per … questi tempi*. Milan: Sonzogno, 1943.

Forgacs, David. *Italian Culture in the Industrial Era, 1880–1980: Cultural Industries, Politics, and the Public*. Manchester: Manchester University Press, 1990.

Forgacs, David, and Stephen Gundle. *Mass Culture and Italian Society from Fascism to the Cold War*. Bloomington: Indiana University Press, 2007.

Forino, Imma. *La cucina: Storia culturale di un luogo domestico*. Turin: Einaudi, 2019.

Fornari, Dario. *Il cuciniere militare: Manuale ad uso dei cucinieri della truppa del R.E. e degli altri corpi armati*. Novara: Cattaneo, 1932.

Forth, C.E., and A. Carden-Coyne. *Cultures of the Abdomen: Diet, Digestion, and Fat in the Modern World*. New York: Palgrave Macmillan, 2005.

Foucault, Michel. *The Birth of the Clinic*. New York: Routledge, 2012.
- *Discipline & Punish: The Birth of the Prison*. New York: Knopf Doubleday, 2012.
- *The History of Sexuality: An Introduction*. New York: Knopf Doubleday, 2012.
- *Power/Knowledge: Selected Interviews and Other Writings, 1972–1977*. New York: Pantheon, 1980.

Fraticelli, Vanna. "Parva sed apta mihi: Note sulla cultura e sulla politica della casa negli anni venti in Italia." *Nuova DWF* 19–20 (1982): 39–47.

Frazer, Julie Riemenschneider. "Mechanizing the American Kitchen: An Examination of the Formation of the 1930's Middle-Class Midwestern Suburban Kitchen." PhD diss., Cornell University, 1997.

Fuller, Mia. *Moderns Abroad: Architecture, Cities and Italian Imperialism.* New York: Routledge, 2007.

Gabaccia, Donna. *We Are What We Eat: Ethnic Food and the Making of Americans.* Cambridge, MA: Harvard University Press, 1998.

Gaifami, Paolo. "Quando la culla è vuota." *Maternità ed Infanzia*, April 1935: 3–5.

Gallop, Jane. *Thinking Through the Body.* New York: Columbia University Press, 1988.

Galton, Francis. "Eugenics: Its Definition, Scope, and Aims." *American Journal of Sociology* 10, no. 1 (1904): 1–25.

Gardella, Ignazio. "Consigli tecnici per la casa." *Domus*, May 1939: 23–4.

– "I servizi della casa: La cucina." *Domus*, January 1939: 56–9.

Garvin, Diana. "Autarkic by Design: Aesthetics and Politics of Kitchenware." In *Food and Material Culture: Proceedings of the 2013 Oxford Symposium on Food and Cookery*, 11–19. London: Prospect Books, 2013.

– "Fascist Foodways: *Ricettari* as Propaganda for Grain Production and Sexual Reproduction." In *Food and Foodways*, 29 no. 2 (2021): 1–25.

– "Riding the Stockcar to Sleep in the Stable: Migrant Agricultural Labor and Songs of Rebellion." In *gender/sexuality/Italy*, 7 (2021): 1–18.

– "Singing Truth to Power: Melodic Resistance and Bodily Revolt in Italy's Rice Fields." In "Speaking Truth to Power from Medieval to Modern Italy," special issue, *Annali d'italianistica* 34 (2016): 373–400.

– "Taylorist Breastfeeding in Rationalist Clinics: Constructing Industrial Motherhood in Fascist Italy." *Critical Inquiry* 41 (2015): 655–74.

Geertz, Clifford. *The Interpretation of Cultures.* New York: Basic Book Classics, 1973.

Gentilcore, David. *Pomodoro! A History of the Tomato in Italy.* New York: Columbia University Press, 2010.

Gentile, Emilio. *Fascismo di Pietra.* Rome: Laterza, 2007.

– *The Sacralization of Politics in Fascist Italy.* Cambridge, MA: Harvard University Press, 1996.

Gerhard, Gesine. "Food and Genocide: Nazi Agrarian Politics in the Occupied Territories of the Soviet Union." *Contemporary European History* 18, no. 1 (2009): 45–65.

Gestri, Romano. *Il problema della Casa Rurale dal punto di vista medico-sociale.* Presented to the IX Congresso Nazionale dell'Associazione Italiana Fascista per l'Igiene, 19–23 September 1934. Bari: Dante de Blasi, 1935.

Ghirardo, Diane. "Architecture and Culture in Fascist Italy." *Journal of Architectural Education* 45, no. 2 (1992): 66.

– *Building New Communities.* Princeton, NJ: Princeton University Press, 1989.

– "Italian Architects and Fascist Politics: An Evaluation of the Rationalist's Role in Regime Building." *Journal of the Society of Architectural Historians* 39, no. 2 (1980): 109–30.

Gianeri, Enrico. *La donna la moda l'amore in tre secoli di caricatura.* Milan: Garzanti, 1942.

Gini, Corrado, ed. *Atti del Congresso internazionale per gli studi sulla popolazione* (Rome, 7–10 September 1931), vol. 7. Rome: Istituto Poligrafico dello Stato, 1931.

Ginsborg, Paul. *A History of Contemporary Italy: Society and Politics, 1943–1988.* New York: Palgrave Macmillan, 2003.

Ginzburg, Carlo. *The Cheese and the Worms: The Cosmos of a Sixteenth-Century Miller.* Baltimore, MD: Johns Hopkins University Press, 1980.

Giuliani, Gaia, and Cristina Lombardi-Diop. *Bianco e nero: Storia dell'identità razziale degli italiani.* Florence: Le Monnier, 2013.

Goody, Jack. "The Recipe, the Prescription, and the Experiment." In *Food and Culture: A Reader*, edited by Carole Counihan and Penny Van Esterik. New York: Routledge, 2008.

Gramsci, Antonio. "Il Mezzogiorno e il Fascismo." *L'Ordine Nuovo*, 15 March 1924. Reprinted in *La questione meridionale* 1935. Rome: Editori Riuniti, 1966.

Gramsci, Antonio, and Valentino Gerratana. *Quaderni del Carcere.* Turin: Einaudi, 1975.

Griffin, Roger. *Modernism and Fascism: The Sense of a Beginning under Mussolini and Hitler.* Basingstoke, UK: Palgrave Macmillan, 2007.

– "Staging the Nation's Rebirth: The Politics and Aesthetics of Performance in the Context of Fascist Studies." In *Fascism and Theater: Comparative Studies on the Aesthetics and Politics of Performance in Europe, 1925–1945*, edited by Günter Berghaus, 11–29. Providence, RI: Berghahn Books, 1996.

Griffith, Brian J. "Bacchus among the Blackshirts: Wine Making, Consumerism, and Identity in Fascist Italy, 1919–1937." *Contemporary European History* 29, no. 4 (November 2020): 394–415.

– "Bringing Bacchus to the People: Winemaking and 'Making Italians' in Fascist Italy." PhD diss., University of California, Santa Barbara, 2020.

Guidi, Maria. "Le nostre industrie: La 'Perugina.'" *Il Giornale della Donna*, 1 May 1931: 6.

Gundle, Stephen. *Bellissima: Feminine Beauty and the Idea of Italy.* New Haven, CT: Yale University Press, 2011.

Hartmann, Heidi. "The Family as the Locus of Gender, Class, and Political Struggle: The Example of Housework." *Signs* 6, no. 3 (1981): 366–94.

Helstosky, Carol. "Fascist Food Politics: Mussolini's Policy of Alimentary Sovereignty." *Journal of Modern Italian Studies* 9, no. 1 (2004): 1–26.

– *Garlic and Oil: Politics and Food in Italy.* Oxford: Berg, 2004.

– "Recipe for the Nation: Reading Italian History through *La Scienza in Cucina* and *La cucina futurista.*" *Food and Foodways* 11, no. 2 (2013): 113–40.

Henderson, Susan R. "Housing the Single Woman: The Frankfurt Experiment." *Journal of the Society of Architectural Historians* 68, no. 3 (2009): 358–77.

Heskett, John. *Industrial Design.* London: Thames and Hudson, 1980.

Hicks, Dan, and Mary Carolyn Beaudry. *The Oxford Handbook of Material Culture Studies.* Oxford: Oxford University Press, 2010.

Hobsbawm, E.J. *The Age of Extremes: A History of the World, 1914–1991.* New York: Pantheon, 1994.

Hodder, Ian. *Entangled: An Archaeology of the Relationships between Humans and Things.* New York: Wiley-Blackwell, 2012.

hooks, bell. "Eating the Other: Desire and Resistance." In *Media and Cultural Studies: Key Works*, edited by Meenakshi Gigi Durham and Douglas M. Kellner, 366–80. New York: John Wiley & Sons, 2009.

Horn, David G. *Social Bodies: Science, Reproduction, and Italian Modernity.* Princeton, NJ: Princeton University Press, 1994.

Huang, Yanzhong. "The 2008 Milk Scandal Revisited." *Forbes*, 16 July 2014.

Huss, Marie-Monique. "Pronatalism in the Inter-War Period in France." *Journal of Contemporary History* 25, no. 1 (1990): 39–68.

"I refettori materni." *Maternità e Infanzia*, May 1935: 5.

"Impianto di una abitazione." *Domus*, June 1937: 28–34.

"Il film 'Alle Madri d'Italia' edito dall'ONMI presentato al festival internazionale di Venezia." *Maternità ed Infanzia*, April 1935: 16.

Ipsen, Carl. *Dictating Demography: The Problem of Population in Fascist Italy.* Cambridge: Cambridge University Press, 1996.

Istituto Centrale di Statistica del Regno d'Italia. *Compendio Statistico Italiano 1939.* Rome: Istituto Poligrafico dello Stato, 1938.

– *Compendio Statistico Italiano 1940.* Rome: Istituto Poligrafico dello Stato, 1939.
– *Compendio Statistico Italiano 1941.* Rome: Istituto Poligrafico dello Stato, 1940.
– *Compendio Statistico Italiano 1942.* Rome: Istituto Poligrafico dello Stato, 1941.
Jerram, Leif. "Kitchen Sink Dramas: Women, Modernity and Space in Weimar Germany."
    Cultural Geographies 13, no. 4 (2006): 538–56.
Jona, Emilio. *Le canzonette che fecero l'Italia.* Milan: Longanesi, 1963.
– "Sul cantare in risaia." In *Colture e culture del riso: una prospettiva storica,* edited by Simone
    Cinotto, 231–77. Vercelli: Edizioni Mercurio, 2002.
Kaplan, Wendy, ed. *Designing Modernity: The Arts of Reform and Persuasion, 1885–1945; Selections
    from the Wolfsonian.* New York: Thames and Hudson, 1995.
Kelly, Joan. "Did Women Have a Renaissance?" In *Becoming Visible: Women in European History,*
    edited by Renate Bridenthal and Claudia Koonz, 175–201. New York: Houghton Mifflin, 1977.
Kertzer, David I. *The Pope and Mussolini: The Secret History of Pius XI and the Rise of Fascism in
    Europe.* New York: Random House, 2014.
Kinchin, Juliet, and Aiden O'Connor. *Counter Space: Design and the Modern Kitchen.* New York:
    Museum of Modern Art, 2011.
Krasny, Jill. "Every Parent Should Know the Scandalous History of Infant Formula." *Business
    Insider,* 25 June 2012.
"La casa della madre e del bambino di Forlì." *Maternità ed Infanzia,* April 1936: 5–11.
"La Cucina Elegante: Specialità di Milano." *Domus,* December 1935: 102–5.
La Cucina Italiana. July 1935. Rome: Società Editrice Demetra.
La Cucina Italiana. August 1937. Rome: Società Editrice Demetra.
La Cucina Italiana. October 1940. Rome: Società Editrice Demetra.
La Cucina Italiana. November 1940. Rome: Società Editrice Demetra.
La donna operaia e lo stato fascista: I quaderni delle corporazioni, no. 14, 2nd ed. Rome: Edizioni del
    Diritto del Lavoro, 1928.
"La lotta contro l'accattonaggio in Roma." *Il Messaggero,* 24 October 1928.
"La storia siamo noi: Luisa, le Operaie e gli Altri, la donna che inventò il Bacio." Directed by Aldo
    Zappalà. Rai Tre, Rai Educational, 2009.
"La tecnica sanitaria nelle costruzioni rurali." *La difesa sociale: Rivista mensile d'igiene, previdenza
    ed assistenza* 2, no. 11 (1935): 484–7.
Landy, Marcia. *Fascism in Film: The Italian Commercial Cinema, 1931–1943.* Princeton, NJ:
    Princeton University Press, 2014.
Lasansky, D. Medina. *The Renaissance: Revised, Expanded, Unexpurgated.* Pittsburgh: Periscope
    Publishing, 2014.
– *The Renaissance Perfected: Architecture, Spectacle, and Tourism in Fascist Italy.* University Park:
    Pennsylvania State University Press, 2004.
Lasansky, D. Medina, and Brian McLaren. *Architecture and Tourism: Perception, Performance, and
    Place.* Oxford: Berg, 2004.
Lavagnini, Milena. Testimony of Milena Lavagnini, "Le mie prigioni," 1930–2000. Transcript of
    manuscript MP/T2 06468, Archivio Diaristico Nazionale, Pieve Santo Stefano, Italy, 2007.
Lazzaro, Claudia, and Roger J. Crum. *Donatello Among the Blackshirts: History and Modernity in the
    Visual Culture of Fascist Italy.* Ithaca, NY: Cornell University Press, 2004.
*Le Case Rurali in Provincia di Mantova: Relazione della commissione nominata dal consiglio
    provinciale di sanità di Mantova nella seduta del 9 giugno 1934* (presented to the township on 30
    April 1935). Mantua: Stamperia Paladino, 1935.
"L'elogio del Duce al Dott. Gianni Mazzocchi Editore della nostra rivista." *Domus,* January 1940:
    21.

Levy, Daniel, and Andrew T. Young. "'The Real Thing': Nominal Price Rigidity of the Nickel Coke, 1886–1959." *Journal of Money, Credit and Banking* 36, no. 4 (2004): 765–99.

Lo Monaco-Aprile, Attilio. *Protezione della Maternità e dell'Infanzia.* Rome: Istituto nazionale fascista di cultura, 1934.

L'Organizzazione Scientifica del Lavoro, ed. "Note di economia domestica." *Domus*, August 1939: xvi–xxx.

—, ed. "Note di economia domestica." *Domus*, February 1937: xvi–xxx.

Lüdtke, Alf. "People Working: Everyday Life and German Fascism." *History Workshop Journal* 50 (2000): 74–92.

Lumley, Robert, and Jonathan Morris, eds. *The New History of the Italian South: The Mezzogiorno Revisited.* Exeter, UK: University of Exeter Press, 1997.

Lupano, Mario. "'Vera' fotografia dell'Italia fascista." In *Dizionario del fascismo: L–Z*, edited by Victoria De Grazia and Sergio Luzzatto. Turin: Einaudi, 2002, inset 1–41.

Macerati, Erminia. *Casa nostra: Trattato di economia domestica.* Bergamo: Società Editrice Commerciale, 1929.

Malaparte, Curzio. *Kaputt.* Milan: Guarnati, 1948.

– *La Pelle: Storia e Racconto.* Roma: Aria d'Italia, 1949.

– *The Skin.* Translated by David Moore. New York: Routledge, 2013.

Maiocco, F. *Il coniglio.* Rome: Ramo Editoriale degli agricoltori, 1937.

Manicardi, Nunzia. *Il coro delle mondine: Immagini e canti dalle risaie padane.* Modena: Il Fiorino, 1998.

Marchetti, Sabrina. *Black Girls: Migrant Domestic Workers and Colonial Legacies.* Leiden: Brill, 2014.

Marcus, Millicent. *Italian Film in the Light of Neorealism.* Princeton, NJ: Princeton University Press, 1986.

Marinetti, Fillipo Tommaso, and Fillìa. *La cucina futurista.* Perugia: Francesco Tozzuolo, 1932.

– *The Futurist Cookbook.* Translated by Suzanne Brill. San Francisco: Bedford Arts, 1989.

Martinelli, G. *E' possibile diminuire il costo della vita?* Arezzo: Editoriale Italiana Contemporanea, 1928.

Matteotti, M. *La classe lavoratrice sotto la dominazione fascista 1921–43.* Milan: Annali Feltrinelli, 1944.

Mazower, Mark. *Dark Continent: Europe's Twentieth Century.* New York: Knopf, 1999.

McLaughlin, Katy. "Portrait of the Artist as a Chef." *Wall Street Journal*, 31 October 2008.

McLean, Eden K. *Mussolini's Children: Race and Elementary Education in Fascist Italy.* Lincoln: University of Nebraska Press, 2018.

Meneley, Anne. "Extra Virgin Olive Oil and Slow Food." *Anthropologica* 46, no. 2 (2004): 165–76.

Mennella, J.A, C.P. Jagnow, and G.K. Beauchamp. "Prenatal and Postnatal Flavor Learning by Human Infants." *Pediatrics* 107, no. 6 (2001): 88.

Merchant, Carolyn. *The Death of Nature: Women, Ecology, and the Scientific Revolution.* San Francisco: Harper & Row, 1980.

Miller, Henry Siefke. *Price Control in Fascist Italy.* New York: Columbia University Press, 1938.

– "Techniques of Price Control in Fascist Italy." *Political Science Quarterly* 53, no. 4 (1938): 584–98.

Minardi, Marco. *La fatica delle donne: Storie di mondine.* Parma: Ediesse, 2005.

Minesso, Michela. *Stato e infanzia nell'Italia contemporanea: Origini, sviluppo e fine dell'ONMI 1925–1975.* Bologna: Il Mulino, 2007.

Moe, Nelson J. The View from Vesuvius: Italian Culture and the Southern Question. Berkeley: University of California Press, 2002.

Molinari, Augusta. "Mondine." In *Dizionario del Fascismo: L–Z*, edited by Victoria De Grazia and Sergio Luzzatto, 154–6. Turin: Einaudi, 2003.

Montanari, Massimo. *Italian Identity: In the Kitchen, or, Food and the Nation*. New York: Columbia University Press, 2013.

Morelli, Lidia. "Arte paesana." *La casa bella* 12 (1929): 33–6.

– *Dalla Cucina al Salotto: Enciclopedia della Vita Domestica*. Turin: S. Lattes, 1935.

– "Elogio del cotone da calza." *La casa bella* 11 (1929): 41–5.

– "Il punto cavandoli." *La casa bella* 9 (1929): 25–7.

– "Introduzione." *Nuovi orizzonti per la vostra mensa: 300 ricette scelta tra le 1224 premiate su 18000 inviate al concorso pomodoro pelati cirio da 3000 concorrenti*. Portici: Tip. E. Della Torre, 1937.

– "L'alloggio a crescenza." *La casa bella* 10 (1929): 32–7.

– "La raplina." *La casa bella* 10 (1928): 37–9.

– *La Vita Sobria*. Rome: Sales, 1941.

– *Le Massaie Contro le Sanzioni*. Turin: S. Lattes, 1935.

– *Le Massaie e l'autarchia*. Turin: S. Lattes, 1937.

– "Mèzari tessuti e mèzari stampati." *La casa bella* 7 (1928): 36–9.

– "Piccoli problemi nella decorazione della villeggiatura." *La casa bella* 7 (1929): 41–5.

– "Una mostra d'arte applicata." *La casa bella* 9 (1928): 21–4.

Moroni, Salvatori, and Maria Paola. "Ragguaglio bibliografico sui ricettari del primo Novecento." In *Storia d'Italia, Annali 13: L'alimentazione*, edited by Alberto Capatti, Alberto de Bernardi, and Angelo Varni, 887–925. Turin: Einaudi, 1998.

Mosse, George L. *The Fascist Revolution: Toward a General Theory of Fascism*. New York: H. Fertig, 1999.

Moyer-Nocchi. *Chewing the Fat: An Oral History of Foodways from Fascism to Dolce Vita*. New York: Medea, 2015.

Muraro, Vaiani L. *L'ordine simbolico della madre*. Rome: Riuniti, 1991.

Mussolini, Benito. *Fascism: Doctrine and Institutions*. Translated by Jane Soames. Rome: Ardita, 1935.

– "Il discorso dell'Ascensione [Address to the Chamber of Deputies]," 26 May 1927. In *Opera omnia di Benito Mussolini*, vol. 22, edited by Edoardo Susmel and Duilio Susmel, 363. Florence: La Fenice, 1951.

Neary, Rebecca Balmas. "Mothering Socialist Society: The Wife-Activists' Movement and the Soviet Culture of Daily Life, 1934–41." *Russian Review* 58, no. 3 (1999): 396–412.

Negri, Ada. "Il companatico dell'illusione." *La Cucina Italiana*, 15 August 1930: 1.

Newlyn, Andrea K. "Challenging Contemporary Narrative Theory: The Alternative Textual Strategies of Nineteenth-Century Manuscript Cookbooks." *Journal of American Culture* 22, no. 3 (1999): 35–47.

Norman, Donald A. *The Design of Everyday Things*. New York: Basic Books, 2002.

Notaker, Henry. *A History of Cookbooks: From Kitchen to Page over Seven Centuries*. Oakland: University of California Press, 2017.

Olivi, Alessandra. "Mangiare 'per due' o mangiare 'quel che c'è': Regimi alimentari della madre in Romagna (1930–1950)." In *Donne e microcosmi culturali*, edited by Adriana Destro, 77–106. Bologna: Patron, 1997.

Opera nationale maternità ed infanzia. *Origine e sviluppi dell'Opera Nazionale per la Protezione della Maternità e dell'Infanzia*. Rome: Carlo Colombo, 1936.

Pagano, Giuseppe. "Case per il popolo." *Casabella* 143 (November 1939): 2–3.

Paluello, Lorenzo Minio. *Education in Fascist Italy*. London: Oxford University Press, 1946.

Palumbo, Elisabetta. *Se otto ore vi sembran poche … Donne nel sindacato agricolo in Italia (1904–1977)*. Rome: Ediesse, 2002.

Painter, Borden W. *Mussolini's Rome: Rebuilding the Eternal City*. New York: Palgrave Macmillan, 2005.

Parasecoli, Fabio. *Al Dente: A History of Food in Italy.* London: Reaktion, 2014.
– "Postrevolutionary Chowhounds: Food, Globalization, and the Italian Left." *Gastronomica* 3, no. 3 (2003): 29–39.
"Parliamo un po' della cucina razionalmente." *Domus,* August 1937: 30–2.
Pascoli, Giovanni. "Risotto Romagnolo." *La Cucina Italiana,* 15 June 1930: 1.
Passerini, Luisa. *Fascism in Popular Memory: The Cultural Experience of the Turin Working Class.* Cambridge: Cambridge University Press, 1987.
Passmore, Kevin. *Women, Gender, and Fascism in Europe, 1919–45.* New Brunswick, NJ: Rutgers University Press, 2013.
Paxson, Heather. "Slow Food in a Fat Society: Satisfying Ethical Appetites." *Gastronomica* 5, no. 1 (2005): 14–18.
Paxton, Robert. *The Anatomy of Fascism.* New York: Random House, 2004.
Payne, Stanley. *Fascism: Comparison and Definition.* Madison: University of Wisconsin Press, 1980.
– *How Fascism Works: The Politics of Us and Them.* New York: Random House, 2018.
Pende, Nicola. "Eugenica e politica demographica." In *L'Economia Italiana.* Rome: Casa di Oriani, 1933.
Per la Protezione della Stirpe. Rome: Istituto Nazionale LUCE, 1933.
Pergher, Roberta. *Mussolini's Nation-Empire: Sovereignty and Settlement in Italy's Borderlands, 1922–1943.* Cambridge: Cambridge University Press, 2018.
Petrini, Carlo. *Slow Food: The Case for Taste.* New York: Columbia University Press, 2003.
Piccini, Vanna. *Per te, donna: Come si vive oggi.* Milan: Mani di Fata, 1932.
– *Scrigno d'oro: Consigli, segreti, ricette per la donna.* Milan: Mani di Fata, 1943.
Piccoli, Umberto. *La bonifica umana e la casa.* Parma: Fresching, 1938.
Pickering-Iazzi, Robin. *Mothers of Invention: Women, Italian Fascism, and Culture.* Minneapolis: University of Minnesota Press, 1995.
Pilcher, Jeffrey M. *¡Que vivan los tamales! Food and the Making of Mexican Identity.* Albuquerque: University of New Mexico Press, 1998.
– *The Oxford Handbook of Food History.* New York: Oxford University Press, 2012.
Pine, Lisa. "Food in Nazi Germany: Consumption, Education and Propaganda in Peace and War." Paper presented at the "Food and History" panel for the Institute of Historical Research, London, July 2013.
Pinkus, Karen. *Bodily Regimes: Italian Advertising under Fascism.* Minneapolis: University of Minnesota Press, 1995.
Pisanty, Valentina. *La difesa della razza: Antologia 1938–1943.* Milan: Tascabili Bompiani, 2006.
Podesta, Attilio. "Case Popolari a Stoccolma e a Praga." *Casabella Costruzioni* 147 (March 1940): 4.
Ponti, Gio. "Attrezzature del lavoro." *Domus,* February 1939: 35–7.
– "Avvenire." *Domus,* July 1940: 27.
– "Casa M. a Milano." *Domus,* October 1935: 1–16.
– "Un appartamento risistemato a Milano." *Domus,* November 1938: 11–28.
– "Un esempio di composizione." *Domus,* September 1936: 15–17.
Purdy, Millard, and James Thurber. "Nickel Soda Pop: It's Disappearing Fast as Costs Push to Six and Ten Cents." *Wall Street Journal,* 2 November 1950, p. 1.
Quine, Maria S. *Population Politics in Twentieth-Century Europe: Fascist Dictatorships and Liberal Democracies.* London: Routledge, 1996.
Raccolta Coordinata ed Aggiornata delle Circolari 1925–1935 Primo Decennale. Rome: Stabilimento Tipografico Ditta Carlo Colombo, 1935.
Randi, Elisabetta. *A cucina del tempo di guerra.* Florence: A. Vallardi, 1943.
– *La cucina autarkica.* Florence: L. Cionini, 1942.

Revelli, Nuto. *L'anello forte: La donna, storie di vita contadina.* Turin: Einaudi, 1985.

Ricci, Fabrizio. *La Perugina è storia nostra: I lavoratori raccontano i cento anni di storia della fabbrica.* Rome: Ediesse, 2007.

Richards, Michael. *A Time of Silence: Civil War and the Culture of Repression in Franco's Spain, 1936–1945.* Cambridge: Cambridge University Press, 1998.

Righi, Andrea. *Biopolitics and Social Change in Italy: From Gramsci to Pasolini to Negri.* New York: Palgrave Macmillan, 2011.

Ropa, Rossella, and Cinzia Venturoli. *Donne e lavoro.* Bologna: Editrice Compositori, 2010.

Rosselli, Emilia. "Alcuni esempi per tende." *Domus* 88 (1935): 48–9.

– "Insalate e insalatiere." *Domus* 89 (1935): 50–1.

– "Lo spogliatoio della signora." *Domus* 90 (1935): 48–9.

– "Stoffe per tovaglie." *Domus* 87 (1935): 44–5.

Row, Thomas. "Mobilizing the Nation: Italian Propaganda in the Great War." *Journal of Decorative and Propaganda Arts* 24 (2002): 141–69.

Sabatini, Roberto. "Luisa Spagnoli: Orgoglio di una città." *Perugia Corriere*, 17 November 2009.

Saraiva, Tiago. *Fascist Pigs: Technoscientific Organisms and the History of Fascism.* Cambridge, MA: MIT Press, 2016.

Sarfatti, Margherita. "La botte piena e la moglie ubriaca." *La Cucina Italiana*, April 1931, 1.

– "Zuppa d'aragosta." *La Cucina Italiana*, 15 October 1930.

Scalabrini, Laura. Testimony of Laura Scalabrini, "Sette pater ave e gloria," 1927–90. Transcript of manuscript MP/10 06139, Archivio Diaristico Nazionale, Pieve Santo Stefano, Italy, 2010.

Scarola, Tiziana. "Le riviste gastronomiche dei primi decenni del Novecento." *Appunti di gastronomia* 45 (2004): 134–40.

Scarpellini, Emanuela. *A tavola! Gli italiani in 7 pranzi.* Rome: Laterza, 2014.

– *Material Nation: A Consumer's History of Modern Italy.* Translated by Daphne Hughes and Andrew Newton. Oxford: Oxford University Press, 2011.

Scavino, Marco. *Se otto ore vi sembran poche: Lotte operaie e contadine in Piemonte dall'Unità a oggi.* Milan: Collana Bancarella, 2001.

Schira, Roberta, and Alessandra De Vizzi. *Le Voci di Petronilla: Storia di una modernissima donna d'altri tempi, uno scorcio di vita femminile italiana dal 1872 al 1947.* Milan: Salani Editori, 2010.

Schnapp, Jeffrey T. "Fascism's Museum in Motion." *Journal of Architectural Education* 45, no. 2 (1992): 87–97.

– "The Romance of Caffeine and Aluminum." *Critical Inquiry* 28, no. 1 (2001): 244–69.

Schnapp, Jeffrey T., and Timothy L. Alborn. *Speed Limits.* Miami: Wolfsonian–Florida International University, 2009.

Schütte-Lihotzky, Margarete, and Peter Noever. *Die Frankfurter Küche Von Margarete Schütte-Lihotzky.* Berlin: Ernst & Sohn, 1992.

Schwartz, Eugenio. *Alimentazione nell'età scolare.* Rome: Ente Nazionale Fascista della Mutualità Scolastica, 1936.

Scott, James. *Weapons of the Weak: Everyday Forms of Peasant Resistance.* New Haven, CT: Yale University Press, 1987.

Scutiero, Antonella. "La Storia: Petronilla, Femminista Ante Litteram." *Lettera D*, for *Elle It*, 5 March 2015.

Serpieri, Arrigo. *La Guerra e le classi rurali italiane.* New Haven, CT: Yale University Press, 1930.

Sheller, Mimi. *Aluminum Dreams: The Making of a Light Modernity.* Cambridge, MA: MIT University Press, 2014.

Sorcinelli, Paolo. "Identification Process at Work: Virtues of the Italian Working-Class Diet in the First Half of the Twentieth Century." In *Food, Drink, and Identity*, edited by Peter Scholliers, 81–98. Oxford: Berg, 2001.

Spackman, Barbara. *Fascist Virilities: Rhetoric, Ideology, and Social Fantasy in Italy*. Minneapolis: University of Minnesota Press, 1996.

Spagnoli, Mario. *L'organizzazione scientifica del lavoro nella grande industria alimentare*. Series 1, no. 10. Biblioteca dell'Ente Nazionale Italiano per l'Organizzazione Scientifica del Lavoro, 1929.

– *Norme pratiche sull'allevamento del coniglio angora per il potenziamento della conigliatura nazionale*. Milan: Hoepli, 1943.

Sparke, Penny. *Italian Design: 1870 to the Present*. London: Thames and Hudson, 1988.

Stanley, Jason. *How Fascism Works: The Politics of Us and Them*. New York: Random House, 2018.

Staro, Placida. *Lasciateci passare siamo le donne: Il canto delle mondine di Bentivoglio*. Udine: Nota, 2009.

Steege, Paul, Andrew Stuart Bergerson, Maureen Healy, and Pamela E. Swett. "The History of Everyday Life: A Second Chapter." *Journal of Modern History* 80, no. 2 (2008): 358–78.

Stormer, Nathan. "Mediating Biopower and the Case of Prenatal Space." *Critical Studies in Media Communication* 27, no. 1 (2010): 8–23.

Suleiman, Susan R. *The Female Body in Western Culture: Contemporary Perspectives*. Cambridge, MA: Harvard University Press, 1986.

Taddei, Francesca. "Il cibo nell'Italia mezzadrile fra Ottocento e Novecento." In *Storia d'Italia, Annali 13: L'alimentazione*, edited by Alberto Capatti, Alberto De Bernardi, and Angelo Varni, 23–61. Turin: Einaudi, 1998.

Terefe, Heyaw. "Contested Space: Transformation of Inner-City Market Areas and Users' Reaction in Addis Ababa, Ethiopia." PhD thesis, Norwegian University of Science and Technology, 2005.

Terra Madre. Directed by Alessandro Blasetti. Rome: Istituto Nazionale LUCE, 1931.

Thomas, Julia Adeney, and Geoff Eley, eds. *Visualizing Fascism: The Twentieth-Century Rise of the Global Right*. Durham, NC: Duke University Press, 2020.

Thompson, E.P. "History from Below." *Times Literary Supplement*, 7 April 1966: 279–80.

Tompkins, Kyla Wazana. *Racial Indigestion: Eating Bodies in the 19th Century*. New York: New York University Press, 2012.

Trabalzi, Ferruccio. "Primavalle: Urban Reservation in Rome." *Journal of Architectural Education* 42, no. 3 (1989): 38–46.

Traverso, Enzo. *The New Faces of Fascism: Populism and the Far Right*. Translated by David Broder. Brooklyn, NY: Verso, 2019.

Treitel, Corinna. *Eating Nature in Modern Germany: Food, Agriculture, and Environment*. Cambridge: Cambridge University Press, 2017.

Trentmann, Frank, and Flemming Just. *Food and Conflict in Europe in the Age of the Two World Wars*. Basingstoke, UK: Palgrave Macmillan, 2006.

Triolo, Nancy. "Fascist Unionization and the Professionalization of Midwives in Italy: A Sicilian Case Study." *Medical Anthropology Quarterly* 8, no. 3 (September 1994): 259–81.

Trubek, Amy. *The Taste of Place: A Cultural Journey into Terroir*. California Studies in Food and Culture. Berkeley: University of California Press, 2008.

Turrini, Elisa. "'L'Almanacco della donna italiana': Uno sguardo al femminile nel ventennio fascista." Storiaefuturo.eu, March 2013. Accessed 20 April 2013. http://storiaefuturo.eu /lalmanacco-della-donna-italiana-uno-sguardo-al-femminile-nel-ventennio-fascista

"Un tipico ambiente utilitario." *Domus*, January 1936: 70.

Vaiani, Luisa Muraro. *L'Ordine simbolico della madre*. Milan: Editori Riuniti, 1991.

Van Esterik, Penny. *Beyond the Breast-Bottle Controversy*. New Brunswick, NJ: Rutgers University Press, 1989.

Valsangiacomo, Nelly, and Luigi Lorenzetti. *Donne e Lavoro: Prospettive per una storia delle montagne europee*. Milan: F. Angeli, 2010.

Vernon, James. *Hunger: A Modern History*. Cambridge, MA: Harvard University Press, 2007.

Verzani, Maria. Testimony of Maria Verzani, "Una storia quasi d'amore: La saga dei Verzani e la sua storia," 1915–73. Transcript of manuscript MP/T2 04236, Archivio Diaristico Nazionale, Pieve Santo Stefano, Italy, 2001.

Vidoni, Giuseppe. "Il problema della casa." *Difesa Sociale: Rivista Mensile d'Igiene, Previdenza ed Assistenza* 5 (May 1933): 201–2.

Villani, Luciano. *Le borgate del fascismo: Storia urbana, politica e sociale della periferia romana*. Milan: Ledizioni, 2012.

Vinaccia, Gaetano. *Per le Città di Domani: Come il clima plasma la forma urbana e l'architettura, La sanità e l'igiene cittadina*. Rome: Fratelli Palombi Editori, 1937.

Virilio, Paul. "A Travelling Shot over Eighty Years." In *War and Cinema: The Logistics of Perception*, Translated by Patrick Camiller, 68–90. London: Verso, 2009.

– *The Vision Machine*. Trans. Julie Rose. London: British Film Institute, 1994.

Vivarelli, Roberto. *Fascismo e storia d'Italia*. Bologna: Il Mulino, 2008.

Wallenstein, Sven-Olov. *Biopolitics and the Emergence of Modern Architecture*. Princeton, NJ: Princeton Architectural Press, 2009.

Walter, Lynn. "Slow Food and Home Cooking: Toward a Relational Aesthetic of Food and Relational Ethic of Home." *Provisions: Journal of the Center for Food in Community and Culture* 1 (2009): 1–23.

Waring, Marilyn. *If Women Counted: A New Feminist Economics*. London: Macmillan, 1989.

Way, Wendy. "The Wheat Crisis of the 1930s." In *A New Idea Each Morning: How Food and Agriculture Came Together in One International Organization*, 129–52. Sydney: Australian National University Press, 2013.

Weber, Cynthia. "Introduction: Design and Citizenship." *Citizenship Studies* 14, no. 1 (2010): 1–16.

Weber, Cynthia, and Mark Lacy. "Securing by Design." *Review of International Studies* 37, no. 3 (2011): 1021–43.

Welch, Rhiannon Noel. *Vital Subjects: Race and Biopolitics in Italy, 1860–1920*. Liverpool: Liverpool University Press, 2016.

Weinreb, Alice. "'For the Hungry Have No Past nor Do They Belong to a Political Party': Debates over German Hunger after World War II." *Central European History* 44, no. 1 (March 2012): 50–78.

Wharton, Tim. "Recipes: Beyond the Words." *Gastronomica* 10, no. 4 (2010): 67–73.

Wheaton, Barbara Ketcham. "Cookbooks as Resources for Social History." In *Food in Time and Place*, edited by Paul Freedman, Joyce E. Chaplin, and Ken Albala, 276–300. Berkeley: University of California Press, 2019.

Whitaker, Elizabeth Dixon. *Measuring Mamma's Milk: Fascism and the Medicalization of Maternity in Italy*. Ann Arbor: University of Michigan Press, 2003.

Willson, Perry. *The Clockwork Factory: Women and Work in Fascist Italy*. Oxford: Clarendon Press, 1993.

– *Peasant Women and Politics in Fascist Italy: The Massaie Rurali*. London: Routledge, 2002.

– *Women in Twentieth-Century Italy*. New York: Palgrave Macmillan, 2009.

Wilt, Alan. *Food for War: Agriculture and Rearmament in Britain before the Second World War.* New York: Oxford University Press, 2001.

Zamarra, Emilia. *Almanacco della cucina per la famiglia Italiana 1939.* Milan: Sonzogno, 1939.

– *La Cucina Italiana della Resistenza.* Milan: A. Barion, 1936.

Zanolla, Linda, ed. *Volumi in Cucina: Storia del progetto cucina.* Milan: Archeo, 2010.

Zappi, Elda Gentili. *If Eight Hours Seem Too Few: Mobilization of Women Workers in the Italian Rice Fields.* Albany: State University of New York Press, 1991.

Zingali, Gaetano. "I provvedimenti mussoliniani per lo sviluppo quantitative e qualitative della popolazione." In *Atti del Congresso internazionale per gli studi sulla popolazione* (Rome, 7–10 September 1931), vol. 7, ed. Corrado Gini, 585–604. Rome: Istituto Poligrafico dello Stato, 1931.

Zucchi, Guido. "I refettori materni." *Maternità ed Infanzia,* April 1935: 5–8.

Zuccotti, Susan. *Under His Very Windows: The Vatican and the Holocaust in Italy.* New Haven, CT: Yale University Press, 2002.

INDEX

Page numbers in italics represent illustrations.